IRAN'S
DIVERSE PEOPLES

Other Titles in
ABC-CLIO's
ETHNIC DIVERSITY WITHIN NATIONS
Series

Canada's Diverse Peoples, J. M. Bumsted

The Former Soviet Union's Diverse Peoples, James Minahan

The Former Yugoslavia's Diverse Peoples, Matjaž Klemenčič and Mitja Žagar

Nigeria's Diverse Peoples, April A. Gordon

IRAN'S
DIVERSE PEOPLES

A REFERENCE SOURCEBOOK

Massoume Price

A B C • C L I O

Santa Barbara, California   Denver, Colorado   Oxford, England

Library of Congress Cataloging-in-Publication Data
Price, Massoume.
Iran's diverse peoples : a reference sourcebook / Massoume Price.
    p.   cm.—(ABC-CLIO's ethnic diversity within nations series)
Includes bibliographical references and index.
ISBN 1-57607-993-7 (hardback : alk. paper)—ISBN 1-57607-994-5 (e-book)
    1. Iran.   2. Iran—Ethnic relations.   I. Title.   II. Series: Ethnic diversity within nations.
DS254.5.P75   2005
955'.004—dc22   2005013791

08   07   06   05   10 9 8 7 6 5 4 3 2 1

This book is also available on the World Wide Web as an e-book.
Visit http://www.abc-clio.com for details.

ABC-CLIO, Inc.
130 Cremona Drive, P.O. Box 1911
Santa Barbara, California 93116-1911

This book is printed on acid-free paper.

Manufactured in the United States of America

Contents

Series Editor's Foreword

WE THINK OF THE UNITED STATES AS A NATION OF PEOPLES, WITH some describing it as a mosaic, a stew, an orchestra, and even yet as a melting pot. In the American vision of diversity, the whole is perceived as greater than the sum of its parts—groups of peoples unify into a national identity. Not all Americans have shared that vision, or, to the extent that they initially did, they considered diversity as groups of people with shades of difference—such as shades of whiteness or variants of Protestantism. Many of the early newcomers would come to represent the core of an American society in which distinctions were expected to fade because a unity was anticipated that would be greater than any one homogeneous racial or ethnic national community. That unity would be forged through a common commitment to the U.S. system of republicanism and a shared set of political principles and values—collectively, America's civic culture. For decades the diversity that was recognized (essentially in terms of religion and nationality) did not appear to be so formidable as to constitute a barrier to nationhood—as long as one did not look beyond the whiteness to the African and Native American (and later Latino and Asian) peoples. By rendering such groups invisible, if not beyond the pale, majority groups did not perceive them as representing a challenge to, or a denial of, the national unity. They were simply left out of the picture until, eventually, they would compel the majority to confront the nation's true composition and its internal contradictions. Even before that more complex confrontation took place, streams of (mostly) European newcomers steadily stretched the boundaries of the nation's diversity, requiring a reexamination of the bonds of nationhood, the elements of nationality, and the core society and values. By World War II and in the ensuing two decades it had become more and more difficult to ignore the impact of the expanding Latino and Asian immigration and arrival of far more diverse groups of European newcomers. To secure their national vision, Americans had (albeit reluctantly and not without conflict) to make profound and fundamental adjustments to many of those components that had served as the nation's bonds, particularly the perception of America as a multicultural society and the belief that pluralism was a legitimate and inherent part of American society and culture.

To what extent has this scenario of a nation of peoples been present elsewhere in the world? Where have others struggled to overcome racial, religious, tribal, and national differences in order to construct—or to preserve—a nation? Perhaps one might even ask where, by the late twentieth century, had others *not* experienced such struggles? In how many of the principal nations has there long been present a homogeneity of people around which a nation could be molded and shaped with little danger of internal discord threatening the overall fabric of national unity? On the other hand, in how many countries has there been present a multiplicity of peoples, as in the United States, who have had to forge a nation out of a disparate array of peoples? Was that multiplicity the product of inmigrations joining a core society as it has been in the United States, or was there a historic mosaic of tribes, bands, and other more-or-less organized entities that eventually adhered as their discovered commonalities outweighed their differences? Do we see invasions from without and unity imposed from above, or the emergence of one group gradually extending its dominance over the others—installing unity from below? Did any of these variations result in nation-states comparable to the United States—the so-called first new nation—and, if so, what have been the points of similarity and difference, the degrees of stability or unrest? Have their diversities endured, or have they been transmuted, absorbed, or suppressed? How much strain have those states experienced in trying to balance the competing demands among majority and minority populations? In other words, where nation-states have emerged by enveloping or embracing (or subjugating) diverse peoples, what have been the resulting histories in terms of intergroup relations and intergroup strains as well as the extent of effective foundations of national unity?

The challenges of coexistence (voluntary or otherwise) remain the same whether two or twenty people are involved. The issue is what traditions, institutions, concepts, principles, and experiences enable particular combinations of peoples to successfully bond and what factors cause others to fall prey to periodic unrest and civil wars? Finally, many upheavals have taken place over the past 150 years, during which inmigrations have penetrated nations that were previously homogenous or were "sending nations" (experiencing more outmigration than inmigration) and were less prepared to address the rather novel diversities. Have these nations had institutions, values, and traditions that enabled them to successfully take on such new challenges?

Examples abound beyond the borders of the United States that require us to examine the claims of American exceptionalism (that America's multi-culturalism has been a unique phenomenon) or, at the very least, to understand it far better. Canada and Australia have had indigenous peoples but have also long been receiving nations for immigrants—however, usually far more selectively than has the United States. Brazil and Argentina were, for decades in the late nineteenth and early twentieth centuries, important immigrant-receiving nations too, with long-term consequences for their societies. Long before there were Indian and Yugoslavian nation-states there were myriad peoples in those regions who struggled and competed and then, under considerable external pressures, strained to carve out a stable multiethnic unity based on tribal, religious, linguistic, or racial (often including groups labeled "racial" that are not actually racially different from their neighbors) differences. Nigeria, like other African countries, has had a history of multiple tribal populations that have competed and have endured colonialism and then suffered a lengthy, sometimes bloody, contest to cement them into a stable nation-state. In the cases of South Africa and Russia there were a variety of native populations, but outsiders entered and eventually established their dominance and imposed a unity of sorts. Iran is representative of the Middle Eastern/Western Asian nations that have for centuries been the crossroads for many peoples who have migrated to the region, fought there, settled there, and been converted there, subsequently enduring tumultuous histories that have included complex struggles to devise workable national unities. In contrast, England and France have been tangling with about two generations of newly arrived diverse populations from the Asian subcontinent, the West Indies, and Africa that are particularly marked by racial and religious differences (apart from the historic populations that were previously wedded into those nation-states), while Germans and Poles have had minorities in their communities for centuries until wars and genocidal traumas took their toll, rendering those ethnic stories more historical than ongoing—but significant nonetheless.

The point is that most nation-states in the modern world are not like Japan, with its 1 percent or so of non-Japanese citizens. Multiethnicity and multiculturalism have become more the rule than the exception, whether of ancient or more recent origins, with unity from below or from above. These experiments in multiethnic nation-states compel us to consider what traditions, values, institutions, customs, political precedents, and historical encounters have contributed to successes (including that of the United States) and failures. What can Americans learn from the realization that their own history—by no means without its own conflicts and dark times—

has parallels elsewhere and, as well, numerous points of difference in the experiences of most other nations? Do we come away understanding America better? Hopefully.

An important objective of the Ethnic Diversity Within Nations series is to help readers in America and elsewhere better appreciate how societies in many parts of the world have struggled with the challenges of diversity and, by providing such an understanding, enable all of us to interact more effectively with each other. Thus, by helping students and other readers learn about these varied nations, our goal is to see them become better-informed citizens who are better able to comprehend world events and to act responsibly as voters, officeholders, teachers, public officials, and businesspersons—or simply to interact and coexist with diverse individuals, whatever the sources of that diversity.

Elliott Robert Barkan

Preface

I RAN IS A VAST AND ANCIENT COUNTRY IN A STRATEGIC LOCATION IN THE Middle East. It borders Russia, Iraq, Turkey, Afghanistan, Pakistan, the Gulf of Oman, and the Persian Gulf and covers a total area of 1.648 million square kilometers, with only 12,000 square kilometers of water. With close to 69 million people, Iran has played a significant role in the political and cultural affairs of the area for more than 3,000 years. Persian is the official language of the country, and 90 percent of the population are Shi'i Muslims. Approximately 8 percent are Sunni Muslims. The other 2 percent are Baha'is, Armenians, Assyrians, Chaldeans and evangelical Christians, Zoroastrians, and Jews.

Iranians speak a variety of Indo-Iranian, Semitic, Armenian, and Turkic languages. Persian, the majority language, is Indo-Iranian in origin. Altogether, 70 percent speak an Iranian language, including Kurdish, Luri, and Baluchi. Approximately 28 percent speak various dialects of Turkish. Speakers of Semitic languages include Arabs and Assyrians, and Armenian Iranians regard Armenian as their mother tongue.

Tribal and nomadic groups have a long history in the country. Many played significant roles as national power brokers and were armed until the 1920s. The twentieth century has been a time of massive change. The Constitutional Revolution of 1905–1906 transformed the country into a new era of modernization. The Pahlavi family ruled Iran beginning in 1925. Their policies propagated building a modern and secular nation at the expense of the more traditional segments of the society and the clergy. A number of ethnic groups also reacted negatively to centralization policies implemented by the government. The establishment of an Islamic Republic in 1979 has had major consequences for Iranians, the Middle East, and global politics in general.

This book traces the origins and histories of diverse peoples of Iran from the earliest times. The relationship of different groups with the central governments is discussed as well as the ways in which these people have influenced each other and what changes they have gone through. Particular attention is paid to the role of the various nomadic tribes and their relationship with the central governments. Some major cultural practices are mentioned briefly, including language and religious practices of the major groups. Most tribal groups consist of many subtribes. However, only the very major groups, mainly clans, are mentioned in this book. *The Cambridge History of Iran,* Volumes 1–7, is used extensively as a source. The system of transliteration adopted in this book is a modified version of that used in *The Cambridge History of Iran.* Spellings of some names that have become very familiar in the West do not conform to this system; I have left those terms in the more familiar form.

I would like to thank Professor Elliott Barkan for his patience and revisions of the manuscript. I would also like to thank Alicia Merritt and Giulia Rossi, ABC-CLIO; Connie Oehring, Oehring Editorial; and my family for their help and support.

List of Maps

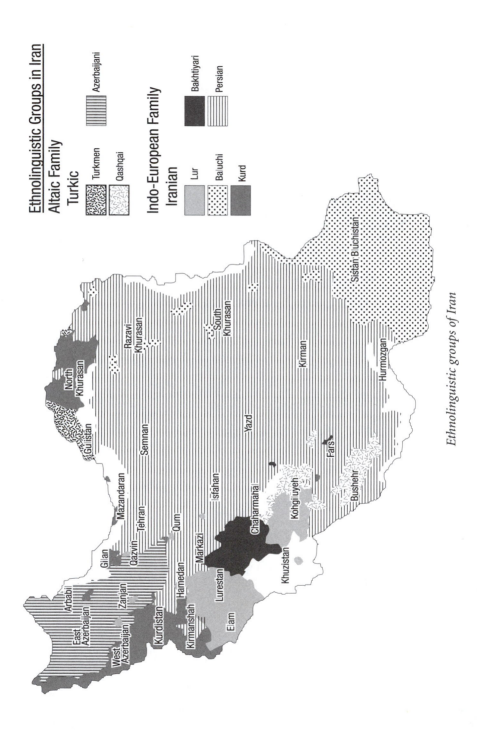

Ethnolinguistic Groups in Iran

Altaic Family
Turkic

- Turkmen
- Qashqai
- Azerbaijani

Indo-European Family
Iranian

- Lur
- Baluchi
- Kurd
- Bakhtiyari
- Persian

Ardabil

East Azerbaijan

West Azerbaijan

Zanjan

Kurdistan

Kirmanshah

Hamedan

Lurestan

Elam

Khuzistan

Markazi

Qum

Tehran

Qazvin

Gilan

Mazandaran

Gulistan

North Khurasan

Razavi Khurasan

Sennan

Isfahan

Chaharmahal

Kohgiluyeh

Bushehr

Fars

Yazd

South Khurasan

Kirman

Hurmozgan

Sistan Bluchistan

Ethnolinguistic groups of Iran

Land and Early History

Physical Setting

IRAN CONSISTS OF A COMPLEX OF MOUNTAIN CHAINS ENCIRCLING A SE-
ries of interior basins that lie at high altitudes above sea level. The Iranian
plateau is set between two depressions, the Persian Gulf to the south and
the Caspian Sea to the north. The country comprises the western and larger
portion of an extensive mountain zone that extends from eastern Asia Minor
and the Caucasus as far as the plains of the Punjab in India. The Zagros is the
most developed of all the mountain ranges in Iran and includes small outer
plains, chiefly the Khuzistan region, interior basins, and the Persian Gulf
coastal regions. The rest of the country includes the Northern Highlands of
the Caspian region, the interior desert basin, and the eastern highlands. Historically, the western end, where the Alburz Mountains reach Iranian Azerbaijan, near Lake Urumia, has been the most densely populated region in Iran.

The Zagros range dominates the entire western portion of the country,
and its northwestern portion is home to a number of ancient east-west routes
extending from Asia Minor to India. Azerbaijan, which shares a border with
Russia, is the most important modern province in this area. The northern
highlands include the Caspian areas and the Alburz mountain range; this
area has been inhabited since ancient times and comprises the two major
modern provinces of Gorgan and Mazandaran. The western section consists
of the modern provinces of Kurdistan and Luristan, named after the Kurd
and Luri peoples of Iran. The ancient province of Pars (Fars) is in the
southern part of the Zagros range and borders the modern Province of
Khuzistan, home to the ancient Elam, close to the Persian Gulf. The interior
desert basins, including modern Isfahan and Kirman, have been major urban centers for centuries. The northeast contains the ancient provinces of
Khurasan and Sistan, once home to the Saka nation.

Early spring pastures and oak woods located at the foot of the Zagros range
(Nasrollah Kasraian)

Pre-Iranian History, ca. 3000–800 B.C.

Archaeological evidence indicates that Paleolithic humans lived in Iran, and the Neolithic records are continuous beginning in the ninth millennium B.C. Many parts of the country dominated by seminomadic tribes, such as the Luristan and Zagros mountain regions, were permanently settled and cultivated by the second millennium B.C. From this time on, settlements declined while the nomadic population increased. The gradual arrival of seminomadic Iranian tribes started at the end of the third and the beginning of the second millennium B.C. and lasted for a millennium. Originally these people formed one group with the Indians, but sometime early in the third millennium B.C., they separated into two linguistically distinct groups: Indians and Iranians. The presence of the Iranian tribes helped to spread the Indo-Iranian language in the Iranian plateau during the second millennium B.C. Indo-Iranian is a branch of the Proto-Indo-European dialect, spoken in the fourth and early third millennia B.C. in eastern and central Europe.

These early migrants were pastoral nomads, cattle breeders, who moved in successive waves mainly on foot accompanied by carts. They branched out into western and eastern Iranian groups. The western Iranian tribes became

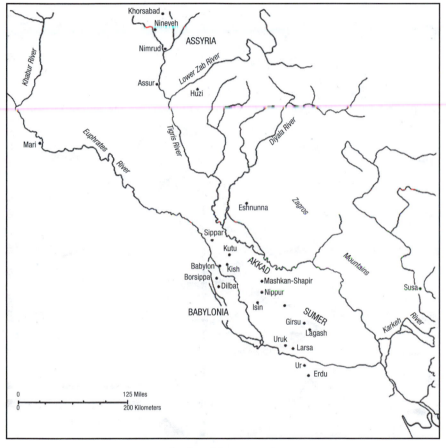

Khorsabad •
Nineveh
ASSYRIA
Nimrud •
Lower Zab River
Assur •
Huzi •
Khabur River
Euphrates River
Tigris River
Diyala River
Mari •
Zagros
Eshnunna •
Sippar •
Kutu •
Mountains
Babylon • Kish •
AKKAD
Borsippa • • Mashkan-Shapir
• Dilbat • Nippur
Susa •
Isin •
BABYLONIA
SUMER
Girsu •
Karkeh River
Lagash
Uruk • • Larsa
Ur •
• Erdu

0 ————————— 125 Miles
0 ————————— 200 Kilometers

Ancient Mesopotamia

the ancestors of the Medes, Persians, and Parthians, while eastern Iranian tribes emerged as Scythians, Alani, Massagetae, Sakas, Chorasmians, and Sogdians.

Well-developed city-states already existed in Mesopotamia (present-day Iraq) beginning around 3000 B.C. and influenced subsequent developments in the area, including the Iranian plateau. By the second millennium B.C. the kingdom of Elam in south (present-day Khuzistan) was a well-developed major urbanized center in Iran. The ethnic composition before the arrival of the Iranian groups was mixed and "very likely included the tribes of the Iranian highlands belonging to the North-East Caucasian linguistic family in the north-west of the plateau, and to the Proto-Dravidian in the south-east. The Elamite, at least in the lowlands, seems to have been related to Proto-Dravidian, the ancestor of the Dravidian languages now spoken in southern India and in some parts of Baluchistan" (Gershevitch, 1985, pp. 2, 3). Susa and Anshan were the most populated and important Elamite centers and had a hieroglyphic writing system as early as 3000 B.C. There might have been peoples or tribes speaking archaic languages unconnected with major linguistic groups of the area. Parts of the Zagros area (present-day Luristan) were inhabited by Kassites, and Kurdistan and the Lake Urmiyeh vicinity were the habitat for other groups, including some Hurrians who had been influenced by Indo-Europeans at some point before their arrival in the Near East. Lullubi and Quti (Guti, Qu-ti-um) people, both from the Zagros region, also shared the area and managed to survive but exerted little influence.

The archaeological evidence indicates that the early penetration of the Iranian tribes into the most eastern region of the Zagros around 1300 B.C. was followed by their gradual penetration to the west along the main roads that crossed the mountain valleys. By 1000 B.C., Iranian groups were already organized into small states or tribes in western Iran and played a significant role in this region, extending beyond their early territories. During the ninth and eighth centuries B.C. the non-Iranian-speaking population still dominated in political terms, but beginning in the second half of the eighth century B.C. the Iranians constituted the majority in many regions of western and northwestern Iran. Elam was in decline, Kassites had been absorbed, and only smaller groups survived, including some descendents of Quti. Early Iranians practiced both pastoralism and agriculture and honored deities, such as Mithra, who had survived from their ancient past. There are no indications of a developed town life among the early Iranians, and settlements for the production of objects were few and small. However, the discovery in 2004 of a new extensive, literate Bronze Age settlement in southeastern Iran might change such assumptions.

Among the groups arriving were the Medes, who migrated to the plateau at the end of the second and beginning of the first millennium B.C. and settled down in northwestern Iran. Petty principalities existed in the area, and opposition by them to the Medes' immigration forced the Medes to unite. In the interior of the country, south of Lake Urmiyeh, lay the kingdom of Mannai, comprising a large part of modern Kurdistan and parts of Azerbaijan. The Medes won their battle to settle in the area.

Early Iranian Dynasties

Medes

The penetration of Iran by Iranians at the beginning of the first millennium B.C. differed from previous invasions because the Iranians were not absorbed by the native population, as other groups were. After a slow penetration lasting a few centuries, they established themselves and eventually became the rulers of the entire region. Medes, along with other Iranian groups, were established in Iran by the ninth century B.C., and their name, along with the name Parsua (Parsuas), shows up in many records. Parsua and Anshan, a major Elamite center in present Khuzistan, are often mentioned together. Eventually the two kingdoms formed Persis, or the Pars (Fars) region of southern Iran. The area consists of a series of steppes leading from the Persian Gulf to the central deserts of Iran and is the home to the first Persian Empire. Early settlements in Pars were primarily in oases where water was obtainable. The size of the settlements depended on the availability of water. Ancient Anshan (Anzan), a major Elamite city center in the area, was inhabited early by migrating Iranian tribes.

The Medes were located farther north, around the area of modern-day Hamadan, along with many other ancient groups and expanded their territory to other areas, including the modern-day Azerbaijan. This area over the centuries has witnessed Kurds, Medes, Persians, Turks, and many others entering and settling in its valleys. Another Iranian group, the Sargatians, settled as far as Tabriz (Azerbaijan) and the frontier kingdom of Urartu (Armenia). The modern province of Khurasan was inhabited by a variety of people and was invaded constantly, while central parts of the plateau and desert areas, because of their harsh physical conditions, remained hostile to settled populations.

These early Iranians on the plateau were not united but lived under minor chieftains. Herodotus mentions six tribes of Medes who paid tribute to the Assyrian rulers of the area. The period is characterized as one of mix-ing, interaction, change, and displacement of ethnic groups, mostly no-mads moving into settled lands with the rise and fall of alliances and alle-giances. Among such groups were Scythians, who arrived from the northern Black Sea by traveling along the western Caucasus into Asia Mi-nor. They made their way along the coast of the Caspian Sea and ended in northwestern Iran. On their way they left artifacts near Lake Urmiyeh, gave their name to the modern city of Sakiz, and invaded Media. Many were ab-sorbed into the local population, and the rest were defeated by the Median tribes and expelled from the area around 600 B.C. They were engaged in agricultural activity, worshiped the war god Ares in the form of a sword cult, made animal sacrifices, and used sarcophagi to bury royalty. Their burial patterns were similar to those of other Scythian tribes in northwest Caucasian territories, with horses and human offerings included in the fu-neral rituals.

The ethnic composition at the time was mixed and also included Is-raelites deported by the Assyrians into Media, which was the beginning of Jewish settlements in Iran. As of 727 B.C. the Assyrians had deported thousands of Israelites and forced them to settle in Media. Close to thirty thousand were forced to settle in Ecbatana (Agbatana, or Hamadan) and Susa in southwest Persia. The next wave of Jewish settlers arrived to es-cape further persecution by Assyrians around 680 B.C., and many settled in Isfahan.

The alliance between Medes and Babylonians put an end to the Assyrian Empire. However, Assyrians are still present and form a small Christian mi-nority in Iran. For a century after the conquest of Assyria, Media became the dominant center of Iranian material and intellectual culture. Median terri-tory stretched beyond its old territory of Azerbaijan, Kurdistan, and the re-gion around Hamadan and extended to the northern part of the central deserts, Isfahan (Paraitekene), Pars, Elam, Kirman/Khuzistan (Carmania), Luristan, and Hyrcania (Caspian/Gorgan area), plus several vassal countries including Armenia.

Medes were Iranians and worshiped ancient Iranian deities. Greek sources also mention the presence of Magi acting as official soothsayers and priests at the courts of the Median kings. Magi, archaic Zoroastrian priests, are mentioned by some ancient historians as a tribe from which religious teachers, priests, and soothsayers were recruited. Very likely the introduc-tion of popular Zoroastrian deities into this earlier form of Zoroastrianism happened in the middle of the fifth century B.C. under the next rulers, the Persians.

Persians

Persians were the other major Iranian group, with at least twelve large tribes, according to the Greek sources. The tribes were mainly nomadic and occupied territories from east of the Caspian Sea to the central desert and Media and Pars in the south. Around 800 B.C. the Persians detached themselves from the Median tribes and, faced with the onslaughts from the north, moved south into the valleys of the Zagros Mountains. They steadily migrated farther southeast, gradually occupied Elamite territory in southwestern Iran, and gave their name to the occupied territories: Parsa (modern-day Fars), which was heavily populated by displaced Assyrians moved there by force. By the time the first Persian rulers appeared, Persian tribes had already formed a tribal union, which was headed by chiefs from the clan of Achaemenid.

Persian Empire, 550–330 B.C.

Achaemenids, the founders of the Persian Empire, are credited with creating the first major multinational empire in the region due to the vast territories they conquered. Cyrus, the first Achaemenid king, ruled Anshan and originally was a vassal of Media. Gradually he attained the support of most Persian and Median tribes, overthrew the Median king, and became the ruler of both the Persians and the Medes in 549 B.C. at Ecbatana (Agbatana), present-day Hamadan. A decade later he conquered Asia Minor and Mesopotamia and, with little resistance, entered Babylon in 539 B.C. He arrived as the righteous prince chosen by the Babylonian god Marduk to restore the old religion that had been ignored by the rulers of Babylon. Cyrus was admired by the Jews for permitting Jewish exiles in Babylon to go home and reconstruct the temple of Jerusalem. He entered Jewish history as a protector and is praised in the Old Testament. Some Jews chose to emigrate to Persia, and as a result, more Jewish colonies were formed in Persian territories. Cyrus was killed battling Queen Tomyris, the ruler of the Saka nation of Massagetae, in what is now Turkestan (530 B.C.). By the time the Persians were defeated by Alexander the Great almost two hundred years later, they had conquered the entire region from Egypt to India, including Asia Minor and Greece, and created the first major polyethnic, multireligious, and multicultural empire in the region. They created a strong and persistent concept of kingship that required strong loyalty from its subjects and was said to be sanctioned by a protector god. They formed a powerful central government backed by efficient administrative and military structures, controlling loosely connected, semiautonomous local and foreign states. However, Achaemenid records "are completely lacking in any name that could define, in a geographic or ethnic sense, the state or kingdom" (Gnoli, 1989, p. 6). The rulers called themselves the kings of the "many lands" or "many peoples" rather than kings of the Persian or Achaemenid Empire.

Engraving of Cyrus the Great (Bettmann/Corbis)

Ethnic Composition

The Achaemenid period was characterized by intensive processes of ethnic mixing, amalgamation of the cultures and religious concepts of different peoples. Achaemenid leaders even staged "marriages" between foreign gods and Iranian deities, such as that "between the Babylonian god Bel and the Iranian goddess Dayna-Mazdayasnish" (Dandamaev and Lukonin, 1994, p. 359). Such mixing was made possible by an increase in direct contact between various parts of the empire because of well-maintained roads and simultaneous use of a number of languages, including Old Persian, Elamite, and Aramaic, for administrative efficiency. Aramaic became the official language of administration and trade in the empire. Schools produced scribes and translators who each knew several languages. However, Old Persian remained the official language at the court. Persian civil servants gave their orders orally, and these orders were then translated simultaneously into other languages, mainly Aramaic and Elamite. Such deliberate policies as maintaining the Persian language despite the primary use of Aramaic and creating their own calendar were part of an imperial strategy designed to maintain Persian authority. Darius, a major ruler of the dynasty, in his inscriptions refers to his own language as Aryan, the root of the name *Iran,* but takes more pride in being a Persian. The Achaemenids also created military colonies throughout the empire, consisting of representatives of various peoples, and carried out mass deportations of entire tribes, settling them at opposite ends of the state.

The archives at Persepolis mention other Iranian tribes: Chorasmians, Bactrians, Sakas, Sargatians (modern Yazd), Caspians, Parthavas (Parthia), and Areiois (from Aria, Herat), in addition to the Medes and Persians. They also mention such Scythian-related tribes as the Sarmatians and other nations under their rule, including the local Elamites, Armenians, Aramaic peoples, Sogdians (non-nomadic eastern Iranians), and Drangians. The latter and other tribes in eastern Iran (modern-day Sistan) were related to the Medes and Persians, spoke the same language, and had the same customs (e.g., the fire cult and the cult of the supreme god Ahuramazda). The country was divided into standard units of administration called satrapy, and Persians were awarded the highest positions as satraps. These units constituted major Iranian provinces plus subjugated countries such as Egypt and Babylonia. Each province or country represented one semiautonomous administrative unit. Altogether some thirty subject peoples were named in the inscribed monuments of the Achaemenid period, and several different groups were sometimes put together under one satrapy. These people moved around

The ruins of the ancient Greek city of Persepolis (courtesy of Dominick F. Rossi)

frequently and were settled, sometimes voluntarily and sometimes by force, in every corner of the empire. The Persians did not use systematic deportation, as the Assyrians did. Sometimes they moved groups for their own safety, and sometimes to improve their situation.

Many groups were given land allotments in exchange for taxes and military service, and they were protected as long as they remained loyal. Archives identify various quarters in the same city housing particular ethnic groups, such as the Sushan quarter named after the city of Susa and inhabited by Elamites, or the Egyptian quarter with its own people's assembly. However, various documents indicate that in the majority of cases different ethnic groups were scattered throughout the empire and fully participated in the socioeconomic life of the country. Persians also expanded their influence into Armenia and were influenced by and had an influence upon Greek inhabitants of the empire. Intergroup marriages are mentioned in surviving documents, and all groups appear as contracting parties and witnesses in various legal texts.

Nomads were restricted to small areas, and true nomads were relatively few in number. Nomadic groups, including those of the Zagros area, were both Iranian and non-Iranian. Some, like the Sarmatians, lived as seminomads, moving high up the mountains in summer and descending to the low ground in winter, as the modern Qashqai tribes of Fars still do. The ancient nomadic tribes were kept under control by encouraging them to become part of the armed forces. In return they were guaranteed maintenance, equipment, and regular supplies. However, the Sargatian tribe from southeast (Yazd) Iran is the only significant nomadic tribe recorded in the army records. Although many other tribes are mentioned, they lived in scattered areas and were treated as marginal. During most of the Achaemenid period, little attempt was made to settle the nomadic tribes of the Zagros, which minimized friction. However, toward the end of the Achaemenid reign, conflict between these tribes and the government increased.

Gradual settling down and assimilation of nomadic tribes took place, as documented in ancient Greek texts with respect to Drangians (modern-day Sistan). After a new capital was established by the Persians in the region, the Drangians, a tribal society of cattle drivers, became farmers, and many started to live in villages. Later the area became a center for extraction of tin, used in bronze production. Centuries later, the Greek topographer Strabo commented that "Drangians were *persisontes,* which means they had become

A Qashqai woman while migrating in spring time, on the tribal path (Il-rah) of Dasht-e-Bakan between Shiraz and Aspas in Fars. (Nasrollah Kasraian)

like Persians" (Gershevitch, 1985, p. 248). Pastoral nomads are also mentioned, and some mountain tribes in remote areas exacted a toll for protecting the roads, indicating one of the ways the central administration managed its relationship with the nomads.

Kurds are mentioned as mountain tribes of Zagros and were engaged in destroying part of the army of the rebellious Persian prince, Cyrus the Younger, around 400 B.C. They were called Carduchi by Xenophon and were described as "rough mountain dwellers resisting all intrusion, fighting with sling stones and shoot[ing] arrows" (Xenophon, 1972, p. 191). At times, along with other mountain tribes, they were referred to as mountaineers invading settlements. By this time they were an amalgam of Indo-European tribes arriving in the area, through different routes and at different times, and lived alongside others, including the Semitic groups. The ancestors of the Kurds were one of the earliest groups with an Indo-Iranian language who appeared in the area. How and at what point Kurds who speak a northwestern Iranian language entered the area is not clear; very likely the Kurds today are not an ethnically coherent group and have a different ancestry.

Persians occupied the highest positions in the state apparatus, awarded loyal supporters, and harshly punished opponents and rebels with little respect for their origins or religious affiliations. At the same time they extensively utilized the cultural, legal, and administrative traditions of conquered nations by granting semiautonomy. Such incorporation enabled the young kingdom to take advantage of the civil and administrative expertise of the conquered nations, though at times such policies endangered the stability of the state. The Persian rulers of the time showed an affinity for the Zoroastrian sovereign god Ahuramazda (wise lord), whom they mention and praise in their inscriptions. First taught among nomads on the Asian steppes around 3,500 years ago, Zoroastrianism is one of the earliest revealed religions. It has links with the ancient Vedic beliefs of India and even possibly to a remote Indo-European past. Most information about the prophet Zoroaster comes from the earliest texts, Gathas, in which seventeen hymns are attributed to Zoroaster himself. Gathas are inspired utterances, many addressed directly to God, and their poetic form is the most ancient of Iranian literary works. The best educated guess for Zoroaster's period, based on linguistic evidence, is between 1700 and 1000 B.C.

Subjects of the empire worshiped multiple gods, and various religious concepts existed among all, including the Persians. Ancient Indo-Iranian nature deities were venerated, along with the distinct Zoroastrianism of the Magi; the ancient Indo-Iranian cult of Mithra; and the goddess Anahita, who was elevated by the Achaemenids. The last two deities were worshiped by many Iranian tribes as far as Bactria, Sogdiana, and Chorasmia. The spread of their cults in the later Achaemenid period was the result of the influence of the religious ideas of the Persians, who encouraged and promoted their native deities, sometimes at the expense of local deities. However, despite such assimilations, the Zoroastrian supreme god, Ahuramazda, remained the most important Iranian deity and the protector of royalty for centuries. The presence of hundreds of sacred objects used by various ethnic groups in the Susa and Persepolis complexes and the allocation of rations for various non-Iranian deities also indicate that there were no restrictions on worship by different nations and groups. Such tolerance was not exclusive to Persians, since in the ancient Near Eastern religions there is no concept of false faith or heresy. Foreign temples and houses of worship, unless exempted, were under an obligation to pay taxes and to support the political line. This principle of religious policy was observed throughout the Achaemenid rule.

Jews

Jewish colonies in Iran were abundant at the time, though the main Jewish settlements were centered in Mesopotamia. There were Jewish colonies in major cities as well. Ezra and Nehemiah, well-known Jewish writers and statesmen, were both employed at the Achaemenid court and were later appointed governors of Jewish territories with their own governmental and judiciary structures based on Jewish texts. Both were influential figures in Jewish history and are regarded as founders of Judaism. They made a deal with the Persian rulers to remain loyal and, as a result, were able to reestablish the Judean society. Ezra produced his code of law during this period and, among other things, prohibited marriage outside the Jewish community. Cambyses (Cyrus's son and successor), who is known to have worshiped Egyptian gods, also patronized the Elephantine temple of the Jews in Egypt. Beginning in the sixth century B.C., there was no Persian deputy in Judah, and representatives from the ancient Davidic House were appointed to be the regional leaders in Jerusalem.

Armenia

The Achaemenid period marks the beginning of centuries of extensive relationships with the neighboring Armenia. Ruled for many centuries by the Persians, Armenia played a major role as a buffer zone between Persians,

Greeks, and Romans. Many wars of independence were fought against Persians, some with success. Armenia became an Iranian province for centuries, on and off. There was widespread cultural exchange between Persia and Armenia, including many royal marriages, adoption of Persian cults and Zoroastrianism by some Armenians, and shared artistic styles. Though Armenians of this period lived and worked in Iran, the present Armenian population in Iran is a by-product of forced settlements in the sixteenth century A.D. and it is not related to the ancient movements.

The Achaemenid conquests, for the first time in history, politically united vast territories from the Eastern Mediterranean to the Indus. Earlier kingdoms disappeared and became integrated within the structures of a unified new state. This unification was successful for a number of reasons, despite rebellions. The Persian concept of ensuring that sovereignty was awarded to conquered nations was different from the later integration and assimilation policies pursued by others, such as the Roman emperors. The nations were left to manage their affairs, though the highest-ranking rulers, such as the governors, were Persians. The subject nations were required to pay taxes and provide military assistance to the Achaemenid rulers. Although the elite of the conquered nations imitated Persian ways, Persian citizenship was not granted to local elites, as was the case with the Romans. Such policies of local autonomy and decentralization of jurisdictions proved effective in holding the empire together until its defeat by the Macedonian king Alexander the Great. At the same time, voluntary and forced resettlements of various nations all around the empire, and easing up of movement among provinces accelerated cultural exchanges between various groups while they maintained their ethnic identities.

The Achaemenid reign in Iran ended when the Macedonian king Alexander the Great broke the eastern Iranian resistance in 330 B.C. Seleucids were Greek rulers of Persia and heir to Alexander's empire after his death. Seleucus, one of Alexander's generals, became the king of the eastern provinces, more or less covering modern Afghanistan, Iran, Iraq, Syria, and Lebanon, together with parts of Turkey, Armenia, Turkmenistan, Uzbekistan, and Tajikistan. His kingdom had two capitals, Antioch in Syria and Seleucia in modern Iraq, a major Persian center at the time.

Seleucid governing policies were different than those of the early Greek period in Iran. Alexander himself did not stay in Iran for long and, while in Iran, attempted to seek support from the Iranians by adopting Iranian customs and usages, wearing local clothes, establishing native military units, marrying Iranian women, and entrusting Iranian aristocrats with functions in his entourage or in the satrapies. However, the Seleucids attempted to

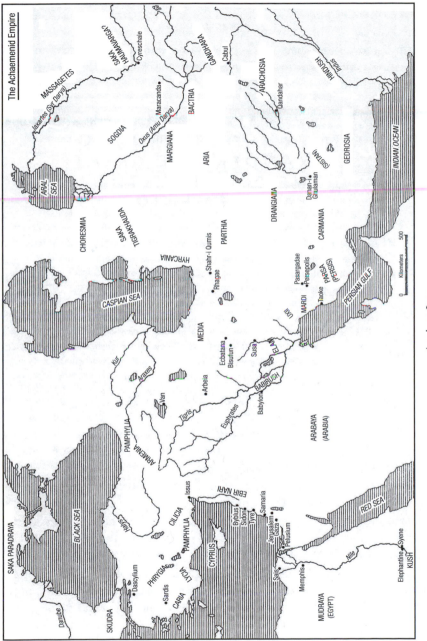

The Achaemenid Empire

Ancient Iran

break with the traditions and methods of the Persian rulers and impose their own. Such policies proved ineffective and were soon abandoned, and they focused on gaining partial loyalty from the people under their rule. They imported Greeks and Macedonians into Iranian lands to work as both administrators and military personnel in newly built towns and accelerated urbanization. At least nine towns were built on the shores of the Persian Gulf, including the major center Iranian Antioch (modern-day Bushire), and others throughout the empire, including the ancient cities of Raga (Rhages, or Ray) near Tehran and Nysa-Alexandropolis in Parthia. However, Parthia, like Bactria, eventually managed to break free from the Greeks.

Atropatene (Azerbaijan) and Persis (Pars)

It is generally believed that Atropatene (Azerbaijan) acquired its name at this period when Atropates, the Median governor of the area from the Achaemenid and Alexander periods, proclaimed independence and called his territory Atropatene (the place of tending the sacred fire). However, the name might be older. The area contained a large number of Medes among other groups and is also known as Media Atropatene. It included the northwestern part of Iran, Kurdistan, Azerbaijan, and parts of Kirmanshah, and its boundaries changed many times. Persis (Fars) remained hostile, dominated by Persians, and no major Greek cities were built in the area. The Persian language, culture, and religion changed little in this region. The development and emergence of the Middle Persian script later on is attributed to the relative independence of such provinces from Seleucid influence. Though Greek arts, civil organizations, sciences, and philosophy were popularized, no attempts were aimed at forcefully Hellenizing the local populations, and the Greek influence barely affected the rural inhabitants. On the whole the Seleucid rulers were not powerful enough to enforce obedience from the numerous kingdoms and principalities incorporated in the empire. They never achieved the relative success of the Achaemenids in maintaining a coherent multinational state controlled by one powerful central authority.

The towns had a mixed population, and in most parts people of different cultural and ethnic origins lived in close proximity, as they had before. More remote provinces maintained the Aramaic language, while a few adopted Greek for administration purposes. Religious tolerance prevailed, but there were problems with the Jewish community, mainly political in nature and because of developments and hostilities outside Iran. The Seleucids moved their capital to Syria and placed garrisons in major areas, including Azerbaijan and Kurdistan. Centrally organized dynastic cults of the ruling Seleucid family existed in some places. Parts of Media Minor and Chorasmia remained independent despite the presence of a Greek polis in central Media. Bactria and Sogdia were fortified and remained Iranian in culture despite Greek settlements. Seleucids also followed the policy of resettlement of various groups; some Kurds were settled in Anatolia for military purposes. Kurds from Media were reportedly fighting against the Romans, but other Kurds in the Roman territories were fighting for the Romans. "From the second century B.C., the Kurds are referred to as Cyrtti by the Greeks. The term was originally applied to Seleucid or Parthian mercenaries of the Zagros, and might not denote a coherent linguistic or ethnic group at this time" (McDowall, 1997, p. 8).

Greeks established many garrison cities in the eastern Iranian territories with large numbers of Greek mercenary soldiers to combat invasions by Indian and Saka groups. By the end of the second century B.C., Drangiana was occupied by the Saka tribes, who then gave their name to the region (Sakastana, or Sistan). The Seleucid presence in Susa was strong, while Aria (Herat), Drangiana (Sistan), and Hyrcania (Gorgan), though under firm Seleucid control, showed little Greek influence. The Greek language was popular among the elite, became the lingua franca, and survived well into the next era, the Parthian period. The Greek script gradually replaced Aramaic, the script that had been dominant in many areas.

Local cults and traditions were maintained side by side with observances of Greek religion. Native Iranians followed their own Zoroastrian and Magi traditions, statues of Greek deities were erected in the cities, and some Greek gods were given Iranian identities. Loyal upper-class Iranians maintained high office, adopted Greek nationality, and became the most Hellenized of all the groups. After the defeat of the Greeks by the Parthians, the next Iranian dynasty, the Greek element survived not only in art and culture, such as Greek science, theater, and schools of philosophy, but also in personal and institutional components such as coinage. It would take more than a century for the Parthians to reduce the Greek influence.

The Parthian Era, 247 B.C.–A.D. 224

The Parthians, belonging to the Iranian nomadic tribe of Parni and part of a major confederacy (Dahae), were the next major Iranian dynasty. They led a nomadic life in the steppe country between the Caspian Sea and the Sea of Aral and were known as fierce horsemen, warriors, and archers, appearing in Assyrian records as early as the seventh century B.C. They defeated the Seleucids, expanded their territories to most of the Middle East and southwest Asia, controlled the Silk Road, and built Parthia into an Eastern superpower. They revived the Persian language and script and the greatness of the Achaemenid Empire and stopped Roman advances into eastern territories. Imperial Aramaic was used widely for administration, and a number of regional forms of this script existed in other provinces. The Persians in the southwest used their own version of the script, which later came to be known as Pahlavi. Parthia at one time occupied areas now in Iran, Iraq, Turkey, Armenia, Georgia, Azerbaijan, Turkmenistan, Afghanistan, Tajikistan, Pakistan, Syria, Lebanon, Jordan, Palestine, and Israel. The Parthians were also known as Arsacids, named after their first king, but became known as Parthians when they moved southward into the Persian province of Parthava sometime before 250 B.C. This was a province listed in both the Achaemenid and Greek sources.

Once established, the Parthians maintained some local petty rulers from the Seleucid period while appointing their own kinsmen as kings in major areas such as Media and Armenia. They were faced with massive invasion by nomads into eastern Iranian territories and Roman attacks on the western frontiers. In Armenia a succession of kings was removed either by Romans or Iranians to guarantee loyalty to either kingdom. Although Iranian religions were popular in Armenia, the eventual acceptance of Christianity severed Armenian relations with Iran, and Armenia became a Roman ally. The challenge of imposing effective control over vast and different cultural units has remained a fixed feature of Iranian society since ancient times and a problem for the central governments.

The Parthian period is known for religious tolerance. The Parthians promoted Zoroastrian religion and literature and maintained the three major cults of Ahuramazda, Mithra, and Anahita. They attempted to eradicate Greek language and script, built a few cities, and expanded the city of Seleucia-Ctesiphon on the Tigris River, which became the capital of the Persian Empire until its collapse in the seventh century A.D. Iran remained a multiethnic and multicultural society, with residents from every race and religion; like the Achaemenids, the Parthians tried to maintain their own superiority. The vassal states of their period were divided into superior and inferior countries, with Parthia, Media, and Armenia forming the most important provinces. Extensive trade with many nations, including the Romans, facilitated cultural exchanges among various traditions. Such interactions included educating royal princes at the Roman courts. This period also marked the beginning of Christian settlements in Iran and, later on, a flow of Christian missionaries and Jewish refugees escaping unfavorable treatment in the Roman territories.

Jews

The Jewish chronicles mention the Parthian period as a good and prosperous one. Centers of Jewish life in the Parthian Empire were situated in Mesopotamia. Jewish chroniclers stated that the Jews enjoyed a long period of peace and maintained close and positive contacts with the reigning dynasty. They sided with the Persians in the rebellions against the Romans in Mesopotamia (A.D. 116) and had a major share of the silk trade, with the support of the Parthian kings. By the second century A.D., a representative of Davidic origin represented the Jewish minority at court. This figure was called the "exilarch" and carried out functions of a political-administrative nature. Religious persecution of Jewish rebels in Palestine by the Romans in A.D. 135 brought many Jewish refugees into the Parthian empire. Like Achaemenids, the Parthians supported loyal groups and punished disloyal ones. The Jewish communities proved to be loyal and reliable and as a result experienced a time of prosperity and cultural-religious creativity.

Christians

Christianity arrived in Iran during the Parthian period as early as the first century A.D., and by the beginning of the third century, church documents in the Syriac language indicates that the Christians in the Persian territories had some 360 churches. Arbela, east of the Tigris River, the capital of the small Persian border kingdom of Adiabene (modern-day Iraq), was the earliest center of Christianity in Iran. There was a large concentration of Jews in Arbela. The first-century Jewish historian Josephus mentioned that a king of Adiabene accepted Judaism about A.D. 36. Such a conversion made Arbela a natural center for a Christian mission at an early date. Nisibis, another major city of the area, was the seat of a Jewish academy of learning. Christianity spread in both villages and cities, and by the end of the Parthian period (A.D. 224), Christian communities were settled all the way from Edessa, an important missionary center, to Afghanistan. The Chronicles of Arbela reported that by this time there were already more than twenty bishops in Persia, and Christians had already penetrated Arabia and Central Asia.

Christianity slowly but steadily continued to advance in various parts of the empire. Though thousands of Persians embraced Christianity, Persia remained Zoroastrian, with many adhering to the cult of Mithra. There never arose an indigenous Persian Christian church, worshipping in the Persian language. The Persian church was of Syrian origin, traditions, and tendencies and for about three centuries regarded Antioch (in Syria) as the center of its faith and the seat of authority.

The Confederation of Tribes and Clans

Parthians were northern Iranians, and their success over southern Iranians was mainly due to the support of the noble families of the Parni clan. Their victory represented the triumph of outer and nomadic Iranian groups over the central, non-nomadic ones, and on the whole they were not well received by settled Iranians. In times of trouble they had to rely on support from their kinsmen in the steppe to the east of the Caspian Sea rather than from Persia or Media. They never attained the same level of central control that the Achaemenids had. There was a loose confederation of major tribes and clans, and never-ending disputes and separatist tendencies of the vassal kingdoms continually threatened their rule. The major clans had a system of petty nobility similar to the European knights, with peasants and serfs depending on them. In times of strength, their main loyalty was to these dependent groups rather than to the kings. Due to its military power, the nobility gained increasing power over the land and its peasants and consequently became rich and powerful enough to defy and resist the kings at times. This fragmentation paved the way for the decline of the Parthian Empire.

At the tribal level a hierarchical system prevailed, and at times of war lesser clans and tribes under Parthian rule were obliged to assist the more noble clans. The noble clans provided the heavy cavalry, and the lesser ones formed the light cavalry. The seven major Parthian tribes remained master warriors, archers, and horsemen and maintained superiority over other groups. Parthians were concerned about their Iranian origin, used a Zoroastrian calendar, gathered religious texts, and popularized literature, mainly oral. The next major Iranian rulers tried to reduce their influence, but their legacy remained in oral and post-Islamic written accounts. In these accounts they were presented as a "legendary Kayanid dynasty from eastern Iran, who constantly fought against their Turanain foes (another legendary dynasty) supported by their legendary Saka hero, Rustam" (Wiesehofer, 1996, p. 134).

One cultural element that survived the Parthians' collapse was the popularity of orator-poet entertainers (minstrels), who presented oral literature almost wholly in verse, accompanied by a musical instrument. The tradition could be the origin of *naghali*, a form of oral entertainment that survived until the early twentieth century. Orators, or *naghals*, entertained the masses at popular teahouses with epic poetry from the pre-Islamic era that is preserved in the *Book Shahnameh* (The book of the kings), which was composed around A.D. 1000. This book contains a section on the Kayanid dynasty of Iran.

The major ethnic groups of the previous period remained, with a number of languages, and both Aramaic and Greek scripts were used. Persians remained in Fars while Azerbaijan was still inhabited mainly by the Medes, some Armenians, and Kurds. Northern Azerbaijan (Russian Azerbaijan) prospered under the Parthians and was called Albania, while the southern part (Atropatene), suffered numerous attacks and invasions caused by the Roman-Parthian conflict. A number of Iranian languages, including Middle Persian, Parthian, Sogdian, Chorasmian, and Bactrian, were spoken as well as Armenian, Aramaic, Greek, and various Caucasian languages. The Parthians finally collapsed due to both internal and external conflicts, and their successors, the Sasanian rulers, in their attempt to link themselves directly to the Achaemenid kings, tried to bypass the Parthian influence. They are often accused of trying to eliminate the Parthian legacy by erasing them from the national history.

The Sasanian Era, A.D. 224–651

Sasanians were minor rulers of Persis (Fars) and of Iranian origin. They defeated the Parthians and organized a nation-state based on the principles of indisputable authority granted by gods and a national church. The name of the country, *Iran*, was derived from the Sasanian concept of Eranshahr (empire of the Aryans) in the third century A.D. and existed in variant forms in the ancient Zoroastrian text, Avesta, and ancient Persia. "By using Eranshahr, the Sasanians created a new 'identity' for themselves and their subjects that became the political, cultural and religious home of all living there" (Wiesehofer, 1996, p. 165). During this period, Iranians asserted their ethnic and cultural identity and created a new calendar and a vast literature in Middle Persian that was referred to as *Pahlavi* by later Muslim scholars. They succeeded in preserving the traditions inherited from the Medes and the Persians and also managed to spread their distinct culture among many neighboring societies. Along with Greco-Roman, Indian, and Chinese, Sasanian remained one of the four major civilizations in Late Antiquity and the Early Middle Ages.

Sasanians divided the country between royal princes, who formed their own minor courts, with kingdoms that included several provinces with mixed populations. Despite efforts to consolidate central authority, the minor kingdoms remained independent enough to exert pressure on the Sasanian rulers but eventually broke down at the time of the Arab invasion in the seventh century A.D. Divergent policies were employed to control the populations of settlements in the vast territories. Urbanization increased, and, at least in the case of Khuzistan, there was a massive migration into large urban centers and a simultaneous decline of farm products. At the same time, large-scale building projects, such as dams, canals, and other irrigation systems, were used to improve farming methods and attract people from the settled villages and small towns in other provinces. Iranian-speaking groups were mainly in the southern provinces, and the western provinces were still influenced by Aramaic speakers. Forced settlements and deportations existed, often associated with the formation of new urban centers, and sometimes included foreign war captives, such as Romans.

Cities had mixed populations. Early in the Sasanian history, religious freedom existed, but with the establishment of a powerful Zoroastrian church, religious persecution increased. Hostilities with Rome also influenced religious policies toward Christians, including Armenians. In the eastern territories, wars with neighbors, including powerful Indian dynasties, resulted in persecution of Buddhists. Due to religious upheavals and new messianic movements, the persecution of religious minorities became systematic, and the religious freedoms granted by previous dynasties in Iran were limited.

Sasanians were the hereditary guardians of a great temple at Fars. Ardeshir, the first king from this dynasty, made great use of religious propaganda as a means of establishing his rule over the vast empire he conquered in the third century A.D. The result was the establishment of a single Zoroastrian church under the direct and authoritarian control of Persia. This church maintained Ahuramazda as the all-powerful sovereign god in addition to the three major cults of Anahita, Mithra, and Varahram (the lord of victory). There were also a number of minor deities, including twelve whose names were given to the twelve Iranian months in the Zoroastrian calendar and are still in use. A single canon of Avestan texts was established, and many festivals were celebrated elaborately with feasts, songs, plays, and prayers to reinforce the system of religious observances. Included were major festivals celebrating the new year (No Ruz, celebrated by the Achaemenids as well);

winter solstice (Shab e Cheleh), dedicated to the deity representing the sun; and Mihregan, dedicated to the deity Mithra. All three festivals are still celebrated by modern-day Iranians. A strong unified and growing body of disciplined priests strengthened the church and implemented its religious codes and observances with great efficiency. Gradually these priests managed to dominate many aspects of the private and public lives of ordinary citizens. However, a separation existed between "throne" and "altar," and at times there was conflict between the two. A long-lasting power struggle would shape the destiny of various religious groups caught between the two. Mazdakites and Manicheans were among such religious groups, which at the end were persecuted despite the support from some kings. Manicheans managed to survive for centuries outside the Iranian territories and influenced mystical movements in both the eastern and the western territories outside Iran.

Jews

In Iran itself, the western territories, including Mesopotamia, remained the main center for Aramaic-speaking groups. The Jewish population of Iran at the time remained predominantly in Mesopotamia, but smaller Jewish communities existed from Armenia to the Persian Gulf as well as in the Caspian area, Media, and Fars. They did not form a majority in any one city, although in central Babylonia some villages were mainly, and even exclusively, Jewish. Early in the period of Sasanian rule, these rulers attempted to convert others to their own religion. They canceled Jews' rights to govern their own affairs, destroyed Jewish places of worship, and forbade the performance of many Jewish rituals. However, a compromise was eventually reached, and many restrictions were lifted. Since Jews were not considered a threat, they were tolerated. The Jewish population of Iran lived in relative peace for almost three hundred years before facing new persecutions and conflict with the late Sasanian rulers. The tensions were eased when Jews supported Iranians in their wars against the Romans.

Christians

Christians had arrived during the Parthian period, and by the late third century A.D. there were both Greek and Syrian Christian churches in Iran. The Sasanian rulers' deportation of Christian inhabitants from the conquered Roman territories into Iran created large Christian colonies in the country.

By the end of the third century independent Christian communities in Iran had been merged. At the beginning of the fourth century the head of the Persian church selected the city of Seleucia-Ctesiphon, the capital of the Sasanian Empire, as his center of authority, with several bishops under his jurisdiction.

Though Rome and Constantinople were the centers of Christian doctrine, many Christian groups, particularly in Mesopotamia, opposed the policies and guidelines emanating from those centers. By the fifth century an independent new church was announced in Iran; the leader was called "catholicos-patriarch of all the Orient" and became partially independent from Rome. The Iranian king approved of the organization of the Persian church on this basis and issued an edict giving recognition to the catholicos as the head of the Persian church. Christians in Iran received a definite standing among the population. They had the freedom to manage their own affairs but were answerable to the state authorities through the catholicos, who became a civil as well as a religious head. The decree also dictated that the election of a catholicos had to be approved by the king, and he became the king's nominee. By the end of the fifth century the Persian church had become totally independent from Rome and later adopted Nestorianism. Relations with the Roman and the Syrian churches were largely severed, and the persecution of Christians eased. In the next century the Persian church grew steadily, with a hierarchy of 230 bishops. Christians were scattered over Assyria, Babylonia, Arabia, Media, Khurasan, Persia proper, Turkestan, Merv, and both shores of the Persian Gulf. The leader, "catholicos of Seleucia," became a powerful entity, and the extent of his jurisdiction matched that of the Byzantine patriarchs. The Armenian and Assyrian churches also existed, and the adoption of Christianity by Armenia created many wars and persecutions on both sides.

Assyrians

Assyrians, one of the oldest surviving Christian groups in Iran, claim descent from the ancient Assyrians, a major Mesopotamian empire originating about 2000 B.C. that was destroyed in 612 B.C. by the Babylonians and the Medes. After this collapse the remnant of the empire was called Urhai and later Edessa. Many Assyrians fled to the secluded mountains of Kurdistan, some settled in Urmiyeh in northwestern Persia, and others scattered throughout Asia Minor. They embraced Christianity in the first century A.D. and soon were divided into two ancient Christian denominations: the

Church of the East and the Syrian Orthodox Church. This division occurred in the fifth century A.D. and appears to have been politically motivated to secure a measure of safety for the Assyrian minority, which was caught between two rival empires, the Persians and the Romans. During the Sasanian era, a majority of the Assyrians in Iran adopted Nestorianism, which created a division between them and the Syrian Orthodox Church but improved their situation in Iran.

Provinces

Sasanians had a hierarchical society controlled by the privileged classes, the priests, the nobles (warriors), and the scribes, with a free, nonslave population. The majority of Iranians were citizens capable of exercising full civic rights. In attempts to increase central authority and improve defense of the four major frontiers, the empire was divided into four military zones. Each had its own commander, and there were four separate armies whose members were recruited from among the minor nobility. The policy provided the minor nobility with more power and reduced the influence of the major landed nobility. The latter were traditionally the backbone of the army and were becoming increasingly more independent from the throne.

The four frontiers included the Caspian area and the northwest region, dominated by the northwest Iranian ethnic and linguistic groups, such as Gilites (modern Gilan) and Dailamites, and included Armenia. Both the Parthian and Sasanian policymakers encouraged the diffusion of the Iranian tribes into Armenia in order to increase the Iranian element in the region and also to use the migrating tribes at times of military conflict. The same policies were used in the Caspian frontier, and by the end of the period many non-Iranian tribes had mixed with Iranians in this area enough to be merged into a common population. In Media a number of Zagros tribes were incorporated into one another, such as different Kurdish groups. "By this time the term 'Kurd' had a socio-economic rather than ethnic meaning. It covered nomads on the western edge of the Iranian plateau, and very likely included many Semitic and even Jewish groups" (McDowall, 1997, p. 9). Azerbaijan had a mixed population, including Persians, Kurds, and Armenians. Beginning in the third century A.D., Azerbaijan was effectively divided between north and south, with the more autonomous northern territories (Albania and later Arran) becoming mainly Christian. The southern territories remained mainly Zoroastrian, and many wars were fought between the two regions, mostly under pressure from the Sasanian rulers, who suspected their Christian subjects of being Roman allies.

The eastern territories and Hyrcania (Gorgan) formed another frontier inhabited by the major Iranian group Dahae and were frequently invaded by the Huns. The next frontier on the southeast, Carmania (Kirman), was essentially Iranian in population and included the bulk of the Persian and the Median populations. Kirman also sheltered nomads, both Iranians and older indigenous peoples. Baluchi tribes were mentioned for the first time during this period. They inhabited the western mountains of the region and were named by the Sasanian administration as one of the seven mountain rulers. The earliest known mention of the area resembling Baluchistan is in the Avesta, and by the Sassanian period the Baluchis had already started moving from areas adjacent to the southern coast of the Caspian into Kirman.

Arabs were scattered close to Armysia (Harmozia, Port of Hurmuz) in the Persian Gulf area. Settlement by the Arabs had started early in the Sasanian period through both migration and transportation. Sistan, which was greatly influenced by Saka migrations beginning in the second century B.C., was beginning to feel the Buddhist influence from India by the third century A.D. The existing evidence of the foundation of new towns, massive irrigation projects, and cultivated land from the Sasanian period attests to an increase in population. The projects were possibly attempts to maintain the Iranian influence in this region. The areas in the southeast had mixed populations, including Indians, indigenous groups, and Iranians.

Conclusion

The empires of the Achaemenids, Parthians, and Sasanians included many territories with Iranian and non-Iranian populations. The problems of dealing with a wide variety of ethnic groups, languages, traditions, and religious concepts while maintaining political and administrative control existed for all three major dynasties. On the whole they were successful in maintaining a balance, since the country as an entity with the bulk of the territories under Iranian control survived from the sixth century B.C. to the seventh century A.D. Throughout this period most groups followed their own laws, practiced their religions, and kept their ethnic identities. Resettlement policies and the foundation of new cities were used to integrate mixed populations and settle nomadic groups. For most of the time, on the whole, religious conformity was not demanded as a means of safeguarding the central government. The ruling principle was reward of loyal groups and punishment of disloyal communities. The Sasanian era was an exception. Never-ending wars and territorial disputes with Rome and persecutions on both sides influenced the religious policies of that dynasty. The emergence of Christianity in Rome and a unified Zoroastrian church in Iran affected many groups in different ways, depending on their allegiances, loyalties, and ideologies. Thus, whereas the Jewish communities enjoyed relative peace, the Christians of the fourth century A.D. as well as the Buddhists, Mazdakites, and Manicheans were exposed to merciless persecutions under Sasanian policymakers.

In this process of mixing of peoples and cultures, the pre-Islamic Iranians cultivated their own traditions and beliefs (such as Zoroastrianism and ideals of kingship) but also eagerly assimilated those of other cultures. The Sasanians collapsed due to internal and external pressures and decades of wars with the Byzantines and the invaders on the eastern frontiers. But by that time the Iranian population had already mixed and had transformed many cultural practices, including Greek, Mesopotamian, and Indian sciences and ideologies, which were to be passed on to the Muslim rulers of the continent.

Timeline

Before 3000 B.C.	Settlements in dry farming areas, including Mesopotamia and Susa in Iran, and presence of far-reaching trade.
3000–2000 B.C.	Migration of seminomadic pastoral tribes and permanent settlements in the Zagros Mountains in modern Kurdistan and Luristan. Major Mesopotamian city-states dominated the area.
2000–1000 B.C.	The arrival of seminomadic populations, including the Indo-Iranian tribes.
1000 B.C.	Iranian groups such as Medes were already organized into small states or tribes in western Iran and expanded into northwestern Iran.
800 B.C.	By the second half of the eighth century B.C., Iranians constituted the majority in many regions of western and northwestern Iran. Medes consolidated their power.
728–550 B.C.	Medes formed the first Iranian dynasty in the region. The beginning of Jewish settlements in Iran.
550–330 B.C.	Achaemenid Persians created the first major empire, and Persian-speaking groups dominated the entire

region. Aramaic was used extensively, but Persians maintained the Old Persian language and their own cuneiform writing.

330–130 B.C.   Greek conquest of Iran and the formation of the Seleucid Empire.

247 B.C.–A.D. 224   Parthian tribes, an Iranian group, ended Greek rule, Middle Persian was developed, and Zoroastrianism was promoted. Christians settled in Iran, and Parthians battled Romans and invaders from the east.

A.D. 224–651   The last major Iranian group, Sasanians, ruled Iran, Middle Persian was fully developed, and a Zoroastrian church was established. Centuries of wars with Rome and the Byzantine empire weakened the empire, and Iran fell to the Arabs/Muslims.

Significant People, Places, and Events

AHURAMAZDA: The supreme god of the ancient Persians, and the most important Iranian deity until the conquest of Islam. His name means the wise lord, and he is popularly known as the wise lord, or lord of wisdom.

ALANI (ALANS): Descendants of ancient Scytho-Sarmatian tribes, they first appeared north of the Caspian Sea, later spread into the steppes of Russia, and gradually took over the eastern provinces of the Roman Empire.

ANAHITA: An ancient Persian goddess, she was associated with waters and fertility and was a patron of women and warriors. Her name means "the immaculate one." She was popularized by the Achaemenids and remained a very important deity with major temples until the conquest by Islamic peoples.

ARAMAIC: The language of many Semitic peoples throughout the ancient Near East. It was replaced by Arabic after the Muslim conquest. However, Christians in Iraq, Iran, Syria, Turkey, and Lebanon have maintained the Aramaic language.

AVESTA: The sacred literature of ancient and modern Zoroastrians. It is written in two dialects, Old and Younger Avestan. The dialects are preserved in the *Yasna,* or sacrificial liturgy, in seventy-two chapters. Chapters 28–53 contain the Gathas, the oldest part of the collection.

AZERBAIJAN: The ancient Iranian province of Atropatene, Azerbaijan occupies the southeastern part of the Caucasus, descending to the Caspian Sea, between Iran and Russia. In 1795 the Russians occupied parts of the area. The region since 1813 has been divided between Russia and Iran.

BACTRIA: Located in northern Afghanistan, this ancient Greek kingdom was an eastern province of the Persian Empire before its conquest by Alexander.

CASPIAN SEA: The Caspian Sea is located in northwest Asia, landlocked between Azerbaijan, Iran, Kazakhstan, Russia, and Turkmenistan. It is the largest lake in the world and is currently a cause of tension between different countries bordering its shores.

CAUCASIANS: The indigenous population of the Caucasus region in southeastern European Russia, including Armenians and Georgians.

CHORASMIA (KHWARAZM): An ancient Persian province, the area is located in present-day Uzbekistan and has been on and off part of the Iranian territories. In the Avestan Gathas it is the country whose king protects the prophet Zoroaster.

DAILAMITE: An Iranian group occupying the Dailam region in Caspian area. They resisted both Arabs and Turks for centuries.

DRANGIANA (SAKASTANA, OR SISTAN): Home to the ancient Iranian tribes Sarangians or Drangians, it occupied modern-day Sistan in eastern Iran. Under the Greek occupation, the Saka nomadic tribes of Central Asia invaded it constantly and eventually gave their name Sakastana (Sistan) to the region.

DRAVIDIAN LANGUAGES: A language and a group. The family of twenty-three languages is unrelated to any other known language family. Presently the Dravidian languages are spoken in India and Sri Lanka.

FARS (PARSUA): The ancient province inhabited by Persians, who gave their name to the area that comprises present-day Fars. The geographical boundary contains a series of steppes leading from the Persian Gulf to the central deserts of Iran.

GILLITES: An Iranian group inhabiting the modern-day province of Gilan. Like other groups in the Caspian region, they resisted Arabs and Turks for a long time. They are the ancestors of the modern-day Gillaki people.

HURRIANS: Arriving from the highlands of Anatolia with their own language, they established themselves at the foothills of the Zagros region by 2400 B.C. They created the kingdom of Mitanni.

HYRCANIA (HYRCANA, GORGAN): Gorgan, meaning "the country of the wolves," is located on the southern shores of the Caspian Sea. With other Caspian kingdoms, it became an Iranian stronghold during the Islamic period, with many pro-Iranian dynasties resisting the Arab conquest for centuries.

KASSITES: An ethnic group with a Zagros Mountains origin; the term applies to both the ethnic group and their language. They first appeared in records in the early first millennium B.C. They are related to Quti and Lullubi, and the origins of the three groups are not clear.

LULLUBI: Ancient group of tribes that inhabited the plains of the Zagros Mountains in western Iran. A warlike people, they appeared around 2200 B.C.

MANICHEANISM: A religion founded by the Persian sage Mani in the latter half of the third century A.D., it aspired to be the true synthesis of the major religions at the time and consisted of Zoroastrian dualism, Babylonian folklore, Buddhist ethics, and Christian/Jewish elements.

MANNIANS (MANNAI): Mannai was a kingdom in the interior of present-day Armenia comprising a large part of modern-day Kurdistan. The Mannians shared the region with the Medes and were finally defeated by them.

MASSAGETAE: Belonging to the Saka nation, these ancient Scythians lived between the Caspian and Aral Seas. They are referred to as *Saka tigrakhauda* by the Achaemenids; Cyrus the Great was killed battling them.

MAZDAKITES: Followers of Mazdak, the founder of a socially radical religious sect challenging both the Zoroastrian clergy and doctrines and the existing social order of the Sasanian period, in the late fifth and early sixth centuries A.D. in Iran.

MEDES: Ancient Indo-Iranian tribes who became the first Iranian rulers of Mesopotamia and Iran, occupying parts of Azerbaijan, Kirmanshah, and Kurdistan.

MEDIA: Ancient territory of northwestern Iran generally corresponding to the modern-day regions of Azerbaijan, Kurdistan, and parts of Kirmanshah.

MESOPOTAMIA: The word means between two rivers and the area refers to the farmland located in a narrow strip of land between the Tigris and Euphrates Rivers in present-day Iraq. It is known as the cradle of civilization.

MIDDLE PERSIAN: Both a script and a language, it became the dominant script of the Sasanian Empire (A.D. 224–651) and was developed from the Aramaic script. This language derived from Old Persian and was extensively in use from the third century B.C. to the ninth century A.D. before evolving into New Persian.

MITHRA (MIHR): An ancient Indo-Iranian deity. The worship of Mithra became a significant cult with major temples in Iran and Roman territories. In Zoroastrian tradition he was the deity protector of the covenant and of loyalty. In modern Persian the name means love and kindness.

MODERN PERSIAN: Language spoken principally in Iran, Afghanistan, and Tajikistan. Persian belongs to the Iranian branch of the Indo-European language.

NESTORIANISM: Followers of Nestorius, the patriarch of Constantinople in the fifth century A.D. Nestorians believed in the doctrine of the two natures of Christ (human and divine) and faced persecution; their bishops fled to Iran. From 488 on, the Persian church adopted Nestorianism.

OLD IRANIAN: A subgroup of Indo-European languages that spread across the Iranian plateau from 1350 to 350 B.C. Of these languages, Avestan and Old Persian are textually preserved. Others, such as Median, Parthian, Sogdian, Carduchi, and Scythian, are known from Greek sources.

OLD PERSIAN: Old Persian was spoken in southwestern Iran and was contemporary with Avestan, spoken in the northeast. The oldest traces of Old Persian date to the sixth century B.C., but it was spoken until the third century B.C. and is preserved in cuneiform tablets from the Achaemenid dynasty.

PAHLAVI: Both a language and a script, Pahlavi is an Iranian language spoken between the third century B.C. and the ninth century A.D. The Pahlavi script evolved from the Aramaic script and was written from right to left. The last Iranian dynasty adopted the same name in the twentieth century.

PARNI: A nomadic tribe from the Central Asian steppe, they were Iranian in origin and are unknown before the third century B.C. Moving south, they joined a major confederation of Dahae tribes. The Dahae disintegrated after the fall of the Achaemenid Empire, and among many groups that emerged out of the larger group were the Parni.

PERSIANS: An Indo-Iranian group who entered Iran around 1000 B.C., conquered the whole area, and created the Persian Empire.

QUTI: Of Zagros origin, they occupied eastern Mesopotamia and southwest Iran in the area now known as the Zagros Mountains.

They appeared around 2200 B.C. and are sometimes referred to as Guti, Gu-ti-um. They belonged to the same linguistic and racial group as the Kassites and Lullubi.

SAKA: A Scythian group invading Iran around the eighth century B.C. and gradually settling down in Iran. They gave their name to the town of Sakiz to the south of Lake Urmia.

SARMATIANS: A coalition of Iranian nomadic tribes who lived on the plains between the Black and Caspian Seas. They had a hierarchical society with slaves, and their women had better status than those in other societies.

SCYTHIANS: Warlike Indo-Iranian nomadic tribes, they occupied an area extending from European Russia to northern China.

SOGDIANA: In modern-day Uzbekistan, Sogdiana was part of the ancient Persian Empire from the sixth century B.C. The name of the country is mentioned in the Avesta, and they spoke the same language as the people of Areia (Herat) and Bactria. Their language is a branch of the eastern Middle Iranian languages.

TURKESTAN: Territory presently stretching from the Caspian Sea to the river Amu-Darya (Uzbek-Afghan border) and inhabited by a number of Turkic peoples. Conquered by many groups, the country became independent in 1990. The Persian influence was the longest and remained until the Mongol expansion in the thirteenth century.

ZOROASTER, ZARATHUSTRA (ZARDOSHT): The ancient Iranian prophet and the founder of Zoroastrianism. Little is known of his historical origins.

Bibliography

Boyce, Mary. *Zoroastrians: Their Religious Beliefs and Practices*. London: Routledge and Kegan Paul, 2001.

Dandamaev, Muhammad, and Lukonin, Vladimir. *The Culture and Social Institutions of Ancient Iran*. Cambridge: Cambridge University Press, 1994.

Fisher, W. B., ed. *The Cambridge History of Iran*, Vol. 1: *The Land of Iran*. Cambridge: Cambridge University Press, 1968.

Frye, Richard Nelson. *The History of Ancient Iran*. Munich, Germany: C. H. Becksche Verlagsbuchhandlung, 1984.

Gershevitch, I., ed. *The Cambridge History of Iran*, Vol. 2: *The Median and Archaemenian Periods*. Cambridge: Cambridge University Press, 1985.

Gnoli, Gherardo. *The Idea of Iran.* Rome: Istituto Italiano Per Il Medio Ed Estremo Oriente, 1989.

Kramer, Carol. *Village Ethno-archaeology: Rural Iran in Archaeological Perspective.* Academic Press, 1982.

Kuhrt, Amelie. *The Ancient Near East, c. 3000–330 B.C.*, Volume 1. London: Routledge, 1998.

McDowall, David. *A Modern History of Kurds.* London: I. B. Tarius, 1997.

Shaffer, J. G. *Prehistoric Baluchistan.* Delhi, India: B. R. Publishing Corporation, 1978.

Wiesehofer, Josef. *Ancient Persia, from 550 B.C. to 650 A.D.* London: I. B. Tauris Publishers, 1996.

Xenophon. *The Persian Expedition.* London: Penguin Books, 1972.

Yarshater, E., ed. *The Cambridge History of Iran*, Vol. 3: *The Seleucid, Parthian and Sasanid Periods.* Cambridge: Cambridge University Press, 1983.

Islamic Conquest

HE RISE OF THE PROPHET MUHAMMAD AND THE RAPID CONQUESTS by Muslim Arabs in the seventh century changed the entire region. According to the Islamic tradition, the Prophet was born in A.D. 570 in Mecca, a very small city on the South Arabian trade routes. At the age of forty, while meditating and praying on a mountain close to Mecca, he received the divine message that Allah was the only god and the source of all authority and being. Muhammad was appointed as the next and the last prophet, and it was his duty to convert others to submit to Allah's will. In the beginning his message did not create any sensation among the tribesmen. His popularity grew, but once he started directly attacking the traditional cults and deities, people turned against him. He was forced to leave Mecca in 622 and migrated with a few supporters to the city of Medina. The migration is called *Hijrat* and is the beginning of the Muslim lunar calendar. From then on Muslims managed to consolidate, defeat their enemies, and unite the whole of Arabia under the banner of Islam. The first expeditions outside Arabia started after Muhammad's death in 632, and almost twenty years later the Muslim Arabs conquered the heart of the Sasanian Empire (including the Iranian capital, Ctesiphon) and rapidly expanded into Syria, Egypt, and eastern Iranian territories. The Muslim Arabs' defeat of the Sasanian Empire created fundamental changes that included a transition from Zoroastrianism to Islam, a change in the script and calendar, and the evolution of the language from Middle Persian into New Persian. Under Islam for the first time since the Achaemenid times, all Iranians, including those of central Asia and on the border with India, came under one rule. The Arab-Muslim caliphs, originally based in Damascus and later in Baghdad, were foreign rulers who successfully managed to Arabize the conquered territories by replacing most of the languages in the area with Arabic. They also attempted to create a unified Islamic culture. They colonized many territories and replaced Christianity as the dominant religion in Egypt, Syria, and many other territories as well as replacing Zoroastrianism in Iran with

Islam. They brought all the different nations of Islam under one jurisdiction, that is, the Islamic legal code, Shari'a, for the first time.

Though Arabization policies did not work as well in Iran as they did in Egypt, Syria, and other territories, the spread of the new religion and the synonymity of the words "Arab" and "Islam" threatened the core of Iranian identity. The fear of losing the old culture, traditions, and language prompted efforts to preserve the Persian style of the Sasanian era by rewriting major literary works such as *Shahnameh,* the pre-Islamic epics and Avestan mythology, in New Persian. This was followed by the mass translation of pre-Islamic books into Arabic and New Persian. The New Persian language, written in the Arabic script, soon spread all over the country, even beyond Sasanian borders, and became the standard language of the eastern territories of the caliphate.

The spread of Islam was another major threat to the national identity. Iranians adapted by shaping a tradition that made Islam look more Iranian, that is, the Iranian Shi'i movement. Following the Prophet's death, the Arab Shi'ites had contested the election of Muhammad's first heirs and believed that the caliphate belonged rightly to Ali, the Prophet's cousin and son-in-law. Later, during occupation by the Arabs, the Iranians supported this cause and made it into a movement of their own. "A legend was made that Hussein, the martyred son of Ali, had married the captive Sasanian princess Shahrbanu, the 'Lady of the Land.' This fictitious figure, which resembles a cult-epithet of the Iranian goddess Anahita, was held to have borne Hussein a son" (Boyce, 2001, p. 151). Iranians organized, opposed the Umayyad caliphs, and eventually led the house of "Abbas," relatives of Ali, to victory in 750 A.D. Once in power, the "Abbasids" betrayed the Iranians, murdered their leaders, and aimed at creating a universal Islamic culture and empire. They built Baghdad outside Ctesiphon in 762 A.D., revived the magnificence of the ancient court, and imitated Sasanian authoritarianism in religious matters.

In the process Islam grew steadily more Zoroastrianized in Iran, and a cult of saints (twelve imams) replaced the practice of venerating the twelve major deities, eyzads. The concept of the last savior who comes at the end of the time to save the world found a place too and was seen in the figure of Imam Zaman (Time Lord), the venerated Shi'i twelfth imam and the savior who appears at the end of the time. Such developments and adaptations made it possible for Iranians to preserve many of their ancient practices and traditions while adopting new ones. At the end, even though Zoroastrianism was reduced to a minority religion in Iran, its structure and rituals found a place in the new religion and are still practiced and revered by many Iranians today.

The colonization of the newly conquered territories by the Arabs was slow, met with fierce resistance, and was initially carried out by establishing military Arab garrisons in the provinces. In the end it had an impact on the ethnic and religious makeup of the country. In the beginning Iranians were left to carry on their own cultural practices. As non-Muslims they paid a religious tax known as *jizya* in addition to the regular taxes and taxes applied to cultivated land. Arabs inherited the Sassanian taxation system but added their own system and increased taxation. The taxes ended up being a heavy burden on the non-Muslim population, and many were converted in order to reduce their tax payments. The land taxes, combined with *jizya*, resulted in mass emigration into the cities. This movement was also encouraged by the introduction of the Islamic system of land ownership, which ended the self-government practiced from ancient times by the village communes in Iran that had partially limited the arbitrary powers of landowners. Land ownership had two major forms: private, with peasants attached to the soil because Islam prohibits serfdom, or the charitable state land, which was maintained by administrators only for income and tax purposes, with little consideration for the peasants and their lives.

The early conquests created a massive class of slaves, mainly war captives, who were divided among the victors and lived under poor conditions. The result was many revolts and the assassination of the second caliph, Umar. The slaves could earn partial freedom if they converted to Islam. It was a qualified freedom, for they became *mawali* (clients) of the Arabs, freed slaves but still dependents and second-class citizens. They fought in the armies for Arabs and, since they never gained status of first-class citizens, ended up revolting and taking sides in factional disputes among Arab tribes. With other Iranians, they were instrumental in overthrowing the first Arab dynasty, the Umayyad, by helping to establish the Abbasid dynasty.

The rest of the free citizens in the occupied territories were regarded as *dhimmis*, "people of the Book," as stated in the Quran. *Dhimmis* can practice their religion but do not have equal rights with Muslims. At first the term applied exclusively to Christians and Jews as those specifically mentioned in the Quran. "Later the concept was expanded, and included the Zoroastrians of Iran" (Frye, 1975, p. 31). The *dhimmis'* status did not apply to others, and Buddhists and pagans were not recognized at all and had to convert. The adherents of other Iranian religions, such as Manicheans and Mazdakites, were subject to persecution and went underground to form secret societies, surfacing occasionally. The cities became conglomerates of people whose status was categorized based on their religion, from the ruling Muslim Arabs as first-class citizens to *dhimmis* and *mawali*. In addition, there was a massive influx of poor farmers into the major towns. The cities became centers for intrigue, revolts, uprisings, and changing loyalties.

The Arabs existed in pre-Islamic Persia in southern and western Iran, but after the conquest a flood of Arab Bedouins arrived on Iranian soil. The earliest centers colonized by the Arabs were Hamadan, Isfahan, and Fars, followed by Qum, Kashan, Ray, Qazvin, and Azerbaijan. Later settlements were formed in Khurasan and Sistan, and among the new immigrants were followers of minor militant Muslim sects, such as the Shi'ites and the Kharijites, who were persecuted in Syria and Iraq. The latter group was responsible for the murder of Ali, and both groups later acquired a following among the newly converted Muslims in Iran.

The Emergence of Shi'ism in Iran

The success of Shi'i in Iran was significant, and the Sunni/Shi'i division was seen as an opportunity by the Iranians to revolt against the Sunni Umayyad rulers. The majority sect in Islam, the Sunni, accepted the first four caliphs chosen by the early Muslims as the rightful leaders of the community. The Shi'ites, on the other hand, recognized only Ali and his children, linked directly by blood to the Prophet, and called such leaders *imams.* Despite the fact that neither Ali nor his children ever came to Iran or had any affiliation with Iran, Shi'i supporters increased drastically with many subsects and participated in many wars and revolts against the caliphs and their agents in Iran. Though Ali was eventually chosen as the fourth caliph, his assassination opened the way for the Umayyad family to consolidate their power. Ali's sons were forced to give up their claims. Later on, Ali's son Hussein was assassinated, and the commemoration of his martyrdom in 680 A.D. has become an important Shi'i ritual, still vigorously observed by Shi'ites during the month of Muharram. The Iranian concept of the imam doctrine incorporated many elements from ancient Iranian practices. "At the bottom of their reverence for the *imam*—the Prophet's successor—and the conception that the leadership of the community was a divine and extraordinary office, lay the Iranians' belief that the *farr-i izadi,* the Divine Power or Aura, should be an essential attribute of the exercise of sovereignty" (Frye, 1975, p. 34). Imams were assumed to have divine powers because of their blood link with the Prophet himself, and the twelve imams became venerated by the Iranian Shi'ites as direct descendents of the Prophet.

Shi'i was originally a political faction with no religious doctrines, but gradually it acquired a religious and even a messianic character. It was believed that there could be an ideal Muslim state completely based on divine law, Shari'a, as stated in the Quran. In this ideal society there was no distinction between secular and religious, and imams, or religious people, ruled instead of caliphs, an idea that was welcomed by the founders of the Islamic revolution in the twentieth century. Despite their popularity among Iranians, Shi'ites were oppressed by the ruling Sunni dynasties and did not succeed in Iran until the sixteenth century, when Shi'i was adopted as the state religion.

Khurasan became the most desirable area for the Arabs, and thousands of Arabs and their families arrived in Khurasan and changed the geographic characteristics of the province. Khurasan later became the home of the holiest Shi'i shrine in Iran, the burial chamber of the eighth imam, Reza, and a major center for Shi'i scholarship. Qum was another favorite area because its arid lands resembled the deserts in Arabia. It has remained the most influential religious center in Iran and is home to another major Shi'i shrine, the burial site of the only female Shi'i saint in Iran, a sister of Imam Reza.

Various Arab tribes settled in different regions, and the masses were gradually absorbed into the local populations and even adopted Persian as their language, with the exception of Iraq. The Mesopotamian territories were Arabized and eventually formed the modern country of Iraq, but the Iranian influence remained there for many centuries. Iranians managed the administration of the new empire, produced major scientific and philosophical literature, and occupied key offices, including that of the prime minister, or grand vizier. The most famous Iranian family was the Barmakids, who occupied the office for a few generations and in the end were removed and persecuted to reduce Iranian influence. The most famous member of the family, Jaffar, is popularized in *Tales from a Thousand and One Nights* as the grand vizier in the popular story "Aladdin."

The Rise of Iranian Dynasties and the New Persian Language

The Abbasid at first intensified policies of centralization, appointed the governors from Baghdad, and made alliances with major Iranian families who promised loyalty. Gradually they allowed provincial governors more freedom and made the office hereditary in some provinces. The local governors were Arabs and used the Arabic language in their local courts. They were given financial and military control in exchange for yearly tributes and acknowledgment of the caliph's supreme position in the Friday prayer and

The new courtyard, golden dome, and Iwan Tala-ye Fath Ali Shah of the Shrine of Imam Reza in Mashhad, Iran (Roger Wood/Corbis)

on coins issued for the provinces. Members of the Abbasid family were appointed as governors to major provinces such as Khurasan, and family disputes and power struggles resulted in several wars between Khurasan and Baghdad. The wars provided the Iranians with some failed opportunities to revolt and fight for independence, and in the end resulted in the governorship of the first semi-independent Iranian dynasty, the Tahirids. By the end of the ninth century, after almost two hundred years, the Tahirids ended the Arab rule by helping the caliphs to suppress mass uprisings in Fars, the Caspian region, Kurdistan, and Azerbaijan (home to a neo-Mazdakite movement with many supporters in most parts of Iran). The Tahirids, despite their formal allegiance to the caliphs and their early involvement in expanding Islamic territory on their behalf, created an autonomous Iran in the east, playing an important role in the dissolution of the political unity of the caliphate in Baghdad. They paved the way for the more independent Iranian dynasty of the militant Saffarids and in the tenth century their successors the Samanids, the first independent Iranian dynasty to rule Iran.

The Saffarids, originally from Sistan, ruled for a short period but were instrumental in the revival and a renaissance of the New Persian literature and culture. Their leaders were from humble origins and did not know Arabic, and as a result they promoted the Persian language. Furthermore, they ended the Kharajites' influence and the Arab culture in eastern Iran. The Samanids, originally from Bukhara, further expanded the revival of the Persian language and used the New Persian script for their administration instead of Arabic. They employed Zoroastrians, built libraries, and supported poets and scientists such as Avicenna (Ibn Sina), the celebrated physician and philosopher. The first major post-Islamic literary works began to appear during this period. The Samanids also made Islam more international by expanding its narrow Arab/Bedouin background and demonstrated that Islamic literature did not have to be in the Arabic language. They created religious literature in Persian, a policy that ended the Arab monopoly of religious studies. A substantial Persian literature flourished that incorporated many elements from the pre-Islamic period and was able not only to compete with Arabic but also to replace it in Iran as the language of the cultured elite and the courts.

The defeat of Arabic as the state language was accompanied by major changes in the languages of Iran. In the Sasanian period the official written language was Middle Persian (Parsi). This language was static and limited as a spoken tongue. Dari, a more flexible version, was used for everyday talk. The two were not different dialects but represented different stylistic levels. Parsi remained the medium of administration and literature, both secular and religious, and its literature is known as Pahlavi. There were also non-Iranian languages, Aramaic (Mesopotamia) and Khuzi, used in Khuzistan. The latter was probably a relic of the ancient Elamite tongue. There were several Iranian dialects as well, such as Azeri, spoken in Azerbaijan; Dailami in the Caspian region; Baluchi and the related Kofch in Kirman (Arabic Qufs); and Kurdish. After the conquest of Islam, many of these dialects were lost, and Dari became the dominant language. It spread considerably and became popularly known as Parsi Dari, which was very close to the current modern Persian (Farsi) in Iran. The new language taking root in the towns eliminated many local dialects, confining them to the country districts and remote areas, and absorbed many Arabic words. Although minor variations existed, as they do today, nevertheless one standard Persian language was used for administration in all the Iranian territories. It became so dominant that it survived the invasion of the Turkish tribes. In fact, Persian became the court language of the ruling Turks and Mongols in Iran, Turkey, and India.

Despite the successful revival of the Persian language and its widespread use, neither Saffarids nor Samanids managed to create a centralized government powerful enough to control all the Iranian territories. Nor were they successful in creating a homogenous culture. Petty local rulers, disenchanted tribes with many revolts, changing loyalties, and the Persian/Arab, Sunni/Shi'i divisions still existed. Both the caliphs and the small kingdoms, such as the Buyids of Dailam, a Persian stronghold with considerable influence, supported one faction against the other. Despite the sympathy for the ancient religion in many provinces, Islam firmly took root in Iran and remained. Centuries of fragmentation and decline followed. Buyids later became key players in the area, occupied Baghdad, and exerted major influence over the caliphs. They expanded their control to Kurdistan, Luristan, and Khuzistan; promoted Shi'i doctrine; and introduced the first public mourning commemorating the death of Imam Hussein. This powerful tradition remains today.

At the same time, like other minor Iranian dynasties, the Buyids celebrated pre-Islamic Iranian festivals with vigor. They saved many of the ancient traditions and established Shiraz in Fars, the ancestral land of the Persians, as a Buyid stronghold just outside Persepolis, the palace complex built by the Achaemenids and burned by Alexander. All these dynasties were Muslim and, at least on the surface, claimed loyalty to the caliphs, who were by now spiritual heads with little military power. The policies of these minor dynasties further helped to establish Islam in Iran. One exception was the Ziyarid dynasty in Dailam, which ostentatiously exhibited its hostility to Islam by minting Sasanian coins and celebrating major Iranian festivals with grandeur. Like other Dailamites, it supported Zoroastrianism and socioreligious protest groups such as a revived Mazdakite movement.

Ethnic Groups

Despite the Arab presence, the country was still dominated by the Persians and the previously existing groups. Inhabitants of the Caspian region, like their neighbors, the Dailamites and Gillites, fiercely resisted the Arabs with local dynasties. Azerbaijan also resisted and gradually gained independence from the Arabs by the tenth century. Minor local dynasties emerged that would safeguard Azerbaijan and continue to resist future foreign invaders. By this time Azerbaijan was becoming increasingly more Turkish owing to the migration of Turkish tribes. The name Azerbaijan appeared after the Arab conquest and meant the same as before, "the place of tending the sacred fire," referring to a major fire temple in the area.

The Kurds in the ranges of the west and the northwest reared sheep in the mountains and created small local dynasties, such as the Shaddadids of Arran (951–1075). They acted as mercenaries at times and ended up with their own minor sects influenced by Zoroastrianism, Islam, and mysticism. Many different Kurdish tribes existed; however, the term "Kurd is used by the Muslim historians and writers from seventh century A.D. to incorporate a number of Iranian or Iranianized tribes, including Kurds, some Semitic, and probably some Armenian communities as well" (McDowall, 1992, p. 11). Several Arab tribes also became Kurdish by culture, through assimilation. For example, the Arab Rawadid tribe moved into Kurdistan in the mid–eighth century but by the tenth century was known as a Kurdish tribe. At the same time many Kurdish groups serving in the Arab armies lost their Kurdish identity and became Arab in culture. The Lurs are associated with the Kurds by the writers of the time, and Luristan itself became part of the Arab province of Kufa. The Lurs resisted the Arab rule and gained more independence in the tenth century. They took sides with the Iranian dynasties and at the same time became exposed to population pressure with the arrival of nomadic Turks in their area. It is from this period that the name *Lur* appears in written records. The Qufs and the related Baluchi tribes in the south gradually adopted the new religion, with pre-Islamic elements surviving as well. The Baluchis are reported by Muslim writers to have been around modern Kirman, and up to the tenth century they occupied the western and northern areas of this region. Gradually they migrated into Sistan and western Makran.

The seminomadic way of life in mountain areas changed very little, but closer to towns the nomad economy flourished because of the Arab Bedouins. The Armenians remained Christians. In the eastern territories, Sogdia, Khwarazm, and Afghanistan, infiltration by various Turkish elements was increasing, though the Persian element and language were strong. Khurasan and the central desert areas were the most influenced by the settlement of the Arabs in the region, and with the largest number of *mawali* at the service of the Arab rulers. The *mawali* and *dhimmis* groups eventually disappeared once the whole country adopted Islam and was under Iranian rule, and the Arabs were assimilated into the local population.

Urbanization continued with new concepts of communal spacing as the city centers became dominated by major complexes containing the mosque, *madrasa* (religious school), and bazaars next to each other and with very close ties. The combination of the three remained until the twentieth century, and the complexes became the centers of resistance and liberation for the constitutionalist movement and eventually the Islamic Revolution of the late twentieth century.

Christians, Jews, and Zoroastrians

The Christians and Jews survived under Muslim rule, but their numbers gradually declined tremendously, and like Zoroastrians many were converted to the new faith. Zoroastrianism became a very small minority sect, with some members emigrating to India in fear of extinction. They created the Parsi community of India, which is still in existence. The Islamic concept of community, *umma,* associated only the believers, that is, the Muslims, with community membership, and as a result the *dhimmis* were placed outside the mainstream with restrictions on their relationship with the larger Muslim society. In the early days of the Arab conquests, many were involved with the administration of the empire and were instrumental in creating an intellectual culture of science and literature. However, they were gradually segregated; were excluded from government employment; and ended up in separate quarters with distinct clothing or labels. They underwent sporadic persecution and lived in isolation until the twentieth century.

Turks

After the Arab conquest, the slave trade became a major business, first with war captives as a commodity and next with Turkish slaves from central Asia. Some were used in the military and others in the service of the local rulers. The result was a considerable though dispersed Turkish population in the major cities. The first Turkish rulers in eastern Iran, the Ghaznavids, emerged indirectly from within the Samanid kingdom by manipulating power struggles and succession wars while functioning as military guards. They replaced the Samanids, supported strict Sunni orthodoxy, expanded their territories, and in the end ruled from Azerbaijan and Kurdistan to the borders with India. They ended pagan, Hindu, and Buddhist influence in the eastern territories; persecuted various Shi'ites, such as Ismailis; and destroyed many libraries. They adopted Persian as the language of the court and overtaxed the natives of Khurasan, causing depopulation, in order to finance their never-ending wars. They struggled against related Turkish tribes invading Iran from central Asia, such as the Qarakhanids. They managed to control the Dail-amite dynasties in the Caspian region, local rulers in Tabaristan (Mazan-daran) and Gorgan, and most pro-Shi'a groups. They maintained peace with the caliphs by acknowledging them as spiritual leaders. They were defeated by the next Turkish group arriving in Iran but managed to maintain small local principalities in the eastern territories well into the twelfth century.

From the end of the Tahirid period, invasions by pagan Turkish tribes from central Asia increased in Iran. At first both the Saffarids and Samanids, and later the Ghaznavids, were successful in holding them back. In the end the newly converted Turkish Muslims succeeded, and the new Saljuq inva-sions altered the ethnic composition of the country through massive immi-gration of Turkish groups into the Iranian territories.

Turkic Domination and the Saljuq Period, 1000–1217

From the beginning of the second millennium until the twentieth century, Iran was generally ruled by non-Iranian dynasties, mainly Turkish and some Mongols. The Saljuq Turks appeared on the scene around the eleventh cen-tury. They had already converted to Islam by the time they arrived and pre-viously had supported wars against the Christian Byzantine dynasties and Armenians. The infiltration of Turkish elements happened through grad-ual migrations, mercenary activity, and military conquests due to the weak-ening of the northeastern Iranian dynasties. Saljuqs belonged to the Oghuz Turks, with a loose confederation of several tribes mainly hiring out their military services to the warring factions of Transoxiana and Khwarazm while moving south in search of pasture land. The Oghuz band became a turbulent factor in the politics of central and western Iran. Their repeated attacks on the Iranian territories created insecurity and forced the con-struction of massive fortifications around towns. One group in particular, the Ghuzz Turks, entered the Persian literature as the plundering Turks and became a symbol of terror and devastation. The Oghuz also established the vernacular language, which later became the literary Turkish Azeri language.

Khurasan was the first major province occupied by the Saljuqs. The oc-cupation of such major centers transformed the nomadic chiefs into terri-torial sovereigns and altered their mode of life from nomadism to a seden-tary lifestyle. They became kingly authorities backed by divine sanction.

These processes were viewed with suspicion by the many Turkish tribes and their lesser leaders. The Saljuq rulers constantly faced challenges from their own tribal people, which resulted in many treaties, alliances, revolts, and changing loyalties. They subjugated the last of the numerous Dailamites, including the Buyids, and managed to keep the local Kurdish dynasties in Azerbaijan and Kurdistan partially under control. Their success in Iran inevitably attracted more Turks from central Asia, and Azerbaijan became the base for their expansion. Political authority in this region was fragmented. Moreover, because Azerbaijan shared a border with Christian powers, systematic raids into the Christian territories were easier. All these factors led to the heavy population of Azerbaijan by Turkish tribes, and at this period Azerbaijan began to acquire the Turkish ethnic and linguistic characteristics that it still has today. By the end of the eleventh century, the Saljuqs had conquered most of the Iranian territories. At times, under more powerful rulers, they managed to keep the country together. But most of the time they were challenged by sectarian strife in Iran and threats from other Turkish tribes in central Asia and Asia Minor and related Saljuq rulers in Anatolia.

The Saljuq rulers called themselves "clients of the commander of the faithful." They fought against Christians and occupied Baghdad, claiming they did so to save Sunni Islam from the influence of the Shi'i. The ruler eventually assumed the title "exalted sultan," and the Saljuqs employed many Iranians from Khurasan who had previously served the Ghaznavid. The Persian language remained, as did the Iranian elite that managed the empire and organized the administration. One was the legendary grand vizier, Nizam al-Mulk (Order of the Realm). Since the Arab invasion, the Iranian elite at the service of the foreign rulers had seen themselves as representatives of the old Persian aristocracy and official classes, with a duty to continue Iranian traditions by cultivating the less cultured foreign rulers. In his *Book of Government,* which has survived, Nizam al-Mulk shows how such policies were implemented by educating loyal guards and officials totally dedicated to the vizier who controlled the administration. The royal tutors would be chosen by the vizier, who himself had been a tutor to the reigning king, Malik Shah. With many loyal connections in the standing army, the vizier had an important role in the nomination of officials for specific campaigns; he also controlled and appointed the chiefs of intelligence and investigation services and the provincial governors. This policy of granting governorship to military leaders later caused the fragmentation of the Saljuq Empire.

The vizier regulated religious schools (*madrasa*) by creating a network of schools to provide a standard, uniform religious education. He opposed Shi'ites and aimed to compete with the intellectual cultures of Muslim

Spain and Egypt. A vast literature, both scientific/secular and religious, emerged in Persian language. He controlled the educated religious elite by providing free education, with generous living allowances and patronage at schools that came to be known as Nizamiyyas. The schools adopted different versions of Sunni scholarship and law, which were regarded by the traditional religious leaders with suspicion and considered more Khurasanian than the standard traditions of the caliphate. The schools remained for centuries, and today the religious schools still practice the same system of free education with allowances and patronage by a particular religious teacher.

Kurds and Other Ethnic Groups

Although Azerbaijan had become a Turkish stronghold, the Saljuqs were less successful in controlling the Kurds and Baluchi population in Fars. The Kurds were fighting the Turks, and also among themselves. They systematically attacked Shiraz and the neighboring cities and halted the trade from the Orient to the Persian Gulf. The Kurds have been establishing minor dynasties since the tenth century. They were already divided into several tribes, and some seminomadic Kurdish tribes effectively controlled Kurdistan and Luristan. Kurdish tribes in the mountainous interiors of Fars and Kurdistan enjoyed a high degree of autonomy. They resisted intrusion by the outsiders and remained a source of trouble for the ruling dynasties of Iran. Some were involved in the Crusades, and one family gained fame by forming the Ayyubid dynasty of Syria, with the legendary Saladin as its most famous leader.

Kurdistan was first used in the twelfth century as a geographical term by the Saljuqs, and the geographical extent of this definition grew and evolved during the succeeding centuries as Kurds moved. The majority of Kurds were tribal, but they did not remain isolated and moved among and beyond non-Kurdish settlements, mixing with local populations. Such processes were mutual, and there were non-Kurdish groups, such as Turks, Arabs, Armenians, and Jews, who became Kurdish by culture. By the time the history of Kurds was written down by a Kurdish prince in the sixteenth century, they were already divided into many groups and had two distinct major languages and many dialects. Little is known about their religious practices at this time, but later sources indicate that Kurds had their own religious mixture and sects. They were influenced by Islam, Zoroastrianism, Mithraism, and Manicheanism, with elements from Christianity and Judaism. They fiercely resisted Saljuq invasions; in the end they were subdued but remained semi-independent.

A woman from the Qahremanlu clan of the Kurdish tribes of Khurasan at their winter quarters (Qeshlaq) in Qorah-meydan (Nasrollah Kasraian)

The Arabs still maintained small emirates on the western edges of the Iranian plateau, with many supporting Shi'i sects. Qufs and the Baluchi mountaineers in Kirman were forced to move eastward into the modern-day Baluchistan. On the whole, the tribal groups in the Saljuq Empire were not under the direct administration of the central government. The Kurds and Arabs were left mainly under the control of their own local rulers. The same was true for Tabaristan (modern-day Mazandaran) in the north, always a Persian stronghold.

Nomadic Turks

By the twelfth century the Turks had become the most significant tribal groups, in terms of both numbers and influence. They kept moving west in search of pasture land and were employed as mercenaries to fight the Christians. Many pushed into Syria and Asia Minor. Though some were incorporated into the regular army and settled down, the majority remained nomadic and seminomadic, moving from winter to summer pastures. Their main concentration was in Iraq, Azerbaijan, Gorgan, and Marv. At times, when the central government was weak, they managed to establish small territorial princes and break away from the sultan's authority. Khuzistan and Fars came under their control for brief periods, and they managed to establish minor kingdoms in these areas. They paid pasture dues and other taxes mainly in kind. These nomadic groups were managed by an administrator appointed by the government to keep the peace among the different tribes and regulate the allocation of pastures and water according to the number of households and followers. Tensions existed between the settled and semisettled nomadic groups. Some nomads such as the Ghuzz constantly overran parts of Khurasan and Kirman and were difficult to control. They were the most serious threat to the Saljuqs and accelerated the dynasty's decline and disappearance from the Iranian territories until their final defeat by the Turkish rulers of Khwarazm, who formed the last major power, the Khawarazm-shahian dynasty, before the Mongol invasion.

Group Conflicts

The Saljuq period was characterized by fragmentation and disputes and power struggles between various Turkish groups, both inside and outside the Iranian territories. There was also discontent among the various Kurdish groups and Arabs of Iraq. Khurasan became a battleground for several Turkish groups and was invaded and conquered many times by various Turkish khans. By the beginning of the thirteenth century, the few remaining pagan kingdoms on the eastern fringes had all been converted. The kingdom of Ghur, in present-day Afghanistan, was the last to accept Islam, but its local rulers were another significant threat to the Saljuqs. In the end they managed to gain independence and formed the Pashto-speaking Ghurid dynasty in Afghanistan. Feelings of protest against Arabs and Turks remained strong among Iranians, but they were channeled into forms other than national organized resistance, such as mob violence *(iyara, ayyar),* organized by powerful leaders with strict codes of conduct. Dissent also emerged as sectarian movements, such as Ismailism and radical Shi'ism. Alid (Alevid) communities became popular among Kurds and other marginal communities, with Ali as the central figure attaining mythical proportions.

Ismaili

Since the early crisis of succession after the Prophet's death, both the Sunni and the Shi'ite sects were subdivided into subsects. Included were the two surviving Shi'i twelve imams of present-day Iran and the Ismaili sect, whose rulers assert descent from the Shi'i imam, Ismail. Ismail was the eldest son of the sixth shi'i imam and is recognized by the Ismaili as the rightful heir. In contrast, the Iranian Shi'i recognize another son as the rightful seventh imam. Ismailis in mediaeval times twice established their own states and played an important role for relatively long periods in the Muslim world and during the Crusades. They were the founders of the first Shi'a caliphate under the Fatimid caliph-imams and also made important contributions to Islamic thought and culture and the development of Sufism. Later, after a schism that split Ismailism into two major branches, one group, the Nizari leaders, succeeded in founding a cohesive state with numerous mountain strongholds. They governed scattered territories stretching from eastern Persia to Syria. They collapsed only under the onslaught of the all-conquering Mongols, lost political prominence, and survived mainly as a minor Shi'i Muslim sect, as they are today. Their most notable follower in Iran, Hassan Sabah, founded the Assassin sect in the eleventh century. He fortified the Alamut Castle in the Alburz Mountains and carried out assassinations of major political and military figures. The Iranian Ismailis were influenced by neo-Mazdakite movements in Iran. On the whole they resented the Turkish rulers of Iran and attracted many followers, mainly in towns and among merchants, members of the elite, and intellectuals.

Ethnic Change

The Turks introduced ethnic, political, and military changes both in Iran and in the rest of the Middle East. The Turks had been in Iran earlier, but during the Saljuq period they arrived en masse and continued to do so until the Mongol conquest of the thirteenth century. Unlike the Ghaznavids, who were of servile origin, the Saljuqs were originally Turkish and military aristocrats. They imposed their political authority over the Iranian world at large: Azerbaijan; the Caspian coastland; Gorgan; Khurasan; parts of Kurdistan, including the Hamadan region; and a large section of Fars became widely Turkish-speaking. The Turkish tribal chiefs were transformed into kings with a sophisticated court hierarchy; an Iranian-staffed bureaucracy; and a multinational, partly slave army to defend their territories. They also fought and sought to control the many nomadic Turkish tribes, which resented such changes because they were instigated by the aristocracy.

The internal and external conflicts halted uniform Turkish domination of Iran, and the standing army shifted from mainly Turkish commanders and their retainers to a mixture of contingents from tributary Arab groups and Kurdish and Persian minor rulers in Kurdistan, the Caspian provinces, Sistan, and other areas. One way to offset opposition by the Turkmen groups was to send them to the frontiers of the empire and to engage them against the Christians or against other Muslim groups, such as the Syrian Ismailis and the Shi'i Fatimids. Another strategy was the practice of granting rulership of provinces or regions to allies, including major tribal chiefs, and the exalted sultan ruled over minor sultans governing major provinces. The latter became more independent as the Saljuq central authority weakened. The Turkish provincial governors founded numerous dynasties, sometimes with no Saljuq prince as their leader. Many disputes and succession wars further weakened the central authority.

Religious Mix

Saljuq Turks strengthened the Sunni faith and reduced Shi'i influence by eliminating the Dailamite dynasties and Ismaili influence and defeating the Fatimids from Iraq and northern Syria. Ismailis remained only in Khurasan, parts of Dailam, and Fars, with little political influence, though their leaders continued to live in Iran until the late nineteenth century, when they moved their headquarters to India. Zoroastrians were eliminated from any positions of power and, like Christians and Jews, remained segregated in their own quarters. All practiced their religions freely and appointed their own religious officials, confirmed by the authorities, paid *jizya*, and sometimes were forced to wear identifying marks on their clothing. Jews at times enjoyed some freedom and occasionally rose to positions of power. Armenians and Greeks sometimes fought as mercenaries for the Saljuq sultans. Jews were mainly involved in trade, and large segregated Jewish communities existed in Hamadan, Isfahan, Nihavand, and Shiraz. Christians suffered mainly because of the Crusades and the lasting suspicion that they supported these wars of Christians against Muslims. Depending on the policies of the rulers and the local politics at times, all these minorities could be persecuted and on the whole remained at the mercy of the rulers.

A substantial Persian-Islamic literature was produced during this period, and there were important technical advances in pottery, metalwork, and astronomy. Omar Khayyám improved the solar calendar used by Iranians at this period. New elements of scale and spatial composition were introduced into architecture. Despite the dominance of Islam and the Turkish military government as unifying factors, local particularism and variety in the social ethics of different groups and communities existed, with divisions between Sunni/Shi'i, Turk and non-Turk, and settled and semisettled populations. The militarization of the government was resented by many, particularly the farmers, whose main function ended up being the support of the army. At the same time, the large influx of Turkish nomads improved the nomad economy and increased produce from their flocks.

The final blow to the Saljuq power in Iran came from the minor Turkish rulers of Khwarazm, whose kings became independent, created their own Khawarazm-shahian dynasty, and extended their power into western and central Iran. They fought both the Saljuqs and the caliphate in Baghdad. However, they did not have enough time to consolidate their power and govern all of Iran because of the Mongol invasion and the conquests of Chingiz-Khan (Genghis Khan).

The Mongol Invasion, 1217–1383

The Mongol invasion of Iran started early in the thirteenth century and lasted for years before the whole country fell. It was accompanied by the massive destruction of major cities, particularly in Khurasan, and the collapse of economic and public order. Factional differences and the refusal of several provinces to help the last Khawarazm-shahian ruler aided the invasion's eventual success. Iran became part of a larger territory comprising the southern Caucasus area and parts of Upper Mesopotamia and Asia, ruled by successors of Chingiz-Khan. The Mongol conquest changed the political geography of the country, added new ethnic components, wiped out the Ismailis, and ended the caliphate in Baghdad. The country was ruled once again by one power. The new borders caused Iran to come into direct contact with the Christian West. The Mongols themselves kept their nationalistic tendencies. Despite the fact that they were gradually converted to Islam, they never abandoned their historical origins or severed ties with their kinsmen in eastern, central, and northern Asia. Persians used the opportunity to try to reduce the Arab influence. The Arabic language as a vehicle of historical writing was totally abandoned and was replaced by Persian. The collapse of the caliphate in Baghdad ended the Arab influence once and for all.

The thirteenth century, after the Mongol conquest, witnessed colossal economic decline, reduction in population and cultivated land, and the migration of multitudes of Mongol and Turkish nomads. The changes caused a decline in urban life and agriculture, an increase in the nomad economy, the expansion of migratory cattle-breeders, and the growth of a peasant insurrectionary movement. Some reforms were introduced later to improve agriculture and reduce tension among the farmers. However, they resulted in large-scale land ownership at the expense of state and petty landowners. The economy of the country did not attain its pre-Mongol level. Large landowners became feudal lords, and the last decades of the Mongol occupation were marked by feudal power struggles and the political disintegration of the Mongol rulers of Iran, known as Il-Khanid.

The invasion of cultivated settled areas by the Saljuqs and other Turkish nomadic tribes had already damaged the urban economy. The total destruction of major cities, including Balkh, Merv, Nishapur, Herat, Tus, Ray, Qazvin, and Hamadan, along with the mass killings of entire populations and enslavement by the Mongols, devastated the country. These depredations resulted in a shortage of professionals and skilled laborers and artisans. Khurasan, Tabaristan, Gorgan, and Gilan, formerly major centers of agricultural products and silk, became wastelands and did not recover for centuries. A few cities, such as Tabriz in Azerbaijan, survived by agreeing to pay heavy tributes, and the city became a major Mongol center. However, Azerbaijan was continuously threatened by the invasion of the Golden Horde, Chingiz-Khan's most direct descendents, combined with other Turkmen groups, who attacked it continuously. This threat combined with the conflict between military clans in the region reduced the area to utter chaos. There was conflict between feudal, mercantile, and clerical classes as well.

These groups kept making alliances against each other with the Mongol military clans. Following the collapse of the Mongols, local dynasties rose in Azerbaijan but were subjugated by the newcomers, the Qara Quyunlu Turkmen. These Turkmen eventually captured Baghdad and Mesopotamia and further expanded their influence into Fars, Kirman, and Khurasan. Some Turkmen dynasties supported Shi'ite movements; they became the predecessors of the Safavids, who made Shi'i the state religion in the sixteenth century.

Khurasan had become a melting pot for different ethnic groups, from Turk to Mongol, including even Indian populations on the eastern borders. This mixing was due partly to military dispositions and partly to cohabitation, as in the case of the Indians. Major agricultural lands became pasture for nomads, and nomads' cattle-breeding ruined grass and crops during their migrations. The nomads also played a significant political role by forming militant feudal aristocracies, plundering the local populations, and becoming the most significant military force in the country. Because there was no organized standing national army, the militant nomads played a leading role and dominated politics until the sixteenth century. They were antagonistic to settled life and regarded themselves as rulers in a foreign hostile land. With most of the old established bureaucracy dead and infrastructures destroyed, the Mongols, unlike previous foreign rulers, did not have the benefit of capable and experienced administrators running national affairs. One exception was during the reign of Ghazan Khan, who employed a very capable Iranian vizier and aimed at certain reforms. Most attempts to rebuild the country failed. New taxation systems introduced to implement reform did not work, and improvements were short-lived. Early Mongol rulers were not Muslims, and religious minorities, including Jews and Christians, gained more freedom and access to the mainstream society. However, restrictions were imposed on them once again after the Mongols adopted Islam.

The Mongol rulers moved frequently, and, despite some settling down, most still followed the tradition of moving between summer and winter camps. Large camps would be set up outside major cities. The Mongol chiefs, great local feudal and noble families, owned large estates with servants and slaves. They sometimes owned and built entire quarters in towns. Although the majority of the military aristocracy of the nomad tribes remained Mongol and Turkish, there were some Iranians and Kurds as well, with the Muslim religious caste mainly consisting of Iranians and some of Arab origin. The civil servants were mostly Iranians.

The Mongol and Turkish rulers introduced a new feudal system based on military fiefs. This new system was decentralized, with peasants and nomads attached to particular families of feudal lords. This was unlike the older centralized feudal state with an established bureaucratic apparatus and settled peasantry. The latter were normally associated with prominent figures, such as the powerful Iranian vizier Rashid al-Din. He owned large estates and had his own very large quarter in Tabriz, complete with craftsmen's guilds, a bazaar, *madrasa,* mosques, and gathering places for dervishes and Sufis. The quarter had local inns (caravanserai) to receive traveling merchants and goods. The two feudal systems were at odds and struggled with one another for control of land and products, contributing to the decline of economic development in Iran.

Discrepancies existed between the Islamic system of land ownership and the Mongol system as dictated in the laws of the *Great Yasa* of Chingiz-Khan. In the latter, the low-ranking Mongol warrior was considered a serf and was attached not to the soil but to his lord and tribal leader. In contrast, the Muslim system did not recognize serfdom, and the peasants were attached to the soil rather than to the person owning the land. In the new system the peasants did not own the land and had to pay rent; their situation worsened further once the *Great Yasa* was implemented. Under this new code their movement from the lands where they were registered was restricted, which meant the binding of the peasants to the soil. Essentially, the peasants became the personal property of the landlord. Both the settled peasants and the nomads were exploited by their feudal lords. They paid taxes both in kind and in money to maintain the Il-Khanid rulers and their families, the state apparatus, and the army. The large influx of Turkish and Mongol nomads also meant occupation, outright seizure of lands owned by established landowners, and dramatic changes in land use to make it more appropriate for the nomad economy. High feudal rents and taxes were excessively out of proportion with the economic development of the country, which had been ruined by the Mongol invasion.

There were many popular uprisings, including major protest movements in the rural areas and among the farmers. Both the uprisings and the economic crisis led to further destabilization of the Mongol rule. The end of the Il-Khanid period in Iran in the mid-fourteenth century created a power vacuum, public and political disarray, the tyranny of petty princes, bloody conflicts between local rulers, and socioreligious movements. One such movement was the Sarbedaran (head on gallows) in Khurasan, which started as a religious messianic movement of the Shi'i creed whose leaders ended up ruling the area for a brief period. The era also coincided with the appearance of Turkmen confederations, moving from eastern Anatolia toward the Iranian highland, including the Qara Quyunlu and the Aq Quyunlu tribes. They first moved into Azerbaijan and then expanded into Fars and Khurasan, with the latter tribe eventually succeeding over the former. All these factors paved the way for the next major conqueror of the area, Timur (Tamerlane), in the fourteenth century.

The Timurid Period and the Turkmen Local Dynasties, 1383–1500

The end of the Il-Khanid dynasty created a power vacuum, with rivalries between three different groups: the princely families related to the Mongols, such as the Jalayirids and Muzaffarids; the local aristocracy; and the supporters of the latter. This third group included followers of Shi'i or extremist religious movements. The power struggles were within and between all these groups, lasting for almost half a century and further dividing the country and halting economic growth. During this turmoil, Timur advanced from central Asia, conquered Iran, imposed unification, and started the Timurid dynasty toward the end of the fourteenth century.

Belonging to a minor military family, and of Turkish origin, Timur was born in Transoxiana (present-day Uzbekistan) in the fourteenth century. He rose to prominence in the service of the local Mongol ruler, claimed to be descended from Chingiz-Khan, and defeated all competitors. He conquered Iran, Mesopotamia, Armenia, Georgia, India, and Syria and managed to defeat and imprison the Ottoman sultan in present-day Turkey. He rose to power in a complex mosaic of tribes and subtribes, local settled populations, and independent military units, and his success was partially based on his ability to gain control through the building of a nontribal power base in his own land. He then waged aggressive campaigns of conquest and plunder against neighboring countries until his death in 1405, when he was on the verge of invading China. His cruelty in war made him a legend, and his plundering of the occupied lands devastated Iran even further. His dynasty, the Timurids, ruled Transoxiana and Iran until the early sixteenth century and became great patrons of Turkish and Persian literature, architecture, science, and arts.

Timur's conquest of Iran brought more Turkmen into the country. At the same time, his policy of moving valuable treasures, slaves, and movable property of all kinds, including riding-horses, pack and domestic animals, and herds, devastated local and nomad economies. Few people survived his invasions; among the survivors were artists, artisans, collaborators, and people loyal to him but also religious authorities, sayyids (claiming descent from the Prophet), Sufis, shaikhs, and dervishes. The latter groups survived because of Timur's respect for religion, though the sects he regarded as heretical were dealt with severely. Timur and his successors saw themselves as the

Timur Beg, or Tamerlane (1333–1405), portrait from Indian colored drawing, lithograph, 1826 (Bettmann/Corbis)

defenders of Islam, and with a few exceptions they promoted Shari'a and theological schools and literature. Patronage of the Sufi and mystic sects eventually led to the coming into power of the next major rulers, the Safavids, direct descendents of Shaikh Safi, a Sufi mystic with a considerable following in Azerbaijan.

The conquest of provinces and cities was followed by resettlement operations on a large scale, both into and away from the Iranian territories, mainly for security reasons. Timur and his successors were more concerned with maintaining power than with introducing a unified and clearly defined system of administration. The old Turkish principle of appointing princely governors continued, but the bulk of the fighting forces remained under the control of Timur or his successors. This made the rulers independent of the appointed governors. Azerbaijan became the most important province, with more Turkmen moving into the area, particularly into Tabriz, the present-day capital of Iranian Azerbaijan. The province was expanded as an administrative unit and at times covered most areas in western Iran, including Fars, Mesopotamia, Isfahan, Hamadan, and Kirman. Other major provinces were ruled by close relatives of Timur or his commanders in the form of fiefs that were hereditary or granted to the governors for a fixed duration. Disruption by different groups, including Turkmen, Kurds, and Lur nomads, were dealt with severely. Minor Kurdish and Lur rulers existed, but they were subdued and the most they could do was to take sides with the warring factions.

Persian remained the language of the court, and Timur is credited with supporting art and culture. In fact, he reestablished the total cultural entity of Iran throughout the massive territories he ruled by patronizing art. He favored Persian literature and consequently spread the Persian language throughout his domain. Despite his nomadic origins, his attempts to make his capital, Samarqand, the grandest city of his time indicate a willingness to make the transition from a nomadic to a sedentary way of life. Like the previous Turkish rulers of Iran, the aristocracy became Persianized by adopting the Persian language and cultural practices, while the bulk of the Turkmen tribes remained nomadic and spoke Turkish. In his efforts to support art and culture, Timur expanded Iranian cultural influence and as a result reduced Mongol influence in Iran. After Timur's death, his empire collapsed, and succession wars broke out. Eventually the empire was divided and never again attained the size it had reached under Timur. The Timurids ruled Iran until the beginning of the sixteenth century, during which time many territories would be lost to the Qara Quyunlu Turkmen. The major provinces became the battleground for warring Turkmen groups such as the advancing Uzbeks and Aq Quyunlu nomads. The latter were established in Azerbaijan by the middle of the fifteenth century and gradually expanded their influence.

The Turkmen dynasties, though powerful at times, did not last, and they were not able to form any sound political organization to ensure their survival. Where they made a difference was in their confederation-forming alliances with other power groups fighting against each other. One such case was the support of the Turkmen tribes for the Safavid spiritual ruler Ismail and the coming into power of the Safavid dynasty in the sixteenth century, which led to the establishment of Shi'i as the state religion in Iran.

Since Mongol times, the larger part of the population had remained Sunni Muslims. By the Timurid period, a major religious change was happening with the popularity of folk Islam, a mixture of different Shi'i sects, mystical/Sufi/dervish orders, and extremist sects. All of these sects, combined with underground political religious activists, prepared the way for the success of the Twelfth Imami Shi'i in the sixteenth century. The Turkish/Persian dichotomy persisted during the Timurid era. The military and governors were Turks and Turkicized Mongols. Persians and occasionally some Turks remained in control of the administration. A significant Turco-Persian culture had formed as a result of centuries of domination by Turkish elements, with a substantial literature produced mainly in Persian and some in Turkish. The Turkish influence increased with the dominance of the next major rulers of Iran, the Safavid, and remained very strong until the twentieth century.

Conclusion

In general, the period from the Arab conquest to the coming of the Safavid in the sixteenth century was a time of decline and disintegration of central authority. In reality the country was divided between different rulers, often of foreign origin. These rulers fought among themselves and against the minor or local Iranian dynasties. The conquests by the Arabs, Turks, Mongols, and Turkmen changed the ethnic geography of Iran and resulted in the development of a strong Turco-Iranian culture. Despite Arab and Turkish domination, Iranians managed to maintain their ethnic identity by a number of strategies. They adopted and changed Islamic ideas and integrated major principles of Zoroastrianism into the new and popular Shi'i creed. Unlike most other countries under Arab rule, they managed to keep Persian as the dominant language, both in Iranian territories and beyond, and expanded and maintained their cultural dominance. Many cultural and religious festivals, such as the Persian new year, remained and helped preserve the continuity of cultural practices. The country remained ethnically diverse, with many groups struggling to gain a foothold. The Arab and the Turkish conquests significantly affected the national and local economies. However, it was the Mongolian and Timurid conquests that devastated the country and accelerated the economic demise of the Iranian territories. The popularity

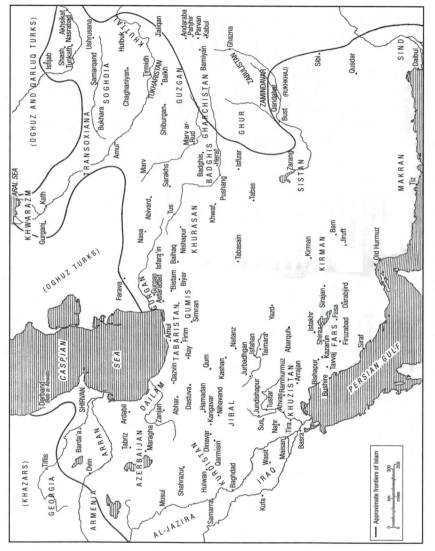

Iran during the Abbasid period, ninth century A.D.

of folk Islam in the end resulted in the establishment of a powerful dynasty headed by a spiritual leader with support from the Turkmen confederations.

Timeline

570	The birth of Prophet Muhammad.
622	Prophet Muhammad, fearing for his life, migrated from Mecca to Medina. This date is the beginning of the Islamic lunar calendar.
642	The Sassanian Empire falls to the Muslim armies of Arabia.
661	Ali, the Prophet Muhammad's son-in-law and the fourth and last of the early caliphs, was assassinated. His death created a major schism in Islam between the Sunni and Shi'ite sects. The Umayyad clan emerged as the rulers of the new Muslim Empire.
680	Imam Hussein, Ali's son, was killed by the Umayyad army in Karbala. His death became the most important Shi'ite mourning event.
696	By this date, Arabic had become the dominant language of the Islamic world.
750	The Abbasids ended Umayyad rule with help from the Persians.
821	Tahirids, a local dynasty from Iran, practically ended the Arab domination of Iran. Their rule ended in 873.
867	The Saffarids of Sistan established Iranian dominance in the eastern Iranian territories until their collapse in 903.
873	The Samanids became the first truly Iranian group ruling Iran, until 999. Persian became the official langue of the court, replacing Arabic.
1010	The Persian epic, the *Book of Kings,* was composed. The book *(Shahnameh)* would become instrumental in the revival and continuity of the Persian language and culture.
945	The Buyid leaders, from north-central Iran, defeated the Arab armies and later captured Baghdad. They collapsed by 1055, but their influence remained for centuries.

1000	The beginnings of Turkish dominance in Iran and the emergence of the Saljuq dynasty.
1220	The Mongol invasion. Chingiz-Khan and his armies devastated Iran. He died in 1227, and his empire was divided between his close kin.
1258	The Mongols sacked Baghdad and ended the Abbasid caliphate. The Il-Khanid dynasty gained control of the Persian territories of the Mongols.
1295	Ghazan Khan, the Mongol emperor of Iran from the Ilkhanid dynasty, converted to Islam.
1405	Timur (Tamerlane) conquered most of Persia and the surrounding areas. The Timurid dynasty of Iran collapsed in 1501.

Significant People, Places, and Events

AQ QUYUNLU: The name means "tribes with white sheep." A major confederation of Turkmen with many subtribes that expanded into Asia Minor and Iran. Very likely they came with the Oghuz Turks into western Asia in the eleventh century.

BEDOUINS: Nomadic Arab tribes inhabiting many territories in the Middle East. Semitic in origin, they formed the bulk of the Muslim Arab armies during the early centuries of Muslim conquest.

BUYIDS: A pro-Shi'ite Iranian dynasty from northern Persia that ruled over parts of Iran for almost a century beginning in the tenth century. They occupied Iraq and exerted great influence over the caliphs.

HIJRAT: The term applies to Prophet Muhammad's departure into exile, from Mecca to Medina. The date this departure took place (A.D. 622) became the beginning of the Muslim lunar calendar.

IMAM ZAMAN: The twelfth Shi'i imam, who is assumed to be hidden and will appear toward the end of time to save the world. The idea is very similar to the concept of the last Zoroastrian savior, Saoshyant. Imam Zaman (the Time Lord) has the title *mahdi*, meaning "divinely guided one," and is expected to appear when the world is in its most corrupt state.

ISMAILIS: Supporters of Ismail, the seventh Shi'i imam. After the death of the sixth imam, a division occurred among the followers. Ismailis supported the eldest son of the deceased imam. Currently most are followers of Agha Khan and are scattered around the world.

JIZYA: A capitation tax prescribed in the Quran and applied to non-Muslims only. Applicable in accordance with the subjects' capacity, the tax became a major reason why many non-Muslims adopted the new fate.

KHARIJITES: An extremist puritan sect in early Islam, entertaining the idea of establishing an Islamic community in which no one, not even the caliph, should deviate from the dictates of the Quran. They attracted many followers in Iran.

OGHUZ TURKS: One of the major Turkish tribes migrating south into Persia beginning in the tenth century. The followers of one of their leaders, Saljuq, became known as Saljuq Turks and ruled many territories, including Iran.

PROPHET MUHAMMAD: Founder of Islam. He was forty years old when he received revelations about the new religion. By the time he died, he had conquered the whole of Arabia under the banner of Islam.

QARA QUYUNLU: The name means "tribes with black sheep." A major confederation of Turkmen with many subtribes, expanding into Asia Minor and into Iran. They were closely related to their Aq Quyunlu tribes, who were their rivals, and entered the area around the same time, in the eleventh century.

QARAKHANIDS: Turkish tribes from central Asia. They belonged to the Qarluq tribal confederation and became prominent during the ninth century in Transoxiana.

QURAN: Muslims' holy book, written in Arabic. Muslims believe that its contents were revealed directly to the Prophet Muhammad.

SHAHNAMEH: The *Book of Kings*. *Shahnameh* is an icon by itself and is a translation of pre-Islamic stories, myths, and the legendary histories of Iranians before Islam. Written in New Persian in the tenth century. Its writer, Firdusi, declared that by writing *Shahnameh* he saved the Persian language. It indeed became the standard in the Persian language and greatly influenced later writers and poets.

SHI'I: Supporters of Ali, the Prophet Muhammad's son-in-law and cousin. The Shi'ites believe Ali and his family are the only rightful heirs after the Prophet's death. He was not chosen as the first caliph and only became the fourth one before being assassinated by the Kharijites.

SUNNI: The majority sect in Islam. They accept the first four caliphs as the rightful successors of the Prophet Muhammad. They do not deny Ali but accept him only as the fourth caliph.

TIMUR (TAMERLANE): The Turkmen conqueror, he established an empire extending from India to the Mediterranean Sea (1336–1405). His name, a European corruption of Timur Lang ("Timur the Lame"), was given to him because his left leg was partially disabled.

TRANSOXIANA: Region north of the river Oxus (modern Amu Darya), present-day Uzbekistan. It included Bukhara and Samarqand, two very important medieval cities.

Bibliography

Boyce, Mary. *Zoroastrians: Their Religious Beliefs and Practices.* London: Routledge and Kegan Paul, 2001.

Boyle, J. A., ed. *The Cambridge History of Iran,* Vol. 5: The Saljuq and Mongol Periods. Cambridge: Cambridge University Press, 1968.

McDowall, David. *The Kurds: A Nation Denied.* London: Minority Rights Publications International, 1992.

———. *A Modern History of Kurds.* London: I. B. Tarius, 2002.

Frye, R. N., ed. *The Cambridge History of Iran,* Vol. 4: *From the Arab Invasion to the Saljuqs.* Cambridge: Cambridge University Press, 1975.

Meiselas, Susan, Martin Van Bruinessen, and A. Whitley. *Kurdistan: In the Shadow of History.* New York: Random House, 1997.

Nicolaisen, Ida. *Nomads of Luristan.* The Carlsberg Foundation's Nomad Research Project. London: Thames and Hudson, 1993.

Van der Leeuw, Charles. *Azerbaijan: A Quest for Identity.* London: Curzon Press, 2000.

CHAPTER THREE

The Rise of Shi'i Islam

The Safavid Period, 1501–1736

THE FIRST SAFAVID RULER BELONGED TO A WELL-ESTABLISHED FAMILY in Ardabil, in Azerbaijan. He was a descendent of a powerful Sufi master and closely related to the Aq Quyunlu Turkmen and Persian aristocracies. Shah Ismail I revived the monarchist tradition of Iran and united the country within a defined territory that more or less has remained the same until now. He became the first militant head of a religious order to be crowned a king. Following the defeat of the Aq Quyunlu tribes and the conquest of Tabriz in 1501, he immediately declared the Shi'i creed as the state religion. This act resulted in the further Iranization of Shi'i Islam and the creation of a powerful class of clergy with considerable influence, which has endured up to the present. Furthermore, by modernizing the military and use of heavy artillery and gunpowder, with help from Europeans, Iran became the only Middle Eastern country that managed to stop the Ottoman invasions at its borders and never came under Ottoman control. Europeans' involvement—mainly English and Dutch at the beginning and others, including Russians, later—was the start of centuries of direct and complex contact between Iran and Europe. It resulted in extensive trade mainly through the Persian Gulf, which ultimately damaged the Ottoman influence and trade and resulted in an increase in hostilities between the Ottoman Empire and Iran.

With both Turkmen and Persian ancestry, Shah Ismail utilized the military support of the Turkmen followers of his Sufi order, but once in power, he placed Iranians in charge in order to control the Turkmen and create a balance. Maintaining this balance between Iranians and Turkmen, and among the latter, who frequently fought against each other, became the most daunting dilemma facing the Safavid rulers, along with the Ottoman and

Uzbek invasions. Ottomans were the main rival, and their invasions and occupations forced the kings to move their capital from Tabriz to Qazvin and eventually to Isfahan in central Iran. There were five major Turkmen tribes, which fought among each other constantly for positions of power at the court. Their leaders were granted major provinces. Later on, to reduce their power, large sections of their territories were annexed and added to the crown lands, an act that undermined some local economies. At times members of the Safavid family replaced the Turkmen governors. The never-ending disputes among the tribes, along with mismanagement by the later Safavid rulers and foreign attacks, eventually weakened the empire. As a result, minor tribes, such as Afshars and Qajars, managed to take over and form their own dynasties after the Afghan invasion and the collapse of the Safavid power.

Ismail's followers regarded him as infallible and as possessing divine qualities as the representative of the twelve imams. The Sufi leader expected absolute obedience and readiness to sacrifice their lives for the grand master from his followers. These followers, named *qizilbash* because of their red headgear, assumed the form of a military and religious organization at the same time. Many conquests that followed enhanced the young ruler's prestige because his followers believed that the victories were the work of God. The same beliefs damaged his position when he was defeated for the first time by the Ottomans in the battle of Chaldiran in 1514. He lost part of his harem; gave up the Iranian territories in eastern Anatolia (Turkey); and was forced out of his capital, Tabriz. Though he went back to Tabriz and regained control, in the eyes of his followers he had lost his invincibility.

The establishment of the Safavid regime in Tabriz in 1501 had a major impact on the development of the identity of the people of Azerbaijan. The shah was a native Turkic speaker and wrote poetry in the Azerbaijani language. It is estimated that during the Safavid era 1,200 Azerbaijani words entered Persian. Tabriz remained the capital and flourished as a result. The occupation of Tabriz by the Ottomans and the Uzbek invasions separated the Turkish population of Azerbaijan from the rest of the Turkish speakers, which increased their ties with the Persians until they became the largest Turkish group adhering to Shi'i. The adoption of Shi'i in both north and south Azerbaijan created a bond between the groups and contributed to the formation of their distinctive and common Azerbaijani identity. Modern nationalists in Azerbaijan regard the Safavids as an Azerbaijani dynasty and an important symbol of Azerbaijani identity and common history.

Turkish and Persian Rivalries

Prior to the Safavid period, a more or less clear distinction existed between the Turks and the Persians, with the latter in charge of the administration (men of the pen) and the former as military heads and governors (men of the sword). Though it is premature to talk of nationalism in Iran before the twentieth century, the two groups nevertheless were very aware of their origins and differences in culture and language. Fully aware of his historical origins as a member of the Iranian feudal elite, Shah Ismail was also the grandson of the last major Aq Quyunlu leader, Uzun Hasan. In fact, it was due to the military support of the Turkmen tribes that he succeeded in the succession wars over his Aq Quyunlu cousins. In their attempts to control the Turkmen, the Safavid rulers, starting with Ismail, departed from the traditional division of military and administrative posts by creating new positions that enabled Iranians to become heads of the administration and military (*sadr* and *amir*). The confinement of the royal princes to the harems, rather than the usual custom of handing them over to the Turkish military aristocracy for training, might have been an attempt to reduce the influence of the Turkmen over the princes. Such policies resulted in a leadership crisis because the princes received no training to prepare them to rule. They also got involved in harem intrigues fueled by their close female relatives belonging to the major Iranian, Georgian, Circassian, or Turkmen groups and their eunuchs. Some later rulers even imported Armenian, Georgian, and Circassian administrators from outside Iran to maintain control. Success of such policies depended entirely on the strength of the individual kings. Although some, such as Ismail I and Shah Abbas I, managed to impose control, others were less successful.

The aristocracies of the Turkmen tribes, like those of the Mongols and the Turks before them, moved from a seminomadic society with many tribal chiefs having a say in affairs to a sedentary one ruled by a monarch with absolute power and divine attributes. During this transition, household and family concepts also shifted from a system based on conceptions of communal decision-making to one of absolutist patriarchal rule. In the past most elderly family members, male and female, had participated in decision-making processes. In the new system the king became the ultimate source of authority. The result was harem intrigues that involved a few very powerful women, including the mothers of future kings. Interference in state affairs by these women, the harem eunuchs, foreign wives, and many concubines, with their plots and back-stabbings, was part of the transition. In the process many Iranian and Turkmen leaders, male and female, lost their lives or positions at the court. The struggles expanded to other domains, notably the language. Turkish became the dominant spoken language at the court, while Persian was used for administration, and Iranians held on to their positions in the bureaucracy.

On the whole, the Turkish elements remained in control of the military faction, despite major reforms in the army by Shah Abbas I (Shah Abbas the Great). He stripped the Turkmen tribal aristocracy of all power and introduced new weaponry and ranks in the army, with help from Europeans. The latter saw Iranians as the only major force against the Ottomans and competed among each other in seeking a power base in Iran. Shah Abbas attempted to create a standing army independent of the warring tribes. Though he was successful and ruled with an iron fist, his successors were too weak to continue in the same manner. It would take until the twentieth century for such an army to be realized.

It is not clear whether other Safavids before Ismail adhered to the Shi'i sect. In order to establish the Shi'i creed in Sunni Iran, the new rulers used force. They imported Shi'a clergy from Lebanon and Bahrain, who created a vast literature in Persian and Arabic. This literature became the standard Shi'i literature in Iran and is still read extensively in the religious schools without much change. They also attacked the holy Shi'i shrines in Iraq many times in order to control the holy sites but in the end could not defeat the Ottomans in charge of Iraq. At the outset the clergy supported the kings' claims to divinity, but ultimately they rejected such notions. Indeed, the clergy declared that they were the rightful heirs to the twelve imams. By the end of their reign, the Safavid kings had lost their position as spiritual heads. The clergy, with a well-established hierarchy, exerted great influence even over the kings. An attempt in 1576 by Shah Ismail II to abolish Shi'i and reduce the clergy's influence failed. Some kings were even forced to impose bans against drinking alcohol and playing music at the court because such practices were regarded as non-Islamic by the clergy.

The use of religion to consolidate power was a major achievement of the early Safavids and had significant consequences. It distinguished Iran from the neighboring Sunni countries, but in the end, it did not contribute much to the unity of the country, which still suffered from conflicts among the warring tribes. It resulted in religious persecution of the Sunni Muslims, including the Kurds, who have remained mostly Sunni. It also helped the downfall of the Safavids during the Afghan invasion, a consequence of the brutal policies imposed to convert Sunni Afghans into Shi'i in the eighteenth century. This resulted in the subsequent loss of the eastern Iranian territories, including Herat and Qandahar (Kandahar). The Baluchi tribes also resisted the Safavid religious and political policies. Like other Sunni groups living near the border areas, they followed separatist tendencies and fought against the Safavid local governors.

Kurds under the Safavids

Many groups functioned as allies or buffer zones between various Turkmen groups, the Ottomans, and the Uzbeks. Safavids made great use of resettlement policies and on many occasions moved and resettled many tribes, such as Kurds, large numbers of Armenians from Armenia, or Georgians from Georgia. These relocations were intended either to stop border invasions or to increase the Safavid power base. Though both Safavids and Ottomans used various tribes in their territories for a number of reasons, their policies toward the tribes were different.

The Ottomans consolidated tribal formations that they found willing and collaborative. In contrast, the Safavids tried to forge large new tribal units out of many smaller groups of heterogeneous origins. In the case of the Kurds, the most significant instance of such tribe formation by the state was that of the Chamishkazaklu, allegedly numbering some 40,000 households originating from Anatolia and Caucasia. They were settled by Shah Abbas I in northern Khurasan around 1600 to guard Iran's frontier against Uzbek intrusion. A centrally appointed tribal chief was chosen to keep the groups together. Gradually they split up into three large tribes, each under an initially centrally appointed but from that time forward hereditary tribal chief. Local Kurdish dynasties were subject to the central authority and were obliged to pay taxes in kind or to provide military service when required. The collection of taxes was the responsibility of the chiefs, and sometimes when the government was weak or involved in major wars the chiefs refused to pay.

The Kurdish ruler of the Ottoman territory of Bitlis (Bedlis), Sharaf Khan, preserved the Kurdish history of the period in his book *Sharafnameh*. Completed in 1597, his account described the differences in the treatment of the Kurdish dynasties at the hands of the Qara Quyunlu, Aq Quyunlu, Safavids, and Ottomans. It included descriptions of Kurdish ruling families; the four major Kurdish clans (Kurmanji, Lur, Kalhur, and Kuran [Guran]); and the names and locations of tens of tribes, many still existing while others have disappeared. Lurs, currently a separate group, are mentioned as a Kurdish clan in this book. They played a significant role in helping the last defeated Safavid prince to regain control but in the end changed their allegiance and, according to some accounts, had the prince murdered.

The persistence of the surviving tribes, such as the Lurs and others, shows continuity over time. However, the tribes' size and degree of organizational complexity fluctuated considerably over time. One example is the separation of the Lurs and their independence as a tribe. Most Kurds of the period were referred to as Sunni of the Shafei school, while Alevid and Yazidi were mentioned, and some were labeled as heretical. Although some tribes were pastoral nomads, others practiced settled agriculture and animal husbandry seasonally, and some were described as settled farmers. *Sharafnameh* recognized the heterogeneity of the tribes and lack of unity, which are said to be characteristic of the Kurdish people. Intertribal conflicts and coalitions and the extent of state interference in the regions under Kurdish chieftains were also noted. For example, the author stated that at the time, the large Mukri confederacy was divided into two opposing factions. Their chiefs, who were closely related, allied themselves with the Safavids and with the Ottomans, respectively. The role of the Kurdish territories as buffer zones enabled the Kurdish chiefs to play one country against another or to seek protection from one against the other. *Sharafnameh* contained several examples of Kurdish ruling families alternating between the Ottoman sultans and the Safavid kings as their patrons. Sharaf Khan, the author, was in the Safavid service himself before changing sides and working for the Ottomans.

Many Kurdish groups did not favor the Safavids because of the Safavid religious policies and hostility toward Sunni Islam. The Kurds were more receptive to the Ottoman policy of ruling Kurdish territory through local tribes. The Safavids tried to appoint their Turkmen relatives or allies as local governors. They had limited success, and Kurds remained hostile. One exception was the prominent Kurdish family of Ardalans, who were permitted to remain in control of the central Zagros range and the fertile valleys to the west. Ardalans were hereditary rulers who had been residing in Sanandaj on the eastern side of the Zagros. Before the rise of the Ottomans, they controlled territories in both Iraq and Iran. They lost their territories in Iraq to the Ottomans but remained prominent in Iran for centuries and became part of the upper-class Iranian society.

Armenians

The present Armenian population in Iran is mostly a result of forced settlements by the Safavid rulers. The relationship between the Armenians and the Safavids was a complicated one that was influenced by the Turkish presence in Asia Minor and events in Armenia itself. In the eleventh century, the Saljuq rulers of Asia Minor forced thousands of Armenians out of Armenia and into Azerbaijan. After the Mongol conquest, the Armenians played a major role in international trade around the Caspian, Black, and Mediterranean Seas. Many Armenian merchants and artisans settled in the Iranian cities bordering historical Armenia. Timur's invasion and the Aq Quyunlu and Qara Quyunlu conflicts depopulated Armenia as more of its people were forced to immigrate into Iran in the fifteenth century. Early conquests by the Safavids extended their influence into Transcaucasia and Armenia. The move resulted in the Ottoman invasion of Armenia. These conflicts lasted for decades. The Safavids and Ottomans deported thousands, destroyed hundreds of villages in Armenia, and depopulated entire regions. Shah Abbas moved thousands of Armenians to Iran, and the Ottomans settled thousands of Kurds in Armenia. The western Armenian territories and parts of Azerbaijan came under Ottoman control. The rest of Azerbaijan remained under the Safavids.

Primary sources estimate that between 1604 and 1605 some 250,000 to 300,000 Armenians were removed from Armenia for settlement in Iran. Thousands died during the harsh forced move. Most were settled in Iranian Azerbaijan, where other Armenians had settled earlier. Some ended up in the Mazandaran region and in the cities of Sultanieh, Qazvin, Mashhad, Hamadan, Arak, and Shiraz. The wealthy Armenians of Julfa in Armenia were brought to the Safavid capital of Isfahan. They were treated better and appear to have suffered less during the migration. They were settled across the banks of the main river in Isfahan, and in 1605 a town called New Julfa was constructed for them. They were granted relative autonomy, sealed by the shah himself. They elected their own mayor, practiced their religion and language, and built many churches (thirteen have survived). They were permitted to ring their church bells and were not restricted with respect to clothing and alcohol consumption. The mayor of Julfa had twelve Armenian villages around Isfahan under his control.

Some of these privileges, such as building churches and ringing the bells for Sunday prayers, were rare in Muslim countries. A poll tax in gold was collected for each male adult. Gradually Julfa grew to become a thriving trade and craft center with about 50,000 Armenians under the protection of the kings. These Armenians ended up with a monopoly of the silk trade and became mediators between Europe, Russia, and India in those countries' dealings with Iran. They also formed a separate ecclesiastical unit under their own bishop, who had jurisdiction over all Armenians of Iran and Iraq. Armenians eventually became one of the first groups in Iran to receive a modern education, mainly due to their contacts with Europe. They ended up playing significant roles in the modern history of Iran and in the Armenian cultural and political revival and nationalistic movements in the nineteenth century. However, not all Armenians or Christians lived as well as those in Julfa. The smaller communities suffered frequent discrimination and persecution. Armenian historians of the period regarded the move to Iran as a catastrophe in their history. Although Armenians managed to create a united, prosperous, and coherent community, at least in Isfahan, by the end of the seventeenth century religious persecution, discrimination, and commercial competition disrupted their communal solidarity.

The religious policies of the Safavid rulers were not coherent and depended on the extent of the power of individual kings. The policies were also influenced by how motivated the kings were by trade prospects with Europe and how much they could resist pressure from the clergy. For example, the religious tax, *jizya*, imposed on non-Muslims was relatively low during Shah Abbas's reign and increased drastically after his death. During his reign, when trade with Europe was a major concern, Armenians were given a monopoly over the silk trade. The control of the revenue from the trade was essential for reorganizing the army and administration, and Armenians were trusted. Shah Abbas permitted Christian missionaries from Europe to build a convent in Isfahan and to carry out missionary activities in Iran and even covered some of the costs. These acts were a deliberate part of a well-planned policy to integrate the Caucasian population in Iran in order to use it more effectively in the power struggles against other groups and warring tribes and in economic rivalry with the Ottomans.

Armenians, like other non-Muslim groups, were granted protection as long as they remained loyal, as was the case with royal slaves known as *ghulams*. These were war captives or purchased slaves brought from Caucasia at an early age. They grew up in the court and were cut off from their ethnic, tribal, or religious ties and identity. They were entirely dependent on the king's goodwill for survival. Some reached the highest ranks in the army and administration and became tutors to the royal princes. The intention was to create a power base internally independent from the Turkmen tribes. The same role was played by the Christian groups imported from Caucasia; for example, by 1604 there were 20,000 Armenian *ghulams*, and by 1616 over 100,000 Georgians had been resettled in Iran. This forced resettlement of the Caucasian population lasted for a century, approximately from 1530 to 1630. Although the kings relied on these groups, they were not always successful in containing them. Shah Ismail II spent twenty years under virtual house arrest due to power gained by Georgians at the court and in the harem.

Assyrians, Jews, and Zoroastrians

Other minorities, such as Jews, Zoroastrians, and Assyrians, had a very difficult time during the Safavid period and faced repeated persecution and forced conversion. Shah Abbas relocated many Zoroastrians from Yazd and Kirman to work in his capital of Isfahan as laborers, weavers, carpet-makers, gardeners, and grooms. Western observers at the court mention a suburb outside Isfahan with 3,000 poorly constructed, unadorned houses allocated to Zoroastrians. The Zoroastrians elected their own leaders, who were confirmed in their office by the government. They were free to produce and consume alcohol. Zoroastrian women did not observe the veil or segregation of sexes in their own communities. The men dressed like other males but could only wear undyed cloth to distinguish themselves from the Muslims. After many resettlements, by the end of the Safavid era and the time of Sultan Hussein many had been forced to convert, with many deaths and much persecution.

Assyrians in Iran faced the same problems, and in addition they suffered from internal conflicts. Some had made attempts since the thirteenth century

Zoroastrians brought their dead to the Towers of Silence, where vultures would consume their corpses. This practice was banned in 1970. (Michael S. Yamashita/Corbis)

to join the Catholic Church in Rome by denouncing Nestorianism. By the seventeenth century many had become Catholic, changed their name to Chaldeans, and chosen Urmiyeh as the center for their patriarch. However, as of the seventeenth century, relations between the Persian Church and Rome were severed. In the end the Assyrians detached themselves from Rome and transferred their patriarchal residence from Urmiyeh to Kotchanes, in Kurdistan (Iraq). The church became divided, with two patriarchs belonging to the Nestorian and the Chaldean churches. The latter transferred their patriarchal residence from Persia to Iraq as well. Their problems were intensified even more due to centuries of hostilities between the Kurds and Assyrians in Iraq and manipulation by both the Ottomans and the Iranians, who used small minorities for their own end.

The situation for religious minorities worsened when a new code known as Jam Abbasi was introduced that imposed many restrictions on the non-Muslims, including Jews. The code controlled dress, residence, building, and traveling and imposed other restrictions as well. There were prescriptions with respect to public and social interactions with Muslims. Safavid clergy introduced the concept of uncleanness of nonbelievers, and the Jewish population of Iran suffered even more under this proclamation. Many were compelled to abandon their religion. A "law of apostasy" enabled converts to Islam from other faiths to inherit the estates of their close kin. This code was not followed through most of the times but remained in effect until the twentieth century. Jewish synagogues were closed, and Jews were forced to proclaim publicly that they had converted to Islam. However, in 1661 a new edict allowed Jews to practice their religion unharmed.

The Sunni majority was treated brutally and was most resistant to the government's conversion policies. The annexation of Afghan territories from Iran in the eighteenth century was a direct result of Safavid conversion policies. It started with the Ghilzai Afghans claiming independence at Qandahar in 1709 and was followed by the conquest of Herat by the Abdali Afghans in 1715 and the invasion of Iran. Iranians continued to claim Afghanistan until the British finally put an end to such claims in the early nineteenth century. Following the Afghan invasion and subsequent uprisings by the Baluchi tribes in the southeast, Uzbeks and Turkmen in the northeast, and Lazgis and Kurds in the northwest, the collapse of the Safavid Empire was inevitable.

Conclusion

On the whole, Safavid Iran was characterized by great ethnic diversity, and many groups maintained ties with related tribes or groups outside Iran. They used such bonds to exert pressure and influence over the government and its agents. Safavids were not entirely successful in controlling all the territories and different groups under their control. Their many resettlement policies created regional problems, some of which continued long after their collapse. The use of the Shi'i religion to exert control was only partially successful. It resulted in annexation of large areas of the country and was followed by centuries of conflict between the Sunni and Shi'i populations, even after the fall of the Safavid. However, the Safavids did manage to create a country within a boundary that has survived. They were far more successful than the previous ruling groups in creating and maintaining a more unified Iran.

Afshar, Zand, and Qajar Periods, 1736—Twentieth Century

Among the tribes moved by the Safavids in the seventeenth century were Afshars and Qajars. These Turkmen tribes were moved from Azerbaijan and resettled in Khurasan and Mazandaran. They became Shi'ites and were loyal to the Safavids. They were settled in close proximity to other groups such as Kurds and Bayats (a Turkmen group that still exists) across Khurasan. The unity or disunity of these varied groups played an important role in bringing into power the Afshar tribes and their leader, Nadir. He brought many parts of Iran under his control but died less than a decade later on his way to suppress a Kurdish uprising in 1747.

An officer in the service of the Safavids and belonging to a minor Afshar tribe, Nadir rose through the ranks to become the protector of the last Safavid kings, who were dispersed after the Afghan invasion. He was more a military adventurer than a tribal chief. It was his brilliant military strategies that enabled Iran to drive out the Afghans. After replacing the decaying Safavid dynasty, he invaded India and plundered and sacked Delhi, the seat of the Mongol rulers of India. He brought back the Indian royal treasures (some taken from the Safavids in earlier raids) that form the bulk of the crown jewels of Iran, which are still on display in a museum in Tehran. His rise to power was linked to the weakness of the central government, a situation that happened repeatedly in Iran. Nadir emerged as the only strongman capable of protecting the king and guaranteeing national security. In the end he overthrew the king and took over.

Nadir declared his own version of Shi'i, the Jaffari sect, named after the seventh imam, Jaffar al-Sadiq. His version was added to the Safavid Shi'i and, as Jaffari Twelfth Imamate, is still the state religion in Iran today. To gain the support of the Sunni groups in Iran, he forbade the Safavid practice of cursing the first three caliphs, venerated by the Sunni. He stopped the enslavement of Shi'i followers by Sunni Muslims on the grounds of their not being orthodox. He sent emissaries to the Ottoman authorities in charge of Mecca and the holy places in Iraq requesting permission for Shi'i Iranians to visit the sites. He also appointed a permanent ambassador to the Ottoman court and tried to ease tension between the two countries and secure the frontiers with the Ottomans without major military conflict. The Ottomans, who did not recognize the Shi'i creed in Iran, supported rebellious groups in border areas with occasional warfare in order to avoid direct confrontation. Baghdad under Ottoman control became a center for refugees fleeing Iran. However, in the end the Ottomans agreed to allow safe passage for Iranian pilgrims with no discussion of the Jaffari creed, and a conditional peace treaty was signed. Such developments were watched closely by the Russians, who were concerned about Nadir's aspirations of subjugating Caucasia and Transcaspia. Russians later consolidated their power, drove the Ottomans out of Crimea, attained a stronger power base in the territories close to Iran, and pacified the region, a task Nadir had intended to undertake but could not accomplish.

Tribal and Resettlement Policies

Nadir's brutality and his forceful demands for money to finance his never-ending military expeditions resulted in many rebellions. He also faced opposition by many tribes, such as the Bakhtiyari, Qajars, Baluchi, Arabs, and Kurds, among others, whom he defeated and often crushed harshly. His treatment of the different groups varied and was designed to guarantee loyalty to his rule. Sometimes he would reinstate local governors after vanquishing them, as was the case in Bukhara and India. He even hired defeated groups to join his army and fight for him, as he did with the defeated Uzbeks and Afghans. At other times he adopted the policy of appointing his own kin and people close to him, but placed them in areas far removed from their hereditary ties in order to reduce the chance of rebellion. In other cases he chose a close relative as governor while appointing a military commander from a different tribe or region. Most tribes of the time were pastoral nomads, and some practiced seasonal agriculture.

Safavids had moved tribes mainly to strengthen the frontiers; Nadir, in contrast, was concerned with maintaining his own power. One example was his resettlement of the rebellious Bakhtiyari tribes in Khurasan, which separated them from their territory and power base and made it difficult for them to forge alliances with their new neighboring tribes. The name *Bakhtiyari* appeared for the first time in fourteenth-century records. They were described as tribes entering Iran from Syria with other very likely Kurdish groups as early as the thirteenth century. This hypothesis has been challenged by the Bakhtiyari, who mention the rarity of Arabic words in their vocabulary as one reason among many to dispute their Syrian origin. By the Safavid period they were established enough to appear in many sources. At his time they were associated with an area near the Zagros Mountains between Isfahan and Khuzistan that now bears their name and is geographically part of Luristan. They are closely related to Lurs, and many still consider themselves to be both Lurs and Bakhtiyari. By the eighteenth century, their leaders were major players in the national power struggles and remained so until the middle of the twentieth century. Part of their traditional territory is named after them, and they played a significant part as armed militants providing military service.

Another example of Nadir's manipulation of the tribes was the creation of the Shahsevan confederacy. The group was composed of a number of Turkmen *qizilbash* tribes, including Takkalu sections of the Shamlu and Afshars, who had immigrated into eastern Transcaucasia in the early eighteenth century. Soon they were mixed with the indigenous Kurdish groups of Shaqaqi and Mughanlu in the same area and adopted the new name *Shahsevan*. At this time there was no confederacy, and the different tribal groups were not united. In the mid-eighteenth century part of their territory was seized by the Russians and the Ottomans. The group split, with some staying in the Russian-occupied land while others went to the Ottoman territory and some remained in Iran. Once Nadir Shah had recaptured the occupied territories, he removed some of the tribes to Khurasan, and after the Russians withdrew, he united the Shahsevan, Mughanlu, and other remaining tribes of northeastern Azerbaijan. Nadir appointed one of his own captains of Afshar origin as the head of the confederacy. The Shahsevan became divided into different groups, some supporting the Russians and others the Iranians. The name means "those who love the shah." One prominent chief, Badr Khan Shahsevan, was instrumental in consolidating and uniting the group, and beginning in his time they emerged as a significant confederation. By the nineteenth century they were divided into two major and often conflicting groups—Ardabili and Meshgini. The two groups constantly fought against each other and were involved in cross-border politics between the Russians and Iranians.

Nadir was threatened by several rebels who were or pretended to be Safavid princes. Fearful of the support of the major tribes for these claimants to the throne, he elevated minor tribes and tribes with no standing that were bound to be loyal to him. Several branches of Afshars remained against him from the beginning. His supporters were varied and included Kurds, Lurs, Turks, and Afghans whose unity was based on military discipline and a common interest in plunder. In the end, his self-serving policies, brutality, and deteriorating mental heath turned many against him. Included were the minor tribes whom he had counted as his major supporters, including many groups in the Persian Gulf, Azerbaijan, Fars, and Khuzistan. Nadir spoke Turkish and employed Iranians in administrative posts, but most, fearing for their lives, ended up seeking refuge elsewhere. His resettlement policies depopulated western Iran. His short reign was so turbulent and bloody that chaos was inevitable. The Iranian historians of his period and later attributed the support for Safavid claimants against Nadir as "the representatives of an Iranian need for unity, continuity, hierarchy and well-ordered government sanctified by tradition" (Avery, Hambly, and Melville, 1991, p. 57). His regional policies of unification were doomed, as were his attempts to create a compromise between the Sunni and Shi'i. However, despite his failure to unify the country, his expulsion of the Afghans and his successful efforts to keep the Ottomans at bay contributed greatly to the identity of Iran as a modern national state.

Nadir's policies of resettlement depopulated entire areas; the estimates indicate that during his reign over 100,000 tribal families were moved to Gorgan and Mazandaran alone. This massive relocation included moving Afshars, Qajars, and other Turkmen from Azerbaijan; Kurds from Kurdistan; Qashqa'i from Fars; Zands from Arak; and some 13,000 Bakhtiyari from Luristan. Even Afghans from Herat and Qandahar were moved and resettled in Iranian territories. Although after Nadir's death many went back to their original territories, it was during the Zand rule that serious attempts were made to restore the country's population. Such massive moves not only damaged the country but also affected the tribes themselves and caused dispersal of the tribal groups that would weaken them even further during the nineteenth century.

Nadir's successors did not last long and were either murdered or deposed. They were manipulated by the various factions and tribes, from Kurds to Arabs and Turks to Uzbeks and Afghans, who supported one claimant to the throne against another. The eastern half of Nadir's domain came fully under the control of the Afghans and eventually became part of modern-day Afghanistan. By 1796 the last of the Afshars, who had been blinded but had survived, was defeated by Agha Muhammad Khan Qajar, who had been castrated earlier by the Afshars. Agha Muhammad Khan Qajar would manage to unite the country once more after the defeat of the Zand dynasty, which ruled for a brief period over much of Iran following Nadir's death.

The Zand Dynasty and the Emergence of the Lurs and Bakhtiyari

The Zands were a pastoral tribal group from the Zagros area. They were Shi'ites and have been named as Lurs and as Kurds by historians of the time, which may indicate that the Lurs had recently separated from the Kurds. Modern scholarship suggests that the Zands belonged to northern Lurs or Lak tribes originally of Kurdish origin. Under the forced resettlement policies of the Safavids and Nadir, they were moved to Khurasan. After the collapse of the Afshars they went back to their native land, near the plains of modern Hamadan. They first became prominent in the 1720s during the Afghan invasion and the following anarchy when Kirmanshah, a Kurdish stronghold, was occupied by the Ottomans for a while. They adopted guerrilla tactics, formed small groups, and attacked the Ottomans. They were later crushed by Nadir. Many of their leaders were put to death and the rest were sent into exile. One exiled small group of thirty or forty families managed to reorganize after Nadir's death and defeated the Ardalans, the hereditary Kurdish rulers of Iranian Kurdistan since Safavid times. Their leader, Karim Beg, like Nadir, was not a tribal chief but had gained prestige and authority because of his leadership abilities. He gathered more supporters, further defeated the Takkalu Kurds, and joined the prominent Bakhtiyari leader Ali Mardan Khan to successfully besiege Isfahan. A Safavid puppet king was chosen, with the Bakhtiyari leader as the regent. Karim left the capital promising loyalty to the Bakhtiyari khan. Following his departure, the Bakhtiyari leader's excessive extortions created an uprising, anarchy erupted, and Karim Khan went back to Isfahan and successfully took over.

In the records of the time the term *Bakhtiyari* was associated with a certain pastoralist ethnic group ruled and united by ilkhans and khans (the paramount and the tribal chiefs). There is a Bakhtiyari dialect in Persian; however, several Turkic- and Arabic-speaking groups are also known as Bakhtiyari. Mainly pastoralists, they also include many sedentary agriculturalist groups. Beginning in the Mongol-Ilkhanid period, their tribal structure gradually changed to include two major interrelated components: the confederation, which consisted of all tribes united under one or two ilkhans, and the individual tribes, some more prominent than others. They had summer and winter pastures and migrated between the two.

By the end of the seventeenth century and the decline of the Safavid central authority, the governorship of the Bakhtiyari region became a prestigious administrative post. During this period a division emerged between two major groups, Haft Lang and Chahar Lang. During Nadir's reign they remained on the periphery and helped him in his eastern campaigns. The leadership

A Bakhtiyari man (Nasrollah Kasraian)

remained with the Haft Lang group, but after Nadir's death they were challenged by the Chahar Lang. One of the best-remembered Bakhtiyari leaders, Ali Mardan Khan, belonged to the latter group and emerged as the most
prominent Bakhtiyari khan at this time. During the Zand era the Haft Lang
was treated as a distinct administrative unit, and the Haft Lang Duraki khans

were addressed using a variety of titles common among the Bakhtiyari representing different already existing ranks. They were and are predominantly Shi'i and did not pose major problems to Nadir but fought many times against the Zands.

After his success in Isfahan, Karim Khan focused on Khurasan. The west, including Azerbaijan, the Caspian area, the Zagros Mountains, Khuzistan, the Persian Gulf coast, and the areas in the vicinity of the central deserts, was dominated by a coalition of Zagros tribes, mainly the Bakhtiyari Lurs. After many conflicts, in the end Karim Khan defeated all, and for the next forty years the area came under his fragile control. Karim Khan was constantly faced with rebellions from Qajars and Afghans, among others. His massacre of thousands of Afghans, reportedly 9,000 in Tehran alone, ended the Afghan resistance. The Qajars remained formidable in Gorgan, Gilan, and Mazandaran and finally emerged as the rulers of the country. Arabs remained in the Persian Gulf coast area, with some minor "pirate" states, and continued fighting against the Zand.

After Karim Khan's death in 1779, power struggles ravaged the country even more. Tribal alliances never proved reliable even among related tribes, who constantly fought each other by supporting opposing leaders. One of Karim Khan's descendents, Lutf Ali Khan, faced treason, broken alliances, disloyalty, and disunity from the beginning of his reign until his brutal murder by Agha Muhammad Khan Qajar. Tribal conflicts fueled by regional warlords and headmen contributed to the rapid decline of the country's infrastructure. The Iranian territories shrank as well. By 1722 the powerful Russian czar, Peter the Great, had fully established his sovereignty over the regions north of the Aras River. Azerbaijan became the only province sustaining allegiance to Iran and paying tribute to the Iranian government.

Nadir alienated the clergy by trying to bridge the gap between Sunni and Shi'i. He also confiscated large sections of the endowment lands belonging to religious institutions. Fearful for their lives, many clergymen sought refuge in Iraq and formed the core of the Shi'i religious infrastructure that has persisted until now around the Shi'i shrines in Iraq. Karim Khan did not seek the sanction of the clergy, nor did he assume any religious role or title. He upheld the Shi'i, built mosques, and eased the return of the clergy and Sufi masters who had also been persecuted by Nadir. Internal security and commerce improved during his fourteen years in Shiraz. Despite Karim Khan's reforms and his popularity, the Zand dynasty did not last. One of the reasons for their failure was their small numbers, which prevented them from imposing their control over the country.

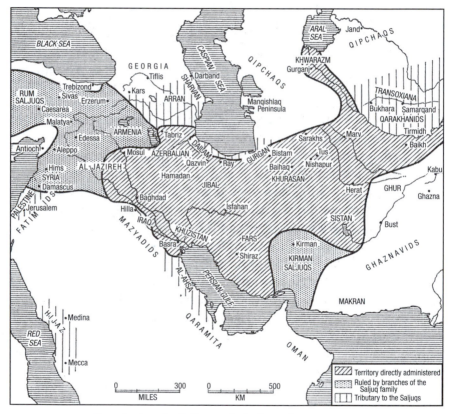

Iran during the Saljuq period, eleventh century A.D.

Ethnic Groups under the Qajars

Turkmen Qajars

Turkmen Qajars, of Oghuz ancestry, had been established in Iran since the fifteenth century and were an original component of the Safavid *qizilbash*. They ruled Iran from 1795 until 1925. The earlier part of their rule was a continuation of the chaotic situation that ravaged the country after the Afghan invasion: tribal wars, loss of territory to the Russians, conflict with the Ottomans, and many massacres by the founder of the dynasty. By this time the Qajars were already divided into many tribes and subtribes. Two major clans dominated the lesser tribes. One provided the ruling dynasty and the other the functionaries and military commanders of the kingdom. The later part of their rule, beginning in 1850, was the beginning of the modernization processes in Iran that resulted in the Constitutional Revolution in 1906 and, finally, the peaceful transfer of the monarchy from the Qajar to the Pahlavi dynasty in 1925.

The success of the first Qajar, Aqa Muhammad Khan, was a result of his ability to end the rivalry between the leading Qajar clans. It was also due to obtaining support from the northern and northwestern tribes to offset the strength of the tribes of the south and the southwest. The result was political consolidation of the country for the first time since the Safavid collapse. He resided in Tehran, which became the capital, and with brutal force subjugated Khurasan and Kurdish chieftains. After his murder, none of the other Qajar rulers proved themselves as effective or as disciplined, and more territory was lost to the Russians. Azerbaijan effectively became divided between the Russian and Iranian Azerbaijan, a division that played a major role in the twentieth century. Nevertheless, Iran was on its way to becoming a modern state.

From the early eighteenth to the mid-nineteenth century, the social and economic organizations of the various tribes did not change much. Tribal groups remained a problem for the central governments. Resettlement policies were commonplace, and with the exception of Shah Abbas I, none of the kings had a lasting hold on all of the different groups and their territories. Abbas I's successors followed the same patterns, and consequently, the distribution of tribes in the eighteenth century was not very different from that of the early seventeenth century. The exception was the loss of several territories and separation of a number of groups from mainland Iran by the nineteenth century. For example, in Safavid times Khurasan still included much of present-day Afghanistan and Turkistan. The territories were inhabited by a number of Sunni Afghani tribes, several Turkmen groups, and the Shi'i Hazara. By the nineteenth century they had all separated from Iran and, despite their many invasions of Iranian territories, remained separate. Many Turkmen and Kurdish tribes settled by Shah Abbas I in the west remained more or less in the same area and still occupy the same territories. To the south more Turks and numerous Arabs stayed, and the Caspian region was occupied by the Sunni Turkmen tribes. Baluchi tribes remained more or less autonomous in the southeast and continued so until the nineteenth century.

The Qashqa'i

One major development was a heterogeneous collection of nomadic tribes, mainly Turks, that formed the large confederation of Qashqa'i by the nineteenth century. The Qashqa'i people claimed origins from a number of ethnolinguistically diverse people from central Asia, the Caucasus, Iran, and Turkey. By the nineteenth century they had asserted a Turkish identity, and Turkish became the dominant language of the group in the twentieth century. They were and are Shi'ites with their own perception of Shi'i Islam as well as regional and distinctly Qashqa'i attitudes and customs. They practiced nomadic pastoralism in the Zagros Mountains. The group had winter and summer pastures and cultivated grain in seasonal pastures for their own use. Their societies were hierarchical and socioeconomically stratified. The elite, the tribal chiefs, increasingly began to play a national role in addition to the leadership of their own confederacy. Gradually they obtained more land, which became a major source of their wealth. The chiefs had advisers, secretaries, and overseers and appointed headmen to administer the various tribes and subtribes. The majority of the Qashqa'i used pastoral and agricultural land that was controlled by the tribal chiefs. Most labor and production was carried out by the Qashqa'i themselves, but at times they hired specialized laborers from outside the tribal units. The Qashqa'i leaders became prominent, and by the twentieth century their elite formed part of Iran's upper class.

The Khamseh Confederation

Another collection of Arab and Turkish tribes and the Persian Basseri remained in the south and by the nineteenth century formed the successful and unique Khamseh confederation. They occupied the area east of the Qashqa'i.

Most people in the area called them Arabs despite their diverse origins. To the west of the Qashqa'i in Fars were the various Luri tribes of Mamasani and Kuhgiluya; all of these groups still exist and have played major parts in the politics of twentieth-century Iran. By the nineteenth century up to one million nomads lived in the Zagros area all the way to Khuzistan and Luristan provinces, with the Bakhtiyari Lurs being the most prominent. The central regions were occupied by a number of Turkish and Kurdish groups, mostly Sunni.

The Kurds

The Kurds occupied territories in the northwest (modern-day Kurdistan), Azerbaijan, Luristan, and the southern areas. They formed a number of prominent groups, including the Zanganeh, Kalhur, Mukri, Shadlu, and Ardalan. Some Kurdish groups that lived close to Turkish groups had become Turkish in culture by the nineteenth century. During the chaos following the Afghan invasion, a number of Kurdish tribes seized several territories in northwestern Iran and close to the Russian border and created havoc. Many settled sedentary Kurds in the area were forced to seek alliances with others, creating their own tribal formations for protection. Many villages and small towns became the protectors of major tribal groups. There is no indication that the Kurds had any sentiments regarding a Kurdish homeland at this period. The battles were between different tribal groups and leaders for supremacy. The Qajars were weak, and the main reason that they could exert some control over the Kurds was the latter's inability to unite. The Ardalan and Mukri chiefs were acknowledged, and the Qajars established family links with them through marriage alliances. The Kurds of Azerbaijan were involved in cross-border politics and sometimes supported the Ottomans against the Qajars. They were instrumental in popularizing mystical leaders from Turkey in Iran and among the Iranian Kurds.

The name *Kurds* was used by the travelers and historians of the time primarily to indicate tribal people who spoke Kurdish. However, many Kurdish groups had no tribal affiliations at the time and lived as both peasants and town dwellers. The tribal people who existed were gradually divided into a few major groups and preserved their own local kinship ideology based on myths of common ancestry. Over the centuries many prominent Kurdish chiefs claimed descent or association with some great figure from the early Islamic period, including Saladin. Another important characteristic of the Kurdish groups at the time was their religious practices. Many remained

Sunni, but cults with unusual practices such as trances, fire-eating, and self-mutilation remained popular among others. The Sufi brotherhoods became popular again after Nadir's death, and local shaikhs gained prominence and many followers. Though by this time there was a distinction between the Lurs and the Kurds, several Kurdish tribes were instrumental in bringing into power the Zand leader, Karim Khan.

Conclusion

On the whole, the tribal population of Iran after the sixteenth century was heterogeneous, with many groups occupying the same territory. Though many of these groups were pastoral nomads, they were not isolated and remained in direct contact with the main urban centers. Their leaders had major family and marriage links to the ruling dynasties. The elite grew up in the increasingly modern courts rather than among their own people. Many were settled in villages, and others moved seasonally.

Prior to the mid-nineteenth century the nomadic tribes in Iran shared similar characteristics. They either enjoyed total independence or had some degree of local autonomy. The introduction of a new quasi-feudal land system by the Turkish groups, while beneficial to the tribes and to regionalism, was detrimental to the power of the central governments. By the end of the Mongol period the Turco-Mongol influence had created new concepts of property organization, land utilization, and the organization of production. Tribes managed their own internal affairs and also exerted influence over neighboring villages and small towns. The wealth of a tribe depended on the quantity of its movables, including animals, light tools, carpets, coins, and jewelry. Possession of land was subject to the needs and location of the tribe's animals. Campsites were the primary units of land and were assigned by tribal leaders. Which group occupied what space changed annually. Grazing lands belonged to the whole tribe and were assigned to tribal members by a tribal assembly headed by the chieftain, with consultation with influential families. Tribes were armed and were the most effective fighting forces in the country. They provided military service to the kings, took sides with warring factions, and manipulated situations by changing loyalties. The tribal chiefs were responsible for revenue collection and payment, maintaining order locally, and providing military assistance if required.

The early Qajars resettled tribes in order to decrease their strength. By the nineteenth century the rivalry between the Russians and the British in Iran and the dispersal of the tribal groups all over the country had in reality reduced their importance as power brokers. They were no longer effective forces in terms of supporting dynastic claims and conflicts. The inability of the Qajars to launch major military adventures had made their military services redundant. Some even resorted to banditry, and the overall economic decline of the country damaged local economies as well. The second part of the nineteenth century provided the most significant challenge to the Qajar rulers. That period was the start of the modernization process in Iran and the beginning of a new era. The new period started with the assumption of the throne by Nasir al-Din Shah in 1848, with help from his brilliant tutor and adviser Amir Kabir.

Timeline

1501	The conquest of Tabriz by Shah Ismail I and the establishment of the Safavid rule in Iran and Shi'i as the state religion.
1507	The Portuguese invaded the Hurmuz Island and port in the Persian Gulf and started a century of rivalry with the British.
1514	The Ottomans had a decisive victory in the battle of Chalidran, and Iran lost eastern Anatolia.
1526	Rebellion by the Rumlu and Ustalju Turkmen tribes. Takkalu tribes also rebelled and attacked Tabriz in 1531.
1555	A peace treaty between the Ottomans and Iran divided Armenia and Georgia between the two countries. The eastern parts of these countries remained part of Iran.
1587	Shah Abbas the Great assumed the throne. He defeated all rebellious groups in Iran and consolidated central power.
1590	Shah Abbas I was forced to give away many territories in Armenia, Georgia, and parts of Azerbaijan and Luristan to the Ottomans.
1597	Shah Abbas I ended the Uzbek invasion of Iran. He welcomed Europeans, including the British, in order to modernize his army and expand trade and unified the coinage in the country.
1642	Shah Abbas II (1642–1666) tried to implement bureaucratic reform and reduce the power of clergy. He

	established trade with the East India Company and gave asylum to several thousand Uzbeks in Iran.
1709	The Ghilzai Afghans rebelled, occupied Qandahar, and established a local kingdom.
1721	Peter the Great, the Russian czar, occupied Baku and increased Russian influence in the area.
1722	Mahmud, a Ghilzai Afghan, attacked Iran, captured Isfahan, and ended Safavid rule. Iran lost Afghan territories.
1736	Nadir Afshar deposed the last Safavid claimant to the throne and declared himself the new shah. He invaded India in 1738. He was a brilliant military strategist whose reign was violent and turbulent.
1750	Karim Khan Zand ruled over most parts of Iran. He died in 1779, and his short rule was relatively peaceful and marked by improvements to national security.
1783	The Russian empress Catherine II signed a treaty with the ruler of Georgia and made the area a Russian protectorate.
1794	The last Zand ruler was defeated by the leader of the Qajar Oghuz tribes.
1796	Agha Muhammad Khan Qajar declared himself the new shah and founded the Qajar dynasty. By his death in 1797 he had managed to consolidate his power and create a powerful central authority.
1813	After a disastrous war with Russia, under the Treaty of Gulistan Iran lost what are now the republics of Azerbaijan, Daghistan, and Georgia for good.
1828	Under the Treaty of Turkmanchi, Iran was forced to cede part of Persian Armenia (modern-day Erivan and Nakhichevan) to Russia and allow the Russians to have a navy in the Caspian Sea.
1848	Muhammad Shah Qajar died.

Significant People, Places, and Events

ABDALI AFGHANS: The most important Afghan tribal group in the eighteenth century. Their most prominent figure, Ahmad Khan Abdali, was chosen by the tribal chiefs as their leader after Nadir

Shah's death in 1741. He later changed his name to Durrani and is regarded as the first king of the independent Afghanistan.

AFSHAR TRIBES: A well-established group in Turkistan, they moved to Iran with the Mongols in the thirteenth century. They settled mostly in Azerbaijan, and their language was Turkish. They were removed by the Safavids in the seventeenth century and settled in Khurasan and Mazandaran.

ARAS RIVER (ARAXES): The river starts in Turkey and flows eastward. It is the international boundary and crossing between Turkey and Iran and between Armenia and Azerbaijan.

ARDALAN KURDS: A major Kurdish group in Iran. The name means "mountain dwelling" or "stronghold." Originally from northern Kurdistan, they moved eastward.

BAKHTIYARI: This major nomadic group is closely related to Lurs and speaks a distinct language closely related to Persian; most are Shi'i. Their name first appeared in written records in the fourteenth century. Beginning in the Safavid period in the sixteenth century, the name applied to both a geographical area and an administrative unit in the Zagros area.

BAYATS: A Turkish group that occupied areas west and northwest of Mashhad in Khurasan in the nineteenth century. They still exist, and most are settled.

CHALDIRAN BATTLE: In 1514 the Ottoman ruler Sultan Selim I launched a battle against Shah Ismail I. He won in a decisive victory, and Iran lost control of eastern Anatolia. Chaldiran is located northeast of Lake Van in eastern Anatolia (the Asian part of Turkey).

CHAMISHKAZAKLU: A Kurdish group from Anatolia and Caucasia, resettled by Shah Abbas the Great in northern Khurasan in the early 1600s.

GEORGIA: Located between the Black and Caspian Seas and bordering on Russia, Azerbaijan, Armenia, and Turkey, Georgia declared independence in 1991 from the Soviet Union.

GHILZAI AFGHANS: A major tribe in Afghanistan. Their leader Mahmud Ghilzai attacked Iran in 1722 and ended the Safavid rule.

GULISTAN TREATY: The treaty was signed between Russia and Iran in 1813 and ended the war of 1804. Under the treaty Iran lost many territories west of the Caspian Sea, including Georgia and parts of Azerbaijan in southern Russia.

HAZARA: The group is mainly concentrated in Afghanistan, but a small group lives in Iran as well. They are assumed to be from Mongolia. Most moved from Transoxiana in the thirteenth and fourteenth centuries. They are pastoral nomads, mainly Shi'ites, and speak a dialect of Persian.

KALHUR KURDS: A major Kurdish tribe in Iran, mentioned as a major group in the sixteenth century. They acquired dominance in nineteenth-century Iran.

KHAMSEH CONFEDERATION: *Khamseh* means "five" in Arabic. The confederation was a powerful group of Arab, Iranian, and Turkish tribes in Iran in the nineteenth century.

MAMASANI: A small city west of Shiraz in the province of Fars. The area has been inhabited by Lurs for centuries. There are still nomadic groups in Mamasani that earn a living from animal husbandry, seasonal farming, and weaving.

OTTOMAN EMPIRE (1350–1918): Following the breakdown of the Saljuq Empire, many small Turkish states were formed, including the Ottomans. Soon they absorbed all of the neighboring states. In 1453 they captured Constantinople (Istanbul) and ended the Byzantine Empire.

QAJARS: A Turkmen group of Oghuz ancestry that ruled Iran from 1796 to 1925.

SHAFI'I SCHOOL: One of the four orthodox schools of law in Sunni Islam along with Hanafi, Maliki, and Hanbali. The four provide different readings or interpretations of legal matters related to the Quran or Hadith literature.

SHI'I JAFFARI TWELFTH IMAMATE: The official religion of Iran. The Jaffari believe in twelve imams, direct descendents of the Prophet Muhammad through his daughter Fatima. They place great emphasis on the works of Imam Jaffar Sadiq, the sixth imam, as the basis of their doctrine.

SUFISM: A mystical sect in Islam. Sufi believe that there is an inner or mystical path to the discovery of God. Sufism has many variations and many sects. Very generally, the Sufi believe that they should surrender to God body and soul.

TRANSCASPIA: An area of steppes and deserts that corresponds to the modern-day Turkmenistan in southern Russia.

TRANSCAUCASIA: A region extending from the Greater Caucasus to the Turkish and Iranian borders. It includes the republics of Georgia, Armenia, and Azerbaijan, among other places.

TURKMANCHI TREATY: This treaty was signed in 1828 between Iran and Russia after Russia's defeat of Iran. Iran lost all territory east of the Caspian Sea, including Erivan and Nakhchivan.

Bibliography

Avery, P., G. R. G. Hambly, and C. Melville, eds. *The Cambridge History of Iran,* Vol. 7: *From Nadir Shah to the Islamic Republic.* Cambridge: Cambridge University Press, 1991.

Floor, Willem M. *Safavid Government Institutions.* Costa Mesa, CA: Mazda Publishers, 2001.

Jackson, Peter, and Lawrence Lockhart, eds. *The Cambridge History of Iran,* Vol. 6: *The Timurid and Safavid Periods.* Cambridge: Cambridge University Press, 1986.

Keddie, Nikki R. *Qajar Iran and the Rise of Reza Khan, 1796–1925.* Costa Mesa, CA: Mazda Publishers, 1999.

Mazzaoui, Michel. *Safavid Iran and Her Neighbors.* Salt Lake City: University of Utah Press, 2003.

McDowall, David. *A Modern History of Kurds.* London: I. B. Tauris, 2002.

Newman, Andrew J. *Society and Culture in the Early Modern Middle East: Studies on Iran in the Safavid Period.* Boston and Leiden: Brill, 2003.

Tapper, Richard. *The Conflict of Tribe and State in Iran and Afghanistan.* Burrell Row, Kent, UK: Croom Helm, Provident House, 1983.

Van Bruinessen, Martin. *Kurds and Identity Politics.* London: I. B. Tauris, 2001.

Modernization and National Identity

The Beginnings of Modernization

B Y THE LATE NINETEENTH CENTURY THE TRIBES IN IRAN WERE ESTI-mated to be one-quarter to one-half of the population of ten million. Tribal leaders made up a major element of the Iranian ruling classes. At times they became part of the court circle and/or competed with the mostly Iranian administrators who had usually inherited their titles and positions from their fathers. Governorships, though often in the hands of close relatives of the kings, were regularly auctioned to the highest bidder. There were some exceptions, such as the governorship of Azerbaijan during the Qajar era that was exclusively reserved for the crown prince. The Qajars dealt with the tribes in the traditional way, by creating divisions and making use of resettlement policies. They maintained extensive marriage alliances and held the offspring of the tribal chiefs as hostages at the court. They collected revenues and tributes from the tribes. By the end of the nineteenth century, major social and political changes and the presence of European powers and Russia in Iran had an impact on the tribal organizations and the country as a whole. Included in the changes were new concepts of government, group identity, nationalism, and national security based on attempts to reform government institutions and taxation and the creation of a regularly paid army based on European models.

Geographic and Ethnic Divisions

Late-nineteenth-century Iran was characterized by geographic and ethnic divisions and great diversity. Poor transportation and communication had kept regions independent and self-sufficient. In the central regions the

A young Qajar prince and his entourage. By Abu'l Hasan, ca. 1860. (Christi's Images/Corbis)

urban population spoke Persian; the villagers spoke Persian, Bakhtiyari, Luri, or Armenian. In the same central plateau the nomads spoke Bakhtiyari, Qashqa'i, Baluchi, Arabic, or Mamasani. In the Caspian provinces the peasantry used Gilaki, Taleshi, or Mazandarani, all Persian-related languages. In the same area the urban population spoke Persian and the Azeri dialect of Turkish, and the nomadic tribes used Kurdish and the Turkmen dialect of Turkish. Azerbaijan was predominantly Azeri-speaking, plus Armenian and some Assyrian. Kurdish, Shahsevan, Turkmen, Afshar, and other tribesmen inhabited the same area. The western provinces were occupied by Kurds, Lurs, and Arab tribes who spoke Afshars, Azeri, Persian, Bayat, and Gurani, among others, and Assyrian Christian settlements. Jews were centered in Isfahan, Hamadan, and other major cities, including Tehran, and some lived in villages near Mashhad, a Shi'ite stronghold. Zoroastrians remained in Kirman, Yazd, and the neighboring villages. The northeastern territories contained all of the major groups plus Jamshids, Tajiks, Afghans, Hazaras, Bayats, and Baluchis. Many of these groups lived as pastoral nomads or settled in villages close to their migratory roots.

The divisions were further complicated by religious differences. As a whole, the country was divided between the majority Muslims and minority groups including the Christian Armenians and Assyrians, Jews, and Zoroastrians. Muslims were divided between the majority Shi'i and minority Sunni. The Sunnis mostly occupied tribal territories at the periphery and included Kurds, Turkmen, Arabs, and Baluchis. In some areas the religious differences were parallel to ethnic differences and were obvious and more homogeneous. In other areas no clear correlations existed between religious and ethnic divisions. The Shi'i majority was divided between official and unofficial sects, and dervishes and Sufi orders also existed. The latter were very popular among the urban populations and other groups, including some Kurdish tribes. Their sectarian heads had great influence and prestige among their followers. Shi'i was also divided among older sects, including Ismaili, which was widespread in scattered villages outside Yazd, Kirman, Mahallat, and Nishapur. There were also new Shi'i schisms, such as Shykhism and the Babi sect; the latter had emerged as a new faith on its own. The divisions were a lot clearer in major towns, where different groups occupied their own districts.

Communal Organization

Communal organization followed the same patterns as the social structure. Communities whether tribal, rural, or urban had their own local and separate networks. The lower strata in the villages, towns, and tribes included peasants, townsmen, and tribesmen. At the highest level it included village landlords, local notables, and tribal chiefs. Cities were complex, with clearly delineated social stratification. The tribal structures were closer to a ranking system than to a class-based society. Land ownership was divided between the crown, religious endowments, minor and major landowners, some absentee landowners, and large fiefholders, with senior members of the clergy and rich merchants also owning large estates. In the cities different quarters existed for various groups, including the religious minorities who lived in their own sections. For example, "Kirman in the late nineteenth century with around 49,000 people had separate wards for Jews, Zoroastrians, Sufis, Shaykhis, Karim-khanis and the Shi'i" (Abrahamian, 1982, p. 16).

There was diversity in religion, languages, and dialects. In the way of life in a given area, for example, pastoral nomads as opposed to settled villagers, diversity existed between the nomadic tribesmen and the urban populations. Even members of the same nomadic tribes lived differently, with some increasingly spending more time in the villages and others continuing their migratory habits. Different nomadic tribes had their own specific features and also shared many similarities in their social structures. The terms *tribe, sub-tribe,* and *clan* were used loosely and could mean different divisions for different groups. Generally the primary social unit among the nomadic tribesmen was the migratory camp. The camp consisted mostly of members of the same clan *(tireh)* and consisted of many households. Depending on the geographic area, it could include from 10 to 100 households.

Tribal leaders inherited their positions. The camps were headed mainly by older members of the more prosperous households. These quite often elected a formal head, who was confirmed by the chiefs. These leaders acted as representatives protecting the group interest against other tribes. At the same time they regulated and maintained internal order with respect to major issues such as land and water allocation. Their authority was based on their role as mediators; they used negotiation and persuasion rather than coercion. Subtribes *(tayifeh)* consisted of a number of camps and were headed either by khans or bailiffs *(kalantar).* The tribe *(il)* was headed by its main khan. The number of tribes varied within different nomadic populations and could be as low as four among the Mamasani and fifty-five among the Bakhtyari. The khans, bailiffs, and heads had similar functions in the tribe, subtribe, and migratory camp. They protected their members against external forces and maintained internal peace and order.

Major Tribal Confederations

In the late nineteenth and early twentieth centuries, three major tribal confederations existed among the Qajars, Bakhtyari, and Qashqa'i. The three had their own dialect and a common genealogy, plus a central authority known as ilkhan, the paramount chief of many tribes. Such figures were elected by the tribal nobles and then confirmed by the government authorities. The confirmation of the tribal chiefs was important and signified official recognition of their authority. The powers and privileges that went with the title were considerable. Such confirmation strengthened an ilkhan's position, particularly among rival prominent families. In cases where there was a family feud, such appointments could be used by the authorities to create a division and weaken tribal unity.

The appointment of an ilkhan made negotiation during crisis such as wars, as well as tax collecting and revenue payments, less complicated for the central authorities. For example, in the case of taxes with the Qashqa'i, the ilkhan appointed a lieutenant known as the *ilbegi* who was responsible for tax collection. After collecting the revenue, he kept some for the use of his immediate supporters and forwarded a portion to the government. Water and pasture were continual sources of conflict between different nomadic groups, members of the same tribal group, and even households belonging to the same migratory camp. In fact, conflict existed at all levels of tribal organization, including rivalries among the family members of the tribal chiefs. The best example of such internal strife was the Bakhtiyari confederation.

Bakhtiyari

The Bakhtiyari confederation had two main divisions, Haft Lang (Seven Feet) and Chahar Lang (Four Feet). Though under one ilkhan, the tribal component of the Bakhtiyari traced its ancestry to two mythical ancestors, one with seven and the other with four sons. The settled Bakhtiyari traced their ancestry to an early property tax that allocated a seventh to the poorer tribes and a fourth to the richer ones. The two branches included fifty-five tribes, each with its own ruling clan and khan and theoretically under one ilkhan. However, the two groups, with 130 subtribes, were constantly in conflict with each other. In the end the Chahar Lang declined, and the Haft Lang occupied the best Bakhtiyari pastures, owned many non-Bakhtiyari villages, and even ruled over a Turkish subtribe. The conflict was extended when the ruling family was further split in the 1870s between the Ilkhani and Hajji Ilkhani families, with claimants reviving and exploiting the old rivalries between the Chahar Lang and Haft Lang factions for their own benefit. With the weakening of the Qajar in the mid-nineteenth century the Bakhtiyari appeared as major power brokers, and by 1880 the first major confederation of Bakhtiyari tribes appeared in written records.

Their most prominent leader at the time, Hussain Quli Khan Duraki, proved to be a shrewd, ruthless, and skilled leader. He established a broad network of social, family, political, and economic ties with the elite, clergy, and merchants. His rise to power was typical for the time: He assumed leadership of his group with help from his brothers against their uncle, whom they murdered. Then he helped the Qajars to defeat the Chahar Lang leader and assumed the leadership of the Bakhtiyari tribes following consolidation of his power. He became the sole representative of Bakhtiyari interest when dealing with the government. This at times created conflict when he had to decide whose interest was more important: his confederation or the government. He also remained in fierce competition with the shah's brother, the governor of Isfahan, and the conflict between the two resulted in many attacks by both sides on villages, settlements, and roads.

A warm oven, a black kettle on a trivet, and the promise of tea in the desert morning. Inside a black tent (Palas). Migratory tribes of the northern border. (Nasrollah Kasraian)

His confederation brought together many major and minor tribes, including nomads and agriculturalists in their own territory and the adjacent areas. The confederation was not stable and was influenced by both internal and external factors. Sometimes it was subject to drastic change due to the intense competition among the ruling families for dominance. The smallest unit in the tribe was families, mainly nuclear families. A household owned flocks and its members worked together as agriculturalists when needed. The yield of the land and the flocks was utilized for the family, and some products were traded as well. The extended family formed a camp, and several related camps were involved in migrations. The pasture rights came with the membership in a tribe or clan. The confederation's territory was acknowledged by the government authorities to contain the northern edge of Fars and the borders with Kuhgiluya and the Arab-dominated south. The confederation reached its peak in the mid-nineteenth century and existed until the 1930s.

The Bakhtiyari leaders' influence also extended to the Lurs, Arabs, and Qashqa'i frequenting the area either as nomads or as agriculturalist-pastoralists and sedentary agriculturalists. They also covered territories occupied by the Persians, the Khamseh confederacy, and Turkish and Armenian agriculturalists. The English authorities in Iran estimated that in "1836 there were 28,000 Bakhtiyari families with a family size of eight. The later reports in 1890 estimated their numbers to be around 29,000 families with a family size of five to six" (Garthwaite, 1983, p. 18). By the end of the nineteenth century the Bakhtiyari were distinguished from the neighboring groups mainly due to the nature of their territory and their socioeconomic structure.

The Bakhtiyari territory in the Zagros area was more compact in terms of size and resources and was located farther from the center. It comprised three major areas: the winter pastures in the uplands, summer pastures on the Zagros plateau, and the mountainous corridor linking the two. Given the inaccessibility of the region, they managed to stay beyond the control of the central government most of the time. The tribal leaders were therefore able to rule with a certain degree of autonomy. The geography and the environment were key factors in Bakhtiyari pastoralism and their biannual migration. Migration was a major aspect of Bakhtiyari self-image and has maintained its key position in the definition of the Bakhtiyari and their ideology.

Hussain Quli Khan's massive land holdings in the area made him one of the wealthiest tribal leaders at the time and a major threat to the ruling shah, who ordered his execution in 1882. The divisions between the families worsened after his death. A violent family quarrel led to twelve years of intense conflict between three factions, Ilkhani, Hajji Ilkhani, and Ilbegi, all closely related, ending only when the leaders feared losing supremacy as ilkhans. Nevertheless, the feud continued well into the twentieth century. Competition with other neighboring groups was also damaging to the individual tribes and the country as a whole. One major characteristic of the Bakhtiyari in the late nineteenth century was their involvement and close cooperation with the British authorities.

The collaboration started with an agreement to permit the British to build a road through their territory. Later it extended to the protection of oil fields for regular payments. Such agreements were a major victory for the Bakhtiyari since they confirmed their authority in the area as opposed to that of the central government in Tehran. Because of the rivalry between the different factions, at times the British authorities divided the promised sum among the rival chiefs in order to avoid conflict. British commercial and strategic interest required stability in the region. In the absence of a powerful central government, the Bakhtiyari were the best alternative. Their rise to prominence alienated the other major confederacy in the area, the Qashqa'i.

Qashqa'i

The Qashqa'i tribes were prominent and played a significant role in Iran beginning in the eighteenth century. Apart from the Safavids and a brief period during Nadir's reign, they remained fairly independent from central authority until the twentieth century. They trace the existence of their ilkhans to the middle of the eighteenth century, indicating the presence of a centralized tribal leader for centuries. During the Zand period they supported Karim Khan and acted as his royal guards, and beginning in that period they lived in Fars and near Shiraz. They were different from other tribal and nomadic pastoral populations in the way that they formed allegiances. Their confederacy included Turks, Lurs, Kurds, Arabs, Persians, and even gypsies. Turkish was their most common language, but it was primarily in the twentieth century that they overwhelmingly became Turkish speakers. These different peoples stayed in Qashqa'i territory and over time assumed Qashqa'i identity. This identity was closely related to their pastoral way of life. At the same time it connoted a tribal organization, a hierarchical society, a shared history, and distinct cultural practices. Most notable of such practices was and is their clothing.

Every Qashqa'i was a member of a lineage, subtribe, and tribe. They identified themselves as being both Qashqa'i and a member of a certain tribe/subtribe or lineage. The confederacy consisted of five large tribes, several smaller ones, and some outsiders. The Shahilu family, whose ancestors formed the

confederacy, was the head of the group and continued to provide the symbolic leaders, even when such titles were eradicated in the twentieth century.
The Qashqa'i continued their nomadic way of life and migrated between Isfahan and the Persian Gulf to the south and southwest. Their association
with territory was based on membership in lineages and subtribes. However,
other factors such as intergroup marriage and labor contracts could change
territorial association and bring different groups together. During the migrations the tents and the camps were under the control of lineage and subtribe elders, headmen, and tribal khans. Autumn and spring migrations were
long, and it was common for subtribes to join or separate on the way. The
groups were patrilineal, and men and women were members of their father's
lineage. Women stayed and migrated with the families of their husbands. The
Qashqa'i were different from other confederations because of their relative
unity and overwhelming support for the Shahilu family, which reduced tensions within the ruling family and created fewer rivalries between different
tribes.

Tribal Rivalries and the Armed Forces

Rivalries extended beyond individual tribes and were detrimental as far as the
country and the armed forces were concerned. The creation of a powerful
army independent from the tribal groups was pursued by the shahs from the
Safavid period with little success. The armed forces during the nineteenth century consisted of loyal bodyguards, mainly Georgian slaves under the command of Qajars, and part-time soldiers. The soldiers, known as the militia,
were recruited regionally. They were under the command of local regional
rulers and were maintained by local taxes. There was a cavalry too, which constituted the main fighting force. The cavalry consisted of different tribal
groups commanded by their own chiefs and motivated by promises of plunder. By the time Europeans arrived to reform the army, they observed that
while the soldiers accepted the Europeans' commands, they would not submit to orders from chiefs not belonging to their own tribe and camped separately. Even when a new short-lived group, a modern army called the "New
Order" was created, the refusal of the members to accept commands from
anyone not belonging to their own tribes disabled the new army. The introduction of the Cossack Brigade was the first attempt in the late nineteenth
century to create a military force independent of the tribal groups.

The tribes and nomadic groups went through many changes during the
nineteenth century. By the end of the century, the formation and dissolution

of tribes and tribal confederacies was bound both to local and wider outside factors. On the whole the tribal dynastic power base was already substantially reduced from the early Qajar period. The policy of "divide and rule" adopted by the Qajar kings, successful attempts to relocate tribes in large metropolitan areas, and forced migrations and relocations had already influenced tribal dispersion in Iran. One European observer in the early 1800s commented that, "apart from the Arabs, whose chiefs were still feared, the different tribes are now so much scattered throughout the provinces, that they have almost lost that union which could render them formidable" (Tapper, 1982, p. 22). Dynastic claims by major tribal chieftains were also tarnished by the presence of Europeans, whose military superiority could not be rivaled by either the Iranian government or the local tribes.

Following the advance of the Russians in the north and the subsequent loss of territories, the northwestern frontiers were closed off. Migratory routes were disrupted, and opportunities for the plundering and looting that were a major source of revenue for many tribes ceased. The same process happened in the areas bordering the Ottoman Empire. The northeastern territories, always a major problem for Iran, were increasingly coming under British influence. Early Qajars intensified attacks against these territories in the hope of recovering Afghanistan, but British protection of Afghanistan ended Iranian attempts to gain control of the region and its tribal contingencies. The support of rebellious tribal groups by outside powers, such as the support of the Yomut Turkmen by the Russians against Iran in the 1850s, was another factor that altered the relationship between local tribal groups and the central government.

The Qajars and the way they ruled also changed drastically throughout their reign. The first Qajar had favored the style of ruling by consolidating power through tribal networks. He avoided life in the capital and palaces and preferred living in the tents among his fellow tribesmen. The following Qajars discarded the tribal system in favor of the opulent royal life and followed the monarchist tradition of the kings. They tried to establish power by creating an extensive statewide bureaucracy and a standing army but, despite introducing some significant changes, failed in both tasks. They did manage to create more modern institutions such as a separate department for finance, a municipal organization for Tehran, and a more efficient court institution. However, they failed to create the stable and viable financial infrastructure essential for running the government or supporting an efficient and centrally controlled military force.

By the end of the nineteenth century the Qajar fighting force had almost disappeared among the civilian population in Tehran and Tabriz. Attempts to create an artillery force and a Cossack Brigade were only partially successful. The Qajars also faced interference from the Russians and the British. The latter at one point supplied the southern tribes in Iran with more modern arms, including rifles far superior in quality to any the government could afford. Efforts at bureaucratic reform also failed, partly because many people were employed through old family and tribal networks that hired family members and loyal supporters instead of people suitable for the newly created positions. The Qajars' failure to create a central bureaucracy enabled the provinces and the local communities to maintain autonomy and independence. Though governors and other major figures were appointed by the authorities in Tehran, in most cases they were chosen from among the local people and then confirmed by the central establishment.

In their attempts to control clergy the Qajars financed holy shrines and appointed religious leaders for the cities (shaikh al-Islam) and for the Friday prayers (imam jom'eh). The clerical establishment on the whole remained independent from the court and at times opposed the legitimacy of the monarchy. The monarchs called themselves the "shadow of the almighty." However, such claims did not go over well with the clergy. The kings were never able to claim any substantial ideological legitimacy as far as the religious establishment was concerned. Without a well-trained army, administrative and financial security, or religious standing, the Qajars mainly ruled by manipulating the existing communal conflicts within their fragmentary society. They retreated when faced with dangerous situations. One direct consequence of such policies was a substantial loss of territory during their reign and the final retreat when faced with the most important political and social event of their time, the Constitutional Revolution of the early 1900s.

Western Impacts on Iran and Modernization

One major aspect of nineteenth-century Iran was the impact of European and Western ideas in terms of military superiority and economic penetration as well as ideological and educational influence. All these factors significantly changed the relationship between the Qajar rulers and Iranian society.

The military superiority of the Western powers and their direct interference, as was the case with the Russians in the north and the British in the south, undermined the Qajar power base. Economic activity in the form of various concessions obtained or bought from the Qajar kings by the British and the Russians threatened local and traditional commercial interests and urban bazaars. The ideological influence popularized notions of equality, liberty, nationalism, human and women's rights, and modern educational institutions. Iranians became familiar with their ancient past and sought new identities free from Arab or Turkish influence. The changes created a court intelligentsia unlike any seen before. The modern printing press made such ideas available on a newly massive scale. The modern schools, though few in number, produced enough educated people to make the realization of the new concepts and ideas a possibility.

This modern intelligentsia introduced new concepts of governing and a modern vocabulary, including such words as *democracy,* still used by the reform advocates. During the process there was a change in the meaning of old concepts and notions. Such terms as *mellat* and *ummat,* which traditionally designated loyalty to a religious community, now represented citizens of a nation with no religious affiliation. The term *mardom* in the past had indicated people without any political connotations; now it had democratic and patriotic implications.

The Western impact started as early as 1800 and originally was in the form of military pressure, mainly from the Russians in the north, who easily defeated the Qajars' fragmented, tribal-based armies. Russian aggression caused the British to take precautionary actions to protect their interests in the region against Russia. The British invaded southern Iran and in 1857 imposed the Treaty of Paris, which legitimized their control of southern Iran. The treaty confirmed the Qajars' sovereignty over Tabriz and southern Iran, but they lost Georgia, Armenia, and all claims to Afghanistan.

The changes improved the transportation system. Iran was connected to Europe via telegraph, and steamboats appeared in the Caspian Sea and the Persian Gulf. The traditional subsistence economy was replaced by cash crops, and the export of raw materials increased. The concessions made to the Europeans were numerous and included a right granted to the two powers to open consular and commercial offices as and where they wished. Their merchants were also exempted from import duties, local tariffs, travel restrictions, and the jurisdiction of the Shari'a legal system. The concessions were later all categorized under the term *capitulation* by the Iranians and created tremendous resentment among all groups and classes, including the Islamic legalists, who viewed the Europeans' exemption from Shari'a courts as an outright attack on Islam itself. The economic concessions threatened local economies and production. By the end of the nineteenth century, Iran, which at the beginning of the century had been isolated from world markets, was being incorporated into European networks of international trade.

The Qajars' response was as expected; they avoided problems when they could and cooperated when the pressure was too great. Early on they even tried to introduce radical reforms instigated by the court. The first attempts to reform and modernize were promoted by the Qajar prince Abbas Mirza, who had been defeated by the Russians in a battle in the early nineteenth century. He concluded that a modern army was essential to the success of the state, so he created modern mobile artillery, dismissed the tribal cavalry as "the mob," built a cannon factory, imported modern weaponry, and put his new army on regular pay. As part of the modernizing process he also hired translators to translate European military and technical manuals into Persian.

His reforms failed because of opposition by his courtiers, tax collectors, and Europeans objecting to the new tariffs. The most vigorous opposition, however, came from the provincial and tribal leaders, who saw the "New Order" army as a threat to their traditional power base. In order to avoid conflict with the tribal rulers, the new army was reorganized many times, and in the end the different units were reduced to tribal contingents commanded by their own tribal leaders. By the time Abbas Mirza died of natural causes in 1833, the "New Order" had already been dismantled.

European involvement in Iran increased dramatically in the second part of the nineteenth century and resulted in rivalry and competition between Great Britain and Russia. The two countries' motives for involvement in Iran were different. England wished to see a strong and independent Iran to serve as a buffer zone against the Russians and their expansionist policies in central Asia and British India. To gain such an objective, it supported reforms in Iran. Russia, on the other hand, wished to check the British presence in Iran, gain access to the Persian Gulf, and expand into the khanates of the Turkmen steppe, to which Iran still asserted some claims. It was also interested in gaining control over the rich territories of northern Iran and the Caspian Sea. Iranians turned increasingly to the British for help in implementing reforms creating a strong and independent Persia. However, neither the Iranians nor the British were able or willing to achieve this objective, for a number of reasons. The two rival outside powers used tribal groups in many different ways in order to gain their own objectives. One example was the arming of the southern and northern tribes to defend either British or Russian interests.

Religious Minorities

The period from the Safavid dynasty to the late nineteenth century was one of the worst for religious minorities. Many restrictions were imposed on every aspect of their lives. They were regarded as unclean and could not come in direct contact with Muslims. Many times they were persecuted and forced to convert. They remained impoverished, underdeveloped, and isolated

Edward VII with the shah of Persia, nineteenth century, London, England (Hulton-Deutsch Collection/Corbis)

from global communities. The restrictions created social structures inside these communities to enable them to avoid conduct with the outside world. As a result they remained inconspicuous and insular. The average urban non-Muslim left his quarters rarely. Most contact with the outside world was through the minority's elite and representatives who were appointed and approved by the authorities. Religious elites, due to their isolation from the outside world, had remained static and fallen behind compared to similar groups in non-Muslim countries. Their communal structures were self-contained, and ritual and social patterns of segregation limited their interaction with other Iranians. The changes that happened in Iran beginning in the middle of the nineteenth century had a major impact on these groups as well.

Babi and Baha'i Movements

The mid- to late nineteenth century was a period of great significance for religious minorities. It coincided with the emergence of the Babi movement and its successor, the Baha'i, a major new religion with thousands of supporters in Iran and outside. The Babi movement was the most significant social upheaval in religious circles. It was a messianic movement that demanded radical change with respect to religious doctrines. Its young leader, Sayyid Ali Muhammad, known as the Bab (meaning "gate"), was a merchant from Shiraz. He proclaimed the coming of a "new age," headed an open campaign against the religious leaders and their authority, and challenged their claims to represent the hidden imam during his absence.

The movement became very popular among the lower and midlevel clergy, and its rapid expansion forced the authorities to suppress it harshly. After a failed attempt to assassinate Nasir al-Din Shah, the assassin was accused of being a Babi, and the authorities, including the reformist prime minister Amir Kabir, ordered the rapid termination of the movement. Most of its leaders were executed, including the Bab himself, who was killed in 1850. The Babis had many female supporters; women's societies; and a female leader, Qurrat al-ain. Improving the situation of women became part of their agenda and that of their descendents, the Baha'i. They had nationalistic tendencies and insisted that sacred literature should be in Persian and that the shrines in Iran should replace the ones in Arabia and Iraq as the most sacred. They introduced a new calendar with ancient Iranian celebrations as the major events instead of Islamic ones.

Amir Kabir and the Babis agreed on the ills of the clerical class and its institutions. They recognized the need for reform and opposed the clergy as a whole. However, the secular Amir Kabir, in his efforts to consolidate the state and impose its authority over the religious groups, was against all expressions of religious dissent. He was murdered in 1852 by the order of the king, and for a time efforts to reform the state were halted. The brutal murder of the Babi leaders, including Qurrat al-ain, deprived the early reformists of a number of charismatic and intelligent reformers. It also removed a serious threat to the leadership and authority of the religious leaders. However, the movement survived; it was split in 1863 between the Azali Babis and the Baha'i, and both groups continued to develop their ideological affiliations. Azali Babis were followers of Subh al-Azal, who became the leader of the Babi movement after the Bab's execution. He had escaped to Iraq, and his leadership was challenged by his half brother, Bahaullah, who became the leader of the Baha'i movement. A number of prominent Azali Babis and Baha'i were involved in the formation of underground societies and schools and contributed to the ideological debates of the time. Although the Azali Babis faded, the Baha'i not only survived but flourished. Up to the Islamic revolution in 1979 the movement grew significantly, and its followers were involved in the socioeconomic affairs of the country.

Christians

Other non-Muslims in the late nineteenth century benefited greatly from the changes caused by the European presence, missionary activity, and the involvement of religious minorities in international trade networks. The missionaries were very important because they opened the first modern schools and provided health care and other community services. The Christian communities became exposed to the European missionary presence. The first attempts by the Europeans to send missionaries to Iran were at the time of the Mongols in the thirteenth and fourteenth centuries. The missions went both to Central Asia and to Persia, with little success. During the Safavid reign more missionaries were allowed in, but under the later Safavid rulers and Nadir Shah, most missionaries were forced to flee and thousands of Christians were compelled either to migrate or to convert.

The second period of missionary work in Persia was begun in 1840 by the Catholic Lazarists. A French civil servant had been sent to Iran in 1838 on a scientific mission by the French Academy and the minister of public instruction. He founded four schools, two in Tabriz and Isfahan for the Armenians and two in Urmiyeh and Salmas for the Chaldean Assyrians. The Lazarists were joined by the French Sisters of Charity and other priests, who took over the schools. The appointment of a new French representative at the Persian court helped the missions. The Lazarists were permitted by the Iranian government to continue their work unmolested, and one of their priests became a great favorite at the court of Nasir al-Din Shah. They built a new seminary and a large new church and trained new priests by teaching them Latin, French, Syriac, and Armenian as well as theology. Besides the seminary, two other colleges were opened, one for boys and one for girls, the latter under the care and direction of the Sisters of Charity. A hospital and one orphanage were also built and were open to people of all faiths, including Muslims. After a while Muslim boys were allowed to attend the schools, and later on Muslim girls were admitted as well. Soon the Lazarists extended their services to Tehran and other major cities. The missionary schools were instrumental in providing modern thought and education for the Iranians, and they were the first girls' schools in Iran. Other denominations followed the Lazarists, and soon a Persian translation of the Bible was undertaken by a Protestant missionary. The missionaries were able to convert some Iranians, and a small number of Christians belonging to sects other than the Armenian or Assyrian churches emerged in Iran.

The first American missionary school was established in Urmiyeh in the 1830s for the Nestorian minority. By 1871 some fifty-two missionaries and physicians had arrived from the United States. In 1870 their work was transferred to the Board of Missions of the American Presbyterian Church, with two divisions. The eastern division covered Tabriz, Tehran, Hamadan, Rasth, Qazvin, and Kirmanshah. The western division supervised work in Azerbaijan and parts of Kurdistan, the Caucasus, and Armenia. More missionaries arrived from other countries, including Russians who managed to convert several thousand Nestorians to the Russian Orthodox Church. The converts were motivated to seek Russia's protection against sporadic persecutions by the civil and religious authorities. By the end of the nineteenth century, Christians were among the best-educated and most modern groups in Iran.

Christians were still divided between different sects, but many had converted to Catholicism. The Armenian church remained strong despite the fact that the Armenians' position in Iran had deteriorated in the eighteenth century owing to persecution and religious schisms among the Armenians themselves. These schisms had divided and weakened the Armenian community. Many Armenians emigrated to Russia in order to escape the unfavorable conditions in Iran. Records from the 1860s indicate that the Armenians of Julfa, near Isfahan, consisted of a population of 300 to 500 families living in poverty. The records of the British Consulate in Tabriz mention thousands of Armenians and Nestorians leaving for Russia, mostly for work as seasonal laborers. The French consul in 1868 reported the Armenian population of Tabriz to be 5,000 and pointed to an increase due to the return of many seasonal workers. By the twentieth century, prospects were much better for the Armenians. They had monopolized the wine-making business and were significantly involved in foreign trade. They traveled regularly between Iran, Russia, and France; a few owned extensive holdings, including wineries. One French observer mentioned that trade in Persia was entirely in the hands of Persians and Armenians. Armenians were employed by many foreign firms and enterprises in Iran and became a major link between Europeans and Iranians. Many moved around in the European colonies; for example, many Armenian families in Iran became dependent on their relatives who were working in India and prospered from the interactions. The Assyrians also prospered but remained less prominent than the Armenians, mainly due to their small numbers.

Jews

The Jewish population of Iran went through similar changes and also benefited from the European presence in Iran. Like Christians, at times of persecution Jews were able to seek protection from foreign representatives. However, they were more exposed to persecution compared to other groups. All accounts by foreign travelers, including a detailed observation and commentary by Lord Curzon, the future British viceroy of India, present a depressing picture of the conditions of Jews in Iran. He commented that "as a community, the Persian Jews are sunk in great poverty and ignorance. They have no schools of their own, except in the synagogues, where they are only taught to repeat their prayers" (quoted in Issawi, 1971, p. 62). Curzon also mentioned that teaching of Persian to the Jews was rare and was carried out only in a few schools or was done privately. The majority were engaged in trade, in jewelry- and wine-making and similar professions forbidden to Muslims. Many performed as musicians and dancers, occupations that were little respected by Muslims. The liquor prohibition of 1904 threatened their involvement in wine-making, but the restrictions were lifted later. Traditionally only non-Muslims could produce alcoholic drinks, for the consumption of non-Muslims only.

Due to persecution in the 1820s and 1830s, many Jewish religious leaders had already left for Palestine. Anti-Jewish sentiments had reached their peak in 1839, when Jewish quarters were looted in Mashhad and many Jewish-owned farms and businesses were confiscated. The emigration of these leaders was a major event in the history of Jews in Iran because it left them without strong religious leadership for generations. Many ordinary Jews also moved to Tajikistan and Palestine to avoid persecution. Like other religious minorities, Jews were confined to their own quarters in urban areas. The presence of Europeans improved these conditions. The first modern Jewish school, "Alliance," was opened in 1898 after a long and frustrating debate and under heavy pressure from Europeans and the International Jewish Alliance. The school was founded by the Alliance Israelite Universelle, and by 1911 there were 11 such schools with 2,225 pupils. The Jewish community was able to connect with other Jewish communities in Europe, India, and Iraq. The Jews played a significant role in trade from the Persian Gulf and in cotton imports from England to Baghdad. However, at the end of the nineteenth century European observers were still commenting on how the Jews were regarded as ritually unclean and in many instances had to stay away from the Muslims they traded with. As well as being merchants and traders, they were engaged in crafts and construction, and some owned small shops. A few were gold- and silversmiths or moneylenders. They were prominent in making perfumes but on the whole remained isolated. The Jewish chronicles report the Qajar period as one of the worst in recent times.

Zoroastrians

The Zoroastrian population had fallen sharply by the early nineteenth century but had started to rise again by 1900. The Zoroastrians reported an increase in their numbers from 7,200 in 1854 to 9,300 in 1892. The majority lived in Yazd, some lived in Kirman, and a few started moving to Tehran. Foreign observers commented on their pitiful situation, and like other non-Muslim minorities they were still subject to the *jizya*. Many became involved in silk manufacturing and weaving. They were helped greatly by the prosperous and well-educated Parsi community of India. They set up a Zoroastrian society in 1855 in Yazd. With help and support from the British embassy, they gathered statistics, and schools had been founded by 1882. Descriptions of the city of Kirman in the late nineteenth century indicate that the population was segregated in separate quarters based on race, religion, and occupation. The Zoroastrian quarter was located outside the city walls, which made it vulnerable to attack by invaders. The Zoroastrians had a local community council *(anjuman)* that represented them in their dealings with the authorities. Many observers commented on Zoroastrian community members who had never left their ghetto and did not speak Persian. They were also regarded as ritually unclean, and well into the nineteenth century they could not ride horses and were allowed to ride only donkeys. At times distinctive clothing rules were imposed by the authorities. Foreign visitors commented on the restrictions imposed on the color of the clothing Zoroastrians had to wear and how they could not carry umbrellas or wear eyeglasses. Like the Iranian Jews, Zoroastrians regard the Qajar period as one of their worst. In response to persecution and segregation policies, the Zoroastrian community became closed, introverted, and static. The impact of the Parsi community of India on the Zoroastrian community of Iran was immense, and the new trade opportunities with India created great improvements in the local communities. They also benefited from the emergence of some talented and influential leaders. The Zoroastrian leaders were articulate and assertive and became very influential during the drafting of the first constitution that guaranteed minority rights. The modern educated Iranians of different faiths who were educated in missionary schools and minority schools made a significant impact in the late nineteenth century. They guided and participated in the developments that led to the success of the constitutional movement in Iran.

Conclusion

Beginning in the middle of the nineteenth century, the most compelling force was the beginning of a demand for change. By now there was a new class familiar with the modern world. Merchants traveled regularly to Russia and Europe, and the printing press was introduced. A new breed of intellectuals rose among all groups, demanding constitutional reform, women's rights, and a secular centralized modern state. Babi, a new religious movement, shook the very foundation of the traditional religious establishment by gaining support and momentum among the clergy itself. Some reformist ministers at the court introduced modern schooling, and underground political parties emerged. The assassination of a Qajar king by a pro constitutionalist shook the Qajars, and a constitution was finally granted. It was revoked shortly afterward by another Qajar king, with help from Russia, but was regained with support from many, including devoted partisans from Azerbaijan and Gilan, tribal leaders, the British, and the religious minorities. These different groups played a major role in the success of the movement. Their involvement indicates fundamental changes in the very concept of nationhood that occurred due to the modernization processes in nineteenth-century Iran. The emergence of such new notions had a significant impact on the tribal component as well.

Timeline

1848	Nasir al-Din Shah assumed the throne. The leaders of the Babi sect announced total independence from Islam and declared Babism a new religion.
1851	The institute of technology, the first modern institution of higher learning in Iran, opened. Amir Kabir, the reformist prime minister, was assassinated by the order of Nasir al-Din Shah. The Babi persecutions continued.
1857	Iran unsuccessfully tried to reclaim Herat from the British. Great Britain imposed the Treaty of Paris instead and ended all claims by Iran to territories in Afghanistan.

1872	Nasir al-Din Shah gave major economic concessions to Baron Reuter, which created major uproar in the country.
1878	Russians were employed to train a Cossack regiment. Nasir al-Din Shah opened the first museum in the country and placed royal collections on display.
1889	The British-controlled Imperial Bank of Iran opened and printed the first Iranian banknotes.
1890	The start of selling concessions to foreign powers by the shah. The first issue of the newspaper called *Law (Qanun)* was published in London and smuggled to Iran.
1891	A tobacco concession was made to an Englishman, Major Talbot. The concession was the beginning of civil unrest in Iran.
1892	The shah was forced to cancel the tobacco concession.
1896	Nasir al-Din Shah was assassinated. His son, Muzzafar al-Din Shah, became the new king.

Significant People, Places, and Events

AMIR KABIR (1807–1852): Mirza Taghi Khan was regarded as the most able political leader during the Qajar era. From humble origins, he rose to become the prime minister. He guaranteed Nasir al-Din Shah's succession to the throne.

BABI: A messianic movement instigated by Sayyid Ali Muhammad in 1844. A young merchant from Shiraz, he regarded himself as the Bab ("the gate") to the twelfth imam and divine knowledge. In 1848 the movement announced its independence from Islam. The Bab was executed in 1850 in Tabriz.

BAHAULLAH (1817–1892): Mirza Hussein Ali Nouri was born in Tehran to a prominent courtier family. He became a Babi supporter and called himself Baha. Later he denounced the militarism of the Babi. He was imprisoned and released during the persecution of the Babis and went to Baghdad in 1853. He was exiled by the Ottomans to Palestine, where he died after completing some major theological works and laying the foundations for the Baha'i sect that was further expanded by his son, Abdul Baha.

BAHA'I: A religion founded by Bahaullah and expanded by his eldest son, Abdul Baha (1844–1921). Originally followers of the Bab, they split

away from Babi after his execution. They believe in the unity of all
religions, nonviolence, and equality of all races and sexes. They are
persecuted in Iran. Their holiest place is in Israel, where Bahaullah is
buried.

BOIR AHMADI AND KUHGILUYA: Closely related Luri tribal groups from
the central Zagros area. They are related to other Lurs in Iran,
including the Bakhtiyari. They are nomadic and Shi'ite and in the
twentieth century the area they inhabited became a province bearing
their name.

CHAHAR MAHAL AND BAKHTIYARI: A province in Iran in the central
Zagros area that borders Isfahan, Boir Ahmadi, and Kuhgiluya and
Luristan provinces. It is inhabited by many Bakhtiyari but has a
mixed population, including Kurds, Turkish-speaking groups, and
Persians.

IMAM JOM'EH: A title assigned to the senior clergyman in charge of the
Friday prayers at the main mosque in each county. Formally
appointed by the Qajar and Pahlavi kings, at times they were so
powerful that their appointment was only a formality as a sign of
recognizing their prominence. They still exist and have become very
involved in the politics of the country.

GILAKI: A northwestern Iranian dialect, Gilaki is spoken in the Caspian
area, particularly Gilan. It is related to other dialects in the Caspian
area, mainly Mazandarani, Gorgani, and Taleshi. None is written, and
all are widespread in the region.

GURANI: A Kurdish group that lives in both Iraq and Iran. The name
applies to both a group and a language related to Kurmanji. They
were mentioned in the sixteenth century as the fourth-largest
Kurdish group. Gurani is closely related to Zaza; both languages are
northwestern Iranian in origin, and neither group considers itself to
be Kurd. They are mainly Ahl i Haqqi.

JAMSHIDIS: A small minority Sunni tribe in northeastern Iran,
primarily concentrated in Khurasan. They speak mainly Persian
with some Turkic (Aimaq) vocabulary. The Aimaqs are originally
from Mongolia, and many Jamshidis still have Mongolian
features.

MAZANDARANI: The dialect, northwestern Iranian in origin, is used
extensively in the Caspian area and the province of Mazandaran.

QURATT AL-AIN: The legendary Babi leader who was murdered during
the Babi persecution in the early 1850s. She belonged to a prominent
clerical family and was married to a clergyman. She left her husband

and family to fight for the Babi cause. Also known as Tahireh ("pure"), she removed her veil in a meeting of Babi leaders and caused a split in the sect.

SHAYKH AL-ISLAM: A title in the ranking system applied to the clergy. In different countries and different Muslim sects, it has different connotations.

SHAYKHISM AND SHAYKHY SCHOOL: Shaikh Ahmad Ahsai, who moved from Iraq to Iran in early 1806, first introduced the doctrine. He was Shi'ite and was equally influenced by Muslim philosophy and mysticism. He went against two dominant schools of Shi'ite thought, was finally excommunicated by the clergy in Iran, and was forced into exile.

TAJIKS: Predominantly Persian-speaking, they live in Central Asia in Tajikistan, Uzbekistan, and Afghanistan as well as some in Pakistan. Culturally, they are closely related to Iran. Most are Sunni Muslims.

TALESHI: This dialect belongs to the northwestern branch of the Iranian dialects. It is spoken in the Talesh region of Gilan and in some parts of Azerbaijan.

Bibliography

Abrahamian, Ervand. *Iran between Two Revolutions.* Princeton, NJ: Princeton University Press, 1982.

Amanat, Abbas. *Resurrection and Renewal: The Making of the Babi Movement in Iran, 1844–1850.* Ithaca, NY: Cornell University Press, 1989.

Avery, P., G. R. G. Hambly, and C. Melville, eds. *The Cambridge History of Iran,* Vol. 7: *From Nadir Shah to the Islamic Republic.* Cambridge: Cambridge University Press, 1991.

Bayat, Mangol. *Mysticism and Dissent: Socioreligious Thought in Qajar Iran.* Syracuse, NY: Syracuse University Press, 1999.

Bosworth, Edmond, and Carole Hillenbrand. *Qajar Iran: Political, Social and Cultural Change, 1800–1925.* Costa Mesa, CA: Mazda Publishers, 1992.

Cole, Juan. *Modernity and the Millennium: The Genesis of the Baha'i Faith in the Nineteenth Century.* New York: Columbia University Press, 1998.

Farmayan, Hafez, and Elton L. Daniel. *Society and Culture in Qajar Iran: Studies in Honor of Hafez Farmayan.* Costa Mesa, CA: Mazda Publishers, 2002.

Garthwaite, Gene R. *Khans and Shahs: A Documentary Analysis of the Bakhtiyari in Iran.* Cambridge and New York: Cambridge University Press, 1983.

Issawi, Charles. *The Economic History of Iran, 1800–1914.* Chicago: University of Chicago Press, 1971.

Ringer, Monica M. *Education, Religion and the Discourse of Cultural Reform in Qajar Iran.* Costa Mesa, CA: Mazda Publishers, 2001.

Tapper, Richard. *The Conflict of Tribe and State in Iran and Afghanistan.* London: St. Martin's Press, 1982.

CHAPTER FIVE

Twentieth-Century Iran

Tribal Groups in the Early Twentieth Century

A T THE TURN OF THE CENTURY THE MOST IMPORTANT TRIBAL GROUPS in terms of political impact were the Kurds, the Qashqa'i, the Lurs, the Bakhtiyari, the Khamseh confederacy, the Shahsevans, and the Turkmen. Some, such as the Mamasani and Kuhgiluya Lurs, had already been pacified by the end of the nineteenth century. Others, such as the Kurds of Quchan and Bujnurd and the Arabs and Baluchis in Sistan and Baluchistan, maintained considerable independence until the early twentieth century. The Ardalan Kurds, a major force in the seventeenth and eighteenth centuries, had already lost their supremacy. The Kurds of Kirmanshah, who were governed by the Kalhur chiefs, came to terms with the central government and maintained power. By the end of the nineteenth century tribal powers had been further reduced due to improvements in national security, partly because of better roads and communication. This reduction was also related to the appointment of some exceptionally powerful governors designated by the capital, British involvement in the south, and Russia's conquest of the northern frontiers. Looting and raiding were reduced in many cases. Voluntary settlement due to new economic considerations in some areas, particularly Azerbaijan, reduced the nomadic population. By the early twentieth century the only major nomadic tribe left in Azerbaijan was the Shahsevan confederacy, which by this time had lost most of its power as well.

The Shahsevan Confederacy

The Shahsevan's demise is a good example of how Russia's involvement affected the tribes. Its members lived both in villages and as pastoral nomads and went into Russian territory for winter pasture. They were mainly Shi'i, and the majority spoke Turkish. Different communities united in one tribe were not necessarily related through descent. They maintained a complex ritual life and favored orthodox religious practices, mosque gatherings, and migratory rites with great intensity.

The group lost considerable pasture land because of the Russian conquests in the early nineteenth century. For some time the Russians allowed limited access to the pastures in Russia because Russian nomads used the same areas. Russian authorities pressured the Iranian government to deal with the problem as well and demanded payment of annual fees for the use of pasture by the Shahsevan. The Iranian government accepted the terms; however, it remained behind in its payments. The Shahsevan failed to observe the limitations demanded by the Russians, and chaos ensued. The Russians applied further pressure until the Iranian government was forced to take severe measures. At some point in the mid-nineteenth century the reformist prime minister Amir Kabir contemplated forcefully settling the whole group. This was the first attempt by an Iranian government to settle all members of a confederation, and it failed. Several more attempts were made, some instigated with support from Russia. In one report the appointed governor, who dealt with the Shahsevan very harshly in the 1860s, stated that he had settled 15,000 families of nomads. The British consul general in Tabriz at the time commented on the inappropriateness of the settling of these tribes and regarded it as a loss for the economy and the country as a whole. In his reports, including some to the Iranian government, he concluded that the efforts would fail and the tribes would revolt and regarded the compensation suggested by the authorities as far below the real value of the losses. He was right in his assessment, and the revolts increased. The Russians were forced to take more action by appointing a permanent office to deal with the Shahsevan-related frontier issues. After many meetings with their Iranian counterparts, attempts were made to regulate these affairs by creating specific codes to deal with criminal activities and civil disobedience. Though the codes were not very effective, order was improved and for a time peace was restored.

Major disturbances started again after a severe famine in the early 1880s that killed half of the nomads. The famine prompted more raids, and disorder followed. Finally the Russians, after several failed plans to regulate grazing patterns and to control the nomads, closed the border altogether in 1885. Many nomads were turned back, and their herds were confiscated. Fugitives who claimed to be escaping persecution and abuse at the hands of the Iranians or their own chiefs were caught and deported. This strategy

A yourt *(the place where the tents of an* obeh *are set up) belonging to Ilsavan (Shahsevan) tribes in their summer pasture. Tents housing nuclear or extended families are set up at a distance from one another and comprise a socioeconomic unit called an* obeh, *headed by an* aq-saqqai *(a white-bearded wise man). Each tent enjoys enough space around it for the cattle. Sabalan mountain foot, near Moil, East Azerbaijan. (Nasrollah Kasraian)*

forced the Iranian government to try to redistribute pasture in its territories in order to accommodate the Shahsevan tribes. This effort marked the beginning of a complex system of grazing rights specific to the Shahsevan. Further disorder in the Iranian territories was dealt with by brutal public execution of two Shahsevan chiefs, after which the nomadic Shahsevan did not create large-scale problems for the Russians or the Iranians for several decades. However, for almost forty years they remained hostile to all external authority. They engaged in minor raids, some with support from nearby villages that had become increasingly impoverished because of the border closure. Their next major involvement in Iranian politics happened during the Constitutional Revolution, when they supported the Qajar rulers against the constitutionalists.

The other factors that drastically affected the Shahsevan were at the local level. In the early 1900s Azerbaijan was the most important province in Iran and was suffering from mismanagement and insecurity. The sale of crown lands to wealthy individuals, including some Shahsevan tribal chiefs, created a gap between the landowner chiefs and the poor pastoralist tribesmen. The closure of the border with Russia drastically changed the economic and political organization of the tribes with the loss of winter pasture. It increased the pasture use fees paid by the tribesmen to the chiefs and created major hardship for many poorer tribes. It widened the gap between the ruling families and the ordinary tribesmen and forced many to settle either in Russia or in Iran. It also created local conflicts—some very bloody and destructive. The Shahsevan formed a coalition in 1909, and most of the tribes joined the Royalists. They ransacked the city of Ardabil and remained a strong force in the region even after the success of the constitutional movement. Their control ended in 1923, when they were finally disarmed by the very powerful war minister Reza Khan, the founder of the next and the last royal dynasty in Iran.

Tribes and Ethnic Groups in the Early Twentieth Century

By the early twentieth century tribal economy and politics had become subject to drastic change from outside forces, such as the European presence. There was also change from within. Many tribal chiefs had become settlers, lived in major cities, and as a result had lost their connection with their subjects. Some of the new-generation elite chiefs were sent to Europe for a modern education, as was the case with the Bakhtiyari leaders. This further increased the gap between the young leaders and their tribes. Some chiefly families such as the Mohammareh shaikhs, the leaders of the Arab tribes in the south, went through less drastic change. The shaikhs remained more traditional, continuing to rely upon and take advantage of the traditionally based royalties.

Bakhtiyari

Bakhtiyari tribes remained a significant force, and in the early 1900s most still lived as nomads. They lived predominantly around Isfahan, with some tribes living in the Khuzistan area. In Isfahan they cohabited with Qashqa'i, Arabs, and Lurs, who also lived in the extreme southern districts. Quite a few tribes were already settled in many villages near their traditional territories in Chahar Mahal and Bakhtiyari. The area already bore their name and was regarded as Bakhtiyari territory. Despite settling down, they had kept their tribal networks and introduced tribal organizations into a peasant region that had its own small village organizations. At times the village and nomad social organizations clashed, and minor conflicts existed.

Bakhtiyari tribes remained a major concern for governments until the mid-twentieth century. Despite the family rivalries of the late nineteenth century, their influence grew due to the efficient leadership of some charismatic chiefs. Their leaders accumulated considerable landed property, and after the discovery of oil in their territory rival family members united and became significant players both in national politics and in the success of the Constitutional Revolution. Bakhtiyari were mainly pastoral nomads. The leaders utilized both their properties and their pastoral base to maintain their own internal power. However, their control over the Bakhtiyari economic base of pastoralism and seasonal agriculture was indirect since most khans by this time lived in the capital and were away from their tribes.

Arabs

The Bakhtiyari's major rival in the southern territories in Khuzistan was the Arab-speaking tribes. Headed by the powerful and wealthy shaikh of Mohammareh (Khoramshahr), Arab tribes occupied most of the area that contained the oilfields. The Shi'i Arabs lived mainly in Khuzistan (the northwestern end of the Persian Gulf close to Iraq), and the Sunni Arabs remained close to the Persian Gulf coast. Persians, Turks, and Lurs also lived in the area, with extensive interaction among all groups.

Prior to the discovery of oil and involvement of the British, the central government did not and could not interfere much in the affairs of the area. It intervened as a mediator during hostilities between the Bakhtiyari and the Arab tribes when the situation went out of hand. The discovery of oilfields in 1908 drastically changed the geopolitical significance of the area, and matters became far more complicated after the establishment of the Anglo-Persian Oil Refinery in 1909. Arab nationalism in the neighboring countries became a factor and was used extensively by the British. In the 1920s there was a failed attempt to create an independent Arab state (Arabistan), initially supported by the British authorities.

The ruling Mohammareh at the time, Shaikh Khazal, had been in power since 1897 after murdering his brother. Exceptionally cruel and ambitious, he had become the most powerful and one of the wealthiest local rulers in the Persian Gulf area. He dismissed the last three Qajar monarchs as weak and puppetlike, paid few taxes, and appointed his own agents in key positions. He increasingly armed his tribes, and the Qajar rulers had little choice other than

A Bedouin cattle-raising family of an Arab tribe in front of their tent between Shush and Ahvaz (Nasrollah Kasraian)

to submit to his requests and ignore his invasions and atrocities committed against many individuals, including his own family members. The extent of his power in the early twentieth century was unique among the tribal leaders. Unlike others, such as Bakhtiyari chiefs who were educated and supported modernization, Shaikh Khazal remained a traditional despot with little interest in the affairs of his own tribes. Tribal members stayed poor and remained among the least educated of all ethnic groups. There is no evidence that they expressed any sentiments regarding any kind of nationalism, whether Iranian or Arab, in the early twentieth century. The shaikh's motives for later attempting to create an independent Arabistan were to serve his interests more than those of the Arab tribes he represented. The early constitutionalist governments were too weak to deal with him. His end came with the rise of Reza Khan.

Turkmen Groups

The Turkmen are not a homogenous group and are mainly Sunni of the Hanafi sect. They posed major problems for the governments following the adoption of Shi'i as the state religion. Most trace their ancestry to Oghuz tribes and live in eastern Mazandaran and northern Khurasan. Mystical sects locally known as Tariqa, particularly Naqshbandi, are popular among them. Many related groups occupy areas in Turkmenistan and Afghanistan. By the early twentieth century the major groups in Iran, the Yomut, Guklan, Tekke, and Salour, had already been involved in decades of cross-border activities, often manipulated by the Russians. Many groups supported the Constitutional Revolution but became dissatisfied when tribal groups, with the exception of Qajars, did not manage to gain representation in the new parliament. Like most other tribal groups, the Turkmen were not consistent in their support of the constitution and at times provided help to the anticonstitutional shah in exile. Following border conflict with the Russians in 1881, the southern parts of Turkmenistan, known as Turkmen Sahra (the desert of the Turkmen) was confirmed as Iranian territory. The area has remained a Turkmen stronghold. They lived as nomadic herdsmen and traded their animal products, colorful woollen fabrics, and carpets. They used their own distinctive tents and insisted on wearing their traditional costumes.

Prior to the twentieth century they continued their relations with related groups outside Iran, but cross-border movements became a lot stricter as of the twentieth century, and settlements increased in size and population. The largest Turkmen tribe in Iran, the Yomut, consists of two major subtribes. Many Turkmen tribes resemble the Shahsevan, but there are differences in patterns of settlements, marriage practices, and organization of the camps. For example, while the Shahsevan young males remain with their fathers for many years, the newly married Turkmen male can establish his own household as soon as he is able to do so. Turkmen such as the Yomut resisted central and chiefly authority. The only leaders they recognized were elected spokesmen. These were normally wealthy men who headed groups of agnates but without any formal authority. As a result they did not have a key paramount chief except at times of major crisis such as wars. Political hierarchy normally was not part of their traditional notions of power. Early in the twentieth century they had large flocks, and the wealth of a household depended primarily on the size of its labor force.

Lurs

Closely related to the Bakhtiyari were the Lurs, with two major Luri dialects both closely related to Persian. Predominantly Shi'i, they lived in the Zagros region to the northwest, west, and southeast of the Bakhtiyari. The first dialect, Lur Buzurg (major Luri), was and is spoken by the Bakhtiyari, Kuhgiluya, and Mamasani tribes; Lur Kuchik (minor Luri) is spoken by the Lurs of Luristan. The two major divisions in the early 1900s were the Pusht-e Kuhi and the Pish-e Kuhi ("beyond" and "in front of the mountains"). These two groups were subdivided into more than sixty tribes, the most important of which included the Boir Ahmadi, the Kuhgiluya, and the Mamasani. Historically the urbanized Lurs lived in the town of Khorramabad, the provincial capital of Luristan. Prior to 1900, the majority of Lurs practiced pastoral nomadism. The alliances they made with neighboring groups made them very significant. Like their Bakhtiyari relatives, Lurs were Shi'i, but their religious affiliation did not make their relations with the central government any better.

Qashqa'i

The Qashqa'i tribes were another major group exerting influence in the early twentieth century. They were stratified, with a wealthy group of chiefly

Shaking the dust off a gelim *and sweeping the tent, winter setting (Qeshlaq) of Lur tribes near Khorram-Abad (Nasrollah Kasraian)*

families. In the early twentieth century they lived in the Zagros region, mainly between Isfahan and the Persian Gulf to the south and southwest. In the spring they moved to summer pastures in the higher altitudes of the Zagros region and during the winter season stayed close to Shiraz. They produced pastoral products and meat and cultivated grain seasonally for their own use. By the early twentieth century there were five major tribes and nine lesser ones. Though Qashqa'i were generally identified by their Turkish language and costume, there were local variations, as is the case today. For example, there are Luri- or Kurdish-speaking Qashqa'i, and identity came with residence as well. Once groups resided in Qashqa'i territory and were affiliated with them, they were regarded as Qashqa'i despite their ethnic or linguistic origin.

Qashqa'i are often described as the most successful tribal confederacy in Iran. The ruling families played a key role in the continuity of the tribe and its identity. One significant factor was the continuity of the ruling elite. The power remained in one family longer than in any other tribal group. The family leaders enjoyed respect and were liked by their tribal members more than most other tribal chiefs, including some Bakhtiyari khans. The ruling lineage traced its ancestry to Amir Ghazi Shahilu, a relative of Shah Ismail Safavid in the sixteenth century. The lineage continued through the founder of the Qashqa'i confederacy, Jani Agha, in the early eighteenth century. His descendents remained as leaders all the way to the Islamic Republic in 1979 and enjoyed popular support among tribal members.

The Shahilu lineage was maintained by imposing restrictions on marrying outside the lineage. Sometimes this meant that women remained unmarried because there were no suitable males. The ruling family maintained its distinctive way of living and costume, including a distinctive hat, tents, and women's colorful clothing, and continued to identify with the Qashqa'i culture and traditions. This was in contrast to other ruling elite such as the Bakhtiyari, who acted, dressed, and lived like other upper-class Iranians in the major urban centers. The elite's adherence to the Qashqa'i culture and traditions made it popular, and thus these leaders maintained the loyalty of their tribal members.

In its relationship with the state the Qashqa'i confederacy followed the same policies, asserting Qashqa'i identity when the governments were weak and assimilating cautiously when the government or its agents were powerful. Other major factors were the solidarity in the ruling family, fewer feuds between families, and the geographical location. The inaccessibility of their pasture land and their distance from the capital and the border regions meant less disruption for the group as a whole. It was not involved in border disputes, and despite its heterogeneous nature and different ethnic origins, it expressed solidarity as a Turkish group. Its members regarded themselves as distinct from their neighbors, including the Persians, whom they referred to as the "Tajik." These neighbors at times could be sources of conflict, but by the early twentieth century many villages and lesser tribes had sought and gained protection from the Qashqa'i.

Kurds

Another major ethnic group, the Kurds, remained a significant force during the nineteenth and twentieth centuries. For almost five centuries the Kurds mainly lived in the Ottoman and Iranian territories. Small Kurdish states existed throughout this period and often acted as buffer zones between the Ottomans and Iranians. They remained independent and hard to control, and their internal organization responded to and was influenced by the British and the Russians in the late nineteenth century. The two major Kurdish states in Iran, Ardalan and Guran, were nontribal and by the late nineteenth and early twentieth centuries had lost power and prominence. The rulers kept living in towns surrounded by a few administrators and officials necessary for running their affairs. Family feuds were very common among the ruling dynasties. Such rivalry often emerged as pro-Ottoman or pro-Iranian factionalism and by the late nineteenth century had extended to include foreign powers. This expansion manifested in the appearance of pro-British and pro-Russian Kurdish factions and the acceptance of the two superpowers as the main political forces in the area.

The Kurdish ruling families, like most other groups, claimed descent from a prestigious lineage with no set rule for succession. Leadership normally stayed in a ruling family. External factors, such as support by the central government for one claimant against another, were also important in the success of the rulers. Leading military chiefs with their followers surrounded the ruler and played an important part in the balance of power. The bulk of the army consisted of the nomadic and the seminomadic armed tribesmen. The states normally contained settlers such as agriculturalists, merchants, a religious class, and Jews and Christians. The ethnic population was heterogeneous, including Turks, Lurs, and Persians. Many migrating groups visited the Kurdish territories during their seasonal migrations, and fringe groups with unorthodox religious affiliations, such as Yazidi and Alevid and the shaikhs, were popular. Tribal confederacies became increasingly irrelevant. By the end of the nineteenth century both the Ottomans and the Iranians, in their efforts to instigate administrative reforms and modernization, had abolished the minor Kurdish states and replaced the ruling families with provincial appointees. Such policies with foreign intervention made a significant impact on the social and political organization of the Kurdish groups.

The immediate result was chaos and a significant increase in looting and raids. The inability of the later Qajars to impose central power and authority created a state of lawlessness. The breakdown of the traditional organizations and the lasting insecurity resulted in the emergence of local Sufi leaders, or holy men, locally known as shaikhs. A phenomenon more popular among the ethnic Kurds, a shaikh is not an orthodox religious leader but is usually associated with the dervish or Sufi orders. Their followers believe in their magical and miraculous powers. Certain communal acts, including cutting one's flesh with swords and swallowing broken glass and fire, have been practiced among them for centuries. These shaikhs were and still are revered by different tribes and have deliberately kept themselves away from tribal loyalties. By the end of the nineteenth century, following the breakdown of the traditional power structures, the shaikhs emerged as the main political leaders of the Kurdish communities.

Another direct result of the breakdown of the power of prominent families such as the Ardalans was the emergence of lesser chiefs at lower levels. The Kurds never stopped making claims about their lost states, and the concept of an independent Kurdistan that emerged in the twentieth century always included mention of these Kurdish states to legitimize Kurdish claims to their own homeland. Another consequence was the emergence of the last confederacies, including the Shakaks, the second-largest Kurdish confederacy in Iran, which played a significant role in Kurdish uprisings in Iran in the early twentieth century. Their rise despite the fact that all other tribal confederacies were declining at the time is related to their significance as border tribes against the Ottomans. They were directly supported by the Iranians to successfully invade Ottoman territories in the late nineteenth century. As a reward, and also to stop them from attacking Iranian territories, they were appointed governors of the border territories. They grew prosperous and remained a major political force in the twentieth century.

The existence of a large group of nontribal Kurds at the beginning of the twentieth century was a distinguishing feature of the ethnic Kurds. Nontribal Kurds were usually tenants, laborers, and sharecroppers with little land. They relied on the protection of the tribal Kurds, who generally owned land and rented it out to others. However, tribal affiliation did not always guarantee protection, and intertribal conflict caused many nontribal Kurds to seek help or protection from groups other than their own. Movement between groups was easy and possible, and at times many nontribal Kurds would join the prosperous tribes and vice versa. The settlements also created an educated intelligentsia aware of the political movements of the time.

The Khamseh Confederacy

The Khamseh was another major confederacy in the nineteenth century that lost most of its influence due to the events of the early 1900s. The Khamseh (Arabic for "five together") was a federation of five tribes of pastoral nomads in the province of Fars in southern Iran. The five tribes were Persian-, Arabic-, and Turkish-speaking. They included the Persian Basseri; Arabs; and the Turkish-speaking Ainalu, Baharlu, and Nafar. Traditionally they migrate semiannually across the Zagros Mountains between the lowlands close to the Persian Gulf and the high summer pastures on the Iranian plateau. The confederation was formed in the late nineteenth century to counter the power of the Qashqa'i. The Khamseh territory bordered the Boir Ahmadi area, and Kuhgiluya Lurs and some Qashqa'i groups migrated through it. In the early twentieth century in the Fars region, the Khamseh allied themselves with the Qashqa'i and the Bakhtiyari groups and played a major part in the political upheavals. However, after the success of the Constitutional Revolution and the following turmoil, the tribal rivalries, particularly between the Qashqa'i and Khamseh chiefs, divided the alliance and reduced their influence.

Basseri members of the Khamseh confederation are Persian-speaking. They practiced pastoral nomadism and migrated within the Fars province, with close ties to Shiraz. They regarded their migratory route as their territory and resisted claims by other groups to these territories. The coordination and allocation of the migratory route were a function of their khan. He devised elaborate schedules and instructed the lesser chiefs and headmen after consultation with other prominent and influential members. Households consisted of extended family and flocks, usually sheep. The members of different households were not necessarily related through male ancestry and included other relatives and a few outsiders. In times of conflict a household could simply move away and join another camp. Problems were solved locally and through the elders or headmen.

Most animal products were allocated to their own use. Each migratory camp had several herding units. The numbers of the tents in the camps were fewer in the winters and increased in other seasons. Many were settling down in nearby villages by the early twentieth century, and a close bond existed between the nomads and their settled kin. Their allegiances were to powerful chiefs and did not necessarily entail common descent. Each camp normally had a headman, who most likely inherited the position but was chosen by consensus and recognized by the Basseri paramount chief and the state authorities. An elaborate migration rite was popular among them, and they paid little attention to orthodox religious practices and preferred local shrines to mosques.

Conclusion

Despite major changes by the early 1900s, tribal and ethnic identities remained relatively strong, and the tribes remained armed, which made them viable military forces capable of threatening government authority. The Qajar rulers were weak and had lost effective control. Many armed tribal groups affected by unemployment and changing economic trends in the surrounding towns and villages used their arms for banditry. These depredations were sometimes carried out with help from government officials to compensate for the tribes' losses and also to deliberately create disorder in border areas especially against the Ottomans. Many tribal groups also suffered abuse by government agents, who increased taxation in order to compensate for loss of revenue. Many Turkmen groups who later sought residency in Russia migrated due to such pressures from government agents.

The most significant event of the early twentieth century was the demand for a modern form of government that led to the Constitutional Revolution (1905–1909). The events transformed the country but at the beginning had little effect on the tribes. The tribal response to the government always depended on the strength or weakness of the central authorities. The upheavals and the subsequent constitutional movement were no exception. Once the movement started, the inability of the government to deal with it was viewed by most tribal groups as another period of weakness that could be taken advantage of. Indeed, shortly before and throughout the movement and after its success, raids by many tribal groups increased. Insurgencies were also carried out by many, including Turkmen groups that revolted and engaged in extensive attacks and raids in the northern territories. Though their motive was very likely looting, one demand by their ilkhan in an attempt to negotiate a peace treaty was that the shah discard the constitution. Another group opposing the reformists was the Shahsevan confederacy. Like the Turkmen groups, it saw the new social order as a threat to its power base.

On the other hand, some tribes such as the Bakhtiyari became strong supporters of the constitutional movement and the liberal nationalists. They provided military assistance when needed. Support or opposition of the movement was primarily based on the ideology of the tribal chiefs and how modern or educated they were. For example, the Bakhtiyari khan, Samsam al-Saltaneh, who was studying in France, came back to Iran in 1908 to help the liberal nationalists and, once the liberals came under attack, provided armed support to the reformists. With the subsequent success of the constitutionalists, he managed to guarantee high positions for the Bakhtiyari elite in the new constitutional government. The tribe was permitted to keep the tax it had collected for the previous year and also received a portion of military tax revenue. The Qajars were Turkic in origin, so several Turkish-speaking tribes supported them against liberal reformists. Azerbaijan itself became the major battleground in opposing the absolutists and fought fiercely in favor of the liberal reformists and the new constitution. The events in Azerbaijan, Bakhtiyari support of the reformists, and the participation of the religious minorities were very important. All these factors, along with support from religious leaders and some dissident clergy, guaranteed the success of the most important event of the first half of the twentieth century—the Constitutional Revolution.

Timeline

1852	Nasir al-Din Shah survived an assassination attempt.
1857	After a failed attempt to regain Herat, the shah was forced by the British to recognize Afghan independence.
1861	Iran lost the province of Merv to the British in Afghanistan.
1873	Nasir al-Din Shah started his first European journey.
1878	The shah traveled to Russia and asked for Russia's help in setting up a Cossack Brigade in Iran.
1879	The first modern police force was formed with help from Austria. The Cossack Brigade under the command of Russian officers started functioning.
1888	Sir Henry Drummond Wolf arrived in Iran from England and began obtaining economic concessions.
1896	Nasir al-din Shah was assassinated.
1897	The Society of Learning was formed by leading intellectuals in Tehran and attracted many prominent supporters.

1904   The first national library was founded in Tehran.

Significant People, Places, and Events

Alliance Israelite Universelle: The society was founded in Paris in
    1860 for the protection and improvement of Jewish life in general. It
    later expanded to North Africa, Eastern Europe, the Middle East, and
    Asia Minor.

Basseri tribes: Iranian nomadic tribes of south Persia. They were united
    with some Arab and Turkish tribes in the late nineteenth century and
    formed the confederation of Khamseh. They are Persian-speaking,
    tent-dwelling pastoral nomads who migrate through the Fars region.

Kurdistan: A province in Iran, it comprises the mountainous area from
    Kirmanshah to Lake Urmia and contains both Turkish and Kurdish
    populations.

Kurds (Carduchi, Cyrtii): The Kurds are mainly in the northwest in
    Iranian Kurdistan, the mountainous region of southeast Turkey,
    northeastern Iraq, and parts of Russia as well as Syria. They have two
    main languages belonging to the northwestern Iranian group of the
    Indo-European family of languages with many dialects.

Lazarists: A congregation of secular priests with religious vows
    founded by Saint Vincent de Paul in France in the early seventeenth
    century. They carried out charity work aimed at assisting the poor.
    They expanded and carried out missionary work in a number of
    countries, including Iran.

Luri: An archaic dialect derived from New Persian and spoken by the
    Luri tribes in Iran. It is closely related to the Kurdish language. The
    term applies to both the language and the people.

Luristan: A province located in western Iran, the area has been home to
    Luri groups for thousands of years. The inhabitants are mainly Luri
    and Bakhtiyari, and the area has been home to many groups,
    including ancient Kassites.

Lurs: An Indo-Iranian group, they occupy western and southwestern
    Iran, and some still live as nomads. Their language is closely related
    to Kurdish, and Kurdish sources as late as the sixteenth century name
    them as a Kurdish tribe.

Nasir al-Din Shah (1831–1896): He started his reign in 1848 and
    almost bankrupted the treasury and the court with his expensive
    trips to Europe and luxurious lifestyle. His autocratic rule resulted in
    his assassination in 1896.

PARSIS OF INDIA: The Zoroastrian community of India. They left Iran around the eighth century A.D. to escape persecution in Iran. They maintained a prosperous community in India and in the late nineteenth and early twentieth centuries helped the Zoroastrian community in Iran.

PISH-E KUHI: The name is applied to a region and also Luri and Kurdish tribes inhabiting the area. The name means "in front of the mountain."

PUSHT-E KUHI: The name is applied to a region and also Luri and Kurdish tribes inhabiting the area. The name means "behind the mountain."

SHAHILU: The most prominent family among the Qashqa'i belonging to the Amaleh group. The chief of the Qashqa'i confederation is usually chosen from the Shahilu family.

SULTAN ABDULHAMID: The last Ottoman sultan. Born in 1842, he was removed by the Ottoman senate under pressure from the group called the "Young Turks." He reigned from 1876 to 1909. He was fluent in Persian and Arabic and had extensive relations with the Qajar kings.

Bibliography

Abrahamian, Ervand. *Iran Between Two Revolutions.* Princeton, NJ: Princeton University Press, 1982.

Avery, P., G. R. G. Hambly, and C. Melville, eds. *The Cambridge History of Iran,* Vol. 7: *From Nadir Shah to the Islamic Republic.* Cambridge: Cambridge University Press, 1991.

Beck, Lois. *The Qashqa'i of Iran.* New Haven, CT: Yale University Press, 1986.

Burke, Edmund, III. *Struggle and Survival in the Modern Middle East.* Berkeley: University of California Press, 1993.

Issawi, Charles. *The Economic History of Iran, 1800–1914.* Chicago: University of Chicago Press, 1971.

Tapper, Richard. *Frontier Nomads of Iran: A Political and Social History of the Shahsevan.* Cambridge: Cambridge University Press, 1997.

Twentieth-century Iran

CHAPTER SIX

Reform and Counter-Reform

The Constitutional Revolution

ON DECEMBER 30, 1906, MUZAFFAR AL-DIN SHAH QAJAR SIGNED A royal proclamation granting approval for the formation of a constitutional monarchy and a National Assembly in Iran. The constitution was based on European models and limited the absolutist powers of the shah. It called for a parliament with elected members that included male representatives from all groups, including the religious minorities. The movement was a success for the intelligentsia and modernism in general. The promoters who drafted the constitution were influenced by European thinkers and modern ideas of state, nationalism, liberalism, and secularism. After many confrontations and a civil war, a civil and criminal code based on European examples with some reservations replaced the ancient Islamic codes, although a clause in the constitution stated that all legislation should comply with the Islamic laws. Some limitations existed, but on the whole citizens of any ethnic or religious affiliation were recognized as citizens with equal rights. The only groups excluded from full participation in the social and political life of the country were women and followers of the Babi/Baha'i faiths. The latter were not recognized as legitimate citizens of the country as long as they practiced their faith. Women were barred from the electoral process, and the family codes remained with little change within the domain of Islam.

The constitutional movement was the culmination of a series of protests that had started in the 1890s. Beginning in the middle of the nineteenth century, the idea of change first arose with respect to the administration of the state but soon covered all aspects of life. The population increase, from around six million at the beginning of the century to ten million at the end, was also a factor. New classes emerged, and there were reformists and dissidents in religious circles. Ideas about women's rights circulated, and modern financial institutions such as banks were sought and established. The reformists were also influenced by the changes and reforms instigated by the Ottomans, such as the *tanzimat* reforms that protected Ottoman citizens despite their religious or ethnic origins. In fact, some of the earliest newspapers that discussed such issues were published in Istanbul and then smuggled into Iran.

The inability of the Qajars to wage significant wars meant decades of peace without major extraterritorial conflicts. Extensive trade with Russia, the Ottomans, India, Britain, and other European countries created a new class of merchants who traveled extensively. This group was among the first instigators of modern ideas. The presence of reform-minded courtiers, such as the legendary secular prime minister Amir Kabir, also boasted reformist ideas. He was responsible for creating modern institutions, including an institute of technology. The emergence of secret societies with political and often radical agendas and connections to similar groups in Russia and Turkey was important too. The participation of many royal princes and princesses in secret societies, some with socialist tendencies, helped the movement. The changes brought different groups together, and some educated non-Muslim Iranians emerged as the principal leaders.

Malkum Khan, of Armenian descent and a key figure in the dispersal of modern ideas as the founder of the popular newspaper *Qanun* (Law), was a product of such changes. His father had nominally converted to Islam and prospered in the nineteenth century. In the service of both the British and the Iranian governments and educated in Paris, Malkum founded a secret society that later became associated with the Freemasons. He made a fortune as a middleman and had a reputation for dubious business practices. He was in contact with a number of key liberal figures, including a reformist Iranian ambassador to the Ottoman court, and published extensively on the advantages of a constitution and modern legal systems. The ambassador persuaded Nasir al-Din Shah to visit Iraq and Europe. No Iranian monarch had visited another country before, and there was opposition from many sources, including the clergy.

The shah's first trip outside Iran was to Iraq, to visit the holy shrines. He was very impressed with the reforms instigated by the Ottoman governor of Iraq. He appointed his ambassador to Iraq as the prime minister and ordered some reforms. The prime minister sought the support of the British in his attempts to modernize, raise funds, and guarantee the territorial integrity of Iran against the Russians in the north. In the process, with support from Malkum, he granted a major commercial concession in 1872 to the famed Baron Julius de Reuter, a naturalized British citizen. The concessions were enormous and were labeled by the British, including Lord Curzon, "as the most complete grant ever made of control over its resources by any country to a foreigner" (Avery, Hambly, and Melville, 1991, p. 187). The concessions created massive opposition, including protests from the Russians, who saw the Reuter concession as a major victory for the British against their own interests.

The situation worsened when the shah decided to visit Russia. The clergy were outraged at the prospect of a Muslim king visiting Christian territory. He traveled to Russia but was forced to leave behind his favorite concubine and all other female companions at the border in 1873. Under no circumstances would the clergy permit Muslim women to visit Christian territory. Flyers circulated in the city proclaiming that a Jew, Baron Reuter, was to be in charge of the country's affairs and that a railroad was to be built going through the holy shrine in south Tehran. Clergy proclaimed the new railway to be the work of Satan, bringing corruption to the Muslim lands. The prime minister was removed from office and later died under suspicious circumstances. The shah was pressured by the Russians as well, and the only major outcome of his trip to Russia was the formation of a Persian Cossack Brigade in 1879 with help from Russia. This was the only modern military force in the country until the early 1920s.

The Reuter concession triggered opposition that culminated in a protest against the tobacco concession of 1890. Most of these concessions were granted to finance the court and the shah's trips to Europe. The shah granted complete monopoly over the production, sale, and export of all tobacco in Iran to another British subject. Tobacco was widely popular in Iran and was consumed by all, including females. The protests brought together many different groups, including the charismatic and internationally known Muslim reformist Sayyid Jamal al-Din Asad Abadi (al-Afghani, 1839–1897), Iranian merchants, secular modernists, and radical elements. A religious decree (fatwa) banning tobacco consumption by all Muslims was proclaimed by the highest-ranking clergy. All over the country people broke their water pipes. Even the women in the royal harem refused to consume tobacco or serve it even to the shah himself. The use of the telegraph, installed by Malkum years earlier, enabled the coordinating committee to be in touch with supporters in Europe, Turkey, and Russia and even the Shi'ite clergy in Iraq. By 1892, after many demonstrations, shootings, and a few deaths, the government was forced to cancel the concession.

The boycott was the first successful mass movement in the country and spread to most major cities. It was overwhelmingly anti-British and increased

Russia's influence in Iran at the expense of the British. Furthermore, it did not end after the tobacco concession was canceled. Mostly from outside the country, Afghani kept writing articles in Malkum's newspaper, which was published in London and smuggled to Iran. The shah and despotism remained the target of many attacks. Afghani later was invited by the last Ottoman sultan to go to Turkey. At the shah's request, the sultan stopped Afghani from publishing material directly attacking the shah. At the same time, the Ottomans financed a pan-Islamic circle in Istanbul and promoted Ottoman-backed Islamic ideas. Included in the new circle were two Azali Babis in exile.

The antishah activities prompted the shah to ask the Ottomans for the detention and return to Iran of three activists, including the Babis. Afghani intervened to guarantee their release and intensified his opposition. In 1895 he was visited by an old and devoted servant who had been released after years of imprisonment in Iran due to his activism. The servant received secret instructions and went back to Iran. In May 1896, on the anniversary of his reign, Nasir al-Din Shah was assassinated by Afghani's servant, Mirza Reza Kirmani, in a holy shrine in south Tehran. For the first time a shah had been murdered because of ideas relating to liberty, equality, and democracy. Thirteen years later, on July 31, 1909, Shaikh Fazlullah Nuri, a very high-ranking member of the clergy in Tehran and a member of one of the most prominent families in the country, was publicly executed by a revolutionary tribunal. He was charged with anticonstitutionalist activities. The execution took place publicly, with masses of people cheering and celebrating. In a matter of thirteen years, the two most important symbols of authority in Iran for centuries, the shah and the grand shaikh, had both been eliminated by a new class of citizens demanding the superiority of the rights of people over those with earthly and divine powers. The end of the nineteenth century in Iran coincided with the rise of secularism; nationalism; and challenges to traditional sources and concepts of leadership, individual rights, and communal organizations and identity.

The Emergence of Nationalism

At the turn of the twentieth century the majority of Iranians lived in rural areas. Most were peasants, tribesmen, and urban laborers and were illiterate. Politically inarticulate and bound to tradition, many resented the foreign presence that had become so visible because it was affecting their livelihood and was viewed by many as a threat to Islam. Tribal loyalties were as dubious as before. The Shahsevan, who had fought the constitutionalists and therefore supported the Russians, did not hesitate to fight the Russians once they had occupied Iran in the north. The Khamseh and Qashqa'i, who had been fighting each other, formed a coalition. Nasir al-Din Shah ruled for almost fifty years and until his assassination in 1896 remained relatively powerful, despite many serious threats to his rule. Most disturbances in his lifetime were social, political, or religious-political in nature rather than extraterritorial. For example, the Babi/Baha'i movement, which started as a continuation of an earlier sectarian religious reformist movement (Shaykhy), ended up as a new religion. Its members demanded equal rights for women, equality, and access to legal systems and rejected the existing clerical institutions altogether. They also sought to have a world religion open to all, with extensive missionary work and international networks. It was a goal they would accomplish by the late twentieth century.

Nasir al-din Shah, despite having some tendency toward reform earlier in his reign, in the end favored despotism. He kept borrowing money from Europeans to finance his trips to Europe and his extravagant lifestyle. His son and heir, Muzaffar al-Din Shah, was forced to spend a great deal of the national revenue paying off his father's debts. The new shah was weak, suffered from ill heath, and like his father kept borrowing money from Europeans and giving concessions in exchange in order to pay for his court and the cost of his trips to Europe. In 1901 he gave William Knox D'arcy, a British citizen, the right to drill for oil in all of Iran for sixty years, except for the northern provinces. The contract would haunt Iranian politics for decades to come. The Russian civil unrest of 1905 had important political and economic consequences as well because Iran was involved in a large volume of trade with Russia. The upheaval in Russia led to high inflation, price hikes, and high levels of unemployment in Iran. Another effect of the Russian crisis was the export of revolutionary ideas to Iran, mainly Azerbaijan and the Caspian territory. The shah was sympathetic to the liberals but was ill most of the time, and his unpopular prime minister censored all of his correspondence and kept him mostly in the dark.

The social and intellectual forces of the revolution had been developing for a long time, but they were translated into action in 1905 when two respectable sugar merchants were flogged publicly. They were accused of price speculations in the market. This punishment was a response to public pressure in order to pacify civil unrest. However, the public saw the actions as settling scores, creating scapegoats, and paying lip service to the real causes of the disastrous economic policies of the late Qajars. Public flogging was a common form of punishment, and never before had the public questioned its merits. The incident was extensively used by the intelligentsia, merchants, and the more educated public to attack the whole system of justice, or lack of it. Underground political societies had already existed in Tehran and most major cities. The activists started dispersing flyers, and in a short period of time everyone was demanding the establishment of a House of Justice. Street demonstrations followed, and mosques became the main centers for political gatherings and discussions. Many proclamations were made; some important members of the clergy supported the movement. Leaflets and flyers were distributed daily. Women participated extensively in public marches and gatherings. Women's secret societies already existed, and more emerged; their members printed flyers, made proclamations, and pointed out the pitiful state of women in Iran.

By the time the movement spread to the provinces, particularly to the relatively progressive Azerbaijan, the demand for the House of Justice had been replaced by no less than a demand for a constitutional monarchy. Despite many leaflets and proclamations about the virtues of a constitution,

Kurdish women at a meeting to demand equal rights, twentieth century. As a sign of protest, some women no longer wear the traditional face veil. (Hulton-Deutsch Collection/Corbis)

the majority had very little idea of what a constitution was. The clergy at first were reluctant, but once the mosques had become the meeting places for the constitutionalists, they joined in. One major characteristic of the clergy supporting the movement was their ideological diversity. They consisted of several high-ranking orthodox Shi'ites, but also included were several powerful dissident clergy with mainly Babi and some Baha'i sympathies. There were also freethinkers and Freemasons, all dressed as legitimate Shi'ite clergy, who gave sermons and elaborated on the advantages of social democracy and a constitution.

The speed with which the movement grew surprised everyone. In a period of one year, beginning in 1905, several major protests and strikes took place. Each protest attracted more people, and by summer 1906 the protesters were demanding a parliament with elected representatives. As a counterattack, the royalists publicly accused the movement's leaders of being Babi. Both the Babi and Baha'i were regarded as heretical, and adherence to heresy was and still is punishable by death. Many reformists, fearful for their lives, moved into a holy shrine in south Tehran. They received unprecedented financial and moral support from the people, merchants, Ottomans, and the British.

After many more strikes and arrests, the death of a young theology student intensified the movement, and more deaths followed. Several of the leaders and their entourages were forced to seek sanctuary at a mosque. By this time a new slogan had been added to the ones used in demonstrations. For the first time "long live the nation of Iran" became as important as "God is great" and other usual Muslim slogans. This was the first time that Iranians had identified themselves as belonging to a nation. "The two main religious sanctuaries used by the constitutionalists in Tehran and Qum became known as 'freedom schools,' with preachers talking about international events, new political ideas, the advantages of a constitutional government, and the rights of a modern nation" (Afary, 1996, p. 55). The authorities took more action and attacked the sanctuary in Tehran, an act contrary to the custom of respecting the sanctity of sanctuaries.

At this point the constitutionalists decided to seek the support of the British as a measure of safety. Fifty of the constitutionalists moved into the British embassy's vast summer compound in north Tehran. In two months thousands more people had moved in and sought sanctuary there. They were mostly financed by wealthy merchants from the bazaar, with some public help. The refugees were organized by leaders from various guilds in Tehran but included people from all walks of life. Students from the modern secular Institute of Technology joined theology students, members of secret societies now coming into the open, and radical intellectuals. Outside the embassy compound, hundreds of women protested daily, lending support to their male relatives inside. They offered their gold and jewelry to support the refugees and distributed flyers and newly published newspapers. The constitutionalists spent twenty-three days at the compound.

The royalists had no choice but to accept the reformists' demands. A royal proclamation was issued consenting to the formation of a parliament. The proclamation was rejected and altered several times. The earlier drafts did not incorporate the phrase *nation of Iran* and called for the formation of an "Islamic consultative parliament," an idea pushed by the conservative clergy. There was conflict between the clergy and secular constitutionalists, who insisted that the parliament must be called a national parliament and not an Islamic one. Reports arrived from Baku that the radical social democrats were ready to attack Iran. A threat by the Persian soldiers of the Cossack Brigade that they would join the revolutionaries left the authorities no choice. Muzaffar al-Din Shah surrendered, and after some discussions a national consultative *majlis* (parliament) was granted. The shah died a few days later, and his son Muhammad Ali assumed the throne. The ratification was the first major victory for the secular constitutionalists and the beginning of a series of confrontations between liberals, radicals, conservatives, secular activists, tribes, religious and ethnic minorities, women, religious leaders, and the new shah.

The First National Assembly

After the shah granted the constitution, a committee was formed to draft an electoral law. Once elections were carried out, the constitution was drafted and approved by the new parliament. The constitution itself was developed quickly and was primarily based on Belgian and French examples. Though it was stated that the document would follow the Shi'i and the Islamic Shari'a, in reality it established a framework for secular legislation and jurisdiction. This finally ended the clergy's monopoly over education and the legal system. The first National Assembly lasted only for twenty months before its violent closure. During the short period of time that it operated, it managed to accomplish a number of major tasks and took a strong stand against European intervention in Iranian affairs. Delegates from Azerbaijan and members of the National Revolutionary Committee and the previously secret societies were instrumental in pushing forward much of the new legislation, to the dismay of the clergy. The Qajar elite and courtiers were also heavily involved in drafting legislation.

The electoral law was the first to be drafted and became a subject of discontent. The country was divided into provinces and departments for electoral purposes, and six classes of voters were assigned: princes/Qajars, clergy, nobles, notables, merchants, and guild members. One of the qualifications for voting was relatively substantial land ownership that could exclude many tribal members, among others. The tribal leaders protested and also objected to the requirement of the ability to read and write in Persian as a condition for election to the parliament. Proportional representation was also a problem; too many representatives were proposed for Tehran, and other areas, including Azerbaijan, wanted more representation. Qajar tribes were recognized as a category by themselves, but other tribes on the whole were not recognized as specific categories. A request was made by the Bakhtiyari, Qashqa'i, and Luri leaders to have a delegate of their own. Though a proposal was discussed, nothing came out of it.

Another major battle was between the orthodox and the dissident clergy. The former wished to block the latter's participation in the coming elections. Royalists and the Qajar elite wanted to maintain the shah's control over the army, while other delegates wished to limit the shah's control. Secularists opposed the presence of the clergy, and factionalism became strife. In the end compromises were made, changes were introduced in the electoral law, and the extent of the property ownership required for qualification as a voter was reduced. Altogether there were thirty-one articles in the code. Religious minorities were all included and would choose their own representatives. However, Babis/Baha'is and women were excluded. Once the electoral law was passed, the first parliamentary elections proceeded. Despite the many conflicts and major problems, the first elections were peaceful, orderly, and straight. Many well-educated and committed reformers were elected. However, the new assembly had 156 deputies, of whom 60 were from Tehran; such overrepresentation created discontent. One of the shah's sons-in-law became the first leader of the parliament. Next, a committee was assigned to produce the fundamental law, or the constitution. When it was composed, the new constitution, with fifty-one articles, limited the powers of the shah and delegated most of the monarch's powers to ministers responsible to the elected delegates of the parliament. The new king, Muhammad Ali Shah, swore to protect the constitution and even approved a longer supplementary fundamental law later; however, he was plotting from the start to restore the monarch's lost powers.

Divisions among the delegates to the first National Assembly existed, but they were mainly ideological and political. Though the clergy tried to impose an Islamic framework, in the end they were overwhelmed by the modern secularists. The constitution was drafted by members of the secular elite who had been educated mostly in Europe, had been active in the political life of the country, and were experienced politicians. Their familiarity with modern political systems gave them an advantage over the clergy. In the first parliament "twenty-one percent of the delegates belonged to the elite and landowning families; 25 percent came from the ranks of clergy; 26 percent were members of trade guilds" (Afary, 1996, p. 69). No group was homogeneous; and there were aristocratic landowners with socialist ideas and clergy with social democratic tendencies along with conservatives, liberals, and moderates in every group. Some landowners became hostile to legislation aimed at land reform and increased taxation, while others supported such actions. Soon the parliament was divided between the radicals, conservatives, moderates, and liberals. The radicals were mostly members of the secret Organization of Social Democrats, with ties to Azerbaijan and the Caucasus. Their presence alienated the more conservative elements to such an extent that some eventually switched to the royalists and the anticonstitutionalist camp. The public was also intensely involved through publications and public meetings. Both radicals and moderates had several publications, while the secularists and the clergy constantly attacked and accused each other.

Absent from the first assembly were religious minorities, with one exception. The new legislation, with some limitations, had guaranteed personal freedoms and rights and equality before the law for all. Included in the codes were the rights of the minorities to have elected representatives in the parliament, as proposed in the electoral law. The clergy on the whole objected to the codes with respect to religious minorities but did not succeed in eliminating them. As a result, the Armenians, Jews, and Zoroastrians were apologetically asked by the leaders of the national assembly not to participate in the elections in order to avoid trouble from the clergy. Jews who had already elected their representative withdrew for fear of reprisals, and the Armenians followed suit. After negotiations, two prominent members of the Muslim clergy were installed as their representatives in the parliament. The secret society that had advocated religious pluralism earlier in the revolution went underground again. However, Zoroastrians resisted, and, backed by the strong pre-Islamic sentiments of the many nationalists and the brilliant maneuverings of a prominent Zoroastrian, they sent their first elected representative to the parliament. Archaeological expeditions by Europeans had shed new light on the pre-Islamic history of the region, and strong sentiments existed among many in favor of the pre-Islamic civilizations of the past, including Zoroastrianism.

The clergy also objected to the passing of bills "guaranteeing compulsory public education and free press and regarded these as anti-Islamic" (Avery, Hambly, and Melville, 1991, p. 204). However, the bills were passed and led to the flourishing of the press and modern literature in Iran. The modern press that emerged published discussions of all major social and political issues, including women's rights. Women's councils and secret societies had existed in all major cities since the early Babi period, and their elite members participated in all major events. Following the success of the constitution, representatives of these groups presented several demands, both to the public and to the National Assembly, to improve women's status. However, they did not succeed in their efforts to obtain equality and remained excluded from the electoral process; nor did they gain any advances in the family codes.

One major debate in the parliament was about how to bridge the gap between the religious law and the modern legal codes. Once the clergy realized that there could be no compromise, many joined the anticonstitutionalist camp. The influential Shaikh Fazlullah Nuri emerged as the most prominent anticonstitutionalist clergyman outside the parliament. The representatives from the guilds tended to be the most reliable and consistent among the first parliamentarians, but even they were divided on the issue of the compatibility of the religious laws with the modern codes. The separation of state and religion became the most important debate of the first parliament, but the issue could not be resolved.

Azerbaijan

At the time Azerbaijan was one of the most progressive provinces in Iran, with extensive links to Russia and Turkey. Major economic, social, and political ties existed between the three. Radical elements from Baku and Turkey had already established themselves in the province. Azerbaijan became the first province in which the opposition between the secularists and the clergy culminated in direct confrontation. During the first parliamentary election local assemblies *(anjuman)* were created in every city to oversee the electoral process. Many continued to function after the elections were over, including one in Tabriz. Many people turned to the assemblies instead of the traditional clergy for their complaints. The clergy saw this trend as a threat and tried to bribe the assembly members. They refused, and one high-profile clergyman, the leader of the Friday prayer, was expelled from Tabriz. Similar actions were taken in other cities, and many prominent clergymen were expelled because of their stand against the constitution and reforms. Azerbaijan members of parliament remained in touch with the local assembly in Tabriz which had opened an office in Tehran as well. This connection and the role Azerbaijan played in the following upheavals proved invaluable to the success of the Constitutional Revolution.

The new shah was determined to get rid of the parliament. He had the support of the Russian Cossack Brigade; some tribal leaders who were disappointed because the constitution did not grant them specific privileges; dissatisfied constitutionalists; and many prominent members of the clergy, some of whom had previously been in the constitutionalist camp. He acted against the new legislation, ignored warnings by the parliament and Tabriz assembly, and refused to sign statements declaring loyalty to the new constitution. His supporters argued that the constitution was illegal in a Muslim society and had to be reversed. The delegates from Tabriz were alarmed. Mass demonstrations broke out in Tabriz and then Tehran and other cities. The scale of the protests forced the shah to temporarily accept the terms. However, he insisted that all new legislation should conform to the Islamic codes. After a failed attempt on his life, the shah first tried a counterattack against the national assembly in an effort to arrest members, which failed; shortly afterward he managed to stage a successful coup. A series of confrontations finally led to the bombing and closure of the parliament by the royalists in 1908. The Russian commander of the Cossack Brigade, who was responsible for the attack on the parliament, later declared martial law and became the military governor of Tehran. Many radicals were arrested, and some prominent leaders of the movement, including well-known constitutionalists, were executed. Others fled, and Tehran fell to the royalists, but uprisings and civil war in Azerbaijan changed the balance of power.

Azerbaijan nationalists and the radical elements in the Tabriz assembly were greatly responsible for the original success of the constitutionalists against the shah. Despite the existence of Russian Azerbaijan and Russia's attempts to attract their loyalty, they supported the nationalistic movement in Iran. The success of liberal nationalistic ideas in Azerbaijan was due to a number of factors. In the early twentieth century Azerbaijan was a prosperous cosmopolitan province with many schools and social services offered by many missionary groups. Azerbaijan, more than any other province in the country, was in contact with the outside world, particularly with both the liberal and the radical movements in Russia and Transcaucasia. Its people also had extensive connections in the Ottoman territories, were exposed to political Turkish literature, and were aware of the changes and the reformist ideas there. Tabriz was at the forefront of the tobacco protest and had taken the most revolutionary actions with respect to land and other reforms. The Azerbaijan people staged strikes and mass protests in support of the supplementary laws and helped obtain ratification despite opposition by Nuri and the shah. This exposed them to the shah's hostility and to the dispatch of Shahsevan tribes, who led a series of attacks and plundered several areas in Azerbaijan.

The attacks led to the consolidation of a militant group called Mujahedin to defend Azerbaijan. The Mujahedin group was a branch of the Organization of Social Democrats and played a significant role in defending the constitution. It became a model organization for others to follow, and soon similar groups were formed in other provinces. They adopted terror as a tool and were responsible for the assassination of the anticonstitutionalist prime minister in 1907. Around the same time, the Anglo-Russian treaty was ratified in St. Petersburg and divided Iran into three zones of influence, with the north and south under Russian and British influence, respectively, and a neutral central zone. The two powers were not to interfere either commercially or politically in each other's zones. The agreement was meant to curtail the German influence that was becoming more pronounced in the region. The treaty enraged Iranian nationalists, and as Russia's influence grew more, they openly started supporting the shah.

After the opening of the first parliament, the Azerbaijan deputies in Tehran formed the core of the liberal nationalist faction. One brilliant and charismatic member, Taghizadeh, became an important and influential politician of the first half of the twentieth century. They also enjoyed the support of militants in Baku and Tabriz, and the delegates from Azerbaijan in Tehran threatened to call on those supporters each time the constitutionalists came under severe attack by the shah. Muhammad Ali Shah had lived in Tabriz, the seat of the crown prince, for many years, and his brutal and self-serving policies had alienated the people of Azerbaijan. After the closure of the parliament, resistance in most provinces, including Tehran, died quickly. However, the Tabriz assembly chose resistance, and the city came under a siege that lasted more than ten months. The defending crowd of 10,000, led by two extraordinary men, Sattar Khan and Baqer Khan, fought the government forces, which ranged in number from 15,000 to as many as 30,000. Included in the fighting force were Armenians, Georgians, and Caucasians. Militants also arrived from Russian territories to support the movement. They demanded a liberal nationalist government and the opening of the parliament for the benefit of the nation of Iran. After the failure of the government forces, the Russians intervened to protect the Europeans inside Tabriz. Their troops finally entered the city at the end of April 1909 and effectively took over the city. The Russians appointed an anticonstitutionalist governor, which added to the hostility toward the Russians. Russian forces remained in Azerbaijan until the Bolshevik Revolution.

The resistance in Tabriz had inspired similar movements in other parts of the nation. Many of the surviving militants left Tabriz after their defeat and headed to Gilan in the Caspian region. There they joined the local revolutionary armed forces and marched toward Tehran. The Armenian commander of the group, Yephrem Khan, later became a national hero as one of the liberators of Tehran. He became known as the Garibaldi of Iran and was appointed as the police chief of Tehran. Proconstitutionalists in other major cities took arms. Isfahan was occupied by Bakhtiyari forces in support of the constitutional movement, and they also headed for Tehran. The majority of Bakhtiyari supported the constitutionalists, with the exception of one small group, headed by a court appointee from the Hajji Ilkhan faction as the paramount chief of the Bakhtiyari groups.

The Bakhtiyari leader from the ilkhan faction united most of the Bakhtiyari, settled differences with the Arab tribes in the south, and moved forward. Inspired by such actions, revolts happened in many cities, and by the time the constitutionalists arrived in Tehran many royalist groups had already surrendered. Another prominent Bakhtiyari, along with an aristocrat and landowner from Gilan, helped the rebels in Tehran. The two groups from Gilan and Isfahan joined forces just outside Tehran in July 1909. The nationalists already had secured many parts of Tehran, and the shah was forced to take refuge with the Russians. He abdicated and was sent into exile in Russia; his son Ahmad, who was still a child, was made the new king. Five anticonstitutionalists, among them Shaikh Fazululah Nuri, were tried and hanged soon afterward.

Five hundred delegates drawn from the dissolved parliament, the guerrilla forces, merchants, guilds, minorities, the clergy, and tribal groups gathered and announced the formation of a Grand Assembly. A new electoral law was ratified, and some changes were introduced. The new codes abolished representation by class and lowered the property requirement as a condition for voting. They reduced the number of representatives from Tehran from sixty to fifteen and created four seats for the religious minorities. Jews and Zoroastrians each had one seat, and Christian Assyrians and Armenians acquired two seats. The second National Assembly opened for business.

The years between Nasir al-Din Shah's assassination in 1896 and the final success of the constitutional movement in 1909 can be identified as the formative period for the political future of the country. The rise of local assemblies and secret societies was a major achievement because for the first time different groups from different religions, tribes, and classes were joined in struggle toward the same goal. Most of the struggles and contradictions that existed during this period would reemerge at some point during the twentieth century. The clashes between tradition and modernity and despotism and liberty; the forging and reinvention of identities, whether ethnic, religious, or cosmopolitan, all still play a significant role in Iran. The understanding and articulation of new concepts such as democracy, liberty, citizenship, and nationality that started during that period are still going on and are continually under experiment by the reformist movement in the country.

Azerbaijan and the Second National Assembly, 1909–1921

The Second National Assembly opened in November 1909; the deposed shah was secure in exile. The nationalist leaders were rewarded and assigned to major posts. Money was borrowed from the first Iranian National Bank for reconstruction. After many negotiations, the bulk of the Russian troops in the northern territories withdrew. An American banker from New York, Morgan Schuster, was hired to reorganize the finances of the country and the tax and custom departments. He won the confidence of the assembly and Iranians in general and among other reforms managed to generate enough revenue to pay for the establishment of a regular gendarmerie, with Swedish officers in charge, to improve security. The parliament approved the bill in 1911, and by 1914 the Gendarmerie had 200 officers and 7,000 men. Under pressure from both the Russians and the British, its size was reduced during World War I, since it was feared that the Swedish officers might be German sympathizers. Many Swedish officers were sent home, but they came back in 1924 after the war had ended. Reforms were introduced in the Cossack Brigade as well. The brigade had been formed in 1878 under a contract that allowed the Russians to stay as commanders for forty years. The brigade was manned by Iranians, but the officers remained Russians. In 1916 the force was expanded, and the number of the Iranian officers increased to 202, almost twice the number of Russians, but until late 1920 it was still headed by Russian commanders. This unit was dissolved into a regular national army that was formed in 1922 by the war minister Reza Khan.

The parliament remained stormy. The divisions started quickly, and within two years there were two main factions split between the minority Democrats with twenty-seven and the majority Moderates with fifty-three members. The Democrats, survivors of the earlier radical societies, were mostly from the northern provinces, including Azerbaijan, and had strong ties to Baku in Russian Azerbaijan. They included the charismatic Taghizadeh. Outside the parliament the Democrat Party leaned toward socialism, and one of its prominent leaders, Haidar Khan, became the first secretary of the Iranian Communist Party. He had connections with social democrats in Baku. He was Turkish speaking, and his inability to fluently read and write Persian barred him from participating in the parliamentary elections. He was instrumental in setting up the first workers' unions in Iran and had a volunteer armed group. Another very active member of the party, Rasulzadeh, was a Menshevik leader from Baku. He had joined the constitutionalists during the civil war. He remained in Iran and published the popular newspaper *New Iran*.

The paper was a party organ that discussed social reforms and promoted socialism's history and the main ideas of its great thinkers, including Marx. The articles published were very significant. The analysis of the social and political systems of the world presented in the paper became, in one form or another, the dominant ideology accepted by Iranian intellectuals until the 1979 revolution. The Democrats proclaimed that the industrialized West had completed its transition from feudalism to capitalism and was at the stage of imperialism. The backward Eastern countries were subjected to this imperialism. Iran was still at the feudalistic stage. Weak and corrupt governments of the East, including Iran's, were a threat to real independence in their countries because they were incapable of protecting their nations against the superior Western imperialist nations.

The new ideology demanded a strong lower house instead of an upper house. Unconditional extension of the vote to all adult males was requested, in addition to equality for all citizens and free education for all males and females. New legislation to protect labor was proposed, along with state control of religious institutions. *New Iran* became the most popular newspaper in the country. The Democrats promoted their own brand of nationalism that was contrary to the nationalistic views of the moderates. They talked about the unity of the nation, including all groups: Turkic peoples, Persians, Muslims, Christians, and so forth. They were Iranians first; "We Are One Nation" showed up frequently as a headline in *New Iran*. They considered the monarchy to be an obstacle to the rule of the people. Soon most radical elements joined the Democrat Party, including a radical Armenian party. However, one group in the Caucasus, the Iranian Social Democrat Party, continued working with the Russian Bolsheviks.

The Moderates were composed of landed aristocracy and the traditional middle class, merchants, artisans, and clergy. They supported a constitutional monarchy and respect for private property. Their program included supporting the lower middle class by providing financial assistance, enforcing a particular type of education and religious ethics, and defending the society against the anarchists, the atheist Democrats, and Marxists. Their nationalism was very much focused around the idea of maintaining national integrity by getting rid of foreign domination. A clash between the two parties, inside and outside the parliament, was inevitable. The conflict reached its peak when a new prime minister and a new regent had to be elected for the minor king, whose appointed regent had died from natural causes. Armed clashes took place, and violence broke out in the streets. The majority Moderates, with Bakhtiyari support, objected to the candidate proposed by the minority Democrats and chose their own. The situation exploded when a very prominent clergyman who was one of the principal leaders of the constitutional movement was assassinated by Haidar Khan's band. The Moderates employed their own forces and attacked the Democrats, killing some, including a prominent member. The Democrats, with help from another group of Bakhtiyari, replaced the prime minister and appointed their own. The police chief, Yephrem Khan, took immediate action with help from a Bakhtiyari group and ordered the disarming of the clashing forces. Democrats obliged and handed over their arms, but the supporters of the Moderates did not. They barricaded themselves but had to surrender in the end. Both groups insisted that the prosperity of the "nation of Iran" was their main goal and produced extensive material on what constituted a modern nation and how to implement such ideas. The role of the Bakhtiyari elite was crucial at the time, and for a few years it exerted major influence by providing military support to different factions.

Bakhtiyari

With the capital in chaos, the tribal groups took advantage of the inability of the central government to impose security. Turkmen raiding and an uprising in Khurasan was followed by rebellions by the Shahsevan in Azerbaijan and the Kurds in Luristan. The Qashqa'i, Khamseh, Boir Ahmadi, and Kuhgiluya Lurs, Arabs, and Baluchi formed a confederation to oppose the powerful Bakhtiyari, who had become major players in the political affairs of the country. Bakhtiyari involvement and support of the Constitutional Revolution made it the most powerful tribal group in the country. The Bakhtiyari paramount chief became prime minister. His younger brother, one of the liberators of Tehran, exerted great influence and had the backing of Democrats. Bakhtiyari nobles controlled the palace guards, war ministry, and governorship of seven major cities, including Isfahan, Yazd, and Arab-dominated areas in the south. The period from 1911 to 1913 is normally regarded by Iranian historians as having been dominated by the Bakhtiyari. They were also in charge of protecting the oil fields, the properties and installations owned by the Anglo-Persian Oil Company. The anti-Bakhtiyari confederation had the full support of Shaikh Khazal, who had lost prominence to Bakhtiyari. He contemplated attacking Mohammareh with help from Baluchi in Kirman, Boir Ahmadi from Bushire, and the Qashqa'i and Khamseh from Shiraz. The coalition failed due to several factors, including internal feuds among the various tribal leaders and even among various chiefs belonging to the same group. The British reported the whole southern region to be in chaos and pointed out that the central government was totally unable to deal with the situation. In October 1911 British troops entered the region and occupied Shiraz and Isfahan. Bakhtiyari were saved and Shaikh Khazal survived, but southern Iran came under British occupation.

Tribes and the Anglo-Russian Occupation of Iran

Rivalries with other groups have been a constant feature of tribal relations in Iran. One such conflict happened between the Khamseh and Qashqa'i. Qavam Shirazi, of a very prominent family from Shiraz, united the Khamseh group. Earlier he had tried to forge a coalition between the Khamseh, Bakhtiyari, and Qashqa'i. The predominantly Persian-speaking Fars had enjoyed relative calm prior to the upheavals that occurred during and after the constitutional movement. The early constitutional governments were weak, went through many disturbances, and were unable to exert control beyond Tehran. Fars was no exception; the roads became insecure, and banditry increased. With Qavam's help, security improved in the Fars region. The move was welcomed by the British, who needed secure roads for their commercial activities. However, the increasing strength of the Khamseh leader in Shiraz and the Bakhtiyari in Tehran alienated the Qashqa'i leader Solet al-Doleh. The conflicts between the three tribal groups escalated, and another rival Qashqa'i khan joined a Khamseh-Bakhtiyari coalition against Solet. The latter managed to get the support of Boir Ahmadi Lurs, who attacked and dispersed the Khamseh forces. After the initial attack, they remained to continue raiding nearby villages and added to the chaos. Solet also instigated an anti-Semitic riot in Shiraz to demonstrate Qavam al-Molk Shirazi's inability to effectively secure the region. Qavam was forced to seek the support of the

British and moved into their compound. His brother was killed by the Qashqa'i tribesmen, and the situation only calmed under pressure from the British after they took control of the area.

The British occupation of the south and new taxation and custom strategies developed by Morgan Schuster were against the Russian interests. Russia sent troops and occupied the northern territories. It sent an ultimatum to the Iranian government threatening to occupy Tehran unless Iran dismissed Schuster and paid for the occupying Russian troops in the north, among other requests. The Anglo-Russian occupation and the Russian ultimatum created the most serious crisis to be handled by the nationalist government as yet. Massive protests broke out in Tehran; Russian property was attacked all over the country. In one incident 300 veiled women showed up in the parliament armed with handguns and threatened to shoot any deputy who agreed to the ultimatum. The parliament voted "no," but the Bakhtiyari prime minister, the regent, the cabinet, and Yephrem Khan decided that "no to ultimatum" meant occupation of Tehran by the Russians. The police chief moved in and closed the parliament. The second National Assembly was halted due to the Russian threat in December 1911. Many protests followed. Attacks on Russian property and individuals linked to Russians and murders on all sides followed. A few days later the deposed shah was back from exile with the full support of the Russians. He landed in Enzali (Anzali) port while his brother attacked Tehran. Iranian forces, paid by revenues gained from reforms implemented by Schuster, defeated his forces. The ex-shah went back to Russia, and Yephrem Khan was killed during the battles.

The country was now occupied by both the British and the Russians. Morgan Schuster was expelled, and his reforms stopped. He later wrote his account of the events in his famous book *The Strangling of Persia*. Taghizadeh and several very prominent politicians were sent into exile, and many fled to the provinces. Tribal groups were directly dealt with by the British and the Russians, who guarded the roads, guaranteed safety, and put down rebellions. The Russians appointed a major landowner from Gilan as the governor of this very important province. The Bakhtiyari, with the full support of the British, ruled in the south and dominated the government in Tehran. One British officer reporting to his Foreign Office noted that the Bakhtiyari khans had imported into the government system their custom of sharing tribal property.

The third National Assembly started only after the outbreak of World War I in December 1914, at the insistence of the Armenian survivors of the police force and the radical Armenian party Dashnak. They lobbied the guilds and threatened to initiate strikes unless the parliament reopened. The

The Russo-Persian War resulted in the dismissal of the American treasurer general of the Persian government, Morgan W. Schuster, at the demand of Russia. After fierce resistance by the Persians, the Russians captured the battle-scarred city of Tabriz. This photograph shows Persian constitutionalists (who backed up Schuster) in the trench of Maralan, about two miles from Tabriz, resisting the invasion of Russian Cossacks advancing on Tabriz. The second man from the left, in dark costume, is the leader of the constitutionalists, who was captured and hanged by the Russians after the battle. (Underwood and Underwood/Corbis)

parliament refused to take sides in the war and formed a committee of national resistance, including both the Democrats and the Moderates. Russians once again intervened and threatened the resistance committee, which fled to the sanctuary in Qum. After the city was invaded by the Russians, the committee fled again, to Kirmanshah. The province was in chaos due to intensive fights between pro-Ottoman Kurdish groups and the British. The start of the war brought the Germans into the power struggle, and they provided guns and ammunition to several groups. Ottomans supported Germany and in turn invaded Iran in order to fight the British. The resistance committee, despite the upheavals in Kirmanshah, established a Government of National Defense with support from the pro-German Swedish officers in the gendarmerie. An alliance was also formed with the Qashqa'i and Baluchi tribesmen. The two groups were armed with rifles supplied by the Germans. In response, the British armed the Khamseh, Bakhtiyari, and Arabs, led by Shaikh Khazal. A native police force, the South Persia Rifles, supervised and financed by the British and Indian forces, was formed in southern Iran. The National Government in Kirmanshah did not survive the British offensive, and by 1916 it had been crushed, with many members in exile or jail. The German influence was effectively halted as well. The Russian Revolution of 1917 disabled the Russians for a while. The British influence increased, and the pro-British league in the government signed a new treaty with the British. The Anglo-Persian Treaty of 1919 outraged many Iranians, who saw it as a sellout to the British government. It also prompted the Russians to take some action.

The Separatist Movements

Gilan

Despite the chaos, factionalism, and support and arming of tribal groups by foreigners, separatist tendencies did not appear to be significant in Iran at the time, despite the flow of revolutionary thought in Russia and Turkey and separatist ideas in the Middle and Near East in general. The failure and un-popularity of a movement in Gilan in the Caspian region also indicated that nationalist tendencies were far stronger than separatist ones among the public. Like the rest of the country, the northern territories, including Gi-lan, faced many upheavals. Like Azerbaijan, Gilan had extensive economic and political ties to Baku. The main port city, Enzali, was prosperous and had boomed due to the increase in trade. Both the port and the capital city, Rasht, by the early twentieth century were among the most important commercial centers in Iran. The area has heavy rainfall and subtropical vegetation and has been a major producer of rice and other agricultural products for centuries, and Rasht has been a main center on the trans-Caspian trade routes. Gilan has a long history of involvement with Russia and Caucasia.

By the early twentieth century a number of progressive and nationalistic societies and radical parties existed in the area, with publications and newspapers. The inability of the national government, following the constitutional movement, to impose effective control enabled a few groups to talk of separatism, but almost everyone wanted to see a powerful national government in the country. The province was prosperous and had its own Iranian-related dialect, Gilaki, and a relatively large middle class and well-to-do merchant population to support independent tendencies. The introduction of cash crops such as tea and tobacco led to many changes among the agriculturalists. Socialist groups and labor movements were strong in the region. However, the population remained loyal and, like the rest of the country during the civil war, defended the constitution and the national government. The Armenian, Caucasian, and Georgian population of the area also supported a strong national government and in fact formed the bulk of the army from Gilan that went to Tehran and helped to defeat the deposed shah. After the Anglo-Russian occupation and the subsequent upheavals, many reached the conclusion that the central government in Iran was too weak to run the country effectively. A few strongmen emerged who wished to overthrow the government and install a more powerful one.

One such movement appeared in Gilan, led by a moderately well-to-do landlord, Mirza Kuchek Khan. A liberal intellectual and a nationalist, he had fought during the civil war and was very patriotic, highly moral, and deeply religious. He formed a small guerrilla group and set an agenda calling for an independent Iran, land and social reform, and Islamic unity. The group called itself the Jangalis ("men of the jungle"). They called their core the Committee of Islamic Unity. They fought the British, Russians, and a German Turkish force moving into their province. They also campaigned against tribal units and bandits, a common phenomenon in Iran in 1915. The Bolshevik Revolution in October 1917 in Russia drastically changed the balance of power in the region and, while eliminating the czars, added a new element, the revolutionary Russians. This group increased its activity in Iran. In 1920 the Bolsheviks entered the main port in the area to retrieve Russian naval vessels abandoned by the White Russians. The area was under the control of the British. Caught by surprise, those forces left the area, and a swift evacuation was ordered.

The British, in fear of Bolshevik penetration of Iran, attacked the Russians in Baku. They failed and were followed back into Gilan by the Bolsheviks. After reaching the area, the Bolsheviks formed an alliance with the Jangalis, who had to choose between the Bolsheviks, the British, or the national government in Tehran. Pressured by radical party members, Kuchek Khan chose the Bolsheviks, who intended to separate Gilan from Iran. The Bolsheviks carried out an antireligious program that tarnished both their image and that of the Jangalis. Most of the people in the area were Shi'i, along with Sunni Kurds moved there previously during forced settlement programs. Before this development, Kuchek Khan had become a legend and had many sympathizers. The alliance with the Bolsheviks cost him and the Jangalis their popular support. The Jangalis formed a short-lived government in Gilan, and despite pressure by the Russians and the hard-liners in his own camp, Kuchek Khan called the Gilan government the Persian Socialist Soviet Republic. However, the Russians, due to the chaotic situation leading up to and following the Russian Revolution, were in no position to stay or carry out major military actions against the Tehran government or the British. They made peace with the central government and left the Jangalis stranded. The separatist movement ended with Mirza Kuchek Khan's death.

Khurasan

Another major revolt that has been regarded as a separation movement happened in Khurasan. The clergy in Mashhad did not support the Constitutional Revolution and only lent support when the constitutionalists won. Mashhad, the capital of Khurasan, contains the burial place of Imam Reza, the eighth Shi'ite imam, which is the most important shrine in the country. The shrine's administration has been one of the wealthiest institutions in Iran for centuries and possesses many properties, villages, and their produce. The shrine was and is financially independent of the local rulers or the kings. The influential administrators of the shrine did not wish to risk any chance of land reform or revolutionary agenda. They stayed neutral as much as possible during the constitutional upheavals. During and after the constitutional movement, banditry increased and tribal raids were normal occurrences. The roads were very insecure, and better and more effective protection was demanded by the people of Khurasan from the new constitutional government.

The weakness of the central government also led to increased activity by the many tribal groups in the region. Many of these groups occupied areas near the boundaries. Mashhad has always been a meeting place of many peoples visiting the shrine. The area is close to Turkmenistan, Baluchistan, and Afghanistan and has remained a center for a variety of different ethnic groups. Cross-border problems always existed, and during migrations and raids over the centuries, many ethnic groups with different languages, religious affiliations, cultural practices, and origins moved in and out of the area. The major languages spoken were Turkish, Persian, and Kurdish along with a number of minor languages and dialects. A significant agricultural center, the area was also inhabited by many pastoral nomads and migrating groups moving through the province. Large urban centers existed, and Khurasan has been home to many significant literary and scientific figures. The geography of the province makes it an unlikely place for the rise of nationalism as opposed to a desire for local autonomy. However, during the constitutional movement and the following upheavals, no obvious separatist tendencies occurred. *Bahar* ("spring"), the most prominent political newspaper in Mashhad, demonstrated deep loyalty for Khurasan and at the same time a devotion to Iran. The newspaper published commentaries demanding better governors for Khurasan and a program of national reform and opposed foreign interference in the affairs of the country. In response to one of these demands, Ahmad Qavam al-Saltaneh, a very prominent personality and one of the most important politicians of twentieth-century Iran, was appointed as the governor. Ahmad Qavam increased security against armed bandits and made other improvements.

With a weak central government in Tehran, the possibility of a coup d'état was a reality. In 1921 Zia Tabatabai, a prominent journalist-politician, staged one with help from a Cossack officer known as Reza Khan. In his efforts to consolidate his position, he ordered the arrest of Ahmad Qavam by the commander of the Khurasan gendarmerie, Colonel Muhammad Pisyan. The latter handed Ahmad Qavam over to the central government and was appointed the new governor of Khurasan. Pisyan's short stint as governor was even more successful than Qavam's. He further improved security, brought armed bandits under control, and inaugurated a number of important reforms.

Pisyan was from Azerbaijan and had an impeccable reputation as a brave and talented nationalist. He had fought for the constitution, and his brilliant management of the province and improvements in a short period made him a local hero. However, the coup d'état did not last long, and Zia was replaced by Qavam as the head of the government, with support from the new emerging strongman Reza Khan, then the head of the Cossack Brigade. Pisyan at the height of his popularity was ordered back to Tehran. He was opposed by both Qavam and Reza Khan; he refused to go to Tehran, and his refusal evolved into a revolt with strong support from the people of Khurasan. Delegations were sent to Tehran, and Pisyan's refusal culminated in the negotiation of a number of demands. His delegates asked for a greater voice in the overall affairs of the country, the establishment of a permanent gendarmerie in Khurasan, and permission for Pisyan to leave Iran for two years. Both Qavam and Reza Khan refused to let Pisyan go, and a Bakhtiyari group was sent to arrest him. They failed, and Reza Khan sent his Cossacks. Pisyan was killed and became one of the heroes of the anti-Pahlavi groups throughout the period of Pahlavi rule. Although Pisyan was accused of leading an independence movement, the support he received from the people of Khurasan, particularly the merchants and intellectuals, is attributable more to his excellent management strategies than to any separatist tendencies either on his behalf or that of the people of Khurasan.

The appointment of officials and governors from Shiraz and Azerbaijan for Khurasan and the employment of Armenians as policemen indicate changing trends in the management of the country. Traditionally, the governors had been appointed from among the local people. They normally belonged to the ruling families and enjoyed the military support of their own group. The new constitutionalist government appointed officials because of their abilities, despite their ethnic origin. Such officials had the support of the gendarmerie, an armed organ independent of the militant local groups. Pisyan's acceptance and popularity were in sharp contrast with the failure of Abbas Mirza's concept of the "New Order," where tribal loyalties had halted any reform aimed at creating an independent military organ supported by the central government.

Khuzistan

The province of Khuzistan in southern Iran remained almost independent of the central government during the nineteenth century. Prior to the establishment of the Anglo-Persian Oil Company refinery, the area had no major commercial center. The majority of the inhabitants were Arabic-speaking tribes, with no middle class or viable merchant community. They did not participate in the Constitutional Revolution; instead their leader, Sheikh Khazal, took advantage of the situation to consolidate his forces against both the government and the competing Bakhtiyari tribes. The discovery of oil prompted the British to increase their presence. They were involved directly in the politics of the region by supplying arms to the tribal groups, creating the southern police force (South Persia Rifles) in 1916, and finally supporting a rebellion by Shaikh Khazal. His revolt, along with the revolt in Azerbaijan, was the most serious faced by the constitutional government. The shaikh was well aware of the threat posed by the emerging strongman Reza Khan. From an early period, he tried to eradicate that threat by attempting to consolidate the Lur, Bakhtiyari, and Khamseh tribes against the central government. He did not accomplish this task mainly due to the support of the majority of the Bakhtiyari for the central government and internal feuding among the tribal chiefs. He used a number of strategies and, after failing in all, sought the support of the British. In his propaganda Khazal claimed that the Arab tribes in the region were recent immigrants who had no connection with the Iranians. He proclaimed himself to be a defender of

Islam against the secularist government in Tehran and promoted an independent Arab Khuzistan, or Arabistan.

The British had had a treaty with the shaikh to support him and initially did so, but then they decided to ally themselves with the central government at the expense of Khazal. In 1924 Reza Khan attacked Khazal's armed troops and ended the rebellion in a matter of hours with almost no loss of life. Reza Khan emerged as a national hero who had defeated a longtime friend of the British and saved the oil fields. This natural resource was increasingly becoming the most important commercial asset of the country. Shaikh Khazal was a relic of the past; his endurance as the strongman of the area was due to a very uneducated and isolated population, a weak central government, and British support. His actions and policies were based on preserving the status quo rather than any Arab nationalistic sentiment. The lack of public support for any Arab nationalism at this point was due to the very high illiteracy rate among the Arab inhabitants. As the population became more educated and more invested in the economic success of the oil industry, the threat of Arab nationalism increased.

Azerbaijan

The most serious threat came from Azerbaijan. Russians had stayed in Azerbaijan since their occupation of the city in 1909 and remained unpopular. The Bolshevik Revolution was welcomed by the people of Azerbaijan, who hoped that the Russians would leave—and they did. Right after the Russian Revolution, a group from Tabriz demanded the removal of the Russian-appointed governor, new elections for the parliament, and the return of the political exiles. Tehran did not respond, and the departure of the Russian troops left a political and military void in Azerbaijan. A strongman emerged in this vacuum.

A member of the Democrat league in the parliament, Khiyabani was a nationalist and a supporter of the constitutional movement. However, like the Jangalis, he was against the weak central government, which was facing a major crisis at the time. The Anglo-Persian Treaty of 1919–1920 was immensely unpopular, and in April 1920 Khiyabani broke with the Tehran government over the treaty. He was a well-educated cleric who had embraced radical ideas while living in the Caucasus. He was against the pan-Islamic ideology propagated by the Turkish government and warned Azerbaijanis in Iran about Turkish plans to annex Azerbaijan. He gained the support of many people from different cities in Iranian Azerbaijan. He established a bilingual newspaper in Persian and Azerbaijani and emphasized his independence from the Democrat Party in Baku. Khiyabani's party, the Democratic Party of Azerbaijan, demanded the appointment of an ethnic Azerbaijani as the governor and the reconvening of the old assemblies *(anjumans)*. These demands were rejected, and Khiyabani took over Tabriz for a brief period and established his own government. This revolt was the most serious threat to the central government at the time. Khiyabani called his domain Azadistan ("land of freedom"). He lost popular support, mostly because of his association with the Soviet Union, did not succeed, and was banished. In 1922 another separatist movement happened in Azerbaijan. This time the revolt was a reaction to attempts by Reza Khan to dissolve the Tabriz gendarmerie and incorporate it into the new national army. This rebellion, headed by Lahuti Khan, who was in charge of the Tabriz gendarmerie, did not attract popular support either, and when Reza Khan's Cossack Brigade arrived in Tabriz, it was greeted enthusiastically.

The Anglo-Persian Treaty of 1919

The Constitutional Revolution, despite its success, had not produced an infrastructure for either a viable democracy or a coherent party system. Several power groups existed, but their survival depended very much on powerful individual leaders or foreign support. Russian interference was halted because of the Russian Revolution, and as a result the British dominated the political scene in the country. World War I, despite the neutrality of Iran, devastated the country. The parliament was disbanded in 1915, and by 1919 it had not resumed its functions. The new shah, barely twenty-one years old, did not have the courage, the will, or the resources to impose any lasting influence. However, this did not stop him from opposing politicians or policies he did not like.

In 1919 an agreement was reached between the British and the Iranian government. The treaty enabled England to fully control Iran's military and financial resources in exchange for assistance to rebuild Persia. In effect the agreement made Iran a British Mandate. The contract was open-ended, with no fixed duration. The parliament was not in session, and therefore the treaty was not ratified by the parliament. Even some cabinet members were disillusioned and angered by the secrecy that surrounded the signing of the treaty. The outrage and accusations of bribery, and the animosity between the shah and the prime minster responsible for this agreement, forced the resignation of the latter. Cabinet after cabinet was formed. Efforts were made to proceed with parliamentary elections in order to ratify the contract. However, the British started to implement the treaty before it was ratified, which created even more problems.

Early in 1921 the British stopped pressing for the treaty and instead decided that a strong government was more beneficial to the stability of the region. The Cossack Brigade at the time was divided between supporters of the Bolsheviks and supporters of the White Russians. The division imposed many problems, and the brigade could not be relied upon. With the support of Reza Khan, the faction supporting the White Russians prevailed. The divisions between the gendarmerie, the British-sponsored South Persia Rifles, and the Cossack Brigade escalated. At one point the British contemplated replacing the Cossack Brigade altogether. The public had lost confidence in the effectiveness of the government, and in 1921 there was a coup that led to the emergence of Reza Khan, his appointment as war minister, and his subsequent assumption of the Iranian throne. The emergence of Reza Khan and the Pahlavi dynasty opened a new chapter in the relationship between the provinces, the tribal groups, and the central government and created new notions of nationalism and a new identity for Iranians.

Conclusion

The Qajars inherited a ruined country and did very little to improve and rebuild it. They lost many territories and had a poor record with respect to human rights and religious minorities. Turkish in origin, they maintained the Turkish language in the court but left the bureaucracy in the hands of Iranians. Most of the Qajar rulers were not powerful enough to impose central authority or fight their powerful neighbors. Consequently, they had little use for the tribal groups in terms of military requirements. Tribal dispersions that had begun earlier continued throughout their reign and helped to weaken the major tribal groups even further. In the end, the most significant challenge to the Qajar rule came with a new class of intelligentsia demanding modernization and a new form of government based on European models. Such changes were introduced due to the European presence and revolutionary ideas in Iran, Russia, and Turkey. Extensive trade with foreign countries damaged local economies. The increasing military and economic presence of the Russians and the British in Iran alienated the public. New concepts of nationhood and identity emerged, and reforms were demanded in every aspect of life. These events culminated in the success of the constitutional movement. The early constitutional governments were unable to implement major reforms and had little control over the country as a whole.

The chaotic situation prepared the way for the collapse of the Qajar rule and the emergence of Reza Khan, the founder of the Pahlavi dynasty.

Timeline

1905	The start of protests that led to the establishment of a constitutional monarchy in Iran. The uproar was caused by the flogging of two respectable merchants in Tehran.
1906	Muzzafar al-Din Shah was forced to accept the convocation of a National Assembly. Iran officially became a constitutional monarchy. The shah died five days later.
1908	The new Shah, Muhammad Ali, attacked and bombed the new parliament with help from the Russian officers of the Cossack Brigade.
1909	Tabriz was occupied by the Russians in April. Muhammad Ali Shah was defeated, and the constitution was reinstated in July. The shah was forced to abdicate in favor of his minor son, Ahmad Shah.
1910	Democrats gained more control in the parliament by making an alliance with the Bakhtiyari. Mujahedin were disarmed. Shaikh Khazal and Solet Qashqa'i started a collaboration.
1917	The Russian Revolution transformed Russia into a communist country.
1918	Northern Azerbaijan in Russia was declared the Republic of Azerbaijan. The Kurdish leader Simqu started a rebellion in Iranian Kurdistan, which ended in 1922. He was responsible for the last major massacre of Christians in Iran.
1919	The Anglo-Iranian Agreement was drawn in London. Known as the Vosouq Contract, it was declared illegal by the Iranian nationalists since the parliament was not in session to ratify it.
1920	The Jangali militants announced the formation of the Persian Soviet Republic in Gilan. Shaikh Muhammad Khiyabani established the Republic of Azadistan in Tabriz. Military forces sent from Tehran crushed both movements.

1920–1921   An Iranian-Russian treaty was agreed between the two
countries, with terms highly favorable to Iran. The
Iranian government declared that the treaty with Russia
was not valid until all Russian troops left Iran. The
matter remained open.

1921   In February 1921, Colonel Reza Khan with 3,000 to
4,000 troops from the Cossack Brigade marched from
Qazvin to Tehran and executed a bloodless coup d'état.

Significant People, Places, and Events

ANGLO-PERSIAN OIL COMPANY: Formed in 1909 by William Knox D'arcy.
Soon he sold most of his interest to others, including the Burma Oil
Company. British Petroleum became the next major shareholder.

ANJUMAN: Local assemblies that emerged before and during the
Constitutional Revolution. The assemblies had members from all
groups, including non-Muslims who worked and fought side by side
with the Muslims.

D'ARCY, WILLIAM KNOX (1849–1917): Born in England, D'arcy made a
fortune in Australia. In 1900 he was approached to finance oil
exploration in Iran. In 1901 he received a concession from the
Iranian government, and in 1908 he struck oil.

MUJAHEDIN: A number of militant Islamic groups use the name. During
the Constitutional Revolution it was applied to local militia defending
the constitution and did not necessarily imply an Islamic association.

MUZAFFAR AL-DIN SHAH QAJAR (1853–1907): The Qajar king who was
forced to ratify the provision for a constitutional monarchy in Iran.
He reigned from 1896 to 1907 and died five days after he signed the
ratification.

QANUN: The newspaper published in early 1890 by Malkum Khan in
London. Qanun means "law." The paper became widely popular and
discussed major issues with respect to reform in Iran and the merits
of a constitution.

QAVAM AL-MOLK SHIRAZI: The Qavam family of Shiraz has been among
the most prominent families in Fars and Iran. It served many kings
over the centuries and at times was persecuted. In the early twentieth
century Qavam al-Molk united many groups, including the
Khamseh, and improved the security of the area. He was not related
to Ahmad Qavam Saltaneh.

QAVAM AL-SALTANEH, AHMAD (1882–1955): Qavam was one of the most significant and influential political figures of twentieth-century Iran. Born in Azerbaijan, he served five times as prime minister. Originally a supporter of Reza Khan, he was pushed aside by the powerful new Shah Reza Pahlavi. He came back as prime minister after Reza Shah's departure in 1941.

REZA KHAN (1878–1944): He was born in Mazandaran Iran. He ended the Qajar dynasty and in a relatively short period restored security and stability to Iran. His attempts to modernize the country were welcomed by many Iranians and opposed by some. He is regarded as the founder of modern Iran.

SAYYID JAMAL AL-DIN ASAD ABADI (AL-AFGHANI, 1839–1897): He was born in Iran to a Turkish-speaking Shi'ite family in Hamadan. He studied theology in Iraq and came under the influence of the Shaykhy school of Shi'ism. He traveled extensively throughout the Middle East, India, and Europe. He opposed European domination and propagated nationalism. He promoted pan-Islamism as a way to fight European dominance.

TOBACCO CONCESSION: In 1890 Nasir al-Din Shah granted the concession to Major Talbot, an English citizen, giving him a monopoly on production and domestic and foreign sales of all tobacco in Iran. The concession was canceled in 1892, and the Iranian government was forced to pay a heavy penalty after the cancellation.

Bibliography

Afary, Janet. *The Iranian Constitutional Revolution, 1906–1911*. New York: Columbia University Press, 1996.

Algar, Hamid. *Mirza Malkum Khan: A Biographical Study in Iranian Modernism*. Berkeley: University of California Press, 1973.

Amanat, Abbas. *Pivot of the Universe: Nasir Al-Din Shah Qajar and the Iranian Monarchy, 1831–1896*. Berkeley: University of California Press, 1997.

Avery, P., G. R. G. Hambly, and C. Melville, eds. *The Cambridge History of Iran*, Vol. 7: *From Nadir Shah to the Islamic Republic*. Cambridge: Cambridge University Press, 1991.

Berberian, Houri. *Armenians and the Iranian Constitutional Revolution, 1905–1911: The Love for Freedom Has No Fatherland*. Boulder, CO: Westview Press, 2001.

Foran, John. *A Century of Revolutions: Social Movements in Iran.* Minneapolis: University of Minnesota Press, 1994.

Ghani, Cyrus. *Iran and the Rise of Reza Shah: From Qajar Collapse to Pahlavi Power.* New York and London: I. B. Tauris, 2000.

Keddie, Nikki. *Qajar Iran and the Rise of Reza Khan, 1796–1921.* Costa Mesa, CA: Mazda Publishers, 1999.

Martin, Vanessa. *Islam and Modernism: The Iranian Revolution of 1906.* Syracuse, NY: Syracuse University Press, 1989.

CHAPTER SEVEN

A New Nation in the Making

Reza Shah and the Pahlavi Dynasty

THE PERIOD FROM 1918 UNTIL THE CONSOLIDATION OF POWER BY REZA Shah was a time of national disunity, economic disasters, political up-heavals, increased tribal conflict, banditry, and poverty. The presence of British forces in Iran practically rendered the central government inef-fective. In February 1921 Reza Khan, the strongman of the Cossack Brigade, marched with his troops from Qazvin to Tehran, where he occupied the cap-ital without bloodshed and proclaimed a journalist as the prime minister. With the parliament in recess, Ahmad Shah recognized the new prime min-ister and, therefore, legitimized the takeover. Many had expected the coup d'état, so it did not come as a surprise, and the shah himself had ordered that there be no resistance. The prime minister of the time, anticipating the coup, had already resigned, and, in effect, there was no government. The takeover was welcomed by the British and their military commander in Iran, who was very impressed with Reza Khan's personality and leadership abilities.

Reza Khan declared martial law and arrested almost all of the politicians regardless of their political affiliation. Despite some anticoup sentiment, on the whole the takeover was greeted with enthusiasm and relief. The new gov-ernment annulled the 1919 agreement with the British. Many younger po-litical activists, including many poets and writers, responded favorably; na-tionalistic sentiments were very high. The motto "Long live the Iranian nation" appeared everywhere, and radical nationalist slogans were used ex-tensively by Reza Khan, now war minister, and his prime minister, who re-signed after three months. From 1921 to 1923, when Reza Khan was ap-pointed as the prime minister, he consolidated his power over an expanding and loyal professional army. He coordinated the operations that ended the Jangali and Khazal movements, put down tribal and regional rebellions,

The shah of Iran, Reza Shah Pahlavi, dressed in his military uniform, 1925 (Bettmann/Corbis)

secured roads, and ended banditry as well as highway robbery. He gained popularity among many in the parliament and a few in the opposition and surrounded himself with young, educated followers who would form the technobureaucratic elite of the Pahlavi era. In 1925 he was officially declared by the parliament as the new king; the last Qajar king abdicated in his favor, and Reza Khan was crowned a year later as the first Pahlavi monarch.

As far as the various ethnic groups were concerned, the period from 1906 to 1925 was a time of disturbance and conflict. During this period, there were major and minor movements in Azerbaijan, Gilan, Kurdistan, Baluchistan, Fars, and Khuzistan. Four of the movements demanded separation, including the Gilan, Baluchistan, Khuzistan, and Azerbaijan rebellions. The separation movements in Azerbaijan and Gilan were directly influenced by foreign elements—mainly radical revolutionary individuals and groups associated with the Russian revolutionaries. Azerbaijan was also influenced by the emergence of national sentiments in the new Republic of Turkey and in Russian Azerbaijan. The Khuzistan and Baluchistan movements were influenced by British involvement. However, internal factors and grievances were equally important in the culmination of the rebellions. Such grievances found new meanings with the emergence of the Pahlavi regime.

The nationalism of the period as it appeared in the local media and in the works of the intelligentsia has several features mostly influenced by European models. It demanded a break with Islamic traditions and, in fact, regarded religion as a barrier to progress. The intelligentsia promoted ancient Persia and its past glories, demanded reform, and pointed out the shortcomings of the parliament and the legal system. In 1935 a new cultural educational institution was formed to purify the Persian language by removing Arabic and other foreign words, and a Persian calendar replaced the Arabic one. A governmental broadcasting agency was created, and all radio programs promoted the state ideology in Persian with no independent or private broadcasting. Ancient pre-Islamic festivals, such as the Iranian new year (No Ruz) were celebrated with grandeur—complete with many government-sponsored parties whose agendas were widely broadcast through the new media.

The traditional aristocratic political elite was criticized, and tribal leaders were portrayed as archaic warlords. The nationalistic sentiments were vocal, articulate, and positive in many aspects, and demanded immediate action. The promoters of the new nationalism were a mixed group that included the intelligentsia, Western-educated bureaucrats, and army commanders. They were heterogeneous in their social, educational, and ethnic backgrounds but were united with respect to the new nationalistic ideas. A new state identity for Iran was in the making, and the idea of a united modern secular state was put forward simultaneously by government agencies and the media. Early in his reign Reza Shah was supported by many because of his swift and overwhelming success in increasing the security in the country and disarming the tribal groups. Later his dictatorial ways created opposition among the more liberal and proconstitution elements. However, the basic policies of the new national order and the notion of a new identity were supported by many—

including most opposing groups. At the same time, changes in ethnic identities were taking place in different parts of the country, and at times these identities clashed with the new state identity promoted by the government apparatus. The most significant of such clashes happened in Azerbaijan and Kurdistan.

Before Reza Shah and the Pahlavi dynasty, the identity of Iran was supraethnic and did not rely exclusively on Persians. The political leadership for centuries was mostly Turkic, and the rulers were aware of their distinct Turkic identity. The Persian elements were also very influential, and in reality both groups ran the country. Other groups such as Kurds, Lurs, and Baluchi survived and kept their identities, but Persian and Turkic cultural elements formed the foundation of the ethnic character of the country and the ruling dynasties. Cultural diversity was recognized, admitted, and worked with. During the nineteenth century, Turkic and Persian cultural elements were fluid and dominated fashion, food, etiquette, and literature. Azerbaijani cultural figures wrote in both Persian and Azerbaijani. Although the government's business was carried out in Persian, there was no prohibition against the use of other languages such as Azerbaijani. The seat of the crown prince was traditionally in Tabriz, where everyone in the court spoke Azerbaijani.

The new state identity in the early twentieth century deviated from this norm by glorifying ancient Iran and emphasizing its greatness. In the process, it identified the greatness of the Iranian nation with the Persians and the Persian language. The king became the central figure and represented the nation as a whole. Loyalty to the king was the same as loyalty to the nation. For the first time a national anthem was created; it focused on the greatness of Iran and the role of the Pahlavi king in restoring the ancient glory and preserving the country. It was played at all public gatherings and was sung by all students in the mornings before the start of the school day. The historical literature that was produced in the 1920s and 1930s was mixed with sentimental nationalism. The use of racist remarks, particularly against Arabs, was characteristic of such literature. The Persian language was linked to the land, and the Aryan origin of Iranians was emphasized and admired to reinforce cultural nationalism.

Military service became mandatory for all young adult males in order to create a unified identity and encourage loyalty to the state. Ethnic clothing was banned from government agencies, and all civil servants were required to dress in European styles. Deviation from the Islamic norms, the promotion of women's rights and women's participation in public affairs, and the Westernization of government policies alienated the clergy and the conservative masses. The new policies aimed at creating national unity estranged other ethnic groups, including some Azerbaijanis. In response, they sought to explore alternative identities. The result gave rise to the question of the identity of Turkic-speakers in Iran as a whole.

Azerbaijan: A Quest for Identity

Azerbaijan, like Kurdistan, was a special case due to the existence of a separate Azerbaijani state in Russia and the impact it had on the Iranian Azerbaijan. Prior to both the Pahlavi regime in Iran and the Stalin regime in Russia, commercial, familial, and cultural interchange and contact between the two was free despite the separation of the two parts after Russia's victories in 1813 and 1828. In spite of being under Russian rule, the Azerbaijanis in Russia adhered to Islam. The literature of the period indicates that the majority of the political activists in Baku and other major cities possessed a Muslim identity and identified more with Muslims in general, including Iranian Muslims, than with Christian Russians. Despite maintaining a Muslim identity, they also remained liberal and promoted secular states. Most viewed Turkic cultural identity as important and referred to themselves as Azerbaijani Turks.

However, such sentiments in favor of Turkic culture rarely manifested into orientation or political action in favor of Turkey. Following the collapse of the Ottoman Empire, the idea of a greater homeland for all Turkish speakers was promoted by a new pan-Turkic movement. Its proponents tried to gain support in north and south Azerbaijan, with limited success. The majority of the Azerbaijani people made a distinction between themselves and the Ottomans. The Shi'i/Sunni division was also a major factor and kept the Shi'i Azerbaijanis separate from the Ottoman Sunnis. However, many people from Russian Azerbaijan traveled between Iran, Turkey, and Russia and imported into Iran new ideas about nationalism and even sentiments about an Azerbaijani identity. This group of educated secular activists made a great impact on the Azerbaijani intelligentsia in Iran. They published in Azerbaijani and even wrote European-style plays in their language and popularized such activities in Iran. Despite the spread of these new ideas, the concept of full-fledged autonomy for Azerbaijan did not exist at the time.

Communication and exchange between the two Azerbaijans were hindered when restrictions were imposed by both the Soviets and the Iranians in the 1920s. The new regulations severely limited movement between the two. Both the Soviets and the new government in Iran aimed at unifying their nations by creating new national identities. In the case of Russia, this process had already been tried for almost a century. Since the nineteenth century, Russia's policies of discrimination against non-Christians had already created a need for exploring collective identity. By the early 1920s a new generation of Azerbaijani citizens in Russia was seeking its roots. The early twentieth century was also marked by a number of significant political movements among Turkic-speaking groups both inside and outside Iran. In 1918 northern Azerbaijan, historically called Albania or Arran, was officially declared the Republic of Azerbaijan, and ideas of a united country began to appear. The Young Turk movement in Turkey, the emergence of a very strong leftist movement in Iran influenced by the Russian left, and affinity for all-out Azerbaijani nationalism among certain groups and factions made an impact. This nationalist sentiment had already been tried by the formation of the short-lived Khiyabani separation movement in Azerbaijan that had been crushed. Reza Shah's plans to promote a new national identity, increase centralization, and extend the government's power to the provinces were bound to create problems between the government and various groups on the periphery.

The centralization policies resulted in the allocation of vast resources to create an infrastructure in the capital and its surroundings at the expense of the provinces. This led to complaints by many, including Azerbaijanis, for decades, and dissatisfaction with such practices still continues. The appointment by the center of all major personnel, including military and police, often with no ethnic link to the area where they were given authority, created resentment. During the administrative reforms many new government ministries were created, all administered from Tehran. One was the newly founded department for tax and revenue collection. The efficiently managed department introduced modern taxation systems and established newly built offices throughout the country. Educated bureaucrats replaced the old khans and local leaders as tax collectors, and the central government made decisions regarding the allocation of taxes.

With the establishment of new ministries such as the Ministry of Education and new legislation making primary education compulsory, Persian became the only language taught in schools. The minority language schools were closed down, and publications in languages other than Persian were effectively stopped. New provinces were created, Persian names replaced many local names, and even ancient cities with non-Persian names were renamed. For example, Urmiya, known by this name for centuries, became Rezaiyeh, named after Reza Shah. The Enzali port on the Caspian Sea became Pahlavi Port. All citizens were required to register, and identity cards and birth certificates became mandatory. In the process people were encouraged to choose Persian names, and in some places the authorities created obstacles for the people who wished to have non-Persian names. In 1935 the Iranian government officially declared that the name *Iran,* instead of *Persia,* should be used as the official name of the country in all international correspondence. The country had always been called *Iran* by the Iranians and neighboring countries, but Europeans still used the name *Persia,* based on ancient Greco-Roman histories. This choice was made to emphasize the unity of the country's entire historical and cultural background, as it had been known by Iranians since the Sasanian period, when the country was called Eranshahr. Reza Shah's crown at his coronation was copied from a Sasanian crown, currently on display in the Metropolitan Museum of Art in New York.

Centralization policies were bound to create problems, and Azerbaijan was at the forefront of the opposition to some of these policies. Events in Azerbaijan were closely watched by the pan-Turkic movement that emerged after the success of the Young Turks in Turkey. The movement tried to establish support groups and movements in both Iranian and Soviet Azerbaijan, but newly powerful central governments in Iran and Russia curtailed such activities.

Iranian Azerbaijan remained at the forefront of the constitutional movement in Iran. Despite the failure of the Democratic Republic, on the whole the majority had remained loyal to Iranian nationalism. Unlike the Qajars and other previous rulers in Iran, Reza Shah proved to be extremely effective in consolidating central power. The success of his government in maintaining control and building new roads and transportation systems brought masses of different groups in direct contact with each other. Reconstruction of the country and a flourishing job market in Tehran resulted in mass migration into the capital from other areas. From the 1920s on, two main trends of identity emerged among Azerbaijani activists in Iran. Many, including the upper classes and those who had lived in Tehran, supported the Persianization of the Azerbaijanis and other minorities in Iran. The most famous Azerbaijani literary figure, Ahmad Kasravi, who wrote the history of Azerbaijan and the constitutional movement, belonged to this group. He rejected any form of autonomy for different ethnic and religious groups in Iran. He defined a nation as the inhabitants of a territorial unit and was against any kind of diversity within such units. Accordingly, Kasravi is known as the father of Iranian nationalism. He supported Persian as the state language. He was extremely antireligious, particularly anti-Islam, and was assassinated by a Muslim underground group in 1946. Most other prominent Azerbaijanis who advocated assimilation into the Persian culture had been educated in Tehran.

Such support for the Persianization of the country by other ethnic groups was not a rare phenomenon at the time; many educated and modern Iranians from all over the country believed that such policies were the only way to build a modern nation-state, end the powers of the tribal warlords, and create a strong and powerful Iran.

Another group of educated elite emphasized the constitution and advocated the establishment of a reformed constitution and a supraethnic regime supporting cultural autonomy for different ethnic groups. Many Azerbaijanis with links to Soviet Azerbaijan and some leftist groups were among this group. Their activities culminated after the abdication of Reza Shah in 1941, resulting in the formation of the Provincial Government of Azerbaijan in 1945. This happened after the occupation of Iran by the Allied forces during World War II. This brief local government and its violent destruction had a major effect on the development of the identity of Azerbaijanis in Iran for decades to come.

The central government was aware of the discontent among Azerbaijanis, and many policies were implemented to reduce any risk. In 1937 Azerbaijan was divided into two separate provinces, and some of Azerbaijan's traditional territories were annexed to other provinces. Tabriz became the capital of East Azerbaijan, and Urmiya, now renamed Rezaiyeh, became the capital of West Azerbaijan. Eastern Azerbaijan included Kurdish territory, such as the major Kurdish cities of Mahabad and Sardasht. The closure of the boundaries between Russia and Iran ended seasonal emigration into Russia from Iran. The effect was devastating for seasonal workers and created massive unemployment and poverty, which led to further emigration to Tehran. Many Azerbaijani workers in Tehran later supported the leftist activists who proposed class identity as the appropriate solution to either Persian or Azerbaijani Turkic identity. The popular and influential workers' movement, led mainly by the Tudeh ("the masses") Party, was not able to solve the identity problem and was divided on the issue. The party became very popular, with many supporters among the intelligentsia and workers, and established branches in many provinces. It had support among the military and was at times financed and coordinated by the Soviets. It played a major role in Iranian politics for brief periods when political parties were legal. The leaders who had grown up in Iran supported the use of Persian in their meetings and among the delegates, but the leaders who came from the Russian Azerbaijan wanted the Azerbaijani language to be used exclusively. The party had popular support among the masses and had discovered that many of the immigrant workers in Tehran did not know any Persian. However, it could not resolve the issue and its publications were written in Persian; some prominent members who insisted on the use of the Azerbaijani language were expelled.

Despite strong dissatisfaction with government policies, there is no solid evidence that, other than a small group of activists, the majority favored separation from Iran. This was well demonstrated by the lack of support for the Russians during the Soviet occupation of Azerbaijan at the end of World War II. Furthermore, a division existed between the masses and the intelligentsia. The majority, particularly in rural areas, remained loyal to formal religious allegiances and remained suspicious of communist Russia. In 1941 the Allied invasion of Iran forced Reza Shah, who had refused to deport German technicians and engineers from Iran, to abdicate. Political liberalization was a consequence of his resignation, and it became possible to publish many political and cultural works in the Azerbaijani language.

Under the Allied occupation, Azerbaijan came under Soviet control, which led to more contact between the two Azerbaijans. The Soviets used Azerbaijani troops in Iranian Azerbaijan and carried out extensive propaganda in the Azerbaijani language in Iran. The literature emphasized the common origins and histories of the now separated lands and the importance of unification. Many people from Baku were involved in such propaganda, and the literature of the period indicates that they also used the opportunity to advance their own ethnic-based agenda. The term *Azeri* became popular and has become the standard term used to identify both the Azerbaijani people and the language.

The Azerbaijan Independent Republic

During the period when political parties emerged in Iran, communism and socialism became popular among the intelligentsia, some of the newly emerging middle class, and organized labor. These movements played a major role in the events of the following decade. The Democratic Party of Azerbaijan (Firgeh Dimukrat Azerbaijan) was established in Tabriz in 1945 under the leadership of Jafar Pishevari, who had spent considerable time in Baku and northern Azerbaijan. The Tudeh Party leadership in Azerbaijan immediately defected to this new party. Both parties were communist and Soviet-oriented, but Pishevari's Democratic Party advocated language rights for minority groups and, unlike the Tudeh Party, wanted less control by the center over the provinces. It also promoted Azerbaijani identity, as opposed to the class identity that was encouraged by the Tudeh Party central committee. Its leaders chose the same name for their party as Khiyabani had previously chosen, and in fact many of their members had been supporters of Khiyabani. In their first declaration, they announced the right to use the Azerbaijani language. By October 1945 they had established the Provincial Government of Azerbaijan, and a similar takeover had established a Kurdish Provincial Government in Kurdistan.

The new Provincial Government in Azerbaijan refused to call itself the Democratic Republic of Azerbaijan in order to avoid accusations of being a Soviet puppet government. With help from Russian troops, it disarmed the local army and police and sent their chiefs back to Tehran. Soviet influence and help was crucial to the establishment of this short-lived government, but many of its goals and declarations reflected local grievances and expectations. A new parliament (All-Peoples Grand National Assembly) was formed in Tabriz, which chose Pishevari as the leader of the new government and dismissed government officials from Tehran. The assembly had 744 delegates and claimed to represent the 150,000 inhabitants from all over the province (Fatemi, 1980, p. 85). Despite the fact that they called Azerbaijan a distinct nation *(millet)*, they denied any intention of separating from Iran. In an effort to forge a distinct history and connection with the past, they called their armed forces Babak, after the legendary leader of the revolt against the Arab invasion of Azerbaijan, and Qizilbash, the name of the Turkic military forces of the Safavid dynasty. Their declarations clearly stated local interests, and at the beginning they had popular support. They also demanded local taxes be retained and used locally for the benefit of Azerbaijan. Their next major declaration proposed the establishment of provincial assemblies as outlined in the Iranian constitution. In 1946 they had a new flag; the Iranian national anthem was abolished, and a university was opened in Tabriz. They presented their demands to the Iranian government and tried to negotiate, with little success. In the end they threatened to secede from Iran if their demands were not met. The demands indicated the importance that Azerbaijanis attached to their ethnic identity. They demanded language rights and relative economic independence for the province; they asked for the use of the Azerbaijani language in the schools; and they called for the allocation of 70 percent of tax revenues for the province in addition to 25 percent of the customs revenues to finance the newly established provincial university in Tabriz. The university was the second one in Iran and set out to use the Azerbaijani language instead of Persian. Fear of communism, the threat of separation from Iran, and the worsening economic situation because of isolation and attempts to sever ties with the rest of the country diminished the new government's popularity fairly quickly. By the end of the 1946 it had lost major support from the population, and the Soviet departure from Iran came as the final blow.

The Soviets were under pressure to withdraw from the Iranian territories for a number of reasons. An oil concession in form of a joint Iranian-Soviet exploration company was made to the Soviets in the north by the Iranian government, subject to approval by the parliament, in an attempt to persuade the Soviets to leave Iran. The concession did not materialize but alerted the Americans and the British, who were seeking their own oil concessions. Oil had become a major issue by 1944, and fierce competition existed between the British, Americans, and Soviets. To create a balance and ease the tension, in 1941 the Iranian parliament had passed a law that forbade the granting of any oil concession until the war was over. However, after the departure of British and American troops from Iran, the Soviets remained. In a bid to persuade them to leave and with support from the communist members of the parliament, the Iranian government granted the Soviet Union a concession for oil in the north. The USSR accepted the deal and evacuated Azerbaijan in May 1946, leaving the newly established Provincial Government with no protection.

In December troops from Tehran arrived in Tabriz. The local government in Azerbaijan tried to negotiate and outline certain demands, but in the end it surrendered. Many people were arrested, exiled, or executed. Some, including the leaders of the Provincial Government, fled to the Soviet Union. Reports of the exact number executed vary according to different sources. The government agencies reported that close to 800 people were killed. Members of the opposition in exile reported 10,000 to 30,000 dead and thousands more deported and emigrating to Russia. The latter figures are very likely exaggerated. However, the impact that the executions and the arrests had on the psyche of the people of Azerbaijan remained for a long time and was used extensively by prominent literary figures until well into the 1960s and 1970s.

Many teachers, poets, and literary figures who had fled to Baku continued to produce literature supporting Azerbaijani ethnic issues and condemning the repression of Azerbaijani people in Iran.

The Rise of Kurdish Nationalism

Iranian Kurdistan had been geographically and politically divided between the northern and southern parts. Both areas maintained distinctive characteristics for centuries. The Kurds living in the northern parts within Azerbaijan and the adjacent areas were closely involved in cross-border matters concerning Iran, Turkey, and sometimes Russia. Quite often they chose to ally themselves with the Ottomans for the practical reason that Istanbul was a lot farther away than Tehran. Being mostly Sunni, they were instrumental in popularizing and spreading minor cults and popular shaikhs from Turkey into Iran. They made alliances with or fought against other groups, including Christian villagers, depending on their motives. Christians were a popular target at times because their deaths seldom led to blood feud. Armenians, Assyrians, and Jews have always lived in Kurdistan, and at times they have been referred to as Christian or Jewish Kurds, indicating a high level of interaction or integration throughout the centuries.

The British authorities in the late nineteenth century reported the situation of the Kurds in Azerbaijan as desperate and blamed their poverty on their exploitation by the land-owning chiefs. They were poor, and their material condition was reported to be worse than that of the Armenians. Prior to 1920 the Kurdish economy in the mountains was based almost entirely on grazing herds and illegal trading across the borders with Turkey. Land was

A black tent (rash-e-mal) *belonging to Jalali Kurds in a camp located in the Arafat summer pastures. These black tents, which are made of goat's hair, are fixed to the ground with long wooden pegs that serve as lateral posts. The tent is then covered all around with straw mats* (hassir). *Near the Turkish border, West Azerbaijan. (Nasrollah Kasraian)*

traditionally controlled by the tribes in these areas, and the tribal leaders organized distribution of pastoral rights for a fee. During the constitutional upheavals, they mostly remained loyal to the monarchy but at times favored local autonomy. Their chiefs resented political activity by merchants and artisan classes in support of the revolutionary assemblies and committees. The weak constitutional government of the early twentieth century created a power vacuum that was used in various ways by different groups, including the Kurds, who fought among themselves and against the government agents in their bid for power.

The majority of Kurds (approximately 75 percent) are followers of Sunni Islam. Despite adherence to this sect, they have not formed alliances with other non-Kurdish Sunni groups such as Arabs or Turkmen. One major difference between the Sunni Kurds and other Sunnis is that the Sunni Kurds are followers of the Shafi'i school of Islam, while non-Kurdish Sunni have mostly adopted the Hanafi school of jurisprudence, the official sect in Turkey.

The southern Kurds lived near Kirmanshah and were mainly Shi'ites. Only 15 percent of the Shi'i Kurds are followers of the official sect in the country; others follow the popular Alevid and other pro-Shi'i sects. Many of the Kurds who practice the official Shi'i sect live around Kirmanshah and speak the southeastern dialect. The Alevids (Alevi) express devotion to Imam Ali, identify their religion as a *qizilbash* religion, and venerate the Safavids. Alevid is a mixture of pre-Islamic, Zoroastrian, Turkmen shaman, and Shi'i ideas that became the basis of a religious sect during the fifteenth century. The religious particularism of the Alevids could be an indication of different origins of different Kurdish groups.

A small minority of the Kurds are followers of the Yazidi religion. They mostly live in Iraq, speak Kurmanji, and have kept in touch with the Yazidis in Iran. They have been routinely persecuted in Iraq and Turkey, and many, particularly from Turkey, have migrated to Germany. The Yazidi religion contains old pagan, Zoroastrian, and Manichean elements mixed with Jewish, Christian, and Muslim beliefs. Sufi brotherhoods were and are very popular among many Kurds, and the prominent Sufi masters have played major roles in local politics. The communal practices of the Sufi also resemble pre-Islamic religious rites and exercises and are not exclusive to the Kurds. The Sufi brotherhoods are locally known as *tariqa,* and at times there have been major divisions among the followers of different *tariqa.* The most popular in Iran is the Naqshbandi group, which was involved in violent disputes with the Barazan groups for decades in the mid-nineteenth century. Another popular sect in southern Kurdistan is the Ahl-i Hagg ("followers of the truth"), who are mainly Gurani speakers. This sect has beliefs very similar to those of the Alevids, including veneration of Imam Ali and a regard for the Safavid dynasty. Both the Alevids and the Ahl-i Hagg include a large number of Zoroastrian religious ideas as well. None of these groups are exclusively Kurdish, and both sects are popular among a number of Turkish and Turkmen groups.

The religious practices of the Kurds indicate deliberate strategies to remain independent from the central governments. In the early twentieth century, the followers of most of the popular sects were predominantly rural, with tribal and kinship ideology being an important element in their lives and belief systems. They stayed together based on their religious affiliation, which was tied to their tribal organization.

The linguistic variety also indicates that the modern Kurds have different origins. The two major languages or dialects, Kurmanji (Northern Kurdish) and Surani (Central Kurdish), are spoken by northern and southern Kurds, respectively. There are also three other languages spoken by a considerable number of Kurds. The Kurds in the Iranian southeast use a dialect that is closer to Persian than Surani. The other two languages are Gurani and Zaza, which are closely related.

The Iranian Kurds played a more prominent role in the political and economic affairs of the country after the constitutional revolution. Kirmanshah was a large city in the early twentieth century with a population close to 50,000. Extensive trade existed between Iran and Iraq, and many goods went through Kirmanshah on the way to Baghdad. The Shi'i pilgrims to Iraq went through Kirmanshah as well, which helped to boost the economy of the region. Both the tribal and the urban Kurds benefited from such activities, and through these economic activities and movements to Iraq ties with the Iraqi Kurds were maintained. The tribal Kurds charged road protection fees and opposed all attempts by the early constitutional governments to secure roads and replace them with the gendarmerie. They increased banditry to prevent competing tribes from collecting road protection fees and attacked the government forces regularly.

During the constitutional struggle the Kurds expelled the monarchists from Kirmanshah and elected a mayor. They were not consistent in their support of the constitution and turned against it when there was an opportunity. The inability of the weak central government to impose any control intensified intertribal conflict in the area, and rivalries between the Kalhurs and the Sanjabi faction of the Gurani at one point resulted in the sacking of 180 villages. The Kurds were involved in the Qajars' failed effort to reverse the constitutional monarchy and, with help from a prominent Kurdish

A nomadic tribal family takes a break in the city of Isfahan, Iran, ca. 1967.
(Courtesy of Dominick F. Rossi)

shaikh, supported the return of the deposed shah. The lawlessness continued after the Constitutional Revolution and was a direct threat to British interests in southern Iran. The British intervened and supported one faction against the other, which led to the defeat of the Sanjabi Kurds in 1918. It was during this period of uncertainty that the beginnings of Kurdish ethnic awareness emerged in Iran.

The Kurdish quest for ethnic identity was closely related to the happenings in Turkey and Iraq and the emergence of new nations in the Middle East. The territory historically occupied by the Kurds had no fixed boundaries and was divided between different countries by the Allied forces following the Ottoman defeat in World War I. Despite promises of self-determination by the British for an independent Kurdistan and many revolts by the Kurds, in the end the Kurdish territory was divided between Turkey, Iraq, and Syria. Iranian Kurdistan was not affected as such because the territory had not been under the Ottoman administration. Nevertheless, the division restricted movement between Kurds in Iran and Kurds in the newly established Iraq. Arab rule over the Kurds and the Kurdish movement in Iraq had and still has a major effect on the Kurds in Iran. The partition of Ottoman Kurdistan by the Allied forces changed Kurdish life, politics, and territorial claims. It was the start of decades of struggle, armed resistance, genocide, and political maneuvering against the governments of Turkey, Iraq, and Iran that still continues.

Since 1918 there have been failed attempts by some Kurdish leaders in Iran to unify all Kurds. Some even considered an independent Kurdistan under British patronage. At the time a chief from the Mukri tribe suggested such a plan to the British representative in Iran, and Kurdish delegates were sent to visit British administrators in Iraqi Kurdistan. A year later there were attempts by more chiefs to gather enough support to stage a revolt against the Iranian government, but they failed, and no action was taken. One leader who did take action was Simqu, of the Shakak Kurds. The Shakak were already divided into three rival factions, and despite Simqu's prominence, he was challenged internally by his rivals. Simqu had previously collaborated with both Russia and Turkey and had been involved in the massacre of Assyrians in Urmiya. He was not trusted by the Iranian authorities, but in 1919 they were too weak to deal with him. Under pressure from the British, who wanted to guarantee security in the area, the Iranian government decided to appoint Simqu as the warden for several highways and to pay him royalties. He later tried, unsuccessfully, to convince the Kurdish chiefs of western Azerbaijan to partake in an uprising and asked for arms from the British. Failing in both efforts, he turned to Turkey for arms and kept recruiting Kurds from that country. By 1920 the Iranians had no choice but to fight him, and initially defeated him. He was pardoned and later was able to recruit more men, get the support of Mukri chiefs, and purchase arms. He made vague remarks about an independent Kurdistan and managed to control a large area for a brief period. His revolt remained fatally handicapped owing to the nature of tribal politics, which were used extensively by and against him. Although many Kurdish tribes supported him, others, including some members of his own tribe, opposed him. His lootings of villages and abduction of Christian women made him feared and disliked by the people in the area. He was finally defeated by Iranian troops and fled to Turkey, then to Iraq, and then, after a promise of amnesty, back to Iran, where he was ambushed and killed.

Simqu's nationalism has been questioned, and no manifesto or political program has survived from his time. His motives were self-serving, and his downfall was in large part because of his inability to forge unity among various Kurdish groups, a problem that has remained until the present time. Reza Shah frequently took advantage of the rivalries among these groups. In his dealings with Simqu, he used tribal auxiliaries from the Kurdish tribes opposing Simqu. The defeat was also due to the fact that Simqu's troops were no match for the new disciplined national army. Though this rebellion was harshly ended, the problem of Kurds defecting to neighboring countries, including Iraq, remained.

Reza Shah put an end to most rebellious activities in the area, and the military position of the tribal Kurds was diminished further. However, they benefited from the land registration scheme under Reza Shah. Land titles previously held by whole tribes were registered under individuals' names, mainly tribal leaders. Gradually many tribesmen became tenants of their leaders. The process increased stratification within the tribal groups. The wealthy tribal chiefs settled down in the towns near their extensive properties, which further increased the gap between the leaders and their tribal members. Due to settlement policies, more Kurdish tribes became sedentary. The tribal relationships were weakened but did not disappear entirely. The paramount chiefs did not survive, but lesser chiefs related by blood to most members of their smaller tribes remained and assumed more responsibility. Some tribes remained semimigratory and semisedentary at the same time. They traveled shorter distances, and poor members were engaged in seasonal work or moved to larger cities as migrant laborers. The number of settlements and villages grew, and many settled permanently.

By the 1930s Kurdish uprisings had largely ended. Simqu and his family had vanished. The chief of the Mukri tribe died in jail. The Kalhur leader was detained in Tehran, along with many other chiefs and their families. They lived well but were restricted in their movements and were watched closely. One of the most prominent leaders, Shaikh Taha, was relieved of his title and position and later died under suspicious circumstances. Tribal groups at the border, such as the Pizhdar, had their flocks seized, their tribal representatives expelled from their villages, and their properties confiscated. The tribal members of Hawraman and other groups that had clashed violently with the government troops were routinely executed in prisons. The situation was so desperate that in 1931 thirty-seven chiefs appealed to the British for help, but with no success. Reza Shah deliberately resettled tribes and took measures to destroy their social organizations. Many were forcibly transferred from Kurdistan and Kirmanshah to Yazd, Hamadan, and Isfahan. In their place he brought in Turkish-speaking groups. On a visit to Kurdistan in 1936, Reza Shah instructed the assembled leaders to stay away from politics and remain loyal to the central government. Had he not abdicated, Reza Shah would have been the most successful leader up to that time in terms of controlling tribal groups in Iran and imposing central authority.

The nationalist fever that affected the Kurds in Iran came from Iraq and not from chiefs such as Simqu. The Iranian government, in efforts to curtail the British influence, offered sanctuary to Kurdish nationalist leaders such as Shaikh Mahmud, who had revolted against the government in Iraq. This policy of supporting Kurdish insurgents in Iraq against the Iraqi government was adopted by subsequent Iranian governments all the way to the fall of the Pahlavi and beyond. However, once the Kurdish leader had moved to Iran, it became obvious that his presence was more a threat to the Iranians than to the authorities in Iraq.

The other major problem that influenced politics between Iraq and Iran was the migratory habits of frontier tribes. With the Iranian government's policies of centralization and establishing government posts and agencies at the border, land ownership, military service, and taxation posed major problems. One major conflict involved the Pizhdar Kurds moving between Iraq and Iran during their migrations. Initially Reza Shah had to gain the support of the rival tribes to maintain order, but once fully in control, he started a policy of disarmament. This required manpower, military tactics, and harsh treatment of the insurgents. The move was intensely opposed by the armed tribes yet was immensely popular with the public and townspeople living close to the tribal strongholds. The tribal loyalties still persisted, and many Kurdish soldiers conscripted into the army under the new mandatory military conscription for adult males willingly sold or handed over their rifles to dissidents from their own tribes. On other occasions the armed tribes would send their rifles across the border to Iraq instead of handing them over to the Iranian authorities. Conscription itself became a major problem and was initially resisted by many. Matters became worse when the government, in its attempts to build a uniform new nation-state, introduced new dress requirements in 1929. Kurds, like many other ethnic groups and clergy, objected to such policies.

Reza Shah managed to overcome most of the tribal-related problems by using military force and a number of tactics such as resettlement and detention. He abolished all tribal titles and prohibited Kurdish dialects, first in schools in 1934, then in all public and government correspondence and notices. Some of the chiefs' landholdings were confiscated, and instead they were granted lands in non-Kurdish territories. The last stroke against Kurds and other major tribes came in 1937 when Iran, Iraq, and Turkey signed a pact recognizing the existing borders, agreed to stop helping insurgents from other countries, and stopped hostilities. This increased the security of the country, ended most rebellions, and increased trade and travel between the provinces. Such improvements were welcomed by the urbanized population, who became free from invasion and extortions by the militant tribal groups.

Reza Shah dealt with the tribal chiefs decisively but left tribal organizations at lower levels intact. This enabled the lower-level leaders to assume leadership, and once Reza Shah was gone, the lesser chiefs were able to restore some tribal organization at lower levels, to some extent. To maintain control and prevent the spread of communist ideology with respect to water and land use, the government required all landowners to register their holdings in the newly established Land Registration Department. The registration of the lands in the chiefs' names had major economic consequences for the nomads and the peasants, who lost most rights to the previously communally owned lands. Their relationships with their chiefs and leaders were in large part transformed. After Reza Shah's abdication, many of the chiefs who had been kept in Tehran went back to Kurdistan, but the changes in the social organization were too altered for many to go back to the traditional power structures and relationships. However, one consequence of Reza Shah's reign was the articulation of a need for a Kurdish identity. This was manifested in the short-lived Republic of Mahabad that was established by insurgents in Iranian Kurdistan after World War II.

The Mahabad Republic of Kurdistan, 1945

England and the Soviet Union occupied Iran in 1941. The British were centered in Kirmanshah in order to be closer to Iraq and the Persian Gulf. The Russians occupied most of western and northern Azerbaijan. The two countries had different concerns and agendas. The British favored the continuity of the central government in Tehran in order to prevent local uprisings—particularly in the Khuzistan oil fields. The USSR and its revolutionary agents preferred a change of government in Iran. They wanted to see a government that was sympathetic to the Soviet ideology of the time. They supported a number of separation movements in Iran, including the short-lived Republic of Mahabad in Kurdistan.

The British were aware of the Soviet policy in the area and soon advised the government in Tehran to reduce any chances of confrontation with the Kurds and to make compromises. The British asked for the return of the exiled tribal chiefs, help in settling any tribe willing to do so, the removal of restrictions imposed on migrations, and the punishment of officers responsible for abuse and executions. The Iranian government was not willing to accommodate the demands and had no power to act in any case. The

Soviets would not give it access to Azerbaijan, and the British prevented it from moving in the south. Government officials asserted that they welcomed British help to restore order in the area since, after the abdication of Reza Shah, disorder had prevailed, but they had not decided what to do with the Kurdish tribes.

The Kurdish tribal leaders approached the British in the belief that it was possible to gain some independence with their help. A government delegation was sent from Tehran to meet with the chiefs and agreed to let the tribes bear arms and wear Kurdish costume as long as they remained under the central government's administration. The chiefs demanded more and wanted their titles and properties restored. Negotiations continued, with no success. Kurds attacked Urmiya and set the city bazaar on fire. They confiscated arms abandoned by the fleeing Iranian forces. Tribes around Sanandaj and Kirmanshah took over the countryside, raided villages, and soon appeared in Tabriz wearing traditional Kurdish costumes and fully armed. Armenians, Assyrians, and some Kurds formed a new party called Liberation and pillaged nearby Azeri villages. The government, unable to send any troops, armed the peasants to defend themselves and virtually lost control of the region. Hama Rashid, a powerful Kurdish leader, seized many villages and cities in central Kurdistan. He looted and burned down houses and confiscated property, and the Tehran government was forced to employ him as a local official.

By 1942 all the Kurdish chiefs had been released from detention or house arrest. Hama Rashid had attacked other Kurdish territory and was forced into Iraq. The Kalhur leader was back from detention, stayed in Kirmanshah, and offered the government help in restoring order in exchange for recognition as the paramount chief of the Kurds. He became the governor of one region and met fierce resistance from both the Kalhurs and other Kurdish groups. He survived and in 1943 was elected as one of the four Kurdish deputies in the parliament. He joined the tribal commission in the parliament and started a series of political maneuverings and the appointment of loyal supporters in Kurdistan. His actions alienated the three other Kurdish deputies, all major landlords from Sanadaj, and serious rivalries between the chiefs and their supporters created more havoc in Kurdistan.

The returning chiefs tried to regain some of their lost powers and privileges but faced a number of problems. Some tribal members questioned the authority of their chiefs. Soviet propaganda about land reform and socialist programs was known and backed by some local activists. Many Kurds who had been settled during Reza Shah's reign did not see the relevance of their chiefs anymore. Towns were growing, and many chiefs resided in the cities and had lost contact with their tribal members. The Soviets were concerned about tribal groups close to their borders. They invited thirty leading Kurdish chiefs to Baku and lent some support for an independent Kurdistan. Headed by Qazi Muhammad, the returning chiefs formed a Kurdish High Committee responsible for health and safety. They solicited other chiefs to put aside their differences and become united; many refused, and only a few chiefs supported the cause. The Soviets informed the group that the USSR supported the minority cause for self-determination but that the timing was not right. Furthermore, the Soviets backed another chief from the Shikak Kurds, close to their border, as the potential leader of the group.

One of the most significant events at the time and after Reza Shah's abdication was the emergence of political parties throughout the country. One such party, the Committee for the Revival of Kurdistan (popularly known as JK or Komala), was established in Mahabad. Its aim was to create an independent Kurdistan. The members were the new urban nationalists, some from Iraq, who rejected tribal loyalties in favor of a united modern Kurdish state. They connected with Kurdish nationalists in Iraq and Turkey. They sought language rights in education and administration and regarded local chiefs as archaic and self-serving. They blamed most of the *tariqa* shaikhs and other religious leaders for keeping the population ignorant. They used examples from Russia showing how, under the red flag of the Soviets, the previously tribal areas were on their way to progress, peace, and prosperity.

Qazi Muhammad joined the Komala, and the Soviets saw the party as a useful organ that in the case of independence could support their interests. Many tribal chiefs also joined the group and sought prominence as leaders. Komala gained popular support, moved into a large new building for its headquarters, and inaugurated its success with a play in Kurdish. In the play Kurdistan was envisaged as a woman (the motherland) violated by hooligans representing the three countries Iran, Iraq, and Turkey. Following further negotiations with the Soviets, Komala was dissolved and replaced with the Kurdish Democratic Party of Iran (KDPI). Prior to the Islamic Revolution, Komala emerged again, in 1969, as the Revolutionary Organization of the Toilers of Kurdistan. The group remained underground until the Islamic Revolution.

Like the Azerbaijanis during their short-lived republic, the Kurds did not demand independence from Iran at the beginning. They stated their aims to be the creation of an autonomous Kurdistan within Iran, language rights, appointment of Kurds as state officials, and the election of a provincial council in charge of administration and social matters for Kurdistan. They also pointed out the difference between the status of the chiefs and ordinary Kurds and stated that all Kurds should be equal with respect to law. The wealthy tribal chiefs tried to distance themselves from the KDPI and did not favor major social changes such as land reform, as did many people with strong religious sentiments. The situation changed in favor of Qazi Muhammad and the KDPI when two prominent rebellious Barazani Iraqi Kurds sought refuge in Iran and arrived with their armed supporters and families. The Soviets instructed Qazi Muhammad to help and placed the two under his supervision. The Democratic Party of Azerbaijan declared independence from the central government, and in December 1945 the KDPI announced the formation of the Kurdish People's Government in Mahabad. By January there was a parliament with thirteen members. Qazi Muhammad was declared the president, and Mulla Mustafa Barazani, the refugee from Iraq, was appointed the commander of the military forces. His appointment was resented from the beginning and created divisions among the Kurds.

The republic collapsed in less than a year, following the Soviet departure from Iran. Once the government troops arrived they burned Kurdish-language books and banned the use of Kurdish as the official language; many executions followed. Qazi Muhammad and a few others were hanged publicly. Barazani was offered the choice to go back to Iraq or be disarmed. He refused both options, gathered his men, and, while chased by the army, marched through the border areas and crossed the Russian border safely. His fifteen-day march created a legend and made him the most popular Kurdish leader of the time.

The creation of the Mahabad Republic is generally associated with the emergence of Kurdish nationalism in Iran. Its aim of creating a Kurdish identity and unity failed mostly because of problems among the Kurds themselves. The divisions, rivalries, and lack of cohesion and unity were centuries-old problems in Kurdish society. These divisions dominated Kurdish culture and hindered any successful articulation of a Kurdish ethnic identity or nationalism viable enough to survive the challenges of the time. Ethnotribal loyalties were still important and added to the problems. In the absence of a genuine and mature expression of nationalism or ethnic identity, the Kurds were forced to accept support from a foreign force. Association with the Soviets, who were occupying the country at the time, created resentment. The leaders underestimated the religious sentiments of the public and an overwhelming antagonism toward a communist regime. One positive aspect of the republic was the emergence of a substantial literature in Kurdish, with daily papers, a periodical for children, a monthly magazine, and radio broadcasting in Kurdish. The beginning of Kurdish written literature in Iran goes back to the end of the nineteenth century, when the first Kurdish-Persian dictionary was published in Tehran. During the Simqu revolt a small press was established in Kurdistan, but it did not survive. During the Musaddiq era, in the early 1950s, publications in Kurdish flourished. Such activities developed the Kurdish language, writing, and literature, and despite the restrictions imposed later on, the Kurdish script and language were fully established. The exodus of some of the elite and educated Kurds to western Europe from Iraq, Turkey, and Iran guaranteed the continuation of such literature in Europe.

The two major movements, the Simqu rebellion (1918–1922) and the Mahabad Republic of 1946, both happened in the same geographic area but were significantly different. The first was an attempt by a powerful Kurdish chief to consolidate power and establish personal authority against the government. In the Mahabad rebellion a new element, nationalism and the quest for a distinct Kurdish identity, was clearly becoming a significant feature of the movement. This quest for a Kurdish land and identity remained a major issue in Kurdistan and still continues.

With eyes cast downward, modest Kurdish "debutantes" pose for a photo near their village in Iran, 1946. (Bettmann/Corbis)

Conclusion

Under Reza Shah and following the establishment of the Pahlavi dynasty, the political economic and social foundations of state structures in Iran were fundamentally transformed. Major bureaucratic reforms and the establishment of modern civil, educational, and administrative institutions had a major impact on all levels of the society. The creation of a modern and loyal paid army ended tribal supremacy and the role of tribal chiefs as major power brokers. The state apparatus aimed at creating a cohesive concept of nationalism. At the core of the new nationalism was the monarchy, which represented the continuity of an ancient civilization. Ancient Iran was glorified, and the Persian language and culture were promoted to create unity and cohesion. At times force and military might were used to implement such ideas, and during the process some civil rights and liberties were ignored and violated. Although many in the urban and rural areas welcomed such policies, intellectuals, members of the clergy, and some liberal nationalists remained hostile. The Persianization of the state met with some resistance among non-Persian speakers, and quests for identity emerged among the marginal groups.

Timeline

1921	Reza Khan occupied the capital on February 21 and proclaimed a journalist, Sayyid Zia, as the prime minister. Ahmad Shah appointed Reza Khan as the commander of the army. Azerbaijan and Jangali movements were defeated.
1921	The Treaty of Sevres was signed between the Allied forces. Kurdistan and other Ottoman territories were divided up between Turkey, Syria, and Iraq. The Bakhtiyari lost their governorship, and by 1923 their titles were abolished.
1922	Reza Khan reorganized the army and defeated the Kurdish, Shahsevan, and Kuhgiluya rebellions.
1923	Reza Khan was appointed prime minister by the parliament. The treaty of Lausanne confirmed the Treaty of Sevres, despite major protests by the Kurds. Kamal Ataturk ("father of Turkey") became the first president of the new republic after abdication of the last Ottoman sultan.

1924	The Republic of Turkmenistan was founded in the Soviet Union.
1925	On December 12 Reza Khan was officially declared by the parliament as the new king, and the last Qajar king abdicated in his favor.
1926	On April 25 Reza Shah was crowned and the Pahlavi era began. Mohammad Reza, the shah's eldest son, was proclaimed crown prince.
1928	The parliament outlawed traditional ethnic clothing for all males, with the exception of registered clergymen. The government started introducing new modern dress requirements.
1932	Labor organizers were arrested throughout the country. The arrests started in 1927, and by 1932 150 people were in jail.
1933	Iran signed a new oil contract with the Anglo-Iranian Oil Company and increased its shares of the profits from 16 to 20 percent.
1935	*Iran* was adopted as the country's official name in foreign correspondence.

Significant People, Places, and Events

AHL-I HAGG: A minor but popular Shi'i sect, mainly in Kurdistan. The followers venerate Imam Ali and have regard for the Safavid dynasty. Their beliefs include a large number of Zoroastrian religious ideas.

ALEVID: A mixture of pre-Islamic, Zoroastrian, Turkmen shaman, and Shi'i ideas that became the basis of a religious sect during the fifteenth century. It is still very popular among many, including Kurds. They venerate Imam Ali.

AZERI: The relatively new term is used to denote both a language and a people. Most people from Azerbaijan call themselves *Azeri* and distinguish themselves from other Turkic speakers.

BARAZANI, MULLA MUSTAFA: The legendary Kurdish commander was born in Iraq in the Barezan region and founded the Kurdish Democratic Party (KDP) in 1946. His family still leads the Kurds in Iraq.

HAWRAMAN: A Kurdish group speaking the Zaza/Gurani language. They live both in Iran (West Kurdistan) and Iraq. They are mostly Ahl-i

Haqqi, but some are Sunni. In 1996 their population is reported to be close to 80,000. Half live in Iran.

LAK (LAKI): A tribal group and a Luri-related dialect, southern Kurdish in origin. They live mainly in Iran. The Zand dynasty was Laki in origin.

MUKRI KURDS: A major Kurdish tribe. The majority live in Iran, and their language belongs to the Surani group.

PIZHDAR KURDS: Border Kurdish tribes living in Iraq and Iran. Their language is Sorani in origin.

SANJABI: A Kurdish tribe and a dialect of South Kurmanji origin. Most live in Iran.

SHAKAK: A Kurdish tribe in Iran, Iraq, and Turkey. Their dialect is of Kurmanji origin.

TUDEH PARTY: The Soviet-backed party was formed in 1941 to replace the banned Communist Party of Iran. The party attracted many charismatic intellectuals. Its first chairman was a Qajar aristocrat. Most of the time it was underground and survived until the Islamic Revolution.

YAZIDI: A minor sect; most live in Iraq, and some in Iran and Syria. Their religion is a mixture of Zoroastrian, Manichaean, Jewish, Nestorian Christian, and Islamic ideas. There are close to 100,000 Yazidi altogether.

Bibliography

Atabaki, Touraj, and Eric Zurcher. *Men of Order: Authoritarian Modernization under Ataturk and Reza Shah.* London: I. B.Tauris, 2003.

Cronin, Stephanie. *The Army and Creation of the Pahlavi State in Iran, 1921–1926.* London: I. B.Tauris, 1997.

———. *The Making of Modern Iran: State and Society under Reza Shah, 1921–1941.* London: Rutledge/Curzon, 2003.

Fatemi, Faramarz. *The USSR in Iran.* South Brunswick and New York: A. S. Barnes and Company, 1980.

Ghani, Sirus. *Iran and the Rise of Reza Shah: From Qajar Collapse to Pahlavi Rule.* London and New York : I. B. Tauris, 1998.

Katouzian, Homa. *Iranian History and Politics: State and Society in Perpetual Conflict.* London: Routledge/Curzon, 2003.

Olson, Robert. *The Kurdish Question and Turkish-Iranian Relations: From World War I to 1998.* Costa Mesa, CA: Mazda Publishers, 1998.

Schulz, Fred. *Nomadism and Colonialism: A Hundred Years of Baluchistan, 1872–1972.* Oxford and New York: Oxford University Press, 2002.

Shaffer, Brenda. *Borders and Brethren: Iran and the Challenge of Azerbaijan Identity.* Cambridge, MA: Harvard University Press, 2002.

CHAPTER EIGHT

Tribes and the State

Major Tribal Groups under Reza Shah

Bakhtiyari

THE DECADE OF WORLD WAR I COINCIDED WITH THE EMERGENCE OF both tribalism and fragmentation in the Bakhtiyari, when the weak central government battled internal and external pressures. European involvement was partially halted due to the war itself. After the war the Bakhtiyari leaders were not able to use any new opportunities to their benefit because of the emergence of Reza Shah. Major khans were aware of the consequences of a very powerful centralized government, but they failed to challenge Reza Shah for a number of reasons. By this time the most important tribal leaders had lived in Tehran for decades and, in reality, had lost contact with their tribes. Another reason was that they based their opposition on traditional loyalties and strategies that had lost their strength in the face of the emerging nation-state. The new and popular concepts of nationhood, as presented by the government and accepted by the public, successfully identified the tribal leaders as ancient feudal warlords. They represented decadence, backwardness, and, in the case of the Bakhtiyari, collaboration with foreign forces. The new army had made them redundant, and the policies of integrating all Iranians into the national economy had created new opportunities that changed the traditional power and social structures. The new courts and judiciary replaced traditional arbitration systems and reduced the tribal leaders' power and influence among their tribal groups.

The first major change implemented by Reza Shah was to remove the Bakhtiyari khans as leaders and place the various groups under the government's direct administration. Prior to Reza Shah, in order to unify the warring factions, an agreement had been made between the two dominant groups, Ilkhani and Hajji Ilkhani, to restrict the leadership within the confederation to the eldest male of each of the two families. This arrangement, with some exceptions, had been followed from the late nineteenth century until the coming of the new dynasty. Reza Shah's moves against the Bakhtiyari and other tribal groups were based on a series of military, economic, and administrative maneuverings supported by his new modern army. The Bakhtiyari lost their governorships of Kirman, Yazid, and Isfahan in 1921 and 1922. By 1923 their right to be accompanied by military retainers had vanished, and Reza Shah removed the Chahar Lang group from authority over the Ilkhani by eliminating their leaders. Non-Bakhtiyari governors, backed by the national army, were appointed and sent to the area. Furthermore, orders were given that all negotiations with the Anglo-Persian Oil Company had to go through the government rather than the khans. All resistance was crushed, and in 1929 three Bakhtiyari khans were executed after a brief uprising. These moves were followed by the abolition of all high-ranking tribal positions. The Bakhtiyari territory was made into a new administrative unit, and more khans were imprisoned and eliminated. In the end many of the remaining prominent khans were forced to sell their extensive land holdings and their oil shares to the central government. The loss of their lands was a major factor in reducing their powers because they constituted one of the major landowning groups in the country.

Despite such major impacts and Reza Shah's centralization policies, the form and function of the Bakhtiyari tribes persisted to some extent. Regardless of all the changes and the state's assumption of the tribal leaders' juridical and administrative powers, many Bakhtiyari continued to align themselves with the Ilkhani or Hajji Ilkhani. Bakhtiyari territory was designated a province along with the neighboring Chahar Mahal, a Bakhtiyari stronghold. This resulted in a more precise definition of physical boundaries for the group, now identifying itself as a social unit with a given territory and with the Ilkhani/Hajji Ilkhani leadership for social and political interaction. Some migrations continued, but they were supervised by government agencies.

The Bakhtiyari followed their biannual migrations, and sheep and goats continued to be significant both in migrations and for their economic survival. The animal products were mainly consumed locally, but some, such as cheese and animal fat, were traded, and wool was used to weave carpets, containers, and tents. Some Bakhtiyari lived as settled agriculturalists, and permanent agricultural settlements existed throughout the territory, as they still do today. The settled Bakhtiyari maintained close ties with their nomadic relatives and shared resources and skills when needed. In the past, both groups

Bakhtiyari men dancing in a group at a wedding. Dastena, near Shahr-e-Kord in Chahar-mahal-va Bakhtiyari. (Nasrollah Kasraian)

had been more or less organized on the same political basis and shared many cultural values and practices. To some extent, the newly powerful central government altered the relationship between the sedentary and nomadic Bakhtiyari. The villagers were not armed and traditionally relied on their nomadic tribes for defense. The disarming of the tribal groups by Reza Shah reduced their dependency on both the tribal groups and the Bakhtiyari khans.

The sedentary villagers practiced dry farming and herded small flocks. Sheep and goats remained very important; horses were rare even among the pastoral nomads, who primarily used donkeys for transportation. The horses were mostly used for riding by men, with the exception of the khans' wives. Both the sedentary and the nomad Bakhtiyari maintained specific territorial boundaries and identified themselves with specific names. Outsiders performed specialized tasks and religious rituals at times needed. Environmental changes were detrimental as far as the pastoral nomads were concerned. The pasture lands in the mountains of southwest Iran were vanishing quickly due to an increase in population, charcoal consumption, and overgrazing. Such factors affected the availability of reasonable pasture to maintain the flocks and increased tensions between the government and a number of different groups demanding appropriate pastures.

Following the government's centralization policies, permanent agricultural villages increased in size and population. One major change was that both the nomads and the agriculturalists managed their affairs through state political offices. The Bakhtiyari confederation, which had emerged in the mid-nineteenth century, was in reality redundant by the 1930s. The major khans had lost all power and considerable wealth. However, individual tribes, which consisted of named units encompassing smaller ones, did survive, though in a more fragmented state. The tribe's primary unit, the nuclear family, functioned with help from the extended family. Pasture rights continued to be derived from membership in the tribes, though at this time a government appointee regulated affairs. There was sporadic opposition in the tribes to the government agencies and their agents, but in the absence of powerful khans and a united front, all such efforts failed.

After Reza Shah's fall, two major Bakhtiyari khans were still living, but their sons and grandsons did not seek to regain a role as great khans. Some property was restored to them, but the new generation had lost both the contact with the tribal members and the motivation to follow the traditional roles expected of them. With family rivalries still existing and an uncertain future with respect to their relationship with the central government, the younger khans were not willing to attempt to reestablish their tribal power. Instead they focused on establishing links with the new royal family and using their influence and wealth to obtain high offices in the government. In the decade following Reza Shah's abdication, two prominent Bakhtiyari attained high positions in the new military and security forces and in the National Iranian Oil Company; the new shah's second wife, Soraya, was a Bakhtiyari.

Qashqa'i

In the twentieth century five major tribes constituted 75 percent of the Qashqa'i population. The same five exist in nineteenth-century records, but estimates of their numbers vary in different accounts. The Qashqa'i were the most united group and maintained loyalty to their popular chiefs. The Qashqa'i paramount chief supported Reza Khan in his bid for power in 1920. Later he was persuaded to become a member of the parliament and moved to Tehran. Once the government started disarming the tribal groups and aimed to control them, conflict was inevitable. Military governors were sent to provinces, and administrators were supported by armed personnel who accompanied nomads during their migrations. Such officers gathered information, assessed taxes, and were instructed to collect the taxes. By 1929 rebellions had started. The Qashqa'i, in particular, resisted the new dress codes. The appointment of a corrupt military governor worsened the situation, and resistance continued even after he was dismissed. Soon the Qashqa'i were joined by other groups, such as the Khamseh and many more. A temporary peace was negotiated, but limited disturbances continued in the region. By 1933 the government had carried out extensive military campaigns using heavy artillery and air raids, curtailed seasonal migrations, and jailed and executed Qashqa'i leaders. The paramount chief died in jail under suspicious circumstances.

In 1933 the parliament enacted a law merging all the major tribal groups of Iran into a single confederacy. In 1934 tribal representation in parliament was officially abolished. Such policies changed the relationships of the tribal groups to their leaders and to the central government, thus significantly altering the social organization of these groups. With the paramount chiefs either dead, in jail, or exiled, the lower levels of the tribal leadership, such as headmen and elders, were able to assert more power. A decentralized confederacy emerged, and the Qashqa'i became more determined to assert a common identity. From this time on they overwhelmingly chose Turkish as their primary language and insisted on wearing Qashqa'i costume. However, they lost most of their herds and pack animals and, due to forced settlements and loss of pasture, suffered severe economic hardship.

Following Reza Shah's abdication, the sons of the last paramount chief, who had been detained in Tehran, went back to Fars. The eldest son was acknowledged as the new leader and tried to restore the devastated tribes in their former territories. He implemented many reforms and was successful in gathering the dispersed groups and restarting the old migratory routines. He paid for reconstruction, implemented an animal redistribution program, and offered monetary assistance to thousands of tribal members. The leadership also sought allegiances with other tribal groups in the area and was involved with a number of other tribal groups in an uprising against the central government in 1946. At the same time they asserted Qashqa'i identity by choosing flags, distinctive hats, and tents that identified them as Qashqa'i. They appealed to the United Nations to be recognized as a distinct minority, but with no success. They managed to gain relative independence for the tribe and participated in local elections, keeping their distance from the central government and thus receiving little interference from it.

Households remained the smallest unit, and a camp was, and still is, a temporary association of several households. A pasture group is composed of several camps remaining in close proximity to each other. Several pasture groups formed a subtribe and were under the supervision of a headman. A tribe consisted of several subtribes and was headed by a khan. The khans formed the elite or the aristocracy of the Qashqa'i. They supported the Shahilu lineage and accepted their supremacy as ilkhans, or paramount chiefs of the confederation. Each tribe had its own summer and winter pastures allocated to it by the paramount chief following consultation with the khans and other interest groups. The khans were responsible for the general affairs of the tribes and mediation at times of conflict, and they designated local leaders, collected taxes, and negotiated with local authorities. Environmental factors, such as rich pastureland, made the nomads more prosperous than other pastoral nomads. Remote and inaccessible migration routes and distance from the capital and borders made them inaccessible to government forces. However, they would later lose this advantage due to new roads, modern methods of warfare, and a new air force. The ilkhans and khans generated their wealth from their properties and other investments and avoided heavy taxes and fees on their own people, which guaranteed the tribal members' loyalty. Their political leadership was more centralized than that of the Khamseh or Shahsevan. They visited Shiraz twice a year during migrations and established commercial, personal, and political ties with the city.

The settled Qashqa'i more or less followed the same three levels of sociopolitical organization and maintained close ties with their tribe, subtribe, and confederacy. No province was named after them, unlike the Bakhtiyari or Kurds, but they were treated as a single administrative unit by government agencies. During Reza Shah's period, when governmental agents were trying to register relevant information, confusing figures were presented to the authorities. In 1940 the Qashqa'i reported 80,000 members for conscription purposes and 400,000 for ration distributions. The composition of the tribes has remained mostly unchanged since the mid-nineteenth century, with an increase in the number of settled communities. The confederation included groups that provided services, such as musicians, blacksmiths, craftsmen, and camel herders. These were part of the confederation but were recognized to be from different origins, such as gypsies and Baluchi. The group enjoyed relative peace for a while before the consolidation of power by Mohammad Reza Shah, who was declared king following his father's abdication in 1941.

Shahsevan

Reza Shah's tribal policies involved pacification, disarmament, and resettlement. His pacification and disarmament of the Shahsevan in their traditional territories, Moghan and Ardabil, happened in 1922 and 1923. Their subjugation was quick and very efficient, and resistance was brief and sporadic. Banditry and armed intertribal rivalries ended, and an unprecedented degree of government control and peace was established. The chiefs who cooperated kept their properties and wealth while others were banished. The Ardabil group lost all its powerful chiefs, but a few relatively influential chiefs remained among the Meshgini Shahsevan in the Moghan area.

However, as in other tribes, the chiefs lost many of their functions, and their relationship with tribal members was altered significantly. Tribal titles such as "khan" were abolished. With the power of major tribes curtailed, some minor tribes declared independence and dealt directly with the government agents, with no need for protection by the larger tribal groups. The Shahsevan kept most of their winter and summer pastures, taxes were regulated, and they paid pasture dues at a specific rate per animal. Azerbaijan lost prominence to Tehran, and with new programs to industrialize the nation, the agricultural sector of the economy was ignored. The decline affected the local economies, and emigration into larger cities became routine.

The resettlement policies, starting in 1930, had major consequences for tribal groups, including the Shahsevan. The nomad families were instructed to stop migrating, settle down, build houses, and cultivate their pastures. Several areas were designated for settlement. Supervisors and other personnel sent to improve irrigation systems and implement the settlement policies accompanied the new settlers. Many nomads settled in villages near their former migration routes, and their presence put additional pressure on the natural resources of these areas. Another major consequence of the settlement policy was a substantial shortage of animal produce due to drought, famine, and mismanagement. The settled nomads were not in charge of individual flocks; instead, a few from the households were appointed to oversee the grazing of a number of flocks. They could not effectively perform the task, and a large number of flocks was destroyed, leading to a shortage of animal products.

By 1935–1936 the government agencies had realized that the settlement policies were not working. The program was evaluated, and some reforms were introduced and some restrictions lifted. Following Reza Shah's departure, many went back to pastoral nomadism, but a large number remained settled or migrated to the larger cities in search of employment. In 1942 the Iranian government established a Tribal Commission in Tehran to inquire into tribal problems, restoration of migratory routes, and return of confiscated properties.

Inside an Ilsavan (Shahsevan) tent. Each tent accommodates an extended family. The inside, where women mostly work, is carefully organized because the tribes keep all their belongings there. Food sacks, fat preserved in goat skin, sour milk, cheese, butter, flour, wheat and wool sacks, etc., are placed at the side, with bedding and gelims and jalims (mats and small mattresses for sitting) in front of them. There is an oven in the middle of the tent beside the chesko (a wooden peg fixed in the center of the tent to which the wooden wheel of the tent top is joined with a rope to protect the tent against winds and storms). Life is centered around the oven. If the son of the family gets married, a section of the tent is given to the newlywed couple until they can afford a new tent. This section is separated from the rest by a curtain. (Nasrollah Kasraian)

Following the occupation of Iran by the Allied forces, the Shahsevan, who were very anti-Russian, remained hostile to the Soviets and the Tudeh and Democratic Parties in Azerbaijan. Their leaders were arrested by the Russians and instructed to support the Soviet-backed groups in the area. Some resistance followed, but they soon gave up, and a prominent Shahsevan was murdered by the revolutionary forces. They later received arms from the Iranian government after the Soviet departure and fought the revolutionaries.

The Shahsevan differed from the other major tribes of the time. In 1923 they did not have a paramount chief; they distinguished between settled and nomadic groups and attached more prestige to the latter. Traditionally, pasture rights came with membership in the tribes, and tribal members supported their own chief. Shahsevan identity was associated with particular names, dress, and behavior rather than pasture, flocks, and tents. The settled groups lived as crop-sharing tenants or laborers on others' lands and were generally denied tribal membership. The Shahsevan used the term *Tat* for such peasants. The Tats were normally without property and formed a residual category among the Shahsevan. Once the nomads were forced to settle, the difference between them and the Tats became irrelevant; however, the distinction remained in the local folk literature and still persists. The tents that were banned emerged as a significant symbol of Shahsevan identity, and like those of the Qashqa'i, were quite distinctive.

Traditionally, the tribal organization was hierarchical and constituted the ruling khans; the noble families and tribes; and the common tribes, or commoners, as they were called. The noble families formed the nucleus of the tribe and claimed descent from the founder of the confederacy in the distant past. The chiefly or noble families bore their ancestor's name and attached major significance to such names. The tribes included another class of workers and peasants, such as Tats, who had no control over pasture or farmland. The lesser or common tribes served under a noble tribe, and their leaders were included in the entourages of the noble groups. The commoners, their leaders, and their chiefs could not assume the leadership of the noble tribes, which was determined by patrilineal descent. After 1941, when many nomads resumed migration, fundamental changes transformed the traditional social structures. Descent and the distinction between settled and nomadic tribes were now irrelevant; instead, pasture and the size of the migrating group became more important. Compared to other groups, such as the Qashqa'i, the Shahsevan suffered less under the settlement policies. This was due to the fact that they resisted less; also, favorable environmental factors, such as good soil and climate and fertile local farmland, were helpful in maintaining a relatively sustainable economy once they settled.

Lurs and Luristan

The province of Luristan is located in the western part of Iran and is named after its inhabitants, various Lur groups. Historically, it covered a much larger territory, including the present-day Bakhtiyari region and parts of Khuzistan. For administrative purposes over the centuries, particularly in the twentieth century, it was divided into smaller units, and parts of it were annexed to other provinces. There are two major groups distinguished by language. Traditionally, the two were organized into several smaller tribes. In the nineteenth century the two main dialects, Major and Minor Luri, were still spoken by many. Currently, the two dominant dialects are Luri and Laki. The two are distinct but closely related. Luri is an archaic dialect derived from New Persian, and Laki is a southern Kurdish dialect. The speakers of the two languages understand each other and speak Persian as well, and both groups regard each other as Lur.

At the beginning of the century many still practiced pastoral nomadism and maintained ties with their settled kin in the villages. Many were settled during the early and mid-twentieth century or migrated to larger cities. Traditionally, the tribal organization consists of four units. The house or tent was the smallest unit and was headed by the male head of the household, which consisted of the immediate and sometimes extended family. The tents resembled the yurts of central Asia. They were dome-shaped, held together by bent semicircular poles, and joined on the top. Several households formed a sublineage connected through a common ancestor and with a specific name, and they normally camped together. The basic unit of sociopolitical organization, the patrilineage, consisted of two or more sublineages claiming common ancestry and occupying a certain territory. The last and the most complicated unit, the tribe, had several patrilineages and was headed by the khans who owned or controlled the land used by the various smaller groups. Until the early 1930s the groups still migrated between summer and winter pastures with their herds, mainly goats and sheep, donkeys, mules, and a few horses, and their distinctive black tents. Most animal products, including wool, were kept for their own use, but they also traded with the local villages.

On the surface they are Muslims and Shi'i but do not follow most of the orthodox practices. They have many local saints and venerate their mausoleums with many unorthodox rituals and practices. Being buried in a cemetery next to a shrine is a major achievement for many Shi'ites and is a popular practice in Luristan. Up to the twentieth century, when it was still possible for Shi'ites to be buried in the holy shrines in Iraq, carrying corpses from Iran to Iraq for burial was a major and thriving business. Orthodox Islam is against the use of tombstones; however, the cemeteries in Luristan display a number of elaborately carved horizontal tombstones with figures of humans, horses, and other motifs and inscriptions. The local shrines are used for a number of reasons, including oath-taking in legal matters, cures for ailments, relief from misfortune, and common Shi'i ceremonies during Ramadan and Muharram. Despite many unorthodox practices, the Lurs, like most of the Shi'i in Iran, mourn the death of Imam Hussein and celebrate the end of Ramadan, the month of fasting.

A man from the Hassanvand Lur tribe inside a black tent beside the warm oven.
Between Khorram-Abad and Andimeshk. (Nasrollah Kasraian)

Reza Shah's tribal policies transformed the existing sociopolitical organization of the group. The tribal groups in Luristan were very resistant and
fought for almost seven years against the government forces, beginning in
1922. By 1930 many of their leaders had been jailed and some executed, their
territories had been occupied, and entire tribes were moved to Khurasan and
forced to settle down in the area. Migration routs were blocked and the black
tents confiscated and destroyed. They were forced to abandon their clothing,
their land was registered, and government agencies took the place of local leaders. After Reza Shah's abdication they were not able to resume nomadism; they
had lost tribal autonomy, and most remained settled. The villages replaced the
tribes as the smallest political units, and the Lurs maintained family and tribal
ties in their settlements. Despite all the changes, the ruling families were still
able to impose some authority and control over the tribal members at the time.

Turkmen Groups

In the twentieth century the bulk of the Turkmen population in Iran occupied territories in Gorgan near the Caspian, mostly in an area that bears their

name, Turkmen Sahra ("the plain of the Turkmen"). They occupy much of the eastern portion of the Mazandaran province and the northern borders of Khurasan and are next to the Central Asian Republic of Turkmenistan. Originally from central Asia, for centuries they maintained contact with related tribes in the western portion of Soviet central Asia and Afghanistan. They all shared the same language, had similar cultural practices, and claimed descent from the same mythical ancestor, Oghuz Khan. They trace their history for a millennium and as of the tenth century had been converted to Islam. They are Hanafi Sunni and are not very orthodox in their religious practices but nevertheless identify closely with Islam. Their language belongs to the Oghuz, or southwestern group of Turkic languages, and is related to Azerbaijani and modern Turkish. Their cultural practices are more similar to those of other Turkmen groups, such as the Uzbek and Kirghiz, than to those of Azerbaijanis or Turks from Turkey. The Turkmen in the area always posed major problems for the governments of Iran, Russia, and Afghanistan. For centuries they were involved in the slave trade and, by raiding and attacking settlements, captured and sold slaves in local and foreign markets. They also lived off banditry and were feared by the villagers who were exposed to their raids. Blood feuds were common and resulted in further raids and killings by the feuding groups. They were not isolated and through their migrations established relatively extensive economic and political links with the urban and rural centers in the area.

They helped the early Qajars to establish themselves and remained relatively autonomous prior to the Pahlavi regime in Iran. The two largest groups, the Tekke and the Yomut, remained more or less nomadic until the 1970s, despite internal and external pressures. The largest settled group, the Guklan, remained southeast of Gorgan. By the early twentieth century they were known for their heavy addiction to and consumption of opium. Other smaller tribes also existed with a number of tribes from other origins that had become Turkmen by culture. They paid special respect to a group of four non-Turkmen tribes who claimed descent from the first four caliphs of Islam. These tribes were regarded as having sacred descent, traveled between all groups, and mediated during crises and disputes. Turkmen migrations were short, and they took advantage of seasonal agriculture due to the favorable climate and soil. The ecology and the environment they lived in were very favorable for agriculture; however, they preferred nomadism to settled life.

Prior to the 1920s the Guklan were under the control of the Kurdish chiefs who ruled over the area. They had a governor appointed by the Kurdish chief and supported by his own Kurdish militia. The governor was responsible for the collection of taxes and normally did not interfere in the internal affairs of the Turkmen. The Yomut remained more independent. Generally, the groups that were close to major administrative centers were under more control than those farther away. Reza Shah's rise to power affected them as early as 1920, when attempts were made by the Iranian government to subjugate them.

Reza Shah's policies initially met stiff resistance from the Turkmen groups. By 1924 a loose confederation had formed between the major groups, but they retreated when they realized the strength of the government forces. Reza Shah firmly established central control in the region, and by the 1930s raiding and collection of tributes from nearby villages had stopped. Many from the Yomut tribes fled to Russia but found the situation even more unfavorable under the socialist Soviet Union. Their land was taken, but the Iranian authorities made allowances for the groups who came back and accepted disarming. The settling of the nomads further increased the tension. They were forced to build houses at their dry-season camps and were allowed to migrate only during the wet season. Government administrators arrived and were established in the area. Government headmen were appointed and made responsible for enforcing government decisions. They watched the Russian occupation of Iran and, for a brief period, were subject to Russian control. After Reza Shah's abdication, the area witnessed chaos and uprisings, and, like other nomadic groups, the Turkmen tried to restart migration and renew nomadism. However, the socioeconomic changes had transformed the traditional ways of life for the Turkmen, as for the other nomadic groups. The southern portion of the Gorgan plain was developed rapidly and became a major industrial center, and the inhabitants of the area became sedentary cotton farmers. Others resumed their nomadic way of life after Reza Shah's abdication, but once the Iranian government consolidated central power, they became subject to government control.

Baluchistan

Baluchistan was the last province to be controlled by the central government. It had remained poor and isolated, but prior to Reza Shah's reign, because of inaccessibility, it had remained more or less autonomous. The area was divided by the British into two sections in the late nineteenth century. Most sections became part of the western borderlands of British India, and the southern territories remained loosely connected to Iran. A very powerful Baluchi khan ruled in southern Baluchistan, and by the end of the nineteenth century he had managed to exert control over most adjacent territories. Reza Shah first tried to negotiate and asked the Baluchi khan to come to Tehran and accept disarming. Upon his refusal, another Baluchi tribal lord was appointed as the governor. A full-scale war broke out, and the Baluchi khan was decisively defeated. Some groups supported the shah against other Baluchi tribes; compromises were made, and disarming was enforced. Iranian Baluchistan's borders were finally fixed in 1928 when west Baluchistan came under the full control of Reza Shah's army following the execution of some prominent Baluchi. By 1935 none of the major tribal chiefs of the area had been able to resist, and they fell under the control of the central government. The modern province is called Sistan and Baluchistan, and the area remained relatively quiet after Reza Shah's departure.

Most people in Baluchistan are Sunni and speak Baluchi, an Iranian-related language. The language has six major dialects and is closely related to Pashto, one of the major languages in Pakistan and Afghanistan. The Baluchi regard themselves as good Muslims and follow the Islamic legal codes with respect to marriage, divorce, inheritance, and death rituals. Imams are normally hired for important functions, and the people have great respect for such figures. By the mid-twentieth century, the majority remained seminomadic or nomadic and the rest were settled farmers or lived in major towns such as Zahidan.

Due to extreme environmental conditions and lack of resources, the Baluchi people have utilized a number of ways to cope with scarce resources and are flexible in their patterns of politico-economic life. These multiple ways of earning an income and organizing political life have enabled them to deal with very unpredictable circumstances. Tribal patterns of authority remained significant among all Baluchi, including the settled population. However, the Baluchi khans, despite owning large properties, never attained the same level of centralization or prosperity as other khans, such as those of the Bakhtiyari. The annexation of part of the British India Baluchistan to Pakistan in 1947 created problems among the anti-British Baluchi population in Iran. There were also some unsuccessful attempts by the Russians to gain some influence in the area. However, the central government remained in control.

The economy in Baluchistan remained subsistence-oriented, with some production for the local markets. Prior to 1935, raiding of livestock, goods, and slaves remained a lucrative business. Marriage was and is preferred between related groups and involves negotiations between senior male family members and material and financial support from the groom's family. The Baluchi maintained their traditional costumes, and the inaccessibility of the

A davvar *(semicylindrical tent made of bent palm branches and a straw mat covering) from a* halk *belonging to a cattle-raising Baluch tribe near Bampur, Sistan-va-Bauchistan (Nasrollah Kasraian)*

area made it difficult for government agents to impose the dress code restrictions. Their black tents are similar to other Baluchi tents, and they have their own designs for rugs and other woven artifacts. The women's clothing is decorated with very elaborate needlework, and the men wear special trousers, long tunics, and turbans. Clothes have social functions, and they mark membership in common or different social categories and groups. The Baluchi stayed fairly unchanged for the next few decades and remained under central government control.

Other Ethnic Groups

Khuzistan was rapidly changing because of the oil industry and its vital role in the country's economy. In the nineteenth century, the agricultural economy of the Persian Gulf area was transformed from local produce into one of cash crops such as opium, mainly due to the trade between Iran and British India. The port of Bushire, on the Persian Gulf, was used extensively for such trade. The oil industry in the twentieth century transformed the area once again. Expenditure in the oil sector and new employment opportunities resulted in the expansion of towns and settlements. The majority of the Arabs remained in Khuzistan, along the Persian Gulf coastal areas, with a few in the central and eastern provinces. Urbanization increased, and both urban and rural Arabs retained their tribal ties. Pastoral nomads still existed along the Persian Gulf coastal plains and kept herds of sheep, cattle, and camels. The rural Arabs practiced farming, and many were involved in the local small-scale fish industry. The opium production was monopolized and regulated by the government and hence lost its importance as a cash crop produced by local farmers. Many from the rural areas joined the new work force in the oil industry and related businesses, mainly as laborers and unskilled workers. There were many Persians, Lurs, and Kurds in the area, among others. The Arabs in Iran are mainly Shi'i with some Sunni, and at this time they had no major sense of ethnic solidarity. There were no significant articulate individuals or groups expressing such affinities.

Gilan, Mazandaran, and Caspian provinces in the north, near the Caspian Sea, became major industrial centers, and many new factories were established in the region. Reza Shah favored the area and had extensive holdings that he had bought from local landlords. The way these properties were purchased remained controversial. Nevertheless, most were developed by industries that set up efficient large-scale production of a number of products and transformed the region. Labor movements and political parties emerged once more and played a significant role in the events of the following decade. The lush environment, abundant rain, fertile soil, and cash crops with capital investment transformed farming and agriculture in the area. Widespread use of local dialects, such as Gilaki, Taleshi, and Mazandarani, continued, but the new generations were educated in Persian, and most welcomed integration and modernization. Modern hotels and a flourishing new industry, tourism, brought people from all corners of the country into the area and its newly established resorts. The area became a cosmopolitan and prosperous region, and its integration into the new modern state was stable and smooth.

Religious Minorities and Early Pahlavi Rule

The spiritual leaders of the religious minorities for centuries had remained isolated and uneducated with respect to their own scriptures. Such literature was in old languages not known by many and was passed on from one generation to another without understanding of the actual texts. Contact with Westerners, the active presence of missionaries, and translations of texts into modern Persian in the late nineteenth and early twentieth centuries changed these religious institutions. The sociopolitical events and modernization processes also improved their social and material welfare in the country.

The religious minorities in Iran, with the exception of the Baha'i, benefited from the constitutional movement. They were instrumental in the success of the movement and were recognized as citizens of the country and, with some exceptions, gained equal rights. The major leadership positions under the constitution, such as premiership, were reserved for the Muslims, but the religious minorities were able to participate in the social, economic, and political events of the century during the Pahlavi reign. On the whole their histories favor the Pahlavi era as their best, with some reservations during Reza Shah's period. Their integration into Iranian society was slow at the beginning but accelerated quickly. Universal education and a standard secular curriculum brought children from all faiths together. Minority schools existed, and children were instructed in Persian, but they also had their own curriculum or religious instruction on a regular and mostly daily basis. All primary schools had a minor course in Islamic studies, in which the principles of Islam were taught. However, members of religious minorities who attended regular schools were not obliged to take courses in Islamic studies. Foreign missionaries were welcomed but had restrictions imposed on them in the 1920s. The missionary schools were open to all, including Muslims, before restrictions were imposed on them from 1931 to 1932. First village evangelism was prohibited, and then, in 1932, Iranians from any religion were banned from attending missionary schools. Such decisions were made following violent clashes and massacres in Azerbaijan and events in Iraq, Russia, and Turkey. Once calm and security were established in Iran under Reza Shah, the religious minorities were able to consolidate and reorganize. The government's policies with respect to the religious minorities were mixed, and political considerations were important. Restrictions were applied at times, particularly with respect to the Armenians, who were suspected of favoring Russia. The Zoroastrians benefited more because of their connection with the ancient past that was being glorified at the time. Most of the restrictions applied were politically motivated and were not religious in nature. Genuine efforts were made to attain the minorities' loyalty, but communist or antigovernment tendencies were not tolerated and could put large groups under suspicion. The general population, particularly in small towns and provinces, remained skeptical of, and at times hostile and prejudiced toward, non-Muslims.

Armenians

Armenians were very involved in the Constitutional Revolution and afterward. However, they kept their affinity for their motherland in Armenia. In the early twentieth century there were around 100,000 Armenians in Iran. The massacres of Armenians in Turkey and the Russian Revolutions of 1905 and 1917 brought many Armenian refugees into Iran. They mainly settled in Azerbaijan, and their close proximity to Transcaucausia and Anatolia exposed them to the political events and ideologies in Russia and Armenia. In the period from 1920 to 1941, loyalty to Armenia was still important. However, traveling restrictions existed between the Soviet Union and Iran, and this curtailed communication between Armenia and the Armenians in Iran. The Russians encouraged Armenians to move to Armenia in Russia, and assistance was periodically provided for such moves. Sometimes the Iranians favored such moves and at other times created difficulties. Most of the restrictions imposed were short in duration. The Pahlavi era gave Armenians ample opportunities to be active in every aspect of life in Iran. The immigrants from Russian territories used their language skills and prospered during World War II because of their close association with the Allied forces occupying Iran. Many Armenian intellectuals joined the Tudeh Party and were pro-Russian at the time. Historically, Russians protected them against Turkish, Kurdish, and Azeri invasions. They felt affinity for Christian Russia, and despite the unpopularity of communism among the general Armenian population, the activists and the intellectuals maintained their support of this ideology. On the whole the Iranian intelligentsia at the time was proleft. The pro-Russian sentiments were used by the government against the Armenian left during arrests and persecutions of communists. Their participation in the arts and entertainment business was substantial, and they were among the first generation of professional actors, musicians, and classical dancers in Iran. They became very prominent in a number of fields, including the oil industry, retail, and caviar production.

Reza Shah's government guaranteed the cultural and religious autonomy of these groups and stopped systematic harassment of them by the Muslim clergy. The Christians, however, encountered some problems from 1938 to 1939, and restrictions were imposed on both the Armenians and the Assyrian Christians. A number of reasons were given for the imposed policy. Such theories range from Reza Shah's admiration for Kamal Ataturk in Turkey and imitating Ataturk's policies with respect to Christians to the rise of Nazi supporters and pan-Iranian groups and caution about the militarization and war situation in Europe. In the agreement signed between Iran and Turkey in

1932, Reza Shah handed over to Turkey a small territory called Little Ararat. The area, which historically belonged to Iran, had an Armenian holy site, and the majority of inhabitants were Armenians. The Armenians of Iran protested but did not prevail. In the late 1930s their schools were closed down, they were banned from employment in the government, and Armenian or Assyrian names of villages, cities, and streets were changed to Persian names. The name changes were applied to most non-Persian names, and they were equally protested by many groups, including the Azerbaijani. The restrictions on schools and employment were soon lifted.

The two major Christian groups in Iran, the Armenians and the Assyrians, had divisions between them. They were also divided on the issue of foreign missionary activities in Iran. Both groups were cautious, but the Armenians were more supportive of the missionaries, while the Assyrians in general were less willing and sometimes resented them. Missionary work and foreign penetration came hand in hand, and the Iranian government, especially Reza Shah, was aware of the two and at times acted vigilantly. Some of the restrictions applied to the Christians in the 1930s could have been a response to foreign penetration, especially in the turbulent period leading to World War II, and more specifically in response to the happenings in Russia and Iraq and the British presence in Iran.

Assyrians

Assyrian Christians are often viewed as the most complex Christian group in the Middle East. Originally Nestorians, over the centuries they have been divided between the Assyrians (Nestorians) and Chaldeans (Catholics). The Assyrians were further divided: The supporters of the West Syrian Church, who remained in Syria, called themselves the Jacobites. Further divisions occurred in the nineteenth and twentieth centuries; some became Protestants, and others joined the Russian Orthodox Church. Most call themselves Assyrians, and there have been debates regarding whether they should be labeled as a distinct ethnic group or a religious community. Even Iranian Assyrians make distinctions between Chaldeans and Assyrians and might refer to themselves as one and not the other. Following the Constitutional Revolution, they asked for two representatives in the parliament to represent the Chaldeans and the Assyrians separately. However, the Iranian governments have consistently recognized them as one group, Assyrian Christians, and assigned only one representative to the whole group. The Nestorians at the time had one diocese in

Tehran, and the Catholic group had three dioceses in Tehran, Urmiya, and Ahvaz in Khuzistan.

The Assyrians predominantly lived around Urmiya. They favored Russia, but they had no vision of an independent motherland. Both groups were at times targets of attacks by neighboring groups that used anti-Christian rhetoric in their political maneuverings. The Assyrians participated much less than the Armenians in the constitutional movement and tried to stay away from political events in the country. Their integration into Iranian society was slow, and they remained isolated. They were divided, and internal conflicts hindered their own development. They had complex relationships with other Assyrians in the Middle East and with the Russian Orthodox Church. Prior to World War I, the Nestorian Assyrians in Iran remained under the jurisdiction and authority of the patriarch in Iraq. Others had already converted to the Russian church, mostly to be able to obtain Russian protection against persecution and attacks by the Kurds and Azeris, who routinely attacked Christians, among other minorities. The Anglican church and other missionary denominations had their own supporters, and internal conflicts among various denominations prevented them from electing a member to the parliament. Assyrians of the later period mostly blame the foreign missionaries and distrust between the Assyrians and the Muslim authorities for the split in their community. The problems were so intense that the Assyrians could not agree on a representative for the Iranian parliament until 1959. The flow of Assyrian and other Christian refugees into Urmiya and Azerbaijan from Turkey in 1917–1918 increased tension among all groups, with violent clashes resulting; many Christians and Muslims perished during this period.

Reza Shah was able to return calm to the area. The Kurdish leader Simqu, responsible for the massacre of Assyrians, was defeated, and the area came under the control of the government forces. Many Assyrians went back to Urmiya and Azerbaijan, and missionaries resumed their activities in the area. The government recognized the potential threat of their presence in Iran; as of the 1920s, restrictions were imposed on missionary work in Iran. The events in Iraq in the early 1930s and disturbances among the Assyrian population there prompted the Iranian government to impose even more restrictions on foreign missionaries. Finally they were asked to leave Azerbaijan to avoid further problems. Between the two world wars, many Assyrians emigrated to Europe, Canada, and the United States, where they remained divided but able to live in peace after centuries of persecution. They used Aramaic for religious purposes and among themselves and Persian for other purposes.

Jews

The Jewish community historically has had more affiliation with the Iranians, but since the Safavid period it has also been subjected to more routine persecutions. Following the upheavals of the early twentieth century many, fearing persecutions that were common during periods of instability, emigrated to Jerusalem. Their fears were justified; from 1906 to 1921 anti-Semitic riots in Isfahan, Kashan, Shiraz, and Kirman devastated the Jewish communities. The constitutional movement improved the situation of Jews, but, like Christians, they could not send a representative to the first parliament.

Reza Shah ended any such attacks on religious minorities. Mass conversion of Jews stopped, and the Shi'ite concept of the uncleanness of non-Muslims was abandoned. Until the early twentieth century, the Jews spoke a language very similar to Persian, distinguishable only by a unique accent. They used the Hebrew script for writing Persian. Their integration into Iranian society was slow at the beginning but improved gradually. Some extremist groups in Iran and their newspapers supported Nazism and the anti-Semitic propaganda disseminated by the Germans, and the Jews became targets of extreme nationalists promoting the superiority of the Aryan race. There were no persecutions, but the anti-Jewish sentiment of this period emphasized their distinct ethnic character and Semitic origin. This focus was unlike the religiously motivated attacks by the clergy that focused on their religion and the animosity between Islam and Judaism. However, such attacks were not very common and were generally opposed by mainstream Iranians and their media. Jewish sympathizers of the leftist groups and antigovernment activists were punished like all other Iranians. In 1931 the Jewish deputy in the parliament was removed and executed. Accounts of his downfall vary even among the Jewish community in Iran; rivalries among the Jews or between Muslims and Jews, a failed conspiracy, and extremist views are mentioned among other reasons for his execution. However, no other Jew was executed, and the Jewish community was not persecuted. Recent scholarship has suggested that he was involved with a number of other Iranians in a group planning anti–Reza Shah activities. For a short time, during the last year of Reza Shah's reign, some restrictions with respect to employment in the army were imposed on Jews. Such restrictions were soon lifted. On the whole, Jews benefited during this period and were able to participate more actively in Iranian society; their situation kept improving.

Zoroastrians

Zoroastrian intellectuals took an active part in the constitutional movement and benefited from it. Unlike Jews and Christians, they refused to relinquish their right to send a deputy to the parliament. Their first deputy was a wealthy and influential merchant with many connections who helped the community greatly. The new secular codes and the presence of their own representatives in the parliament led to a major shift in the status of non-Muslims. They were barred from electing Muslims or being elected by Muslims, which restricted their full integration into the Iranian community; however, they were able to voice their concerns in the parliament. Segregation policies and *jizya* religious taxes were abolished, and Zoroastrians integrated more freely into Iranian society. Many were merchants, and some would become among the wealthiest entrepreneurs in the country. Zoroastrians remained in Kirman and Yazid, but more started emigrating into the capital. They had schools in Tehran, adapted more easily than some other minorities with respect to the language, and sympathized with and supported a new generation of Iranian activists and scholars focusing on pre-Islamic research and glorification of ancient Persia. Although their schools and temples were subjected to rules and sometimes restrictions imposed on all religious minorities, the glorification of ancient Iran made them a special case.

Ancient Zoroastrian symbols were adopted by the government as state emblems. When Iran asked all foreign nations to address the country as Iran and not Persia in 1935, it was stated that the name *Iran* existed in a variant form in the ancient book of Avesta (the Zoroastrian holy book) and was the true name of the country. Zoroastrians welcomed the new state ideology, and their leader and deputy in the parliament at the time worked very hard to improve the situation of his community.

Baha'i

The Baha'i are the descendents of Muslim (and some Jewish) Iranians and as such share the same language, culture, and history. Estimates about their numbers in Iran vary, and due to many persecutions and lack of legal status, reliable statistics are hard to obtain. The Iranian constitution did not recognize them as legitimate citizens, and they are regarded by many to be heretics and also accomplices in the British interest. The Baha'i believe in universal peace and tolerance of all religions and consider their own to be the best one in which all other creeds can converge. Following the nineteenth-century division between the Baha'i and Babi, the majority followed Bahaullah and his son Abdul Baha, who became the successor and the sole interpreter of his father's teachings. Due to the harsh treatment of Baha'i in Iran, early in the twentieth century they moved their headquarters out of Iran. They also started missionary activities in the United States, Canada, and Europe. Prior to his death in 1921, the Baha'i leader established the twin institutions of "Guardianship" and the "Universal House of Justice." The two worked side by side; the Guardianship's function was interpretation, while the function of the Universal House of Justice was legislative. The two remained independent but complemented each other. Baha'i faith grew extensively under the leadership of the Oxford-educated son of Abdul Baha, Shoghi Effendi.

The Baha'i enjoyed peace and prospered from 1926 to 1934. They were permitted to hold large public meetings with government agents and police present as a protective measure. They expanded the number of their schools, libraries, community projects, and cemeteries with no harassment. In 1930 for the first time they started openly building a national Baha'i center in Tehran. More Baha'i women became involved in the affairs of the community. They also started locating, identifying, and purchasing Baha'i holy places in Iran. National conventions were held beginning in 1927, and a Central Spiritual Assembly was elected to regulate their affairs. Despite their lack of legal status, employment in the government institutions of the period was open to them, and they were not barred from attending any of the educational institutions. Some achieved high positions in the country, especially in finance, and their high visibility was used against the government by the anti-Baha'i clergy and their supporters.

The emerging nation-state was secular, and religious differentiation was losing its dominance. This change facilitated the partial assimilation of the Baha'i into the Iranian community. However, some restrictions existed. They could not openly publish their religious literature, and Baha'i marriages were not recognized. This was mostly due to the fact that they did not have legal status, so unlike the recognized religious minorities, they could not carry out marriages in their own independent institutions. Such Baha'i institutions existed but were not recognized as legitimate. The government did not attempt to legalize their status because of opposition by the clergy. As of 1934, there was a sudden change of government policy, probably under pressure from religious authorities and also because of the political situation. Baha'i schools were closed, and their public meetings were banned. Such restrictions were political and happened to most religious minorities, ethnic groups, and political organizations. However, the Baha'i case was different.

Snow lies on the ground in front of a domed Baha'i temple in Chicago, Illinois, 1985. (Kit Kittle/Corbis)

Fanatical Muslim groups resented them and used such occasions to launch attacks against them. Anti-Baha'i sentiments lasted for a decade, and problems culminated in 1944, when attacks on the Baha'i community initially increased but were then controlled.

Baha'i believe in the propagation of their faith and continued their missionary activities despite systematic persecution in Iran. Initially they had officially appointed teachers at the local level, both residents and visitors who propagated the faith. With the number of Baha'i increasing, they started having local spiritual assemblies in various communities, with many classes to enable the general Baha'i populace to take part in the propagation as well. As of 1930, the Baha'i were encouraged to expand to the neighboring countries. Their advocates were called pioneers and were sent all around Iran as well. Following the restrictions imposed on them in Iran as of 1934, they reduced their activities in Iran for the time being. Despite easing tensions later on, they were never able to gain legal status in Iran; the public remained skeptical about their faith, and they remained a target of the clergy and fanatical Muslims.

Shi'i Religious Institutions

The majority of Iranians, close to 88 percent, are Shi'i; 10 percent are Sunni; and the rest are followers of other religions. The Baha'i probably constitute the largest group among the non-Muslims, but due to their persecution and lack of legal status in Iran, their exact numbers remain unknown. The success of the constitutional movement was a major setback for the clergy because they lost their prominence in the legal system. Shari'a, the Islamic code, was gradually abandoned with respect to most criminal, civil, and penal codes. It survived in the family and inheritance laws. The clergy maintained their extensive land holdings, including land owned by mosques and shrines and the religious endowment lands administered by the clergy. Reza Shah's establishment of modern government agencies further reduced their influence. All births, deaths, divorces, and marriages were to be registered in the appropriate government institutions. Traditionally, the clergy had managed such affairs. Modern educational institutions and a new accreditation system by the Ministry of Education ended their dominance in the field of education. Courts replaced their arbitration and judicial functions, and secularization trends diminished their popularity among the educated and the newly emerging middle class. Major religious mourning ceremonies commemorating Ali's and Imam Hussein's deaths were regulated, and self-mutilating practices, such as beating oneself with swords, and public slaughter of animals were banned altogether. The clergy had always used such emotionally charged occasions to raise sentiment among the public. The first half of the twentieth century was a time of setbacks and defeats for the Muslim clergy in most Muslim countries, and Iran was at the forefront of such anti-Islamic sentiments and policies.

Clergy resisted all such policies, with some success. They were attacked by the new intelligentsia for being archaic and draconian. In response, the clergy accused proponents of secularization of Westernization, corruption, and anti-Islamic sentiments. They reestablished and reinforced their traditional learning centers, known as the *hawza-i ilmi* (center for religious learning), in the major shrine cities such as Qum and Mashhad. The institutions became the most articulate centers of opposition to the Pahlavi dynasty in Iran for decades. High-ranking religious leaders and their entourages moved back to Iran from the holy cities in Iraq as of 1920. Under the leadership of prominent figures, a number of prestigious and wealthy religious learning centers were established. One minor religious figure at the time was Khomeini, the first leader of the Islamic Republic in 1979. Social and ethnic divisions existed within the ranks of the clergy. Of the three major religious leaders who emerged during the Islamic Revolution, one had the overwhelming support of the Azerbaijani population and was from this province.

Reza Shah's campaign to introduce European-style dress codes further isolated the clergy and made them look backward. He also introduced specific measures and tests for granting religious titles, and members of the clergy who did not pass the requirements were forced to abandon their turbans and traditional attire. The legalization of alcohol consumption and the compulsory emancipation of women were major blows to traditional Islam. The emancipation of women is still regarded by the clergy to be the most vicious attack on Islam by any ruler in Iran.

However, the final assault occurred when attempts were made to register the religious endowment lands and place these extensive holdings under the supervision of a government department. The lands were a legitimate Islamic institution, properties donated to the Muslim community for its benefit. The state was responsible for their administration. In the past, with the clergy in charge of all legal institutions, they had assumed the administration of the properties and were entitled to 10 percent of the annual income. From 1934 to 1968, a number of laws were passed, and eventually an organization independent of the clergy and under the direct supervision of the prime minister assumed administration and control of the properties. Such policies diminished substantial profit and income and were resisted by every possible means.

Women and Emancipation

Before and after the Constitutional Revolution, women's groups and societies emerged in Tehran and other major cities. Many participated in the movement but did not gain full benefit from the new constitution. They were barred from the electoral process, and the family codes were not modernized and remained within the domain of Shari'a, the Islamic legal code. Reza Shah's modernization policies benefited women, and compulsory universal education for all children opened up new opportunities despite opposition to such acts by the clergy and the more conservative segments of the society. In 1931 the marriage ages for girls and boys were elevated to fifteen and eighteen, respectively. Under the Islamic codes, girls as young as nine could marry with their fathers' consent. Women were also given the right to initiate divorce under certain conditions. A government-sponsored women's organization (Ladies' Center) was established with leading female activists of the time in charge. One of the most daring acts of Reza Shah was his compulsory emancipation of women. In 1936 Reza Shah and his wife and daughters attended the graduation ceremony at the Women's Teacher Training College in Tehran. All women were advised to come unveiled. Emancipation of women was officially inaugurated. Unveiling was made compulsory, and women were barred from wearing the traditional Islamic outer cover called the *chador* and the scarf in public.

The emancipation was a continuation of the earlier policies with respect to dress codes, with the aim of modernizing and unifying the diverse nation. The act was a direct assault on one of the major institutions of Islam: female veiling. The modern classes benefited from the act. The traditional women and dedicated religious groups felt assaulted, and many remained indoors and would not go out. The tribal and rural women had hardly ever followed the tradition of veiling and hence were not affected by the new law. Following Reza Shah's abdication, the restrictions were lifted. The changes and the new educational and employment opportunities had a significant impact on the status of women and their participation in public life following centuries of isolation and veiling. In the following decades they became one of the best-educated and most liberated groups in all of the Middle East.

Conclusion

With the exception of the Qashqa'i, most tribal groups in the country were fundamentally transformed between 1921 and the abdication of Reza Shah.

They became more marginal, were disarmed, and were forced to settle down. They lost relevance as major power players due to the creation of a modern army independent of the tribes. Beginning in 1941, many tribal groups tried to resume old patterns, but most did not succeed. The trend toward permanent settlements continued voluntarily. The changing economy was a major factor, and tribal groups' isolation and autonomy were further reduced with the advent of modern roads, communication, and education. The tribal chiefs in reality had lost support among many of their members, and many living in Tehran or Europe were not in direct contact with their tribes. Many prominent Bakhtiyari and other members of tribal elites remained close to the court. They exerted influence in national politics as individuals rather than as tribal leaders. New concepts of nationhood emerged, and a new national identity was forged and propagated through the media and implemented by the government apparatus. In the process some political rights and civil liberties were curtailed. The Azerbaijan and Kurdistan populaces remained divided with respect to fundamental concepts, such as national and ethnic identities. In both Azerbaijan and Kurdistan, the population identified more with the Iranians than with the Turks or the Kurds from Turkey and other neighboring countries.

Many among the emerging prosperous middle class favored integration into Iranian society, while the intellectuals and the leftist groups continued debates about liberty and identity. In the northern territories near the Caspian area and in the central provinces, the powerful central government and its Persianizing policies were welcomed, and many identified with the new nationalism. The power and influence of the clergy were radically curtailed. Modernization processes were applied to women and religious minorities, with some reservations. These groups had historically been treated as second-class citizens.

Timeline

1927	The Swiss-educated minister of justice, Davar, introduced more secular laws and transformed the judicial system. Compulsory military service for male adults was introduced.
1929	The first railway system in Iran, the Trans-Iranian Railway, was inaugurated.
1933	The Qashqa'i faced extensive military campaigns and raids, and the parliament enacted a law merging all the

major tribal groups of Iran into a single confederacy. The first modern university in Iran, Tehran University, was established.

1934	Tribal representation in parliament was officially abolished. All tribal titles were eliminated, and the use of Kurdish dialects in schools was prohibited. Baha'i schools lost their license to teach.
1936	Reza Shah with his wife and daughters attended the graduation ceremony at the Women's Teacher Training College in Tehran. All women were advised to come unveiled. Emancipation of women was officially inaugurated.
1937	Iran, Iraq, and Turkey signed a pact recognizing the existing borders and ended hostilities. Azerbaijan was divided into two separate provinces.
1938	Armenian schools were closed for a short period.
1940	A prominent Zoroastrian was gunned down because his son in Germany, despite his father's opposition, was broadcasting pro-Nazi sentiments.
1941	Iran was occupied by the Allied forces. Reza Shah was forced to abdicate in favor of the crown prince.
1942	The Kurdish chiefs were released from detention. A Tribal Commission was formed in Tehran, and migratory routes were restored.
1945	The Provincial Government of Azerbaijan was formed. It was followed by the Mahabad Republic of Kurdistan.

Significant People, Places, and Events

BUSHIRE (BOOSHEER): The most important Iranian port in the Persian Gulf. It has been inhabited for over 2,000 years. Nadir Shah intended to make it the home of a naval fleet. It was extensively used by the British from the mid-eighteenth century on. It became a major port during the Pahlavi era, and has remained so.

GUKLAN: A Turkmen tribe, originally from central Asia. They are Sunni, and their language closely resembles those of other Oghuz-related groups and is related to Azerbaijani, Crimean Tartar, and Turkish. They live close to the border with Russian Turkmenistan.

HANAFI SUNNI: One of the four schools of law in Islam, it is named after its eighth-century founder, Abu Hannifa. It is considered to be one of the more liberal schools of law and traditionally is nonhierarchical and decentralized. It is the official sect in Turkey.

LUR BUZURG: The language of the Lurs is divided into two main dialects, Minor and Major Luri (Luri Kuchek and Buzurg). The division is also related to the geographic location. The southern part of Luristan is known as Lur Buzurg. It is inhabited by Bakhtiyari and includes districts of Mamasani and Kuhgiluya, also inhibited by Lurs.

LUR KUCHEK: Indo-European in origin, Minor Luri is associated with the northern part of Luristan. It is mainly inhabited by Feili Lurs divided into Pish Kuh ("east of Luristan") and Pusht Kuh ("west of Luristan").

SALOUR (SALUR): A major Sunni Turkmen group in Iran. From the eighth until the eleventh centuries, along with the other Oghuz Turks, they inhabited the area between the Caspian Sea and the Aral Sea in central Asia. Their woven products and rugs are well known.

SHOGHI EFFENDI: The eldest son of Abdul Baha and the Guardian of the Baha'i faith from 1921 to 1957. The Oxford-educated Effendi transformed the Baha'i faith into the modern world religion that it has become.

TEKKE: A Turkmen group living mainly in Iran. Of Oghuz origin, they are closely related to another major Turkmen group, Salours. They converted to Sunni Islam during the Saljuq period and emerged as significant forces in the sixteenth century. Their rugs are famous.

TURKMEN: Of Oghuz origin, they started arriving in Iran in the eighth century. There are close to two million Turkmen in Iran. They inhabit the area along the northern border of Iran close to modern Turkmenistan. Their language is Turkic in origin, and they speak a number of dialects.

Bibliography

Barth, Frederick. *Nomads of South Persia: The Basseri Tribe of the Khamseh Confederacy.* Oslo and New York: Universitetsforlaget and Humanities Press, 1964.

Beck, Lois. *The Qashqa'i of Iran.* New Haven, CT: Yale University Press, 1986.

Garthwaite, Gene Ralph. *Khans and Shahs: A Documentary Analysis of the Bakhtiyari in Iran.* Cambridge: Cambridge University Press, 1983.

Karsh, Efraim. *Empires of the Sand: The Struggle for Mastery in the Middle East, 1789–1923*. Cambridge, MA: Harvard University Press, 2001.

Katouzian, Homa. *Musaddiq and the Struggle for Power in Iran*. London and New York: I. B. Tauris, 1990.

Kingston, Paul W. *Britain and the Policies of Modernization in the Middle East, 1945–1958*. Cambridge: Cambridge University Press, 2002.

McDaniel, Tim. *Autocracy, Modernization and Revolution in Russia and Iran*. Princeton, NJ: Princeton University Press, 1993.

McLachlan, K. S. *The Boundaries of Modern Iran*. New York: St. Martin's Press, 1994.

Menashri, David. *Education and the Making of Modern Iran*. Ithaca, NY: Cornell University Press, 1992.

CHAPTER NINE

Great Expectations

Mohammad Reza Shah and Consolidation of Power

PRIOR TO THE OCCUPATION OF IRAN BY THE ALLIED FORCES, REZA Shah had been asked to deport all Germans, including engineers and military attachés, from Iran. Reza Shah and the government both refused. Soon afterward the Allies occupied the country, despite its neutrality, and forced Reza Shah to abdicate. Reza Shah was sent into exile, where he died. After the abdication, his twenty-two-year-old crown prince was declared shah with approval from the parliament. The new Pahlavi ruler followed the same policies of modernization, Westernization, and secularization. During Reza Shah's short reign, the country had been significantly transformed into a modern nation-state with a new identity, a functional bureaucracy, major educational institutions, and modern communication systems. Most important of all, a national modern army had been created totally independent of the tribes and the local militia. After Reza Shah's abdication, Iran remained occupied by the Allied forces, political parties emerged, censorship stopped, and many restrictions imposed during Reza Shah's times were lifted. The new shah was too young and had too few resources to exert any real power. Many of the major crises, such as the revolts in Azerbaijan and Kurdistan and pressure to give oil concessions to foreigners, were tackled by the government and the parliament. The most serious challenges remained the occupation and the question of oil concessions. Russians stayed beyond the agreed time limit, and in 1946, Prime Minister Qavam al-Saltaneh signed an agreement with the Soviets and gave them a concession for oil in the north, subject to approval by the parliament. The parliament did not approve of the agreement, and it was dropped. The Tudeh Party had gained popularity and had a faction in the parliament. Following defeats in Azerbaijan and Kurdistan and the Soviet departure, it lost ground, and after a failed assassination attempt against the shah the party was banned by the parliament.

Oil remained the most serious question. In 1933 Iran had signed a new agreement with the British, validating the previous contracts with minor changes, and the Anglo-Persian Oil Company remained fully in control of the oil fields in the south. The agreement was overwhelmingly in favor of the British and remained a subject of intense criticism in Iran. The occupation had caused serious economic hardship, and the British were more despised than ever. The oil strike of 1946 was the start of a major anti-British movement in Iran. It led to the shooting of the strikers, assassination of a prime minister, and prominence of the liberal aristocrat Dr. Musaddiq. It continued with the nationalization of the oil fields following a long debate and international crisis, the defeat of the monarchists, and the shah's flight to Europe. Following a U.S.-backed coup d'état, after only a few days in August 1953 the shah was back, Dr. Musaddiq was ousted, and the Tudeh Party was banned.

The era was a unique period in Iranian history. Powerful national figures debated a major issue in the parliament without any fear of a commanding monarch or tribal divisions. A modern army was able to guarantee security without much hassle from tribal warlords and local militia. Around the globe new nation-states were emerging as European colonial rule diminished. Democratization and nationalistic processes were happening in the country at the same time. Dr. Musaddiq assumed the premiership following the assassination of the prime minister by the followers of an extremist Islamic sect. Musaddiq was the leader of the opposition and the chairman of the National Assembly's Oil Committee. His nationalization policy was based on his firm belief that as long as foreign forces remained in control of such vital resources, Iran could not function as a fully independent sovereign state. Extensive dialogue at the international level and an appeal to the International Court failed, and Musaddiq's government unilaterally annulled the previous oil agreements and nationalized the vital natural resource. The National Iranian Oil Company became the subject of intense international debate and was regarded by many as a serious threat to the flow of oil in the region, since other oil-producing nations in the region might follow the same path.

The movement, despite its massive popular support in Iran, failed for a number of reasons, including foreign pressure; a boycott of Iranian oil by the major international consumers, including the British; very poor leadership; lack of economic resources to compensate for the financial losses; disastrous economic conditions and the near bankruptcy of the country; and opposition by the Tudeh supporters. The conservatives of all groups, including factions in the parliament, army, and clergy, feared that instability and chaos could result in a takeover by the communists, so they supported the monarchy. The Cold War had started, and the Soviet-backed Tudeh Party had become very prominent. It opposed Musaddiq because nationalization would end the granting of any oil concession to the Soviets. The opposition created major divisions inside and outside the parliament and weakened the movement. The Tudeh members, despite a heavy presence in the army at the time, did not rescue Musaddiq or oppose the military coup d'état. Musaddiq was ousted and remained under house arrest until his death in 1967. The psychological impact of the defeat was enormous and remained for a long time. Musaddiq is still remembered as the father of nationalism in Iran and has become a symbol of national resistance and efforts to achieve independence and sovereign integrity. The Tudeh in particular and the leftists in general are still regarded as Soviet collaborators, and the shah became identified as a puppet of the United States.

The following decade was a time of consolidation of power. Political parties were banned. The parliament was dissolved and reopened with members selected and approved by the authorities. The media and press were censored. The few political parties that existed and were approved by the authorities were dissolved in 1975, when one party formed by the government, Rastakhiz ("resurgence"), replaced the two existing parties. A new oil contract was signed with a consortium of countries, including the United States, Great Britain, and eight other European countries. Iran shared the profits equally with the other nations. Oil revenue increased almost tenfold from 1953 to 1961. Financial and military aid poured in. The United States became the closest ally of the new government. The army, police, and a new organ, the gendarmerie, based on the French system, were reorganized and became powerful and well equipped, along with a secret agency to oversee security. State institutions rapidly expanded and monopolized power. Urbanization increased, and educational and health institutions grew rapidly. School texts emphasized Iran and Iranians with no distinctions between different ethnic groups. Economic plans were implemented; communication and national security improved. Changes, such as annexation, were made in the provinces and their administrative units, aimed at improving control over potentially troublesome territories such as Kurdistan and Azerbaijan. The royal family on the surface remained respectful of the religious groups; the shah and his wife made frequent visits to holy sites and shrines and even went to Mecca as pilgrims. The bazaars, important centers of urban protest, were left alone, and the merchant class benefited greatly from the booming economy. The leaders of the clergy condemning underground Islamic extremist sects remained close to the court and had easy access to the shah himself.

The government adopted a modified version of Reza Shah's plans with respect to the tribes, nomads, and other ethnic minorities. New offices were created to deal with specific problems such as pastoralism. Pastoralism was to continue but on new terms, with a long-term development policy of planned and designated locations for settlement of the nomads but with less coercion. Traditional pastoralism was discouraged in favor of modern agroindustrial projects and complexes. Traditional pastureland was often allocated for such projects. Government loans and the newly established Planning Organization assisted the projects financially and at times provided technical help. New breeds of animals, assumed to be far superior to the local flocks, were imported. Such expenditures were made possible by extensive revenues from oil, an outcome of the emergence of the Organization of Petroleum Exporting Countries (OPEC). OPEC is a permanent intergovernmental organization that was created in 1960 by Iran, Iraq, Kuwait, Saudi Arabia, and Venezuela; more members joined later on. Its functions were to coordinate and unify petroleum policies and prices among the member countries. In a decade it became a very powerful organization and, following an oil boycott, caused a sharp increase in oil prices that led to an energy crisis. The revenue from oil increased immensely, and the oil-producing countries benefited hugely. Iran was able to spend billions on development projects. The Planning Organization became the major vehicle through which many major development projects were planned and implemented. Included were key agroindustrial complexes and many plans for agricultural development and improving or replacing livestock in Iran. Cultural organizations emerged as well, with art and entertainment festivals presenting the ethnic diversity of the nation by displaying various groups in traditional costumes with ethnic musicians and dancers. However, some, like the Shahsevan, would not participate in such displays.

In the following decade the Planning Organization created many development plans to help transform the country into a modern industrialized nation. Implementing such plans required security and stability, and the government was very successful in maintaining both. The state continued sending military personnel to supervise tribal affairs and expanded the state apparatus among the tribal and nomadic groups. The success of such policies depended on the individual groups and how resistant they were to the imposed supervision and control. Such groups as the Qashqa'i, which had managed to restore some of the old migratory and power structures, resisted. Others, like the Bakhtiyari, remained loyal as a group, although some individuals emerged as potential threats. The Bakhtiyari enjoyed even more prominence after the shah fell in love with and married his second wife, an upper-class Bakhtiyari. They became permanent fixtures at the royal court, but, following the shah's divorce from Queen Soraya, many were gradually ousted from the royal inner circle. Of all the nomadic groups, the Qashqa'i remained the most persistent in following their old lifestyle, and the government was forced to take more radical action. The survival of such groups depended on their adherence to a well-defined ethnic identity and historical origin, and many attempts were and are made to clearly present and reinforce their distinct identities and histories. The age of tribalism was over in the country due to the government policies and to major sociopolitical and economic changes in Iranian society as a whole. Land reform and the White Revolution were the last major attempts by the government to introduce changes and modernize the centuries-old system of land ownership and management.

Land Reform and the White Revolution

Land reform was a demand that had been made by many political activists and radical groups since the start of the constitutional movement in Iran. It was used extensively as a propaganda tool by the separatist movements in Azerbaijan and Kurdistan, but it never was implemented because no one was sure how to conduct such a program. Traditionally, tribes bore arms and protected rural areas. For centuries they were involved in complex and extensive relationships with the peasants and villages in their areas. Iran had never had a feudal political economy comparable to Europe's. Inheritance patterns divided the land considerably, and large-scale private land ownership was weak and tenuous. Land ownership was based more on military privilege than on aristocratic rights. There was no serfdom; peasants had few obligations, and crop sharing was the dominant form of paying rent or tribute to the mostly absentee landlords. State and religious landholdings were the most extensive, and centers of power were always in the main urban centers.

During Reza Shah's reign a number of new patterns emerged. An efficient tax administration increased tax revenue collected from the landowners and at the same time reduced income from the lands. State monopoly of trade in the main agricultural products increased efficiency, modernized means of production, and at the same time was detrimental to small agriculturalists and major landlords using traditional techniques. The Land Reform legislation of 1962 was initiated by the relatively independent prime minister,

Amini, and his minister of agriculture and encouraged by the John F. Kennedy administration in the United States. The shah had become a subject of criticism because of his secret police and his government's human rights violations. The U.S. administration saw reform as one way to deal with the situation in Iran, and, following research and analysis, encouraged Iran to start with land reform. The landholdings of individuals were to be limited in size. The legislation limited the size of private holdings to one village. The rest of the lands would be divided among the peasants, and cooperative societies were to be set up with some financial and technical assistance from the government. The peasants were to pay the owners over the years, and the government also paid some compensation. Landholdings that used wage labor were excluded. More amendments and legislation were added after the fall of Amini's government to cover all aspects from the relationship between the landlords and the peasants to tenancy contracts and sale of the land. The headmen, the traditional power holders in the villages, were also to be replaced by a council composed of the peasants who had gained land titles following the Land Reform act. The many changes introduced during the course of the reform have remained a subject of controversy and criticism until the present time.

The reform was followed by the White Revolution, in which six more points were added to the reforms, including electoral rights for women and the formation of education and health corps to serve in remote areas. It also included nationalization of forests, the sale of state factories to private enterprises, and profit sharing for industrial workers. The intention of the Land Reform legislation was to create independent farmers; its implementation, among other things, led to the elimination of sharecropping and the emergence of commercial farming at the expense of small traditional farmers. However, some farmers did benefit from the reforms, and an increase in land prices ultimately was materially beneficial to many who received land. The most articulate opposition to the moves came from the religious sector under the leadership of a lesser-known clergyman called Khomeini. The effects of Land Reform in various regions were different, and even the prominent nomadic groups were affected differently because of the diversity of the socioeconomic patterns and structures among these groups.

Qashqa'i

The five major Qashqa'i tribes, Amaleh, Darrehshuri, Kashkuli Bozorg, Shish Boluki, and Farsi Mardan, occupy territories in southwest Iran. They migrate between winter and summer pastures in the lowlands and highlands of the Zagros Mountains. They cover a vast territory and during migrations go through five different provinces; therefore, administration and coordination by the government have been and are major tasks. Most are sheep- and goatherders and in the mid-twentieth century around 400,000 still practiced pastoral nomadism. Despite their diverse origins—Turk, Kurd, Lur, Arab, Persian, and gypsy—they call themselves Turks and differentiate themselves from the other groups, including the dominant Persians, whom they refer to as *Tajik*. In the past their identity was expressed through allegiance to khans, a confederacy, tribes, or subtribes. Following attempts by the Pahlavi to settle and integrate them into the larger Iranian community, they started attaching more significance to their distinctive costumes, tents, hats, and Turkish language. The female clothing is very colorful and distinctive. The women wear several layers of colorful skirts with long tunics, vests, and colorful headscarfs and use jewelry extensively. The most striking feature of the male clothing is their distinctive hats made of felt.

Cultural practices, such as weddings, music, dance, rituals, and migratory rites, have become significant vehicles through which a common identity is expressed and articulated. They are Shi'i Muslims and have a lax attitude toward formal religion. The most important Islamic tradition they follow was and is the Feast of Sacrifice (Id-e Qorban). The day marks the willingness of Abraham to sacrifice his son to prove his loyalty to God and is observed by Muslims everywhere by the sacrifice of an animal and performance of prescribed purification rites. The animals that the Qashqa'i sacrifice are normally purchased for the purpose and have to be of superior quality; the meat is shared among all members of a camp. They eat little meat and believe that if they do not share the meat, misfortunes will result. The day before the feast is reserved for remembering the deceased by gathering to share a meal and recite prayers in Arabic and verses in Turkish. Women are prohibited from slaughtering animals, but when men are absent or animals are dying and should be consumed quickly, they do slaughter the animals. The Qashqa'i follow the Islamic codes with respect to slaughtering animals and impose prohibitions on using the meat, wool, and skin of animals that were not killed or did not die the right way. However, quite often they overlook such prohibitions and trade the prohibited products with peddlers and other outsiders.

They also observe the Ashura, the tenth day of the lunar Arabic month Muharram, when Imam Hussein's death is commemorated. Their observations have never been as elaborate as those performed by the majority Shi'i Iranians, but they have incorporated their own rituals into the event, and the occasion is locally called *shozenda.* The mourning rituals during Muharram are very elaborate in Iran and last for several days; the Ashura is the peak of these observations. Processions with standards *(alam)* are a common feature of the occasion, and the Qashqa'i nomads make their own standards using tent and loom poles. They make a long wooden cross and dress it with female clothing using red skirt, black tunic, and black scarf. They fasten bells to the vertical poles. They believe Imam Hussein's small army used the same kind of standard, and they give several explanations for the female clothing, including one that suggests that the clothing worn by Arabs at the time of Imam Hussein resembled the costumes Qashqa'i women wear. The bells are to attract attention and tell others to join the occasion. The rituals normally take place in a local cemetery where people form a circle around the standard, with males and females clustering at opposing sides. Verses in Persian and Turkish are recited by all. The men pound their chests, as most Iranian males do during the rituals, and many wear black shirts. Small bush fires around the procession are common, and communal meals are served at the end of the day. Ramadan, the month of fasting, is observed mostly by a few elderly. People traveling do not need to follow the fast. They regard migration as traveling, and many do not feel obliged to fast as most Muslims do. The Islamic calendar is lunar, and it does not fit well into migration patterns that are based on a solar calendar. In general, the Qashqa'i observe Islamic traditions only when they can accommodate them in their lifestyle.

Sometimes they mock settled villages and some of their unusual practices, such as tree cults that involve placing rocks or fabrics on or close to the trees. But they do not disturb such sites and sometimes follow the same practices. During the secular Pahlavi period they used the services of formally trained religious figures for important functions, such as marriages or the funerals of important figures. Nomadic rites, such as rain ceremonies, were still commonplace at times of drought, but sometimes the better-educated headmen did not approve of such practices. During the rain ceremony, they dress a young boy as a bride but make him look more like a clown. Verses are sung by this figure, who claims he is a bride bringing the wind and the rain and asks for sweets and other small treats. He is normally showered with some water and carries a sack that he opens when he asks for treats. The occasion is a merry one, is popular with children, and normally ends with a communal meal and get-together. Migration rites are common and vary with different groups. The most common is the setting of small campfires by women and children in the vacated campsites of households that have left earlier for migration. In the past such fires would be kept burning for a few days until the departed people were assumed to have reached their destination.

The Qashqai'i are mainly monogamous, but some wealthier individuals have always practiced polygamy. The Qashqa'i women, compared to those in settled areas and villages, have fewer restrictions, do not wear the veil, and participate in many camp activities. They do not like to marry their daughters to outsiders, but such marriages do happen and have become a lot more common because of the decrease in the number of nomads and available young men. Marriages among close kin are common, particularly among paternal cousins. The male heads of the family ask for brides for their sons and take charge of negotiations with respect to wedding gifts and bride price.

Wedding camps are set up for marriages, and the more people who are invited and show up, the more prestigious the wedding. Local clergy are invited from outside towns and villages to perform the ceremony. Red or white are bridal colors, and the brides cut their bangs and forelocks short for the occasion. A bride has her own tent, and until recently it was customary for the bride to remain out of the public view for three days after the marriage and for her clothes to be checked for signs of blood after consummation of the marriage to confirm her virginity. However, many such practices have lost their significance during the last few decades. An elderly woman who is regarded as a ritual specialist makes a fire pit outside the bridal tent and places stones on the pit to indicate the start of a new household. It is common for the brides to keep dressing in her bridal colors until the couple has a child.

Musicians are always invited; they are mostly outsiders who move around the camps and villages to perform at weddings. In the past, before the establishment of permanent and mobile health units, the musicians performed other tasks as well, such as circumcision, dentistry, and barbering. Ceremonial clothing is worn by men for a wedding, and a stick-fight dance is performed. This particular dance is exclusive to the males. All people dance, but males and females form different circles. There are no prohibitions with respect to females dancing or watching them dance. All members of a camp help: Women prepare the meals, but men and women eat separately during the wedding feast. A wedding lasts for several days, with new guests arriving and previous ones leaving as it goes on. Presents are brought for the newlywed couple, which could be anything from sheep and goats to animal produce to carpets. A bride moves in with her husband's family and becomes part of that household until her husband is able to set up their own tent. However, the youngest son and his wife are obliged to stay with his parents and look after them in old age.

As with most other people in Iran, weddings are postponed for a year after the death of a close relative. The Qashqa'i remember their dead during the burial; on the third, seventh, and fortieth days; and on the first anniversary of the death. The dead are also commemorated by all on certain days, such as the day before Ashura or the new year, and also on Thursdays. The Qashqa'i follow the burial patterns of Muslims. Women still play a major role during childbirth, but such activities are becoming more and more a function of trained health professionals. No Ruz, or the Iranian new year, is celebrated by the nomads. The heads of households buy new clothing for all members, including hired help and people on contract. Animals are slaughtered, and extended families get together for the new year feast. People pay their respects to the elderly and the most prestigious tribal members by visiting them and sometimes presenting gifts to the chiefly families.

The Qashqa'i cultural practices did not change much during the 1950s and 1960s, but their sociopolitical structure was influenced greatly by the government policies. Their economic situation was altered even more following the Land Reform, the White Revolution, and new regulations with respect to pasture and land use. By 1954 the government had reached the conclusion that for effective control over the group it had to remove the popular ilkhans. It sent the paramount chief and his family into exile and effectively stopped communication between him and his confederation. Military personnel were appointed as administrators, but it was decided that it would be more beneficial to appoint some local and less important khans as allies. The underlying policy was to give privileges to lesser khans and divide the loyalty of the group. However, the appointed khans continued administering the affairs in the customary fashion and did not help the government administrators to expand their power or control. In 1960, given the lack of cooperation from the local khans, the government once again abolished all tribal titles and placed the administration of the group under the direct and full control of government institutions.

Land Reform, Pasture, and Qashqa'i Society

The Land Reform act of 1962 and the subsequent nationalization of pasture had serious consequence for many nomads and for pastoralism and tribal migrations throughout the country. In some cases the reforms radically changed the relationship of nomads to land, pasture, other nomads and tribes, and their own tribal chiefs. The Land Reform program nationalized all pastures, ceased to recognize the authority of tribal rulers over their tribes, and placed pasture use under the control of appropriate government agencies and military units. On the whole, Land Reform and the nationalization of pasture were detrimental to the Qashqa'i and their relationship with their environment. Under the provisions of the Land Reform Act, peasants or settled agriculturalists who were residing permanently on their land were entitled to receive parcels of land. Seminomadic pastoralists did not qualify. Furthermore, land belonging to the tribal chiefs that had been used communally was divided among the settled residents, who did not necessarily belong to the established tribes of the regions. All functions previously performed by tribal chiefs were assigned to armed government agents, and many more gendarmerie posts and stations were established throughout the territories to supervise the nomads' activities.

There was sporadic resistance to these actions, but it did not succeed. After the arrest and executions of a few Qashqa'i, the government was fully in control. Following the nationalization of the pastures, the nomads needed permits for all activities. The scheduling of migrations and the allocation of pasture, campsites, and water were controlled by government agents, mainly military personnel with little or no experience in such affairs. In Qashqa'i territory, the allocation of traditional lands to settled non-Qashqa'i increased tension in the local population, and protests against the government's policies increased, but with little success.

Land Reform resulted in the widespread expansion of cultivation at the expense of grazing land. The best pasturelands were lost, and the nomads were left with inferior lands. The introduction of motorized irrigation pumps by the cultivators lowered the water tables and degraded the pastures even further. New legislation with respect to forest and range nationalization had more or less the same deleterious effects on the nomadic way of life. New government organs, such as the Ministry of Natural Resources, were created with the aim of preserving forests and wildlife. They employed forest rangers to supervise the areas and prohibited grazing, hunting, and cutting live vegetation for firewood. However, since no effective provisions were made for the nomads to be compensated or to use alternative means, such actions continued illegally, and more tensions were created.

One major blow to the Qashqa'i was the transformation of one of their best pasturelands, Dasht Arjang, west of Shiraz, into a huge hunting reserve with limited access for local users, both settled and nomadic. Large private and government-owned industrial complexes were also established in many areas customarily used by the pastoralists. The expansion of the oil industry and appropriation of thousands of acres of land to be used in the new expanding sector and major oil-related industries, such as refineries, airports, and large-scale military complexes, deprived many nomads, including the Qashqa'i, Bakhtiyari, Arabs, and Lurs, of their traditional territories. Some of these changes were natural and inevitable consequences of industrialization, urbanization, and modernization. But many were deliberate and serious attempts by the government to settle the nomadic tribes. In 1962 the government officially declared that tribes did not exist in Iran anymore, and the term *tribe* was not to be used in official correspondence. Soon it had to admit that it had not been able to eradicate tribal patterns, and other strategies were employed. One such action was the introduction of mobile schools and a tribal education program.

The Tent Schools of the Qashqa'i

The tent schools were initiated in 1954 by a well-educated Qashqa'i, Muhammad Bahmanbegi, who was the director of the program. A government employee, he became the most significant link between the group and the government and enjoyed popular support among the Qashqa'i. In 1954 he opened seventy-three tent schools with specially trained teachers. At the time the Qashqa'i nomads, because of their earlier support of Musaddiq, were not very popular with the government. However, Bahmanbegi managed to persuade the authorities to experiment with the new schools. His program was very successful, and in a decade the tent schools covered all of the tribal groups. The tent schools were established in summer and winter camp locations and did not move with the tribes. Instruction was in Persian, included both males and females, and had a major impact on the literacy rate among the tribal groups in southwestern Iran. Symbolism asserting the authority of the government was used, including a picture of the shah, a map of Iran, and the singing of the national anthem before classes. The curriculum was the standard one used in the country, and although no mention was made of any tribal groups or their way of life, the schools were welcomed.

By 1970 a few changes were introduced in the curriculum, aimed at creating a more modern image of nomadism. In this new image there were no khans, children had books in their hands instead of weapons, and ideas and concepts that would ease their integration into Iranian society were promoted. The new curriculum also presented a new image of women and encouraged their active and positive participation in their communities. By the 1970s a significant number of the teachers at the tent schools were women, mainly of Qashqa'i origin, and the tent schools were regarded as the most successful program ever introduced among the nomadic groups in Iran. Bahmanbegi introduced other measures as well, including a tribal carpet-weaving school focusing on Qashqa'i designs, a tribal technical school, and training programs for midwives and paramedics. He sent talented young

Boyer Ahmad students taking a test at a tribal school near Ardakan, Fars.
(Nasrollah Kasraian)

Qashqa'i to universities with scholarships and trained a number of people to improve the quality of livestock.

He had the backing of the Qashqa'i because his programs created new employment opportunities and education and improved their health and technical know-how. He also glorified the Qashqa'i people and reinforced the assumption that they were a unique group among the Persians. The tent schools were placed in subtribes and came to represent these groups, helping to preserve the existing structures. Bahmanbegi resisted sending non-Qashqa'i teachers to the schools and started a teacher training program for the group. He also urged the female students and teachers to wear their traditional costumes and used the most ornate features of the Qashqa'i costumes to create a national Qashqa'i costume model for women to follow. The male teachers and students were dressed as modern Iranians, and he expected them to be fully integrated into the larger Iranian society. Hence, the women became the bearers of tradition and identity. In the absence of the traditional ilkhans, Bahmanbegi emerged as the most powerful Qashqa'i with extensive support from both the nomads and the government. The Qashqa'i emerged as the most coherent and united nomadic group in Iran.

However, the changes were overwhelming, and many Qashqa'i settled down voluntarily. With the positions of ilkhans and khans abolished and most away from their territories, the local headmen, elders, and minor chiefs assumed some of their responsibility. With rising tensions between the government agencies and the nomadic tribes, the government was sometimes forced to use the services of these people. Many more governmental departments and auxiliaries were created, and some attempts were made to introduce reforms because government officials realized that many of their measures were ineffective. There was also pressure by Western anthropologists conducting research and publishing reports demonstrating the devastating effects of government policies on the nomadic tribes of Iran. It is estimated that by the end of the 1960s between 30 and 40 percent of the Qashqa'i had settled down, a major hike from the end of the 1950s, when around 15 percent were settled.

Qashqa'i nomads were one of a number of groups that had attracted international attention, mainly because of their exotic way of life. Faced with increasing interest in the group by foreign dignitaries, researchers, filmmakers, private collectors, journalists, and tourists, the authorities launched a number of programs. Handicraft productions were supported, and such products were exhibited and sold in government shops. In 1977 a Festival of Popular Traditions was created for the various ethnic groups to exhibit their clothing, music, dances, and artifacts. Young men and women in their traditional clothing were to dance in public. Many groups resented such activities and particularly objected to their young unmarried daughters wearing makeup and dancing for an alien public. Despite opposition and clashes, such displays went on. Many Qashqa'i came to feel that their assimilation into the Iranian nation was inevitable. They started paying more attention to articulating their identity in a number of ways. The Office of Tribal Education under Bahmanbegi became a very important apparatus through which such articulation was reinforced.

Bakhtiyari

The term *Bakhtiyari* applies to both a region and a group, historically consisting of both pastoralist nomads and settled groups. The centralization policies of the government in the twentieth century affected the Bakhtiyari social structure significantly at the highest levels and changed the dynamics of the relationship between the khans and their tribal members. The Bakhtiyari leaders, unlike the Qashqa'i ilkhans, accepted the imposed centralization, the new nationalistic concepts, and the value of the prominence of a powerful modern state. They cooperated with the country's leadership and were assimilated into the state apparatus despite hostility by some individual members to the Pahlavi rule. Compared to the Qashqa'i, the Bakhtiyari leadership, with some exceptions, remained fragmented and divided. The tribal groups were heterogeneous and contained a number of Turkic- and Arabic-speaking and sedentary groups. Mutual interdependencies existed between the nomadic and the sedentary groups. These groups also maintained extensive relationships with the urban Bakhtiyari in major cities, including the capital, and the ruling families and the chiefs were subject to more changes due to their extensive involvement in national politics. The tribal groups were less affected by national politics and remained in their traditional territory, extending from Luristan to Khuzistan and westward to Isfahan and all the way to the border with Iraq. Most of their territory, close to 60 percent, is mountainous, and the length of their migrations varies based on a number of factors, including the location of their summer or winter pastures. Land Reform reduced the remaining powers of the surviving khans. To compensate, they intensified their investment in other sectors, lobbied for high positions among the elite, and enjoyed prestige and power in the court while Queen Soraya was still married to the shah.

Within the tribe, the family remained the smallest unit. Several related families constituted a larger unit approximating a descent group. Such groups formed a camp; depending on the location, among other factors, a camp could contain three to twelve tents. Members of a camp shared herds and helped each other during the migrations. Help was particularly needed when crossing bridgeless rivers. The nomads relied heavily on cereals planted in summer and winter pastures in addition to the herds, mainly sheep and goats. By the 1960s the number of Bakhtiyari who practiced nomadism was estimated at around 250,000. The government's policies did not favor nomadic pastoralism, but coercion was not used as it had been during Reza Shah's period. However, more people settled down, due to major socioeconomic changes in the country and new educational and employment opportunities.

Many ordinary Bakhtiyari started farming on the lands provided by the Land Reform Act; others worked in the oil fields, and some even migrated to the Persian Gulf countries such as Kuwait. The most significant changes happened at the highest levels of leadership and among the elite families. The elite managed to maintain some power by integrating into the upper classes and assuming some prominent national leadership positions. The elite families remained divided, and the modern younger elite generation began recovering tribal histories and attempting to discover and document their origins. Consequently, a number of stories and myths of origin were gathered. Most dealt with the ruling families and their genealogies, asserted the Bakhtiyari economic and military role, but provided little information about the more common tribal members and lesser khans. Despite centralization during the Pahlavi era, the form and function of the tribes, with the exception of the ruling families, remained more or less the same in the surviving nomadic groups. The tribes still aligned themselves into the two major divisions, Ilkhani and Hajji-Ilkhani. The inaccessibility of their migratory routes, especially in the mountains, allowed some autonomy during the migrations, despite the control of these routes and allocation of the pasture by government agencies.

Another major change that affected most nomadic groups in the 1960s and 1970s was the impact of a new modern market economy. Traditionally and up to the early 1960s, the pastoral nomadic economy had relied on periodic exchanges of pastoral products for locally manufactured products and agricultural produce with villages around the migratory routes. Extensive networks existed between the migratory nomads and settled villages and small towns, and both groups benefited from the exchanges. Urban markets and foreign imports replaced a lot of the locally made products and eliminated the relationships between the nomads and the villagers on their routes. The result was a great need for cash, since the new market economy was based on cash exchanges rather than barter. Many of the poorer nomads, including the Bakhtiyari, went into debt. Their products were less desirable because of foreign imports, modern factories producing dairy products, and modern slaughterhouses and imported meat from Australia and other countries. Settling and migration into the cities increased. The Bakhtiyari who continued nomadic pastoralism became more impoverished. It is estimated that by the early 1980s almost half of the Bakhtiyari nomads had given up nomadism.

Shahsevan

After the closure of the Russian borders in the nineteenth century, the Iranian authorities allocated 364 pastures to the elders of the tribal sections of the Shahsevan. At the turn of the twentieth century, it is estimated that around 10,000 nomadic families were living in the Moghan and Ardabil areas in northwestern Iran. By the 1960s over 100 of the pastures were under cultivation, and the rest were occupied and used by descendents of the original

The spring migration of the Shahsevan from their winter pastures, on camelback along a motorway, between Ardabil and Sarab in East Azerbaijan. Some Shahsevan (now called Ilsevan) tribes spend their summers in the highlands of Bozqush and winter in the plain of Dasht-e-Moghan. Most of the tribes migrate as far as 150 kilometers. (Nasrollah Kasraian)

assignees. The number of Shahsevan pastoral nomads at this time was estimated to be around 40,000. The area remained under the administration of the East Azerbaijan province, which had a population of 500,000 in the 1960s.

The effects of and response to Land Reform were detrimental to the chiefly families and to pastoral nomadism in general. Many major landlords divided their lands among family members before the date on which the new legislation became effective. In this way they avoided losing their lands. But once the pastures were nationalized, they lost a significant source of income from grazing rights, fees, and leases. The appointment of government agents and military officials with little know-how worsened the situation and resulted in more loses. The most fundamental changes occurred in the relationship of the nomads with their chiefs. The chiefs lost most of their power and influence among their tribes, both locally and nationally. The wealthiest of them moved into the major cities and were integrated in the upper strata of the urban and national communities. By the 1960s twenty of the most active former chiefs had formed a loose coalition, with extensive marriage and other social ties among themselves but with little connection to their former tribes. The emergence of large agroindustrial projects, a new dam, and the resulting disappearance of their best pastureland further reduced nomadism in the area. Following the oil boom, the government undermined the livestock economy still more by subsidizing imports of meats and dairy products. However, some nomads persisted and continued their migrations.

The Shahsevan are Shi'i Muslims by faith and speak Azerbaijani Turkish, a language that is spoken by the majority of the inhabitants of Azerbaijan. Some features of their culture, such as their distinctive felt-covered tents, resemble those of related groups outside Iran, including the Ghuzz Turkic tribes of central Asia. Their winter quarters in Moghan are close to the Russian border, and their summer pasture is located between Ardabil and Tabriz, important urban centers for centuries. In the 1920s and 1930s Reza Shah's government pacified, disarmed, and resettled them. In the 1940s they resumed pastoral nomadism and tried to revive the old confederacy, and a loose decentralized coalition was forged between a number of major tribes. By the 1960s the abolition of tribal titles and Land Reform had deprived the coalition of its economic and political foundation and infrastructure.

The smallest social unit, the household, consisted of a man, his wife or wives and children, his sons and their wives and children, and his elderly parents. They occupied the same tent and shared work, food, and space. Young married sons stayed with their father and needed his permission to set up their own tents; they might lose their inheritance if the father did not approve of the move. They followed the inheritance laws of Islam, which were incorporated into the family codes. In the Islamic system of inheritance, a daughter's share is half of a son's, and a wife inherits very little. Rights to pasture use are also inherited by children from their fathers. In general, the Shahsevan regard women as minors, and only postmenopausal women are regarded as mature adults.

The Shahsevan regard themselves as good Muslims and are much stricter in observing formal religious practices, such as daily prayers and mosque attendance, than other nomads. During the Pahlavi era, when public religious rituals were discouraged, they observed most of the prescribed ceremonies such as commemoration of Imam Hussein's death, the Feast of Sacrifice, and fasting during the Ramadan. Despite the government's ban on bodily mutilations, some groups still practiced such acts, but the Shahsevan did not follow such practices to the extreme that some Shi'i Iranians did. Most religious practices have changed little during the last few decades, and nomadic groups still follow more or less the same procedures. During Ashura and on the tenth day of Muharram, family members get together in a large tent and bring carpets, shrouds, and hangings with religious texts and pictures of the Prophet Muhammad and Imam Ali and transform the tent into a temporary mosque. Religious figures are always present, and more prosperous members look after them during their stay. Expenses are shared, but the prosperous elders contribute more and gain prestige from such actions. They follow other religious occasions with the same intensity, particularly during the Feast of Sacrifice, when communal meals are an important part of the events. A major occasion for the Shahsevan that has lost a lot of its significance was circumcision and the related feast or feasts, depending on the wealth and status of the host. Entertaining guests with music, dance, and food was a major component of the occasion, and the operation happened when all guests had arrived on a date announced earlier. The Shahsevan rarely celebrate the occasion elaborately today, but it is still recognized as an initiation for boys.

Marriage is preferred among members of the same tribe but outside their immediate camp group, although such patterns are harder to maintain. The groom's father or other prominent male members of a family normally ask for the bride's hand from her related males. If the proposal is accepted following negotiations with respect to bride price, wedding gifts, expenses, and so forth, a betrothal is arranged fairly quickly, and a ring is presented to the bride. The groom is not involved and takes part only in the actual wedding. It might take up to a year for the groom's family to fulfill all the requirements. A wedding takes place in the groom's camp, and his family is responsible for all the expenses. Feasts, games, music, and dance are important parts of the festivities. Elaborate ceremonies involve picking up the bride from her own camp. After the wedding, the bride normally stays in a tent for three days and is visited by her husband only at night. After the third day she is allowed to come out, her veil is removed, and she is exposed to all and assumes her functions in the new household. Young males have a say in choosing their partner, but most girls do not. Young brides have to obey the more senior women and are not fully recognized as mothers until they have produced sons. Polygamy is practiced among the wealthier members, and multiple wives cohabit in the same household.

The Iranian new year is observed by all and involves spring cleaning, purchasing new clothes, visiting relatives, giving of gifts, and communal feasts. The feasts, with music, games, and entertainment are similar to wedding parties. Like other Iranians, the Shahsevan observe the ritual of jumping over the fire on the last Tuesday of the year (Chahar Shanbeh Suri). They follow the death rituals all Muslims observe. Religious figures are always involved, and they are brought in from the villages and nearby towns. More cere-monies and communal feasts occur on the third, seventh, and fortieth day after the death, and on the anniversary of the death.

During the Pahlavi era, when all migrations were strictly controlled, the nomads were allowed to settle unmolested for twenty-four hours at desig-nated spots during the migrations before reaching the summer and winter pastures. Such regulations had a major impact on the relationship of the set-tled villages and the nomadic groups and interrupted a whole series of in-teractions, from trade to performing labor. The main herds were sheeps and goats, but like most other nomads they kept a range of different animals such as cattle, donkeys, horses, dogs, and sometimes camels. The produce from the animals was mainly for local consumption, and some was sold to the vil-lages. The emergence of city-based dairy companies created a new market. The nomads' milk is bought wholesale and they establish tents on the sites and make cheese on a large scale, then transfer the cheese back to town. They rear animals for sale as well, and at times, for a fee, they rear animals for in-dividuals. They charge grazing fees for outsiders who do not have grazing rights, and renting pastures is also a viable economic activity.

The period from the 1960s to the 1970s witnessed a rapid decline in Shah-sevan pastoral nomadism due to major socioeconomic change, aggressive government policies, an unfavorable market for pastoral produce, and in-appropriate planning. With the loss of many of their pastures, they lost se-curity of tenure and the right to cultivate their pastures. The expansion of village populations and farms along the migration routes deprived them of campsites and appropriate grazing. They compensated by changing their tra-ditional modes of movement. Trucks and motorcycles were frequently used to move from one area to another. Some changes were beneficial; their car-pets became popular in the international markets, and their revenue from such traditional crafts increased. However, on the whole the disruption of their nomadic pastoralism was immense and hard to reverse.

Conclusion

The decades following World War II were times of immense change as the country was transformed into a modern nation-state. Twentieth-century Iran was multicultural, cosmopolitan, and constantly changing. Turks, Kurds, Turkmen, Baluchis, and Arabs, among others, lived everywhere, with no re-strictions imposed to ban them from participating in different aspects of life in the country. Many had become Persianized, and although by this time it was hard to determine who was Persian, the Pahlavi policies of glorifying the ancient past and the Persian language were used by many to create reconstructed histories that placed Persians as a distinct group in the country. However, many identified with being Iranian rather than Persian.

The deployment of major programs such as land reform and nationalization of pasture had a detrimental effect on pastoral nomads. Some, such as the Qashqa'i, remained hostile, and their leadership suffered as a result. Others, such as the Bakhtiyari, remained loyal and occupied high positions in the national government and elite. The rapid increase in urbanization, major economic changes, and the creation of tribal schools resulted in voluntary settling of many tribal groups and new employment opportunities for them.

Timeline

1941	Mohammad Reza Shah ascended to the throne following his father's forced abdication.
1943	Elections for the crucial fourteenth parliament started. The Tudeh Party presented twenty-three candidates, of whom eight won in the elections.
1944	On International Workers' Day in May, the Tudeh Party announced the merger of four union federations into the first major trade union in Iran. With sixty affiliates and close to 100,000 members, the Tudeh Party reached its peak during this period.
1946	Prime Minister Qavam signed the Northern Oil Concession with the Russians. The parliament rejected the agreement. Russian forces evacuated Iranian Azerbaijan. Three Tudeh Party members were appointed as cabinet ministers by Qavam. Major strikes were organized by the Tudeh Party, and several labor leaders were arrested.
1947	Parts of British India Baluchistan were annexed to Pakistan by the British.
1950	Prime Minister Ali Razmara was assassinated after nine months in office. He was succeeded by the nationalist Mohammad Musaddiq. The Iranian government recognized Israel.
1951	The parliament nationalized the oil industry in April. The Anglo-Iranian Oil Company was disabled, and the

	shah and Musaddiq collided. Britain boycotted the purchase of Iranian oil.
1953	The shah and his wife, Soraya, were forced to leave Iran. They came back after only a few days in Europe with the help of Western countries, including the United States. Musaddiq was overthrown, and the Tudeh Party was banned.
1957	The first Tehran Jewish Congress was inaugurated, and the World Jewish Congress was permitted to open an office in Tehran.
1962	The Land Reform Act was implemented in Iran.
1963	The White Revolution, or the Shah and People's Revolution, was officially proclaimed.

Significant People, Places, and Events

AMINI: The prime minister during the Land Reform Act of 1962. A Qajar aristocrat, he was independent of the shah and was encouraged by the Kennedy administration in the United States to implement some reforms in Iran.

JUMPING OVER THE FIRE (CHAHAR SHANBEH SURI): This festival was originally a purification rite and part of an ancient ancestor cult. It is one of the most popular national festivals in Iran and is celebrated on the last Tuesday of the year. At sunset all Iranians will jump over bonfires and celebrate with music and feasting.

MIHREGAN FESTIVAL: The change of seasons was celebrated by the ancient Iranians through No Ruz and Mihregan (Mitrakana). Originally dedicated to the deity Mihr (Mithra), it was an ancient harvest festival. It is celebrated by modern Iranians to commemorate knowledge and learning and coincides with the beginning of the school year.

MOHAMMAD REZA SHAH PAHLAVI (1919–1980): The second and the last Pahlavi ruler, he introduced many economic reforms and improved the military strength of the country. His political actions, dissolving all political parties and forming a one-party system, were opposed by many. His social reforms with respect to women were also opposed by the clergy. His popularity has grown tremendously in Iran two decades after the Islamic Revolution.

MUSADDIQ, MUHAMMAD (1882–1967): The leader of the popular movement that resulted in nationalizing the oil industry in Iran, he became the prime minister, was opposed by the shah, and was eventually overthrown with help from the CIA and Great Britain.

NO RUZ (NEW YEAR): The Iranian new year is a celebration of the spring equinox and has been celebrated since Achaemenid times from around 500 B.C. It has been influenced by ancient Mesopotamian festivals, among others. Its current form is closely related to the new year celebrations during the Sasanian period, seventh century A.D. It is the most important national festival in Iran.

NATIONAL IRANIAN OIL COMPANY (NIOC): On April 27, 1951, Dr. Musaddiq presented the parliament with nine-point legislation prepared by a special Oil Committee. The new legislation was approved on April 29, and NIOC was formed with a three-member provisional board of directors. Its formation created a significant international crisis.

ORGANIZATION OF PETROLEUM EXPORTING COUNTRIES (OPEC): OPEC was created at the Baghdad Conference in 1960 by Iran, Iraq, Kuwait, Saudi Arabia, and Venezuela. More members joined later. Its objective is to coordinate and unify petroleum policies among member countries.

RASTAKHIZ PARTY: In 1975 the shah replaced the two legitimate state-run political parties with one called Rastakhiz ("resurgence"). When criticized by foreign journalists for being a totalitarian, he commented that those who did not agree with the system should leave the country.

Bibliography

Beck, Lois. *Nomad: A Year in the Life of a Qashqa'i Tribesman in Iran.* Berkeley, CA:University of California Press, 1991.

Gasiorowski, Mark J. *Mohammad Mosaddeq and the 1953 Coup in Iran.* Syracuse, NY: Syracuse University Press, 2004.

Goodell, Grace E. *Elementary Structures of Political Life: Rural Development in Pahlavi Iran.* Oxford: Oxford University Press, 1986.

Hooglund, Eric James. *Land and Revolution in Iran, 1960–1980.* Austin: University of Texas Press, 1982.

Katouzian, Homa. *The Political Economy of Modern Iran: Despotism and Pseudo-Modernism, 1926–1979.* New York : New York University Press, 1981.

————. *State and Society in Iran: The Eclipse of the Qajars and the Emergence of the Pahlavis.* London. I. B.Tauris, 2000.

Tapper, Richard. *Frontier Nomads of Iran.* Cambridge. Cambridge University Press, 1997.

————. *Pasture and Politics, Economics, Conflict, and Ritual among Shahsevan Nomads of Northwestern Iran.* London: Academic Press, 1979.

CHAPTER TEN

Ethnicity versus Nationality

Azerbaijan

THE MAJORITY OF PEOPLE IN AZERBAIJAN ARE SHI'I MUSLIMS, AND THEY speak Azerbaijani Turkish as their first language. In the post–World War II period and during the Musaddiq era, most political restrictions were lifted in Iran. Literary activity started again in Azerbaijan, mainly within the framework of cultural societies, groups, and prominent literary figures. Expressions of Azerbaijani identity became a popular theme of literature at the time. However, such activities were curtailed following the collapse of the nationalist government. Azerbaijanis have an extensive literary tradition, including modern literature. Poetry has always been the most popular literary form in Iran in general and among the Azerbaijanis. The most popular literary piece of the period, published in Azerbaijan in 1954, was a poem called "Greetings to Heydar Baba" (a hill in a village). The poet expressed his feelings and identity as an Azerbaijani and praised his land, culture, and language. The poem became extremely popular in both Soviet and Iranian Azerbaijan and in many other Turkic-speaking regions, an indication of a need or desire for expressions of identity.

The creation of a number of cultural organizations mainly backed by Mohammad Reza Shah Pahlavi's third wife, Queen Farah, who had family ties in Azerbaijan, contradicted policies of censorship and control. Such organizations promoted ethnic production of handicrafts and carpets. They produced and published books on folklore and literature of different groups, including children's books. Some literature of the same nature was also published independently, mainly in the 1960s and 1970s by Azerbaijani literary figures who managed to explore their collective identity through such publications. Some very prominent literary figures with Azerbaijani origins also emerged. They sympathized with the leftist groups in Iran and promoted both Azerbaijani culture and opposition to the Pahlavi regime. Many of these works were written in Persian, and some very clearly represented a shift from conceiving oneself as a Turkic Muslim to conceiving oneself as an Azerbaijani with a language called Azeri instead of Turkish. Literature in the Azerbaijani language also existed, but its influence was limited due to the underground nature of such publications. The most articulate form of ethnic expression was music and the emergence of popular Azerbaijani singers, musicians, and composers who wrote their music in Azerbaijani; some attained national popularity.

Criticism of government policies by intellectuals remained articulate and at the same time marginal because of censorship. They criticized cultural and ethnic oppression and labeled the government policies as Persian chauvinism. They challenged the state's articulation of their origins as Iranians who had adopted a foreign language because of successive Turkic invasions. The Azerbaijani thinkers of the period were divided among themselves and did not produce a coherent ideology about their origins or autonomy. Many remained leftists, mainly Marxists, and saw most of the struggles as being based on class divisions as well as national and provincial chauvinism. Such personalities and their literature rejected both Persianization and Azerbaijani nationalism, along with the relevance of ethnic origins to contemporary political questions. By the late 1970s a few concessions had been made with respect to the Turkish language in Azerbaijan. Tabriz University conducted a few courses in Azerbaijani, and the ban on publishing books in this language was somewhat relaxed.

A major characteristic of the quest for identity at the time was based on the constructions of origins and histories. Some Azerbaijanis used the existence of distant local dynasties and khanates in Azerbaijan, prior to the influx of Turkish groups, as proof that earlier in their history autonomous local governments, such as a Turkish nation, had existed in Iran. The Kurds used the same arguments while trying to reconstruct their histories. The government's launching of literary corps, to establish schools in remote areas and expand education, was received with some hostility by Azerbaijani nationalists and intellectuals. The schools followed the standard curriculum in Persian. They were well received by the general public, and although many still refused to send their daughters, there was little objection to sending boys to such schools. Many saw it as an opportunity to improve the future of their male offspring. Gaps existed between the intelligentsia, mainly between the leftists and the secularists on one side and the masses of people still bound by tradition and religion on the other. Such gaps might explain the massive support given to Muslim groups and the rejection of the leftist intelligentsia during the Islamic Revolution. A small number of underground militant groups emerged in Azerbaijan with leftist and Islamic ideologies. The Islamic group, the Mujahedin, gained massive popular support in Iran following the Islamic Revolution.

In the 1970s, following the rise of oil prices, extensive development projects were carried out throughout the country. Different provinces were developed differently and unequally. Technological advances, expanding communication systems, and mass migration to major cities, particularly Tehran, brought together many people of different origins. The central provinces in Iran prospered more and became more receptive to the government ideology of "one nation all Iranians" compared to the provinces at the periphery. Unequal development increased resentment and migration. Azerbaijani immigrants had a major presence in Tehran, mostly in the construction business. Statistics indicate that the rate of migration from rural Azerbaijan to Tehran and Tabriz was the highest in Iran by the 1970s. Many succeeded economically, assimilated into the Persian culture, and had extensive holdings and connections in the bazaars and retail trade. Others lived in the poorer neighborhoods but remained together as cohesive units with their own mosques and religious leaders of Azeri origin. Although the upper and modern groups joined the upper-class Iranians and assimilated better, the masses and the less educated remained religious, and many supported the Grand Ayatollah Shariatmadari. He was one of the highest-ranking clergymen in Iran and was from Azerbaijan. Following the Islamic Revolution, he was stripped of his rank and remained under house arrest until his death.

Azerbaijanis in the urban centers had their own mosques or went to selected ones that they dominated and listened to sermons in their own language. Many other immigrant groups in major cities also had their own mosques and gathered for various religious functions. In the absence of the old leaders, khans, tribal chiefs, political parties, and community centers, the mosques became the most important gathering places for many, including the immigrant groups. These were the only organized places with a structure where they could express solidarity. The mosques became the most important centers of opposition to the Pahlavi regime during the Islamic Revolution. The Azerbaijanis are considered to have been the most successful ethnic group in Iran in terms of assimilation into large urban centers; at the same time they have managed to keep coherent groups and are very successful in retail businesses. This success is often attributed to the fact that the Turkic people were in power for many centuries and had established themselves economically, politically, and socially before the recent changes.

A poor man wearing a ghaba *stands outside a mosque, Tehran, Iran. (Courtesy of Dominick F. Rossi)*

Despite the closure of the borders between Soviet and Iranian Azerbaijan, radio broadcasts from Baku remained a major link between the two. After the Azerbaijani movements were crushed, many activists from Iranian Azerbaijan went to Baku as refugees. The Soviet government for a long time supported propaganda aimed at uniting the two territories and only gave up when relations between Iran and the USSR improved greatly in the 1970s. In Baku many publications, exclusively in Azerbaijani, by both exiles and locals tackled the question of Iranian Azerbaijan. The cultural institutions, such as museums, displayed items from Tabriz and other locations from Iran as though they belonged to one united country. The radio broadcasts, especially music, also bound the two regions. However, communism remained unpopular among the masses. Hence, propaganda from Soviet Azerbaijan was often regarded as attempts by the Russians to spread communism in Iran and were not generally effective.

Kurdistan

The Kurds today number around twenty-six million worldwide. They constitute close to 23 percent of the populations in Turkey and Iraq, 8 percent in Syria, and close to 10 percent in Iran. They also live in smaller numbers in Armenia, Republic of Azerbaijan, Europe, and North America. They are often described as a nation without a country. Compared to the Azeri in Iran, their sense of belonging to a distinct community remained much stronger during the second half of the twentieth century. Their situation in Iran was different from that of the Kurds in Turkey or Iraq, who were denied existence as Kurds. In Iran, although the Persian language was used to unify all Iranians, there was no outright denial of Kurdish identity, but there was an insistence that they remain passive and subject to government control. The policies of secularization effectively reduced the clergy's influence, and centuries-old divisions between the Sunni and Shi'i became irrelevant. At the same time the Sunni clergy were able to function without any real harassment from Shi'i institutions, and they maintained their distinctiveness from the rest of the Shi'i population in Iran.

Kurdistan as a territory remained divided between different countries, and the idea of a Kurdish state shared by all Kurds emerged with little evidence that such a united land or territory ever existed. Myths of early Kurdish states, heroes, and common ancestry became very popular and are still reconstructed despite obvious problems, such as the two distinct Kurdish languages and substantial historical evidence showing diversity in origins.

Saladin is one common hero whom many Kurds identify with and use as proof that powerful Kurdish states existed, even though he was Arab in culture and acted as an Arab Muslim ruler with no reference to a Kurdish identity. He ruled over and commanded parts of the Arab empire and defended it against the Crusaders. Such reconstruction of identity started with the new territorial divisions after World War I and has remained very important in the course of seeking origins and common roots.

Iranian Kurdistan has remained an important region for agriculture and livestock breeding. It accounts for about 30 percent of cereal production in Iran. Originally stock breeding was carried out by the nomadic tribes migrating between summer and winter pastures. Such movements created tension between settlers and the nomads and among the various nomadic tribes competing for pasture. In the second half of the twentieth century, with the nomadic tribes disappearing and settling down, the villagers carried out the stock breeding in addition to raising cash crops such as cotton. There are almost seven million Kurds in Iran, living mainly in the provinces of Kurdistan, West and East Azerbaijan, Zanjan, and Kirmanshah. There are many poor Kurdish immigrants in major cities such as Tehran. Most stay together, wear Kurdish costume, and speak Kurdish languages among themselves.

The policies of modern Iranian governments with respect to the Kurds were greatly influenced by the Kurdish uprisings in Iraq, the Cold War, and border disputes between the Iranian and Iraqi governments. Following the collapse of the Mahabad Republic, the Kurdish Democratic Party of Iran (KDPI) was forced underground. Two small groups survived in Mahabad and Sanandaj. By 1954 they were united with the intention of overthrowing the monarchy; creating an independent Kurdistan in Iran; and liberating all Kurdistan, including territories in other countries. Kurdish broadcasts from the Soviet Union and Cairo condemned monarchies in Iraq and Iran and encouraged Kurds everywhere to unite and aim for their own nation-state. In 1958 the Iraqi monarchy was overthrown and the new leader, backed by the Soviet Union, openly lent support to the Kurdish people in Iraq. Mulla Mustafa Barazani returned to Iraqi Kurdistan as a national hero, and the Iranian national army was immediately deployed in Kurdistan and at the border with Iraq.

Barazani attempted to unify the Kurdish Democratic Parties in Iraq and Iran under his leadership. However, the Iranian members were quickly arrested, and the party in reality had ceased to exist, with the exception of a few members who had survived. This small group emerged later as a new Revolutionary Committee, established links with Iraq, and supported Kurdish resistance there. By 1961 the Kurds of Iraq were rebelling against the Iraqi government, and Barazani sought refuge in Iran. In exchange for help from Iran he denounced the new KDPI, arrested its members in Iraq, fought some of them in Iran, and handed over their leaders to the Iranian government. Barazani remained in Iran and received support from the Iranian government, the United States, and Israel against Iraq. His actions alienated the Iranian Kurdish resistance movement. In 1973 a new Revolutionary Committee, headed by Abd-al Rahman Ghassemlou, a well-educated Iranian Kurd in exile in Europe, was formed. Ghassemlou assumed the leadership of the Iranian Kurdish resistance until his murder by the agents of the Islamic government of Iran in 1989.

Ghassemlou's movement did not achieve any major victory or extensive support in Iran. Its few supporters collaborated with the two main, but very small, underground militant groups in Iran: the Marxists, Feda'i-Khalq ("ready to die for the masses"); and the Islamic group Mujahedin-i Khalq ("holy warriors for the masses"). Their impact was mostly psychological; they gained recognition, and Ghassemlou himself was well respected and known among the Kurdish population. During the Cold War the Soviets remained very active in the region. The emergence of pro-Soviet leaders in Syria, Egypt, and Iraq created complicated political maneuverings between these countries, Iran, Israel, and the United States. The latter established major military bases in Iran to offset further Soviet expansion in the area. Some Iranian Kurdish groups sought the support of the Soviet Union, which further complicated matters and created divisions. Kurdistan remained under the full control of the Iranian government and, like the rest of the country, went through significant socioeconomic changes.

The ethnic composition of Kurdistan was very mixed by the middle of the twentieth century. Persians, Lurs, Azeri, Christians, Kurds, and refugees from Iraq lived in the major cities and the many villages in the area. Northwestern Kurdistan (Urmiya-Mahabad) remained more developed than the mountainous south. The illiteracy rate was high among the rural people and the few surviving tribal groups but was beginning to improve. Many previously nomadic groups were settled by then, and a powerful class of landlords existed. With the disappearance of the chiefs and their social, economic, and political roles, a loose bond existed between the notable landlords and their peasantry. The elite were not necessarily Kurdish, and they included the enterprising Azeri, who controlled and owned large properties and many commercial ventures.

The effects of the Land Reform Act were both economic and psychological. The state challenge to the affluent landlords and the massive propaganda against them through the national media cost them a lot of their prestige. In Kurdistan they ceased to exist as powerful political forces despite the fact that it took almost ten years to implement the reforms, and quite a few had managed to maintain holdings by dividing their assets among family members. Socioeconomic factors were also responsible for this shift of the political power. Communication had improved substantially, with the Iranian national radio stations broadcasting to every corner of the country. The improved literacy rate created more opportunities and confidence among lower-income groups. The adverse effects of the modernization, industrialization, and pasture policies reduced profitability of small-scale farming, and large numbers immigrated to major cities, including Tehran. Many Kurds moving to more prosperous provinces became aware of the backwardness of their region and sought explanations. It was in this climate of change and transformation that a new quest for identity emerged among the Kurds, independent of organizations such as the KDPI.

The government was rapidly funding major industrial projects in Khuzistan and in central and northern Iran. Provinces such as Kurdistan and Baluchistan remained far behind the average national growth rate. The population increase was a factor, in addition to the border problems with Iraq that reduced the trade between the two countries. A new generation of mobile young Kurds, working all over the country in more prosperous regions, eventually wanted changes with clear political consequences. Kurdish broadcasts from abroad, massive attacks on Kurds in Iraq, and the support of the Iraqi Kurdish rebels by Iran and in the Iranian territories made the question of ethnic identity an issue for a new generation of Kurds. The policies of Persianization, assimilation, and restrictions of publications in other languages created resentment.

Kurds responded by insisting on wearing their costumes and promoting Kurdish cultural practices such as music and dance. Radio broadcasts in Kurdish from neighboring countries, including the Soviet Union, prompted Iranian broadcasters and the Voice of America to broadcast Kurdish-language programs in Kurdistan. The radio and later the TV broadcasts promoted the use of Kurdish language even more, and Kurdish music and dance became an important element of Kurdish identity. Many members of the chiefly families joined the upper classes and held important positions in the central government. Some were allowed to keep their lands after Land Reform. However, the question of Kurdish nationalism did not go away, and compared to the Azerbaijani population the Kurds remained far more persistent with respect to identity issues and questions. Such issues were reinforced because of the situation of the Kurds in Iraq.

By the 1970s and after many onslaughts by the Iraqi leaders, including Saddam Hussein, close to 100,000 Iraqi Kurds had arrived in Iran as refugees. The critical situation and the mass exodus created a major crisis between the Iranian and the Iraqi governments and increased the prospect of war between the two. In 1975 an agreement was reached between the shah and Saddam Hussein at the OPEC conference in Algeria. Border disputes were resolved, and both countries accepted the border agreements reached in 1913 and 1914. Furthermore, they were each to cease support of rebellious groups in the other's country. Within hours of the agreement, the Iranian forces withdrew. Barazani and thousands of his supporters moved back to Iran, where they were disarmed. Barazani died from an illness in the United States in 1979. His body was flown to Iran, and he was buried in Kurdistan near the Iraqi border and later moved to his homeland. Despite many mistakes, changing sides, and causing major divisions among the Kurds, Mustafa Barazani has gained mythical proportions among them. His family name still bears considerable influence; his son Massoud took over the leadership of their followers after his father's death. The new Kurdish self-consciousness and identity emerged as a significant factor after the collapse of the Pahlavi regime and has remained one of the most important issues in the Kurds' relations with the Islamic government of Iran.

Turkmen, Arabs, and Baluchi

The period from 1945 to 1979 was a time of immense change for Iran as a whole and the ethnic groups in particular. Development financed with the oil revenue transformed the country. The socioeconomic changes, mass media, and prosperity transformed traditional patterns and concepts of life. There was a massive increase in urbanization, a large educated middle class, and growth of national identity for many. In the provinces that were more developed and became prosperous, the urban and the rural populations identified with the state national identity. In the peripheral provinces and those where non-Persian groups were the majority, ethnicity and quest for identity took a different route. In these areas resistance grew as communal identity based on one's immediate village, tribe, and language gave way to a broader national identity imposed from the center. The various ethnic groups in Iran responded differently; some favored integration, including the people in the prosperous and modern provinces of Gilan and Mazandaran near the Caspian area, Khurasan, and central Iran. However, even in the same territory the desired degree of integration differed greatly depending on the

Flames of burning gas shoot high into the air and brighten the night sky from a pipeline in the Iran desert. These flames burn waste gases near an oil refinery, Bandar Mah Shar, Khuzistan, Iran, 1970. (Roger Wood/Corbis)

people's ethnic origins and culture. The Turkmen groups in the Caspian region were such a case.

Turkmen make up about 2 percent of the population of Iran. They remained more independent than other ethnic groups following Reza Shah's abdication. However, by the late 1960s the socioeconomic changes were too drastic for any group to be able to continue traditional patterns of existence, and government control had been fully established in the area. Different groups' responses to changes also depended on the ecology of the regions where they lived. For example, groups in the northeastern portion of the Gorgan Plain were and still are able to maintain some pastoralism. The area is arid and thinly populated, in sharp contrast to the fertile southern portions of the plain that became centers of modern agricultural production. In the absence of major tribes and tribal sociopolitical power structures, the people in that area maintain identity by adhering to their unique cultural practices.

The Turkmen groups have distinctive clothing and tents and have maintained many of their cultural practices such as music, dance, horseback riding, and wrestling. Their marriage alliances no longer have political significance but create important social alliances between households. The bride price, which is heavy, is raised by the groom's family and after the marriage stays in the bride's family's household. It is regarded as a burden by many and is a reason why poor families delay marriage for years. The Turkmen have kept their patterns of residence by descent. Closely related groups stay together, and women participate in many activities and generate income through weaving carpets and elaborately decorated fabrics. They follow the Islamic codes with respect to inheritance, death, and marriage. They prefer marrying among relatives and groups they know; however, such patterns are becoming harder to maintain. They remained resistant to settling down and participated in migrations whenever they could, even if only for brief periods. The major agroindustrial complexes and rapid development in the region had a significant impact on their lifestyle, and many voluntarily settled down. They did not have a lot of contact with related tribes in the Soviet Union, and there were no major groups with separatist tendencies. The majority was concerned with maintaining their cultural practices, and they were able to do so. However, there were sporadic complaints about the lack of language rights. On the whole their community prospered during the 1960s and 1970s.

Arabs remained in Khuzistan and constituted 3 percent of the population of Iran. By the 1970s Khuzistan had gone through massive industrialization. Major international ports, oil-related industries, and petrochemical factories transformed the area. Many of the Arabs became Persianized, and the region's prosperity made the central government popular. Ethnic clothing remained popular, and there was a sharp gap between the modern educated sector and the less-educated traditional groups living in more remote areas. The Bakhtiyari people remained relatively quiet. Many of their leaders had been assimilated into the Iranian upper class. However, there was a rebellion led by a prominent Bakhtiyari, the head of a major department in the army and later the secret service. He ended up fighting the government forces, defected to Iraq, and was later killed. However, this rebellion was not due to ethnic grievances on the part of the Bakhtiyari; it had more to do with power struggles at the national level.

Iranian Baluchistan remained isolated and has always been regarded as the most underdeveloped area in Iran. It is the second-largest province and includes Sistan; the two were grouped together for administrative purposes and formed one province. By the 1970s the Baluchi people constituted 2 percent of the population, and many remained seminomadic. The harsh, arid climate of the region restricted agriculture and small-scale farming. By the 1970s development plans had been started in the region, and a new university had been established. The local television and radio stations broadcast Baluchi music, and there were some programs in the local language as well. However, the area remained poor and underdeveloped. There were uprisings in Pakistani Baluchistan in the 1970s, and the Iranian government, fearful that the conflict might extend to Iran, helped Pakistan to suppress the movement. Because it is close to the Pakistan and Afghanistan borders, the province became a major route for smuggling and later drug trafficking. Such activities reached their peak after the events in Afghanistan and Iran in the early 1980s and had a major impact on the local socioeconomic patterns.

One major difference between Baluchistan and the other provinces, such as Kurdistan and Azerbaijan, was the role of traditional leaders. Despite disarmament and crushing of the traditional power structures, some Baluchi traditional leaders remained influential and assumed leadership at times of crisis. The area remained so underdeveloped that education and new opportunities were basically available only to the well-to-do families, mainly the chiefly families, who remained the link between the government and the local people. There was a large influx of poor Baluchi to nearby major cities such as Mashhad in Khurasan.

The ties between Pakistani Baluchistan and Iranian Baluchistan remained strong. The underground organization the National Front of Baluchistan, the only opposition group in Iran, had extensive ties with Pakistan and, in fact, was created by a Pakistani Baluchi. The group was active between the 1960s and 1970s in Iran and was led by three prominent Iranian Baluchi tribal chiefs. They managed to organize a small militant group composed of members of the three tribes. In the end they made peace with the Iranian government, and those in Pakistan came back to Iran, openly supported the regime, and denounced the National Front.

Religious Minorities

Religious minorities on the whole prospered during the period leading up to the Islamic Revolution. Many regard this period as their golden age.

However, there was no major change in their legal status. They were still legally barred from leadership positions, though the government did not observe the restrictions and there were many prominent non-Muslims in a number of high positions. However, the legislators were not prepared to risk opposition by the clergy and more conservative elements by demanding change with respect to religious minorities. The Baha'i were given equal opportunity but remained without legal status. The religious minorities faced more discrimination in the smaller towns and the provinces, which motivated them to migrate to larger cities and the capital itself.

Members of religious minorities participated freely in the social and economic life of the country. Many were involved in and even owned major commercial and industrial enterprises. Missionaries and their schools were replaced by international schools, which were very popular and continued to educate the elite and the upper classes. There were small numbers of Roman Catholics, Protestants, and Anglicans, mainly converts from Islam or other Christian groups. Churches were built, and their spiritual and political representatives were acknowledged and were present in major state functions. The younger generation was rapidly integrating into the larger Iranian society. Despite ease of integration and many improvements, on the whole the religious minorities remained marginal.

Armenians

Following the occupation of Iran and after World War II, there was confusion in the Armenian community. Many hoped to return to Armenia in Russia following the Allied forces' victory, and some did leave easily with Soviet support through Azerbaijan. More expected to go, and the Iranian government facilitated their departure, but the Soviets refused to grant immigrant visas to all who wanted to leave. The exact numbers are not known. One newspaper in Tehran in 1946 quoted a figure of 60,000. However, that number is probably exaggerated and very likely represents the number of people who wanted to leave but could not. A few thousands and sometimes entire villages left for Soviet Armenia. The majority who left were poor urban workers and small traders. During Muhammad Reza Shah's reign, the Armenian internal autonomy was maintained and restored. Armenians participated freely in many aspects of life in Iran, but unlike earlier periods, when they had been very active in politics, especially leftist groups, they participated a lot less in politics.

They became professionals in a number of prestigious fields and had a strong presence in the music and arts arena. There were no restrictions with respect to the use of the Armenian language. Popular Armenian pop singers and actors emerged and became national icons. Many publications in Armenian and Persian dealt with their history and the massacre and genocide in Turkey. The constitution prohibited non-Muslims from attaining the highest positions in the country, a prohibition that remained in force during this period. Armenians were not favored in the army because they still revered Soviet Armenia. Tehran, Tabriz, and Isfahan became major centers for Armenians, and by the 1970s there were close to 300,000 Armenians living in Iran, with thirty churches and close to fifty schools. Most Armenians were urbanized; half of them lived in Tehran, and the rest remained in other cities, including Isfahan and parts of Azerbaijan. Both the Armenians and Assyrians used Bibles in their own languages, and Persian translations of the Bible were made available to the non-Christian public without harassment from the Muslim clergy. The Armenians have kept their loyalty to the Armenian Apostolic Church and have remained separated from the Eastern Orthodox Church. However, there are divisions among them; many support the patriarch in Lebanon instead of the one in Armenia. Iranian Armenians have been immigrating to the Armenian Republic for half a century. They were the largest Christian community in Iran, and on the whole, despite increasing integration, they remained marginal to some extent.

Armenians celebrate all the major Christian festivities. Prior to the revolution of 1979, thousands of Muslims participated in their celebrations, including the New Year's Eve celebrated by all Christians, which was a major event in the big cities such as Tehran. They have a number of major holy sites in Iran, and they have managed to repair and extend such complexes. The Armenian quarter in Isfahan became a major tourist destination for Iranians and foreign tourists alike. Their major old churches and buildings were registered as national heritage sites and as such were protected.

Assyrians and Chaldeans

Most Assyrians became urbanized during the 1960s and 1970s, but a few Assyrian villages remained near Lake Urmiya. The Assyrians remained part of the Assyrian Church of the East (Chaldean/Nestorian Church), with close ties to the Assyrian Church in Iraq. At times they provided help to the persecuted Assyrians in Iraq. By 1979 there were about 30,000 Assyrians in Iran; half of them lived in Tehran. Their numbers decreased in Iran during World

War I, when they fled to avoid intense fighting between the Russians, Turks, and others. Many died, and others fled to Iraq. During the Pahlavi period some came back to repopulate their old villages, but many ended up in the urban areas instead. The Chaldeans remained in Khuzistan or migrated to Tehran, while 40 percent of the Nestorians (Assyrians) remained around Urmiya and the rest moved to Tehran. The period from 1945 until the Islamic Revolution was a peaceful time for the Assyrians. Their community prospered, but they remained more cautious than the Armenians. Their integration into the larger Iranian society was slower. They started connecting more with the Assyrians outside Iran, mainly through the Assyrian Universal Alliance, which had opened a branch in Iran.

Jews

The Jewish population of Iran prospered greatly after World War II. Jewish schools had their own curriculum in addition to the Persian one, and

An Iranian woman decorates a storefront with Christmas decorations in Tehran, December 23, 2003. Christmas, not commonly celebrated in Iran, where the majority religion is Islam, is celebrated by the Assyrian and Armenian minorities, who are Christians. (Morteza Nikoubazl/Reuters/Corbis)

Modern Hebrew was incorporated into the curriculum at the Jewish schools. Publications in Hebrew existed, and Jews were permitted to build new synagogues and to hold government jobs. The formation of the state of Israel in 1948 had major consequences for the Jewish population in the Middle East. Jews were expelled from most of the Arab countries and were forced to settle in Israel. The Iranian government provided safe passage for Iraqi Jews who were expelled from Iraq and were on their way to Israel. Some of the wealthier Iraqi Jews remained in Iran and were given residency by the government. At the time anti-Jewish sentiments appeared in the bazaars, and some businesses boycotted trading with Iranian Jewish merchants. In 1950 the Iranian government recognized Israel, much to the dismay of the religious establishment there and in the rest of the Arab world. Following the establishment of the Jewish state of Israel, thousands of Iranian Jews emigrated to Israel. It is estimated that between 1948 and 1953 close to one-third of the Jews in Iran left for Israel. During the Musaddiq era anti-Jewish sentiments appeared once again. The weakness of the central government meant more power for the clergy, who used the occasion to attack Iranian Jews and Israel and to demand that Iranians join the anti-Israel struggles and war by the Arab nations. Once the central government solidified its power, such activities ended.

During the 1950s the Jewish community in Iran established and expanded many links with international Jewish agencies. It received support from the Alliance Israelite Universelle and a number of other international organizations, including the American Jewish Joint Distribution Committee. This organization was established in Iran in 1947 and laid the foundation for many social, medical, and educational activities for the Jews in Tehran and the rest of the country. Though strong links existed between Iranian Jews and Israel, on the whole the remaining Jewish population of Iran did not support Zionism.

By the early 1960s close to 8,000 Iranian Jews were attending Jewish schools sponsored by the Alliance Israelite Universelle. They had also established hospitals; medical, youth, and women's centers; and charities to help poor families. They had a council in charge of their community affairs, and since the constitution permitted them to conduct private and judicial affairs in their own courts, they had their own institutions to deal with such issues. The support of Israel by the Iranian government created close ties between the two countries. Jews were allowed to hold the Tehran Jewish Congress in 1957, and the World Jewish Congress was given permission to open an office in Iran. By 1948 the Jewish population of Iran was around 60,000, and by the 1970s there were about 80,000 Jews in Iran. Despite earlier emigration to Israel, the numbers remained more or less the same. By the 1970s about 55 percent of the Iranian Jews lived in Tehran and enjoyed freedom and equality, with many prominent Jews in the country. Jews also immigrated to Iran from Iraq, Afghanistan, Russia, Poland, and Germany. Some of the European Jews who immigrated made substantial contributions to improving the lives of Iranian Jews.

Like Armenians, the Jews of Iran regard the period from the 1950s to 1979 as their golden age. Their economic status improved significantly, and many assimilated well into the larger Iranian society. By 1979 around half of the Jewish children in elementary schools attended Hebrew schools and learned Hebrew. Like the rest of the Iranians, many Jews were becoming more secular and did not insist on religious education. By the late 1960s, with the exception of Israel and South Africa, Iran had the wealthiest Jewish community in all of Asia and Africa. The majority of the Jews were middle class by this time; they were very well educated, and 10 percent of the Jewish population was regarded as extremely wealthy. The rapid improvement in the life of the Jewish population of Iran is attributed to the policies of the government, and specifically to the very close relationship between Iran and Israel. Such association proved to be detrimental to the Jews of Iran following the Islamic Revolution.

Zoroastrians

The Pahlavi era was a time of immense change for Zoroastrians. The government policy of glorifying ancient Persia was a source of pride for this religious community. Many research institutes in Iran, Europe, and North America were founded to explore different aspects of the ancient religion. Many nationalist organizations emerged promoting the ancient faith, some with very clear anti-Islamic sentiments. By the 1970s the number of Zoroastrians in Iran is estimated to have been around 30,000 to 35,000, with new temples, schools, and libraries. The grand celebration of major pre-Islamic festivals created more awareness of the ancient Iran.

Four of the national celebrations in Iran are pre-Islamic in origin: No Ruz (New Year); jumping over the fire on the last Tuesday of the year (Chahar Shanbeh Suri); celebrating nature on the thirteenth day of the first month of the year (Seezdeh Beh Dar); and the Yalda Festival, which celebrates the end of the winter and rebirth of the sun and is a very popular family affair. Despite centuries of opposition by Muslim rulers and clergy and attempts to eradicate the celebrations, people refused to abandon them. Their promotion by the Pahlavi regime benefited the Zoroastrian community.

Zoroastrian symbols became popular and were worn as jewelry, used as decorative items, and even used as state symbols. The monarchy adopted ancient Persian ceremonial names and replaced all Arabic titles and terminology. Most Zoroastrians, like other minorities, moved to Tehran; the rest remained in Yazid and Kirman. Extensive links were established with the Parsi and Irani communities in India, and some Zoroastrians in those countries were encouraged to move back to Iran. The Irani were Zoroastrians who had emigrated to India in the eighteenth century but had maintained contact with the community in Iran.

The community went through some major changes with respect to identity issues and modern interpretations of ancient works. Meticulous scholarly works by Western academics provided a new understanding of the major principles of the ancient religion, though some of these findings were rejected by the leaders of the Zoroastrian community. The result was the emergence of new schools of thought in the community, which led to divisions. One major issue still unresolved has been the refusal to accept new converts. With the popularity of the ancient faith among mainstream Iranians, some wanted to convert and were refused admission. Because the community was very small, there was pressure from within to accept converts, and the issue created some division.

Baha'i

The Baha'i never gained legal status, but they also benefited from the Pahlavi religious policies, and a few prominent Baha'is occupied key positions in the government. Such treatment was not welcomed by the clergy and more religious groups. Prominent Baha'is were among the first victims of the new revolutionary government. On the whole, they enjoyed peace and prosperity from the late 1940s until 1979, with some exceptions. They encountered problems during the fasting month of Ramadan in 1955, when some anti-Baha'i activities supported by some clergy took place. The dome of the Baha'i center in Tehran was destroyed. The government's involvement outraged international agencies, and such activities stopped. The Baha'is designed and implemented a number of plans for developing the community, and as of the 1950s women were eligible to be elected to the local and national spiritual assemblies.

The community in Iran grew in terms of numbers and complexity. By the 1960s there were around 150 national committees in Iran. The center in Tehran had expanded and had a printing office, a major library, and a youth club; thousands of people served the community in Tehran alone, with many functioning as teachers of the faith. The Baha'is had one more encounter with the Iranian government in 1975. At the time the shah had introduced a one-party system in the country, and all groups were asked to join it. The Baha'is insisted that they were not political and refused to join, and tensions emerged. They were mostly employed in the private sector, and although there were Baha'is in very high positions, on the whole they did not favor employment in government agencies since they were required to state their religion on application forms. Some clergy and the extremist Muslim groups continued their denunciation and harassment of the Baha'i in the 1960s and 1970s. Prejudice against them existed at all levels, and many preferred to remain inconspicuous.

The Baha'i international community prospered under the leadership of Shogi Effendi, and by the time of his death in 1957 the Baha'i faith was well established and had expanded to every continent. Baha'i literature was translated into many languages, but it was not openly available in Iran. The world center of the Baha'i faith in Haifa, Israel, expanded considerably. By 1963 the Universal House of Justice in Haifa had nine members elected to govern the international Baha'i community. This system of governing has more or less remained. They have no clergy and became increasingly community oriented, providing many services to their members. The community in Iran also grew, with many converts from all faiths. They had no restrictions with respect to practicing their faith but participated with some caution in the sociopolitical life of the country. Their exact numbers are not known, but prior to the Islamic Revolution they were estimated to be one of the largest religious minorities in Iran, probably *the* largest. It is estimated that their number there in the late 1970s was 150,000 to 300,000. The number of Baha'i worldwide is estimated between six and eight million, and Iranians have a significant presence as leaders in the Baha'i world community.

The Baha'i rituals have similarities to Islam. There is fasting and daily prayers. Alcohol and recreational drugs are prohibited. They have their own special marriage vows and are monogamous; chastity outside married life is required. Marriage requires permission from many members of the groom's and bride's families, since they believe that a marriage is a union of two families and not just two individuals. Their divorce is simple, and the equality of sexes is an important element of the faith. They have their own calendar; celebrate No Ruz, the Iranian new year; and end their fasting period on March 21, which in most years marks the first day of spring and the first day of the first month in the Persian calendar. Their fortune would change drastically with the coming of the Islamic Revolution.

Women and the Pahlavi Reforms

Reza Shah's emancipation policy drastically changed the position of Iranian women by opening up new educational and employment opportunities. After Reza Shah's fall, independent women's organizations emerged, including the National Women's Society and the Council of Iranian Women. Such organizations lobbied for equal rights, opposed polygamy, and demanded changes in family and inheritance laws. Most such organizations lost their independence once the new shah consolidated his power. By the late 1960s the Organization of Iranian Women, headed by the shah's twin sister, had close to 350 offices nationally and 113 centers and covered 55 other women's organizations. It carried out extensive health, education, and charity work. In 1962, following the White Revolution, women gained electoral rights, and further improvements were made in the family laws. The Family Protection Law was ratified in 1968. However, the government could not implement major reforms in the family codes because of opposition by the religious sector. Polygamy was restricted but not eliminated, and the marriage age was increased to eighteen years of age for girls. Women gained more rights with respect to custody and divorce. Abortion was not legalized, but the existing penalties were removed, and birth control was promoted.

Among the prominent clergy opposing such reforms was Ayatollah Khomeini. He was forced into exile following his opposition to the White Revolution. The religious groups objected in particular to the involvement of women in the education and literary corps and in the military service, which had become mandatory for women as well. Women's magazines mushroomed all over the country, a ministry for women's affairs was formed, and female members of parliament and senators were elected or appointed. Queen Farah was officially nominated by the parliament as the regent, since the crown prince was a minor at the time. This was the first time a woman had officially gained such a position. The equal-opportunities mandate guaranteed women's employment in the government sector. By 1978 33 percent of university students were female, with two million in the workforce. About 190,000 were professionals with university degrees. There were 333 women in the local councils, 22 in the parliament, and 2 in the senate. Religious leaders and more traditional groups objected to such changes. Some prominent clergy encouraged women to follow the Islamic dress code, and from the early 1970s on, some women began appearing at universities and institutions of higher education wearing Islamic attire. The situation for all women would change drastically following the Islamic Revolution; like

Farah Diba, empress of Iran, during a state visit from the king and queen of Spain. Tehran, Iran, 1970s. (Michel Setboun/Corbis)

religious minorities, women lost many of the rights they had gained earlier in the century.

The Twenty-five Hundredth Anniversary of Iranian Civilization

By the 1970s Iran, known as the Island of Stability, had become a military superpower in the area second only to Israel. It played a significant role in balancing power in the Middle East and had excellent relationships with Russia, Israel, European nations, and the United States. Towns and cities were growing rapidly, and favorable economic opportunities in the larger cities brought hundreds of thousands of immigrants together from every corner of the country. The authorities were convinced that they had managed to create a coherent identity among Iranians that surpassed ethnic and other cultural divisions. The shah's coronation in 1967, twenty-six years after his assumption of power, and the shift of the beginning of the Iranian calendar from the Prophet Muhammad's *Hijrat* to the beginning of the Achaemenid period, were manifestations of such beliefs. In 1971, in an opulent and very expensive occasion, many world leaders, including kings and queens, were invited to Iran to celebrate the twenty-five hundredth anniversary of the Iranian civilization. The shah was awarded the title *Arya-Mihr* ("the light of the Aryans") by the parliament. The ceremonies took place outside the ancient Achaemenian palace, the Persepolis complex, near Shiraz. The ceremonies coincided with nomadic migrations, and the Qashqa'i were instructed to postpone their migrations through the area for several weeks. The grand ceremonies went ahead, emphasizing the continuity of the monarchical tradition of Iran with the king as the ultimate savior of the ancient land. Members of the Iranian army were outfitted in Achaemenian military costumes and marched through the ancient gates. In a speech in front of the tomb of Cyrus, the first Achaemenid king, in full view of the world media, the shah declared, "Cyrus, rest assured, we are awake." Such acts were intended to reinforce the notion that Iran was and had been a united entity that had overcome centuries of invasions.

Conclusion

During the last two decades of Pahlavi rule, major economic development projects were carried out. The increase in oil revenues created many new employment opportunities and resulted in mass movement from the rural into the urban areas. Due to events in Soviet Azerbaijan, Turkey, and Iraq, governmental strategies to deal with the rise of ethnic identities were devised, taking into consideration such global issues as the Cold War, Iraq, and the Palestine-Israel conflict. The people of Azerbaijan, constituting almost one-quarter of the population of Iran, became the most articulate group with respect to their identity quest. However, as with the Kurds, their leaders did not manage to present a coherent history or concept of ethnic origins, were divided, and did not have mass appeal.

The policy of Persianization met with success among most urbanized Iranians and a number of other groups. Gilakis, Mazandaranis, and most people in the central provinces assimilated easily into the new nation and considered themselves to be Iranians. Baluchis and Lurs continued to emphasize their ethnic distinctiveness despite being of mainly Iranian origin. Turkish-speaking groups maintained their notions of distinct origins and regarded themselves as different from the Turks in Turkey. Many were Persianized and assimilated well into the larger Iranian society.

Women participated extensively in the affairs of the country, and some improvements were made in the family codes. The non-Muslim minorities had different relationships with the government, the Muslim public, and international groups. The Jews, Assyrians, and Baha'is participated less visibly and actively in major national events. Jews in particular suffered from lack of strong leadership because of the emigration of generations of prominent and influential leaders to Palestine and Israel. Armenians and Zoroastrians, in contrast, enjoyed more solidarity and had better communal organizations and leadership. They participated more in national events and were instrumental in improving their own legal status until 1979. The modern and educated Iranians were tolerant and valued equal opportunities for all. The clergy on the whole, and the more traditional and fanatical elements in particular, remained opposed to most religious minority groups, particularly the Jews and the Baha'is.

Timeline

1960	The shah was pressured by the United States to permit independent candidates to run for the twentieth parliament. The accusations of vote-rigging forced the authorities to stop the elections. The prime minister, Eqbal, was removed.

1961	Dr. Amini, the new prime minster, dissolved the twentieth parliament. He exiled General Bakhtiyar, the head of the secret police.
1964	The clergy opposed the shah's reforms, and the outspoken Khomeini was exiled. Khomeini is sent first to Turkey and then to Iraq, where he stayed from 1965 to 1978.
1967	The shah was crowned as the king of kings in a lavish ceremony watched by the world media. He was granted the title *Arya Mihr* ("the light of the Aryans") by the parliament. Queen Farah became the first Iranian queen officially crowned by a king and became the regent to the throne.
1971	The anniversary of 2,500 years of Iranian civilization was celebrated at Persepolis.
1973	The fourth development plan starting in 1968 ended, and Iran enjoyed a major industrial and infrastructure development.
1975	The shah dissolved the two existing government-backed parties, and Iran officially becames a one-party system. The beginning of the Iranian calendar was changed from the Prophet Muhammad's *Hijrat* to the start of the Achaemenid dynasty.
1978	In September massive demonstrations against the shah led to riots and strikes. Martial law was imposed.
1979	In January the shah and his family left Iran, and Pahlavi rule ended. The shah died of cancer in Egypt in 1980.

Significant People, Places, and Events

ASHURA: The tenth of the Arabic month, Muharram. It is believed to be the date when Imam Hussein was murdered. The death is intensely mourned by the Shi'ites. The rituals include self-mutilation by males with chains and swords, marches, plays, and communal meals.

FARAH DIBA (PAHLAVI): Muhammad Reza Shah's third wife. She played a major role in the cultural and political life of Iran. She was the first queen in the Middle East to participate extensively in public affairs and became a role model for other First Ladies in the area. She was appointed regent by the parliament. This was the first time a woman had officially been granted such a position.

FEAST OF SACRIFICE (ID-E QORBAN): One of the most important Muslim festivals. It concludes the end of the pilgrimage to Mecca and lasts for three days. Arabs call it Id al-Adha. The festival involves slaughtering animals such as rams or cows to commemorate Ibraham's (Abraham's) willingness to obey God by sacrificing his son. The story is very similar to the story in the Bible, with Ishmael being sacrificed instead of Isaac.

FEDAI-KHALQ GUERRILLAS: The independent underground militant group was an amalgamation of two leftist groups in 1971. It expressed no loyalty to the Soviet Union. After the Islamic Revolution it split into two groups. Most of its leaders and many activists were executed, and many more went into exile. It emerged outside Iran in 1983 and formed the Iranian People's Democratic Party in exile.

GYPSIES: The Iranian gypsies are known as Koli and Luli. They originally migrated toward Europe from a region between India and Iran in the fourteenth and fifteenth centuries. They have been nomadic for centuries and were involved in making handicrafts such as baskets and sieves and some iron work. There are very few gypsies in Iran, and they are not recognized as a special group.

IRANI ZOROASTRIANS: Zoroastrians who emigrated to India in the eighteenth century from Iran. They have maintained their contact with the Iranian Zoroastrians.

LAND REFORM: The program was implemented in 1962 and was intended to modernize agricultural sector. Almost 90 percent of the small-scale sharecroppers became landowners as a result. It reduced the influence of major landowning families. The reforms were hastily done and had major problems because they were poorly planned. However, the small farmers benefited because of the increase in land prices.

MUHARRAM: The month (in the Arabic calendar) when Imam Hussein was killed by the armies of his rival Yazid, the son of the founder of the Umayyad dynasty. The period is a month of mourning for Shi'ites. Historically Muslims are not supposed to wage wars in this month.

MUJAHEDIN KHALQ: A militant underground Muslim group in Iran. Formed in the 1960s, it was labeled as an Islamic Marxist group by the Iranian authorities. It emerged as the most serious opposition to the Islamic government. It was violently persecuted by the Islamic authorities, and thousands were executed. The survivors went to Iraq and were supported by Saddam Hussein. They were labeled by the U.S. administration as terrorists but recently were granted amnesty by the U.S. government following the occupation of Iraq.

RAMADAN: The Muslim month of fasting. All healthy adult Muslims are required to fast from sunrise to sunset during the month and to refrain from sexual activity while fasting.

SADEH FESTIVAL (JASHN I SADEH): Sadeh means "100" and is a midwinter feast marking the 100 days before No Ruz. It had lost its significance until it was renewed by Zoroastrians in the twentieth century; it has become popular among many Iranians.

SEEZDEH BEH DAR (GETTING RID OF THE OMEN OF THE THIRTEENTH DAY): This festival happens on the thirteenth day of the first Iranian month and ends the No Ruz celebrations. All Iranians will spend the day in nature. Originally it has been a celebration of ancient deities, protectors of rains and waters.

TURKMEN SAHRA: An area in the ancient province of Gorgan (modern-day Golistan) in the Caspian region in northern Iran. A Turkmen stronghold, the area is very fertile and has been home to many Turkmen tribes for centuries.

WHITE REVOLUTION: In 1963, through a referendum, more measures were added to Land Reform. Included was nationalization of pasture and forests. The reforms were intended to improve the shah's image internationally. Some measures, such as electoral rights for women, were opposed by the clergy, including Khomeini.

YALDA FESTIVAL (SHAB I CHELEH FESTIVAL): Yalda means "birth," and the festival is a celebration of the winter solstice on the longest night of the year. It is Zoroastrian in origin. Some of its rituals are similar to those of Halloween. It is celebrated by all Iranians.

Bibliography

Afkhami, Mahnaz, and Erika Friedl. *In the Eye of the Storm: Women in Post-Revolutionary Iran.* Syracuse, NY: Syracuse University Press, 1994.

Atabaki, Touraj. *Azerbaijan: Ethnicity and Autonomy in Twentieth-Century Iran after the Second World War.* London: Palgrave Macmillan, 1993.

Avery, P., G. R. G. Hambly, and C. Melville, eds. *The Cambridge History of Iran*, Vol. 7: *From Nadir Shah to the Islamic Republic*. Cambridge: Cambridge University Press, 1991.

Bruinessen, Martin Van. *Agha, Shaikh and State: The Social and Political Structures of Kurdistan*. London: Zed Books, 1992.

Fawcett, Louise. *Iran and the Cold War: The Azerbaijan Crisis of 1946*. Cambridge and New York: Cambridge University Press, 1992.

Irons, William. *The Yomut Turkmen*. Ann Arbor: University of Michigan Press, 1975.

Koohi-Kamali, Farideh. *The Political Development of the Kurds in Iran*. Hampshire and New York: Palgrave Macmillan, 2003.

Mirsepassi, Ali. *Intellectual Discourse and the Politics of Modernization: Negotiating Modernity in Iran*. Cambridge: Cambridge University Press, 2000.

Moghadam, Fatemeh E. *From Land Reform to Revolution: The Political Economy of Agrarian Relations in Iran, 1962–1979*. London: I. B.Tauris, 1996.

Mortensen, Inge Demont, and Ida Nicolaisen. *Nomads of Luristan*. London and New York: Thames and Hudson; Copenhagen: Rhodos International Science and Art Publishers, 1993.

Salzman, Philip Carl. *Black Tents of Baluchistan*. Washington, DC: Smithsonian Institution Press, 2000.

Vaziri, Mostafa. *Iran as Imagined Nation: The Construction of National Identity*. New York: Paragon House, 1993.

Backlash

The Islamic Revolution and Its Aftermath

THE PAHLAVI VISION OF A MODERN, WESTERNIZED, SECULAR IRAN with military superiority, economic growth, and a homogeneous cultural identity was shattered in 1979 when massive protests throughout the country on an unprecedented scale forced the royal family to leave Iran. A number of reasons have been offered for this failure. Unequal development resulting in a gap between the rich and the poor, the absence of civil and political institutions, violation of the constitution, inability of the leadership to understand and evaluate the dynamics of change in a traditional Muslim society, and some economic problems and mismanagement are a few that are commonly mentioned. Before the shah's departure, an interim government was formed composed of well-known politicians, mainly supporters of Dr. Musaddiq and members of his banned party, the National Front. This government was to be in charge until a decision was made about the monarchy by the parliament. The shah's departure paved the way for the return of Ayatollah Khomeini, the consolidation of power by militant Muslim groups, and the eventual proclamation of an Islamic Republic. The interim government was headed by a prominent Bakhtiyari as the prime minister. Shapur Bakhtiyar was an old associate of Dr. Musaddiq and a well-known member of a group opposing the shah. He was chosen because of his antishah record in order to gain popular support; his appointment had nothing to do with the emergence of chiefly Bakhtiyari families. He lasted for thirty-seven days and was then forced to flee to Europe. He was assassinated by agents of the Islamic Republic in Paris in 1991.

The shah left the country on January 19, 1979. Ayatollah Khomeini was back in Iran by February 1. On April 1, 1979, Iran was declared an Islamic Republic, and on January 25, 1980, the first Iranian president was elected.

An estimated 400,000 demonstrators against Shah Mohammed Reza Pahlavi fill the campus of Tehran University carrying huge portraits of Ayatollah Ruhollah Khomeini and other opposition leaders, January 13, 1979. (Bettmann/Corbis)

However, power struggles emerged, and in the confusion the new leadership proved ineffective. The hard-liners consolidated power very quickly and surrounded Khomeini, and in no time the new prime minister (appointed by Khomeini) and the newly elected president, Bani Sadr, were both forced out of office. Assassination of more moderate ayatollahs and members of the parliament soon followed. During the first few years of the new regime, all opposition was brutally crushed; universities and many high schools were closed down for a few years. Many fled the country, and thousands were imprisoned or executed. Unlike the Constitutional Revolution, in which the clergy had lost most of their power, the Islamic Revolution brought them back in full force with unparalleled power. The first revolution (1906) had been fueled by Western ideologies such as nationalism, liberalism, secularism, and socialism. In the revolution of 1979, a thoroughly clerical constitution with Islamic codes was created with conscious efforts to condemn such Western concepts as nationalism and democracy. In fact, such notions were regarded as heretical and incompatible with Islam. The Nation of Islam replaced the Nation of Iran; the constitution stated the importance of the Arabic language (because it is the language of the Quran, all Muslims are obliged to learn it), and it became a major part of the curriculum. Names of cities and places were changed, and many Arabic names and terms replaced the Persian ones. One of the first acts of the new government was to abandon all cooperation with the United States and Israel and, consequently, issue a declaration of full support for the Palestinian Muslim cause. The Palestinian leader, Yasser Arafat, was invited to Iran and was received as a hero; he became a symbol of Muslim resistance and unity. The revolution transformed the country into a theocratic state ruled by the Islamic codes. It led to the emigration of nearly three million Iranians to other countries and created a large group of refugees fleeing persecution; harassment; and deteriorating economic, social, and political conditions in Iran. The exodus continues even today. The revolution promoted radical Islam, divided the clergy, and devastated the country through eight years of war with Iraq. The long-lasting Iran-Iraq War produced close to a million deaths on both sides and thousands of wounded and had a major effect on the population distribution in Iran. Khuzistan, the Persian Gulf areas, and the territories close to the Iraq border were at the forefront of the war. Many large areas of terrain are still full of land mines. Major cities were bombed and entire villages depopulated, along with the areas around them. War refugees settled in a number of other major cities, including Tehran, Shiraz, and Isfahan. Arabs, Kurds, Lurs, and Bakhtiyari were forced to settle in unfamiliar areas to avoid the hostilities. Although many people returned to their cities, many more remained in or migrated to major cities such as Tehran.

The constitution of the Islamic Republic was a major setback for human rights and the rights of women and religious minorities, including Sunni Muslims. Prior to its establishment there was major opposition to the clergy and the way they selected participants to draft the constitution. The constitution itself was opposed by many, but the revolutionary government either silenced or took no notice of the opposition, and it was ratified in November 1979. Article 4 proclaimed that all penal, financial, civil, economic, administrative, cultural, military, political, and other laws and regulations must be based on Islamic Shari'a. This principle applied absolutely and generally to all articles of the constitution itself as well as to all other laws and regulations. The state religion remained Shi'i Jaffari Twelfth Imamate, and non-Shi'i Muslims were barred from occupying leadership positions in the country. The constitution named Zoroastrians, Jews, and Armenian and Assyrian Christians as the only recognized religious minorities, with no mention of Baha'i, evangelical Christians, or any other religion. In reality, the constitution provided only a qualified commitment to the principle of nondiscrimination on the basis of religion or ethnic identity. Although in some articles it clearly stated equal rights, other articles contradicted this principle and reserved the highest positions for Shi'i Muslim Iranians. Since all codes must comply with Shari'a, discrimination is inherent despite guarantees of equal rights. The constitution did not specifically mention any ethnic minority. However, it guaranteed freedom to use and publish in minority languages alongside Persian. The school texts remained in Persian (Article 15). Article 19 guaranteed equality for all citizens, despite their ethnic origins. However, in practice such provisions have not been observed.

Article 15
The official language and script of Iran, the lingua franca of its people, is Persian. Official documents, correspondence, and texts as well as textbooks, must be in this language and script. However, the use of regional and tribal languages in the press and mass media, as well as for teaching of their literature in schools, is allowed in addition to Persian.

Article 19
All people of Iran, whatever the ethnic group or tribe to which they belong, enjoy equal rights; and color, race, language, and the like, do not bestow any privilege.

The new clerical leaders condemned Pahlavi's policies, especially modernization and emancipation of women, and declared that returning to old traditions and norms was their priority. Compulsory veiling of women was legislated, birth control was condemned, alcohol was banned, and unsuccessful attempts were made to segregate the sexes. Ayatollah Khomeini affirmed that nomadism and tribalism had suffered tremendously at the hands of the previous regime and that it was time for the noble tribes to go back to their old ways. In no time demands were received from various provinces for partial autonomy and language rights, among others. In a matter of weeks there were armed clashes in Kurdistan and Turkmen Sahra, followed by bombings and attacks on oil pipelines and communication centers in Khuzistan. Pan-Turkic groups emerged and demanded autonomy in Azerbaijan. The Kurdistan conflict was the first and the most serious, resulting in mass killings by the newly and loosely formed Revolutionary Guards.

Kurdistan and the Islamic Republic

The modern province of Kurdistan is much smaller than its previous territories and includes eight major cities; the provincial capital is Sanandaj. The province borders West Azerbaijan and has a mixed population, including many Azeri and Kurdish groups, Kirmanshah with a large Kurdish population, and Iraq on the western border. Elam in southern Iran is also heavily populated by Kurds. The area is home to Iraqi Kurdish refugees, although many returned to Iraq after Saddam Hussein was ousted. Its economy in the eastern areas is based on small-scale agriculture and animal husbandry by the settled agriculturalists and some seminomadic groups that have survived. Carpet-weaving and handicrafts are also important. There are close to seven million Kurds in Iran, and the Islamic government often views them as a major concern.

Prior to the Islamic Revolution, Kurdistan remained one of the few places where underground organizations were able to carry out some limited activities. The Kurdish Democratic Party of Iran (KDPI) remained the most prominent of the banned organizations, along with non-Kurdish Marxists, Islamic militants, and Komala. The latter had attracted many radical Kurdish intellectuals in Iranian Kurdistan and gained recognition among some workers, peasants, and Kurdish women. The KDPI's emergence as a viable political organization was to a large extent due to its charismatic and well-educated leader, Abd al-Rahman Ghassemlou. Born into a landowning family of the Mukri tribe, he left Iran after the collapse of the Mahabad Republic. He lived in Prague and returned to Iran in the early 1950s. He was imprisoned after Musaddiq's fall and later returned to Prague, obtained his Ph.D., taught economics, and went to France after the Soviet invasion of Czechoslovakia. In 1973 he was chosen as the leader of the KDPI. By the time of the revolution he had returned to Iran and helped to transform the KDPI into a party with a large membership and a clear agenda for Kurdish autonomy in Iran. The KDPI under Ghassemlou promoted nonviolence, while Komala saw armed resistance as a viable strategy for dealing with the Kurdish question.

The revolution was well received in Kurdistan, and all major groups supported the mass movement against the shah, with the exception of some prominent Kurds who had close ties to the government. Following the shah's departure, the area became a stronghold for groups including the liberation army in support of the monarchy, the previously banned Marxists, and the Islamic Mujahedin. The banned groups were directly involved in the uprising against the monarchy and participated in violent clashes with the military. Following the success of the revolution, they all went public. Both Komala and the KDPI rallied for the support of the Kurdish people in Kurdistan. Kurdish autonomy became the most debated issue in Kurdistan, followed by widespread discussions in the national press, which was still able to function freely prior to its closure by the new revolutionary government in the early 1980s.

By the late 1970s the Kurds in Iran had a general awareness of being a separate people. Such distinctions were mostly based on who was and who was not a Kurd rather than knowledge of the Kurds' historical origins and ethnic identity. Such assumptions about identity and unity of the Kurdish people existed despite major divisions in language and religion and non-Kurdish minorities who lived among Kurds and had extensive social and economic ties with them. The linguistic diversity, including a large number of different dialects—some incomprehensible even to other Kurds—and a substantial number of Persianized Kurds who barely spoke Kurdish, remained a dividing factor.

Religious affiliations also divided the Kurds. Although the vast majority are Sunni, they differ greatly in the degree of their devotion and their loyalty to orthodox Sunni practices and rituals. The popularity of mystical sects, notably the Naqshbandi and Qaderi, and loyalty to competing shaikhs and various Shi'i marginal sects, in addition to the secular Kurds, created significant divisions as well. Prior to the twentieth century Kurdish society was stratified, with tribal chiefs heading seminomadic groups and ruling families governing the affairs of the settled Kurds. Both groups lost their prominence in the twentieth century, but some ties remained, and such associations were manifested during political rallying supporting one group or faction against another. The mystical shaikhs also managed to maintain most of their power over their followers and still exert local influence. In mass uprisings or support for particular movements, it has been the shaikhs and not the political parties who have been able to mobilize people. One such shaikh was Mulla Mustafa Barazani's brother, Shaikh Ahmad Barazani, who was able to mobilize thousands of supporters in times of need. The question of ethnicity in Kurdistan was even more complicated by the fact that some groups mostly identify themselves with their religion or language, such as Alevid, Yazidi, or Gurani.

There is no doubt that in Iranian Kurdistan, as in other Kurdish areas outside Iran, the Kurds mostly define themselves in terms of ethnicity. However, their participation in ethnic nationalism is not necessarily tied to their ethnic identity. For example, many Persianized Kurds reject any notion of an independent Kurdistan and clearly associate themselves with Iran rather than Kurdistan. Partially overlapping identities exist and it is not uncommon for a Kurd to consider himself first a Muslim or a Qaderi or Zaza speaker, or even Azeri or Persian, in addition to a Kurdish identity. There were major differences between Iran, Iraq, and Turkey with respect to the Kurds, who were far more brutally oppressed in Iraq and Turkey. Their adherence to their Kurdish ethnicity and nationalism was a lot stronger in those countries. However, this was to change with the success of the Islamic Revolution in Iran.

Early in the 1970s the Kurds in Iraq, encouraged by Iranian and U.S. promises of support, were aggressively fighting against Saddam Hussein. In 1975 the shah and Saddam signed an agreement in which important border concessions were made to Iran in exchange for its ending military and financial support of the Iraqi Kurds. As a result, close to 100,000 *peshmerges* ("ready to die") guerrilla fighters arrived in Iran and were settled in temporary refugee camps. As early as 1976, guerrilla attacks and factional fighting were happening between the Patriotic Union of Kurdistan (PUK) and the Kurdistan Democratic Party (KDP) close to the border areas. Attacks on the Kurdish territories in Iraq brought thousands more unarmed or regular refugees, mainly with their families, into the towns in Iranian Kurdistan. The presence of a large number of refugees and militant Kurds played a decisive role in the uprisings against the Islamic Republic in 1979. The situation was further complicated when the Iranian branches of the Kurdish Democratic Party and Komala emerged and were restructured in Iranian Kurdistan. Another popular leader was Izzaddin Husseini, a Sunni shaikh, who managed to rally a large number of Kurds around him. At this time another clergyman, Ahmad Muftizade, who had been educated at the prestigious Muslim institution Al-Azhar in Egypt, emerged in Sanandaj.

Following the revolution and the return of Ghassemlou, the KDPI remained prominent around Mahabad. The Komala stayed active farther to the south in Sanandaj. There were very violent clashes between the Shi'i minority and Sunni Kurds and major conflicts between peasants and landlords who had lost land during the Land Reform period and wanted their properties back. There was fighting between Kurds and the proshah military, and between Kurds and the new Revolutionary Guards sent from Tehran. The fact that such clashes happened very quickly in Kurdistan was due to the complicated situation there and the presence of a large number of displaced and armed militant Kurds from Iraq.

As early as one week after the success of the revolution, representatives and delegates, some Kurdish, were sent by the government in Tehran to talk to the Kurdish leaders in an effort to calm Kurdistan. The leaders of the KDPI and Komala and Shaikh Husseini emerged as the most prominent Kurdish personalities, and the three presented their demands to the representatives from Tehran. In one gathering, they managed to bring nearly 100,000 Kurds together to impress the authorities. They demanded autonomy, freedom to use the Kurdish language, the allocation of more financial resources to develop Kurdistan, a Kurdish assembly, the punishment of the anti-Kurdish military, and the expulsion of Barazani and his group. Barazani was accused of collaborating with the shah's regime. They also wanted a new province to include the many Kurdish areas previously divided and annexed to other provinces. Their claim went far beyond Kurdistan and included West Azerbaijan, with a large Azeri majority, and Kirmanshah and Elam, which had a Shi'i majority and was mainly Lur in origin. Shaikh Husseini, a Sunni cleric, was declared the leader of the Kurdish people. He had become the spokesman for the KDPI and was also a member of Komala and the Marxist militant non-Kurdish group the Fedai Guerrillas. The choice of a shaikh was a clear indication that the leadership in Kurdistan was aware of the religious sentiments of the average Kurds and the sensitivity of an Islamic government in dealing with the leftist-oriented groups in Kurdistan.

Both the Kurds and the Azeri boycotted the referendum on the new constitution, and more violence followed. At one point the government even offered the Kurds a plan for local administration through two provincial assemblies in Mahabad and Sanandaj. It also promised to guarantee cultural autonomy and freedom of Sunni practices in Sunni areas. However, none of the proposed concessions materialized, and more Revolutionary Guards were sent to the area. The regular army at this point was in chaos because of many desertions, executions, and massive dismissals, and the revolutionary government did not trust it. All the top commanders and half of the middle-ranking officers were removed, devastating its operational abilities. The creation of a military force of Revolutionary Guards, which existed side by side with the regular army, had already begun and was rapidly expanding. The Revolutionary Guards (Pasdaran) and their auxiliaries and affiliated military units have remained the most important military force loyal to the Islamic government.

The revolutionary government was divided. It was not able to respond to Kurdish demands, and further violence broke out in every corner of Kurdistan. The events there and the denunciation of the Kurdish uprising by Ayatollah Khomeini, who called on the nation for a holy war *(jihad)* against the resistance, left no illusion that the central government would give in to demands for autonomy. Summary executions of Kurds were broadcast through the media with explicit images that created terror and forced thousands to escape to Iraq. There was violence between different Kurdish factions, but it was mainly directed against the revolutionary army and the agents of the new government in Tehran. The Barazani group took the side of the Islamic Republic, became a significant military force in the area, and fought the Iranian Kurds. By the summer of 1979, more troops had arrived to establish the central government's control over the area. The Kurds managed to exert control over towns in early 1980 and over the rural areas by 1983. At this time most were forced to retreat into Iraq, which had been engaged in a devastating full-scale war against Iran since 1980. Komala and the KDPI split, and both ended up carrying on small-scale guerrilla activities in the border areas for a few years and blaming each other for their failure.

Because of the divisions that existed right from the beginning and throughout the conflict, the Kurds were not able to form a coherent united front. None of the major groups managed to maintain massive popular support, and many Kurds remained suspicious of the leftist ideologies of the leading groups. In the beginning the KDPI and Komala were able to attract large crowds, but they lost popularity in the aftermath of military operations and chaos in the area. The KDPI remained active in Mahabad and Komala in Sanandaj; the latter remained committed to armed struggle. In 1979 the KDPI reached a compromise with the government and declared a cease-fire, but it was undermined by Komala's repeated attacks on the government forces. The Iraqi government supplied arms to some factions to fight everyone else and the government in Tehran. There were also the so-called traditional conservative elements, shaikhs, clergy, local leaders with influence and followers (agha, mainly old tribal chiefs), promonarchists, and landlords, all with their own agendas. The new government was able to use some of these elements, including some of the conservative clergy. Although Sunni and pro-Kurdish, they did not support the leftist groups and were willing to work with the new regime.

As weak as it was in the beginning, the new government had clear policies with respect to the minorities. Government officials were aware that if they lost in Kurdistan or made serious concessions, they would have to face demands from all other groups as well. They did not accept the Kurds' pledge of local autonomy and viewed them as separatists. Shaikh Husseini and other Kurds opposed some of the major principles of the constitution, such as the position of the "Supreme Spiritual Leader" with unlimited power and a Guardian Council composed of clergymen with powers superior to those of the parliament. Such opposition resulted in the barring of prominent Kurds such as Ghassemlou, who was elected to be present at the seventy-three-seat Assembly of Experts (for the drafting of the new constitution), from major decision-making processes in Tehran. Further divisions in the KDPI and Komala weakened the Kurds from within and ended any hope of attaining any degree of autonomy in Kurdistan. Iraq, with support from the United States, Western Europe, and most other countries in the region, attacked Iran in 1980, and the long war changed the dynamics of politics in Iran and Kurdistan.

The eight-year war between Iran and Iraq had major consequences for the Kurds. It provided a golden opportunity for them to negotiate with the government in Tehran and gain some concessions. However, they failed due to poor leadership and bad decisions. By 1982, amidst the war, the Kurds had been pushed back and lost more territories under their control; by 1983 all the major groups had been forced to resort to guerrilla tactics. The KDPI reluctantly joined the National Council of Resistance (NRC) formed by the deposed president of the Islamic Republic and the militant Muslim Mujahedin, who had suffered mass eradication under the revolutionary government. The NRC operated from Iraq during the war, which diminished any popularity it had in Iran. The KDPI eventually left the NRC, and this decision and increasing criticism of Ghassemlou's autocratic ways divided the group further. The KDPI still exists; Komala formally disappeared but reemerged in 1991 as a new minor group.

The Kurds suffered because of Iraqi attacks on the region. Their towns became major targets of Iraqi artillery, and indiscriminate bombing by the Iraqi forces, clearly aimed at eradicating Iraqi Kurdish camps in Iran, devastated the region and resulted in mass evacuation of towns and villages. On the Iraqi side, the government depopulated, mined, and cleared hundreds of villages in the border areas and moved their Kurdish populations away from the border for better control. The Iranians also cleared areas and placed land mines. The border region was and is littered with land mines, but despite being labeled a danger zone, it was used by the rebellious Iraqi and Iranian Kurds and other groups. The banned leftists and militant Mujahedin active in the region also used the area for campsites for their military operations. The no-man's zone, as it is called, became a popular route for smugglers, particularly following the Iraqi invasion of Kuwait and the resulting imposition of economic sanctions on Iraq. Smuggling became a major economic activity in the area and connected many Kurds in Iran and Iraq. It is not regarded as a criminal activity, and its widespread practice is recognized as an essential and viable way of making a living under the harsh realities of life in Kurdistan. The U.S. invasion of Iraq in 2003 and the lifting of sanctions will no doubt have an impact on the smuggling economy that will lead to further deterioration of the Kurds' lives unless alternative economic strategies are put in place.

Kurdistan has remained quiet for a long time, with the exception of occasional sporadic clashes. A garrison of thousands of troops was established in the area in the early 1980s and managed to keep everything under control. One major protest happened following the arrest and during the trial of a popular Kurdish leader in Turkey in 1993. However, the uprising was soon crushed, and in the absence of legitimate political parties and organized resistance, there is currently no viable opposition to the central government in Kurdistan. The end of the war in 1988 and Khomeini's death in 1989 were fresh opportunities for the Kurds, but such hopes vanished when Ghassem-lou was assassinated during talks with representatives of the Iranian government in 1989.

Azerbaijan and the Islamic Republic

Currently Azerbaijan consists of three provinces in Iran: West Azerbaijan, with its capital in Urmiyeh; East Azerbaijan, with its capital in Tabriz; and the third province, Ardabil, with the city of the same name as its capital. A nearby province, Zanjan, with its capital in the city of the same name, also has a dominant Azeri population. There are significant Azeri communities in and around Hamadan, Tehran, Qum, Khurasan, and many other parts of Iran. Turkic speakers constitute close to 25 percent of the population in Iran, and the Azeri form close to 85 percent of Turkic speakers. They are the largest minority group in the country, and it is estimated that close to one-third of the population of Tehran is Azeri migrants. Although this figure has not been substantiated, it indicates the presence of a large Azeri population in Tehran.

The lifestyle of the urban and rural Azerbaijanis is very similar to that of the Persians, and there is extensive interaction and marriage among the Azeri and the rest of the population. Shi'i is the majority religion, and at the time of the revolution, in 1979, the most prominent religious leader in the country, Ayatollah Shariatmadari, was from Azerbaijan. He had a good relationship with the monarchy and was responsible for saving Ayatollah Khomeini from persecution during the uprisings against the shah's White Revolution. It was due to his intervention that Khomeini was made an ayatollah and was sent into exile in Iraq rather than being imprisoned. After the success of the revolution, literary journals and newspapers in the Azeri language appeared all over Azerbaijan. A number of organizations and small parties were formed, most advocating some form of national and cultural autonomy within Iran.

Following the revolution, the radical Muslims in Tehran formed the Islamic Republic Party. They very quickly consolidated power, harassed other political groups and parties, and created their own militia. Ayatollah Khomeini was back in Iran in February, and by March his supporters had arranged a referendum on the future of Iran. They provided only two choices: a monarchy or an Islamic Republic headed by Ayatollah Khomeini. The referendum was opposed by many, including the Kurds and the people of Azerbaijan. However, on April 1 Iran was declared an Islamic Republic by the overwhelming majority vote.

Azerbaijan became an important center of opposition to the antidemocratic maneuverings of the new government. The Assembly of Experts and the resulting constitution created even more opposition prior to, during, and after the document's ratification. A new organization, the Islamic Republic's Muslim People's Party, was immediately set up in Azerbaijan with the full support of Ayatollah Shariatmadari, who openly criticized the policies of the government in Tehran. The party became a major organ in Azerbaijan, with many influential figures, and at one rally managed to attract hundreds of thousands of people for support. In a matter of ten months peaceful negotiations and demonstrations evolved into armed clashes and occupation of military and police posts and television and radio stations in Azerbaijan. The most serious clashes happened prior to the drafting of the new constitution and eventually led to the virtual house arrest of Ayatollah Shariatmadari in Qum.

Unlike the opposition in Kurdistan, the movement in Azerbaijan was more concerned with the establishment of a democratic constitution and national government than with provincial grievances. In their demands and negotiations with the authorities in Tehran, the resisters insisted that the key officials in the province should be chosen under the supervision of Shariatmadari. The struggle became one between powerful clergy rather than an ethnic uprising. The moderate Azerbaijani clergy were no match for the radical militants in Tehran. Shariatmadari was put under house arrest and stripped of his credentials. The party was divided and lost popular support. The uprising had remained mainly in East Azerbaijan and was not supported by all Azeri, who in the end participated in the referendum. In contrast to previous uprisings in Azerbaijan, the leftist groups had a minor presence and did not make a significant impact. They were divided and fought among themselves, and the Tudeh Party in particular had lost credibility because of its earlier associations with the Russians. The Islamic militants, the Mujahedin, emerged as the most popular opposition group, with thousands of youth supporting its inexperienced and relatively young leadership.

The main factors influencing separatist tendencies were events outside Iran. The breakdown of the Soviet Union in the early 1990s and the establishment of an independent Republic of Azerbaijan in the former USSR had significant effects on the formation of ethnic demands in Iranian Azerbaijan. Communist ideology gave way to nationalistic and ethnic ideas in the new republic. The Azeri intellectuals who had escaped to Baku after World War II, along with the Azeri nationalists there, had kept the question of a united Azerbaijan alive in the press and media. A new genre of literature had emerged that focused on ethnic and nationalist issues, often with nostalgic overtone. This kind of literature was broadcast from Baku into Iran for decades and became more popular in Iranian Azerbaijan in the early 1980s. Propaganda with nationalistic fervor was broadcast that emphasized the Turkish language and a separate identity and origin for the Turkic speakers, and presented exaggerated or inaccurately reconstructed histories and mythologies. The separatists even attacked well-known historians such as Kasravi, who had promoted the Iranian origins of Azeris.

Once the Azerbaijan Republic was established and the Soviet influence was reduced, extreme nationalist sentiments became a significant factor in the republic's political life. Despite the fact that the majority of Azeri live in Iranian Azerbaijan, the republic has made claims of sovereignty and unity of Azerbaijan that have remained an important political issue. Several political organizations such as the Liberation Front of South Azerbaijan have been financed and established in Iran. Such organizations are not legitimate; however, they are backed by the media from Baku and are well known in Iranian Azerbaijan. Television broadcasts from Baku have reconstructed histories and maps with plays, music, and poetry that reinforce the notion of a united Azerbaijan. Such programs are broadcast in Europe and North America as well, and Azeri television networks on these continents make great use of such productions. Extensive social and media networks have been established in these countries that promote the same ideas through publications, websites, concerts, and regular meetings. The accounts portray the Iranian section as lost territories from the mainland in the north and Azerbaijan as a totally independent country with no historical links to Iran.

The wealthy Iranian Azeris are encouraged to invest in the republic, and facilities are provided in efforts to persuade them to move to Baku and other cities in the republic. Travel between the two is made easy by both sides, and there is a flow of Iranian Azeris moving from Iran to the republic for work and investment opportunities. The pan-Turkic groups in Turkey have also supported the separation of Azerbaijan from Iran. There is a large number of Iranians in Turkey at present. The government of Turkey provides facilities for the Turkic-Iranians and finances some organizations among them, promoting pan-Turkism and the idea of a large united Turkish territory for all Turkic-speaking groups. The political events of the past few years, the violent conflict between Armenia and the Republic of Azerbaijan, and political crisis in Turkey have introduced changes. Both Turkey and the Republic of Azerbaijan have reduced their activities in support of an independent Azerbaijan in Iran. Both have tried to negotiate economic cooperation with Iran and are cautious about covert activities there.

The Islamic Republic has its own agenda. It has been trying to gain influence in the independent republic and Turkey. It has built several mosques in association with charities in the Republic of Azerbaijan and has been trying to entice the republic's populace to come to Iran for visits and pilgrimage. It has been accused of supporting radical Muslim groups in the republic and in Turkey. Such activity has been a major diplomatic issue between these countries at times. There have been major clashes between government forces and the Azeris and other Turkish speakers on several occasions. A demand in 1994 by representatives from Qazvin to make this city and the neighboring towns with a large Azeri population into a province was defeated in the parliament and created many local clashes. Nationally, Azeri people have always been subjects of jokes and ridicule. The production by Iranian television networks of comedies using such stereotyping created even more resentment and conflict. Such examples are used extensively by nationalists in the Republic of Azerbaijan against Iran and as proof that Azeris are mistreated there.

There has been conflict with respect to the parliamentary elections as well. In one case the authorities in Tehran refused to accept the legitimately elected Azeri candidate for the parliament. They rejected his credentials and barred him from taking his seat. This representative, who was elected by very strong vote, promoted a secular democratic government in Iran and emphasized ethnic rights within a democratic federal government. He was arrested and spent three years in jail before he was released due to international pressure.

The Islamic Republic and the Pastoral Nomads

The policies of the new republic with respect to pastoral nomads have been varied. On the whole, the government has not used coercion as its main strategy. It has attempted, like governments before, to re-create tribal systems in a manner compatible with the new state. The Islamic Revolution was an urban phenomenon, and the tribal groups did very little to guarantee its success or failure. The settled members in the cities participated in the street demonstrations, and the local chiefs tried to reclaim their lands, but with no success. The nomads were called the "treasures of the revolution" by Ayatollah Khomeini and were classified as the second-most-oppressed group, af-

A woman from the Turkish tribe of Hamadan (Nasrollah Kasraian)

ter the clergy, under the Pahlavi regime. In the areas, such as those dominated by Turkmen, where active militant groups were present, there were violent clashes. In other areas, such as Baluchistan, the presence of powerful chiefs and monarchists also created violent clashes. Other tribes, such as the Shahsevan, had relative calm in their areas; the Qashqa'i chiefs suffered the most, while the regular tribespeople stayed away from most of the violence. The 1980s were a time of conflict and war. War-related shortages and restrictions, and the sanctions preventing the import of U.S. goods because of the hostage crisis, created a boom in local produce, including dairy and other livestock products, that benefited the nomads and agriculturalists.

A new organization, the Jihad for Rural Reconstruction, was created shortly after the revolution. The organization was staffed by local people, used local resources, and implemented many programs designed to reconstruct an infrastructure in the remote and deprived parts of the country. On the whole it was successful in some tasks, such as the supply of clean running water and electricity. However, some areas such as Baluchistan remained backward, with little improvement compared to other areas. The most effective organizations with respect to the nomads have been the Organization for Pastoral Nomadic Affairs and the Forest, Watershed, and Rangeland Organization. Both are mainly staffed locally. The first is responsible for the pastoral nomads and is affiliated with the Ministry of Agriculture. Since the mid-1980s it has implemented a number of major tasks and reforms with respect to the nomadic population. By the early 1990s the government agencies were convinced that settlements were the future for the nomads. However, they did not use force, and a number of options and incentives were made available to the nomads to motivate them to settle voluntarily. Paramount and major chiefs and their families have been eliminated from almost all processes because the government agencies regard them as exploiters of common people. Leadership positions are normally negotiated between the elderly of a group and government agents. Language rights do not exist, and tribal schools follow the national curriculum that is all in Persian. Relatively successful efforts have been made to employ local people for a variety of tasks, including security and policing. A number of programs have also been made available to improve the lives of nomads who want to continue pastoral nomadism. One of the most successful so far has been the creation of the so-called pastoral habitats among the Shahsevan nomads.

The pastoral communities of Iran currently compromise about 2 percent of the total population, or close to 1.4 million people. In the previous centuries the number of pastoralists has varied between half and one-quarter of the general population, so there has clearly been a sharp decrease in pastoral nomadism in Iran in the twentieth century. The nomads currently produce close to one-third of the country's livestock products. It is generally believed that pastoral nomads in dry lands produce more economic gains per hectare than the traditional sedentary production systems. However, the emergence of major agroindustrial complexes in Iran has and will make produce by pastoral nomads unprofitable. Ecological damage to pastoral habitats in Iran has made a significant impact already, with loss of pasture due to overgrazing and population pressure. Iran's population has almost doubled since the revolution. Originally the clergy proclaimed family planning to be a non-Islamic practice. However, they reversed their policy, and Iran has been very successful with respect to lowering the average birth rate. Recent studies and surveys by the government and international agencies indicate that the pastoral nomads are aware that their way of life is not sustainable in the future. However, they prefer to maintain, save, or revive pastoral nomadism as long as they can. The Shahsevan experimental pastoral habitats might be a move in the right direction.

Shahsevan

During the last decade before the Islamic Revolution, pastoral nomadism declined rapidly in Iran; the Shahsevan were no exception. Major factories and large agroindustrial projects were developed in the area, with foreign companies as partners and shares being sold to the general public and the local people. By the late 1970s the Shahsevan had lost their best winter pasture in the Moghan Plain. In one move alone, close to 1,800 nomadic families were evicted from the area. They also lost security of tenure and the right to cultivate pastures in other areas. During the revolution, the nomads played little part because the revolution was mainly urban in nature. The settled tribal members who lived in the nearby towns participated in street protests, and three of their chiefs were killed by the radical revolutionary elements. Such events made the nomads cautious. After the success of the revolution, they took over the industrial complex in Moghan and demanded restoration of their former pasturelands. A loose coalition was formed, and thirty chiefs and some 400 Shahsevan went to Qum to visit the two prominent ayatollahs, Khomeini and Shariatmadari. The latter criticized them for taking over the industrial complex, and the former declared them to be the treasures of the revolution. By the end of the visit very little had been accomplished; nevertheless, they presented their demands. They wanted their former lands to be restored to them for pasture use. The Forestry Department and the gendarmerie agents had to leave the area, and a number of social, educational, and health care facilities were to be established by the government. They also demanded financial aid to start over again.

In the end some measures were taken: The agroindustrial complex was disbanded, some land was returned to the Shahsevan, and it was demanded that they change their name from Shahsevan to Elsevan ("those who love the people"). Their name was officially changed, but the nomads did not accept it, and after a decade the old name was used widely and officially and the new one abandoned. After the war and in the 1990s, the agroindustrial complexes were back in full force. The cities and local towns had grown immensely. Further changes were introduced when the area was divided into two provinces for administrative purposes. More pastureland, close to 18,000 hectares, was taken away and allocated to the Ministry of Agriculture for further large-scale development in the Moghan area. The old industrial complex was changed into a new and larger complex called Pars Abad and has grown into the second-largest town in the new subprovince, with close to 50,000 people living and working there. A new major dam was constructed, and more areas have been allocated for extensive agroindustrial projects.

However, a number of steps were taken to improve the situation of nomads. The war created food shortages, and the nomads benefited from the strong local markets. The new Organization for Pastoral Nomadic Affairs, despite some problems, on the whole has been relatively successful. One of the reasons for its success has been its employment of locals to provide services. In the case of the nomadic tribes, such as the Shahsevan, they used educated nomads to provide essential services, education, security, and pasture-related tasks such as allocation. The Shahsevan enjoyed some revival until the early 1990s. In 1993 the government policies with respect to nomadism changed, and settling the nomads is on the agenda once more. However, force is not used, and many nomadic groups are voluntarily settling down. Major social, economic, and demographic changes inevitably have led to more settlements. The Shahsevan's local Organization for Pastoral Nomadic Affairs did oppose the government's settlement ideology, but the Shahsevan have also reached the conclusion that settlements are inevitable. They have devised their own plan to suit the needs of the pastoralists and provide incentives for those who want to settle, but they have tried to improve the lives of the nomads who want to continue.

The remaining pasture lands are divided into nine new units called pastoral habitats. Each habitat, like a campsite, has a central base with power, water supply, a bath house, and health and school facilities. There are tracks from the center to winter campsites around the periphery. The nomads can stay at the campsites at the periphery or live in the center. Some of the campsites are in inaccessible areas in the mountains. New roads have been constructed for Jeeps and other suitable vehicles, mostly government owned. The settlements have enabled the government agencies to keep good control over the nomads, but the nomads have also reacted positively to the plans. The first such habitats started operation in 1995, and so far they have remained. They have proved to be profitable, and despite the presence of major agroindustrial complexes and migration to the cities, the number of nomadic families has increased.

In 1987 the number of Shahsevan families who practiced nomadism was close to 6,000 families, more than it had been in the 1970s. By 1995 close to 8,000 families were practicing pastoral nomadism, and the rate has remained stable. Some problems still persist; farming by settled farmers on the summer pasture lands is an issue. The current system used for issuing grazing permits has problems, but improvements are planned. Most planning is done locally. The chiefly families are not favored and have lost their positions. Some quietly live in the area and have farming and livestock enterprises. The government agencies do not deal with them, and leadership among the nomads is negotiated between the elderly of the groups and the local Organization of Pastoral Nomadic Affairs with no reference to the chiefs. The tribe and the subtribe remain the main pastoral nomadic units.

Qashqa'i

The Qashqa'i nomads are part of a larger confederation of close to 800,000 people in southwest Iran that includes non-Qashqa'i groups. Close to 250,000 Qashqa'i still practice pastoral nomadism. They form close to half of the Turkic-speaking population of Fars. Although many have settled down since the 1960s, many retain pastoralism on a part-time basis and as one of several strategies. During the second part of the twentieth century they had to migrate or live at new places, and their patterns of residence changed. Tents became too expensive and too cumbersome. Instead, many began building huts and small brick houses on their summer and winter pastures. Their migration routes are the longest and the most difficult of all of Iran's pastoral tribes. They have to rely heavily on government planning and agencies for their seasonal migrations. Many changes have occurred during the last thirty years, most in response to significant socioeconomic changes, population pressure, and expansion of the agricultural sector. Pack animals,

Qashqa'i migrating on the tribal path of Dasht-e-bakan, north of Shiraz in Fars. (Nasrollah Kasraian)

especially camels, are not much used, and mechanized vehicles have become much more prominent during the migrations. This by itself has introduced major changes because the Qashqa'i can get fairly quickly from one location to the other and not all family members need to travel together at the same time. Males can be working in towns or on their farms and join the rest of the family later without much loss of time. Children mostly attend schools, which means they cannot be used as labor at all times. Women might not accompany the herds, and additional manpower has to be employed. Water management is a serious problem, and the nomads are not able to use natural surface waters anymore. The introduction of farms, orchards, and large-scale agricultural businesses has reduced both surface and underground waters. The government agencies have taken responsibility for providing water at designated locations.

With all this, significant changes have happened with respect to power structures, chiefly lineage, and local Qashqa'i are now appointed by the government agencies in charge of security and most local affairs. There have been changes in rituals and related practices as well; some, such as celebrating the rain or rituals related to protecting animals, are not practiced regularly anymore or have become simply symbolic. The favorable attitude of the government toward tribalism and pastoral nomads until the mid-1990s encouraged nomads to continue migrations; nevertheless, many more are settling down. The nomads are aware of the difficulties but are attached to their way of life. Despite many changes, there has been a collective effort among the Qashqa'i to somehow preserve their way of life.

The Islamic Revolution took place with minimal involvement by the tribal groups. Qashqa'i participated in street demonstrations in the cities but did not provide armed assistance or any major leadership. When they appeared in demonstrations, they showed up fully dressed in their costumes and with slogans in Turkish. Both males and females participated in demonstrations. Their numbers were small, but they were very visible, as they intended to be. The two surviving brothers who had assumed the positions of paramount khans were both in exile, in Europe and the United States. They cautioned the Qashqa'i to show restraint, and they recommended no call to serious or military action. They did contact Ayatollah Khomeini, who was in France at the time, and asked if they should attack the military and police. They were told no but were asked to maintain order in the Fars province if needed.

Just before the shah's departure in January 1979, a local Qashqa'i leader recruited fifty armed guards to protect an oil field in an area the Qashqa'i regarded as their territory. One paramount khan, Naser Khan, came back just before the shah's departure and assumed leadership of the tribes after decades of absence from Iran. He was greeted like a hero in Tehran and was offered the governorship of the Fars province. He was escorted by hundreds of cars and thousands of Qashqa'i to Shiraz, where he paid a visit to the major shrine. His brother Khosrow Khan, the second paramount chief, and several other members of the family returned as well, some from detention in Tehran. They became involved in negotiations with the new revolutionary government, and for the first time the daughter of one of the khans emerged as a leader with substantial influence. Another younger member of a ruling family was appointed by the new government to receive and accompany representatives from the Sandinista government of Nicaragua who were visiting Iran. Although they did not hold any official titles, the khans exerted great influence in Fars and were approached by all groups in the province on a number of occasions and for a variety of reasons.

It did not take long before the Qashqa'i and the new Revolutionary Guards antagonized each other. The new government, with its organ, the Islamic Republic Party, relied heavily on mobs of the poor and uneducated militants grouped into factions such as Hezbollah (followers of the Party of God) or the Revolutionary Guards. The guards soon took over most police and army units and were responsible for many illegal and violent acts against individuals or groups opposing them or the new Islamic government. Qashqa'i leaders, despite their support of the revolution, did not accept the guards as legitimate, nor did they sympathize with the antidemocratic moves of the new regime and consolidation of power by the clergy.

The two khans had many problems resuming leadership and revitalizing the older ways of life, and they drifted apart. The economic base of the group had been totally undermined during the last few decades. The pastures had been nationalized; many of their properties had been confiscated and developed into major industrial and large-scale agricultural businesses by non-Qashqa'i. Many Qashqa'i at the time were already settled down, and new classes had emerged. The middle class was living in towns and had been assimilated into Iranian society. Such groups had mixed feelings about resuming older patterns of nomadism, while the seminomadic groups wanted a return to the traditional ways. A wealthier new class, many with no ties to the ruling lineage, did not favor the two khans' leadership either, and some felt threatened by actions to repoliticize the group.

Most expected that the two khans would play significant roles in the new nation and would manage to restore some of the old pasture lands and rights, but the khans were not able to do much more than keep the Revolutionary Guards off their immediate grounds and expel some non-Qashqa'i from some of their pasturelands. Such acts created even more problems. Regional autonomy was not feasible. The removal of government agencies in charge of pasture allocation created chaos, and the khans were not able to produce workable plans with respect to allotment in time for the migrations. Conflict with respect to pasture use emerged among the various Qashqa'i groups. The khans had lost considerable wealth and did not have financial resources. The government institutions in charge of dealing with the tribal groups were eventually reinstated by agents of the new government.

Conflict emerged among the members of the Shahilu clan as to how to deal with problems and divisions among the close-knit family group. What role the women should play became an issue as well. The new generation of younger males and females had been educated mostly in Western countries and had different ideas, while the older generation valued age, experience, and lineage. Traditionally, powerful women existed, but they exerted influence through their sons and other male relatives. The new professional Qashqa'i females demanded direct roles and influence and dismissed gender as a criterion for leadership. The prominent families who had remained in Iran or had come back earlier in the 1960s and lived in Tehran had access to networks of influence, whereas the two paramount khans, who had lived outside Iran, had no such resources.

The tribal schools had produced generations of educated Qashqa'i with national rather than tribal sentiments. Leftist sentiments also existed among the younger urbanized population, and they objected to any leadership by the ruling lineage. The government itself had not fully consolidated power, and parallel power groups existed, which made negotiations difficult. All these factors effectively halted efficient management of the group at the time. Ayatollah Khomeini made a number of speeches favorable to the tribal groups and praised their way of life. Posters and stamps were printed with pictures of different ethnic groups fully dressed in their traditional attire. Included were pictures of Kurds and Qashqa'i.

The tribal, ethnic, and opposition groups demanded a federal political system with autonomous provinces. The establishment of the Islamic Republic introduced new elements into the relationship between the tribes and the central government. The theocratic nature of the government and the constitution meant clergy rule and the imposition of Shi'i ideology on all groups. The Qashqa'i leaders, unlike Kurdish leaders, remained undecided and ambivalent. They were not sure how long the clergy would last and whom they should deal with. Due to decades of exile, they were hesitant about their own position and were aware of their inadequate understanding of the dynamics that had occurred during their absence. They decided to stay away from national politics and wait to see what would happen. They further hoped that once parliamentary elections were carried out, they would end as the undisputed Qashqa'i leaders in the parliament and could then exert influence. They presented three candidates, but only Khosrow Khan, one of the paramount chiefs, gained enough votes in the first run of the elections.

The elections coincided with the takeover of the U.S. Embassy in Iran and the hostage crisis. Originally sixty-six members of the U.S. Embassy were taken hostage in November 1979; in the end fifty-two remained and were detained for 444 days. The revolutionary group at the embassy presented documentation indicating that the Qashqa'i khan had direct links with the Americans. In fact, all they had was the mention of his name in one document. The authorities seized the opportunity to label him an American agent, rejected his credentials, and disqualified him as a candidate for parliament. Soon he was kidnapped; he resisted, was beaten up, and went missing. He was released soon after but was taken into custody again; in the end he bribed his way out. Several prominent Qashqa'i were arrested; most managed to escape to the tribe's stronghold near Shiraz.

The two khans and their entourage set up a military camp and managed to stop the Revolutionary Guards from taking over the camp. They were

joined by other khans and their families, and also people from the neighboring tribes such as the Boir Ahmadi and Basseri. They were portrayed in
the media as antirevolutionaries and for two years managed to hold on and
move from camp to camp. Altogether close to 600 prominent khans, their
families, and their bodyguards remained together, and on occasion they were
joined by other insurgents such as Mujahedin, or leftists, and Kurds fighting the revolutionary government. Their popularity grew with the nation as
a whole because they had defied the revolutionary government for months.

The war with Iraq relieved them briefly from government attacks. The
same war enabled the government to quickly consolidate power and extend
the scope and the power of the Revolutionary Guards to combat the Iraqi
offensive. Soon the army was used to crush all resistance inside the country.
The Revolutionary Guards evolved into a major fighting force with their own
artillery and air power and have remained independent of the regular army.
The insurgents were forced to separate into smaller camps, sometimes with
limited access to food and medical supplies and with little distinction between the khans and their retainers. Women were present in the camps and
participated in all activities. Some, including Naser Khan and his daughter,
managed to escape from the camps. The insurgents were finally defeated;
many prominent members, including Khosrow Khan and khans of the Boir
Ahmadi, were executed.

Despite the presence of a large number of armed Qashqa'i in the region,
the insurgents did not receive major military or financial support from the
tribe as a whole. This was a major shift in the relationship between the ruling lineage and the average tribal member. Historically they would have been
supported by full force. The lack of support was due to a number of factors
and significant changes in the tribal economic and power structures. The
massive merciless persecutions and indiscriminate and summary executions
of all opposition by the government were major deterrents. Violence on this
scale was unprecedented and terrified people, leading to mass defections and
exodus. The paramount chiefs did not present any viable plan or ideology
that could make a significant change in the lives of the Qashqa'i and make
the sacrifices worthwhile. The group had survived and some had done quite
well without any chiefs for decades. Many did not see the chiefs as relevant
enough to raise arms in their support. In contrast to the past, there was no
possibility of confiscating property and animals during attacks and no
promises of reward or profit.

Attempts to attack military garrisons in the hope of capturing arms had
devastating consequences, including air raids, and the Qashqa'i were no
match for a modern army. A very important element was the government's

clever and effective handling of the crisis. Government officials separated the khans from the Qashqa'i people and condemned the chiefs as self-serving warlords seeking lost land and pasture for their own benefit. They did not interfere in the daily routines of Qashqa'i life and did not stop migrations; on the contrary, they provided much-needed assistance. They could not disarm the group easily and therefore did not attempt to do so. The pastoralists benefited from the food shortages and price hikes; the demand for dairy products increased nomadism, and many others kept cultivating land for the much-needed agricultural products.

There were setbacks as well; many of the Qashqa'is' woven products were intended to be exported, but the war and sanctions against Iran because of the hostage crisis limited access to international markets. The government's mismanagement and inconsistent policies with respect to carpet and rug exports had a negative impact on the carpet and rug industry, major products produced by many tribal, rural, and urban groups. Restrictions on music and dance applied to all, including tribal dances and music during weddings and other celebrations. Women were asked to conform to Islamic attire; even in towns many did not comply.

Land tenure became the most pressing problem for both the Qashqa'i and the government authorities. Following the revolution, there was chaos with respect to land tenure, with thousands of claims. The government issued, created, and then abandoned a land reform bill. In 1982 another bill was presented to the parliament to impose land reform. It was vetoed by the Guardian Council on the grounds that it was against Islamic principles. The government policy remained inconsistent and contradictory. In some areas lands were distributed to the peasants. In others, such as Baluchistan and Kurdistan, the government took sides with larger landowners as a precautionary measure against the local radical rebels.

The Revolutionary Guards and government agents did not move into Qashqa'i territory until 1983. Once they did move in, they recruited youngsters from among the tribes and formed local Revolutionary Guards units in the areas. The war and massive casualties among all, including the Qashqa'i youth, intensified anger and hatred against the Islamic government, and sporadic clashes took place. In return, government propaganda started picturing some Qashqa'i individuals or groups as bandits and antirevolutionary and un-Islamic, but this approach was soon given up. Tribal schools continued to function but at a decreased level for a while; then they picked up again. Coeducational classes at the tribal teacher-training college, high school, and tent schools were banned, and the number of female participants decreased initially but later resumed its former rate and in the end increased.

Despite the increasing religiosity of the country and promotion of the Shi'i religious practices, Qashqa'i have kept their independence and have avoided participating in state-sponsored religious events. They have not welcomed the building of new mosques and the presence of Shi'i clergy in their towns.

The Islamic Republic marked a new era for the Qashqa'i. The paramount and secondary khans virtually ceased to exist, and the midlevel leaders depended on the state for management and resources. The Shahilu lineage that had been in control for centuries, united and respected, lost many members and wealth. The surviving new generation is mostly outside Iran, with little connection to their family histories or the Iranian Qashqa'i. The apparent hereditary paramount khan, the son of Naser Khan, died in the mountains during the conflict with the government, and many others were executed. Naser Khan's daughter, after spending months in the mountains, managed to escape with help from the Baluchi and for a while assumed a leadership role outside Iran. However, as a ruling lineage her family has effectively ceased to exist.

Bakhtiyari

The Bakhtiyari group stayed away from the political events following the revolution. After Shapur Bakhtiyar was ousted as the prime minister, many prominent Bakhtiyari were arrested, and many more left the country. The Bakhtiyari people live mainly in Khuzistan, and many are employed in the oil industry. Their language belongs to the western Iranian group of languages, is closely related to Luri, and at times is called Luri or Bakhtiyari. Their number is estimated to be 800,000 to 1 million, with less than one-third practicing pastoral nomadism. The pastoral nomads produce meat and dairy products and still migrate between their traditional territories west of Isfahan to the Khuzistan plains for winter pasture. Their migration routes are very difficult, and at times they have to cross mountain passes that are as much as 10,000 feet high. They have stayed away from national politics. Their chiefly families have lost all prominence in the country, and many have had their assets and properties seized by the Islamic government. They have no paramount chiefs any longer, and the younger elite mostly live outside Iran. More nomads are settling down voluntarily, and like other pastoral nomads they are dependent on the central government for their migrations.

Turkmen

The majority of Turkmen live in the northeast, and their traditional territory is now divided between Khurasan, Mazandaran, and Gorgan (modern-day Gulistan). They do not have a province named after them. Since the collapse of the Soviet Union, their close proximity to the Republic of Turkmenistan has enabled them to establish more links with related groups in the republic. There are close to two million Turkmen in Iran, and they are not guaranteed a representative in the parliament as are the Christians or other legitimate religious minorities. This issue has been a problem for some groups who do not have a province in their name and therefore are not guaranteed representation. In the last parliamentary elections there was significant support for some Turkmen candidates, but they did not gain enough votes provincially to make it. The main groups, Guklan, Yomut, Tekke, and Salour, mainly live in Khurasan and Gorgan. They engage in a number of traditional activities, such as horse and cattle breeding by the Guklan and Yomut and very fine rug weaving by the Tekke. The traditional tents, as popular as they are, are becoming too expensive to use, and motorized vehicles are now frequently used during migrations. Most are Hanafi Sunni, and a minority support mystical sects such as Naqshbandi.

The area witnessed chaos and intensive armed clashes following the Islamic Revolution. A month after the success of the revolution, violent clashes started in the Turkmen Sahra region because of a name change. The name of the main port, formerly Bandar Shah ("king's port"), was to change to Bandar Islam, but the Turkmen wanted it to be called Bandar Turkmen. Although the dispute was minor at the time, the active organizations in the region used the opportunity to make a series of demands and ended up engaging in conflict that led to many deaths and the influx of more troops from Tehran. The main active organs in the area, the Political and Cultural Center of the Masses of Turkmen, Feda'i Guerrillas, and Mujahedin, assumed leadership and made a number of proclamations. Their demands included language rights; the return of previously confiscated land, mostly managed by the Pahlavi Foundation; the cancellation of land taxes and fees; limits on foreign exports that competed with local products; a number of social, medical, and educational issues; and the appointment of local people to official posts.

The Turkmen also wanted the regular army and Revolutionary Guards to leave the area and leave them in charge of security. They did not demand either autonomy or separation, and the leadership was not organized or articulate enough to gain popular support. The movement was dominated by leftist intellectuals, university teachers, students, and professionals, who had little connection to the average Turkmen. The government in Tehran blamed the monarchists, imperialists, and leftists for these problems, and a number of delegates, including high-ranking clergymen, were sent to the area to negotiate. The Turkmen objected to and boycotted the referendum and seriously challenged the Assembly of Experts and the new constitution. Broadcasts from Turkmenistan in the Soviet Union encouraged the Turkmen to fight and gain independence. However, the situation calmed down, and although sporadic opposition continued, the banning, arrest, jailing, and execution of the most active groups and individuals in the area effectively curtailed opposition.

Predominantly Turkic-speaking, the Turkmen have been struggling to gain minority language rights, with little success. They object to national television broadcasts being mostly in Persian and have demanded more local programming. In the early 1980s more violence broke out in the region. The Turkmen objected to the presence of Revolutionary Guards who intended to enforce the compulsory Islamic dress code and veiling among the Turkmen women working in the fields. Many have remained seminomadic, practice agriculture seasonally, and follow traditional migration patterns. Their society has remained male dominated with little change compared to the Qashqa'i. The literacy rate has increased among the younger generation, both men and women, and improved education will in the long run likely influence gender relations. Persecution and the Iran-Iraq War have resulted in the defection of many Turkmen to Turkey. Like many other minority groups, they insist on wearing their traditional clothing when they can. The Iranian population has increased since the Islamic Revolution, and all cities have grown. The presence of large urban centers is making an impact on the lives of marginal groups, and they are becoming more integrated than in the past.

Baluchistan

The province is located in the southeast of the country, bordering Pakistan and Afghanistan. It consists of two sections, Sistan and Baluchistan, with regional differences existing between the two. For example, in Sistan religion is more important, while in Baluchistan ethnicity plays a more vital role in people's lives. The Iranian Baluchis are mainly concentrated in the Makran highlands. In 1979 only one-quarter of the total population of Baluchistan lived in the cities. Its population has more than doubled from around

600,000 in the early 1980s. Currently close to half a million live in the capital city of Zahedan. The province has remained one of the poorest and least-developed areas in Iran. At the time of the Islamic Revolution in 1979, it was a few months before the extent of the changes in the rest of the country was felt in Baluchistan. The majority is Sunni and has close ties with related tribes in Pakistan and Afghanistan. The area was affected by the revolution in many ways, and also by the events in Afghanistan. The war against the Russian-backed government and later the Russians, the civil war, and the emergence of the Taliban in Afghanistan caused a steady flow of refugees from Afghanistan into Iran through Baluchistan for decades.

By the time the Taliban was overthrown following the September 11 terrorist attacks on the United States, there were close to two million Afghani refugees in Iran. Most refugees in Iran are integrated into the larger Iranian society and are working; very few live in refugee camps. Following the collapse of the Taliban regime, international agencies and the Iranian government have facilitated the return of the Afghanis to their country. So far the return has been mostly voluntary, and over 900,000 Afghanis have returned. Many Afghani refugees in Iran speak a Persian dialect very similar to modern Persian and are culturally well assimilated. However, their presence, especially in the border areas, where they are not distinguishable from the local population, has had some consequences.

After the revolution several of the Baluchi tribal chiefs who were in exile or lived outside Iran went back to their strongholds. Baluchistan did not have a strong presence in the referendum, but the tribal leaders were active and participated in the election of the first president and the parliament. The new revolutionary government reached the conclusion that the local tribal leaders could be in charge of security in the area for the time being. They armed a number of prominent leaders and their groups and allowed the conditional return of other tribal leaders from outside Iran. Not all the returned leaders were received well or complied with government policies, and some were later forced to leave Iran and cross the border into Pakistan.

The authorities in Tehran were reluctant to rely on the religious leaders in the area. Normally referred to as Mulavi, such leaders were Sunni who had been educated mostly in the religious schools in Pakistan and had close ties with Saudi Arabia. A number of Sunni Muslim groups existed, with some supporting radical movements, that denounced Shi'i Islam. One influential group, the Party of Muslim Unity, headed by a Sunni clergyman, originally supported the revolution but then opposed the constitution and Shi'i supremacy. The party was divided between different factions and was forced to move to Pakistan. Leftist groups also emerged in the area and initially had some impact but in the end did not prove significant. They resented the return of the local khans and accused the Islamic Republic of being reactionary and betraying the ideals of the revolution. Promonarchy forces were also active in the area, and all the active groups for some time created chaos in the region. Foreign involvement increased as well, with Iraq, Pakistan, and Russia supporting different factions and trying to destabilize the region. Most groups appropriated the Sunni/Shi'i divisions and focused on how a Shi'i government could threaten the area. The intensification of opposition to the Russians in Afghanistan prompted the Soviets to reduce their activity in Iran. They withdrew their support for the leftist insurgencies in Iranian Baluchistan in exchange for the Iranians cutting back their aid to the Soviet opposition in Afghanistan. However, the Liberation Movement of Baluchistan, orchestrated from the Pakistani Baluchistan, remained and is still active to some extent.

A characteristic of the antigovernment movement in Baluchistan was divisions based on tribal loyalties and the role of the tribal chiefs. Such chiefs had remained more influential in Baluchistan than in other areas. For example, three promonarchy leaders who formed the core of the anti-Islamic front after the revolution belonged to the chiefly families. All three were members of the parliament prior to the revolution and had the support of their tribal groups. In the 1990s several Iranian Baluchi chiefs were assassinated in Pakistan. They too had relied on their tribes for support and had maintained the loyalty of tribal members. New and modern classes, in particular the educated Baluchis, emerged as important groups following the revolution, and they were also able to use tribal connections at times.

There were clashes with Iranian government agents, but on the whole there was no independent or genuine movement for separation or autonomy compared to those in Kurdistan, Azerbaijan, or the Pakistani Baluchistan. This difference was mostly due to the backwardness of the area and the high illiteracy rate. The clashes remained tribal in nature and were complicated by foreign interference. In their attempts to control Baluchistan, some groups were relocated, many organizations were banned, and non-Baluchi were given incentives to move into the area. During the last two decades a number of prominent Sunni leaders, shaikhs, and imams have been executed or kidnapped or have vanished. Several Sunni mosques have occasionally been closed down, and new Shi'i institutions and mosques have been built in the area. Sunni are discriminated against nationally, and the presence of a large number of mainly Shi'i government appointees from outside the region has created violence and tension on a number of occasions. Sectarian tribal clashes happen as well, but many are related to smuggling and narcotics networks in the area.

Religious Minorities and the Islamic Republic

The total population of Iran is about 68 million, of which approximately 98 percent are Muslims, with the Shi'i constituting 93 percent, the Sunni 5 percent, and others 2 percent. The majority of the Sunni reside in Kurdistan, the Turkmen area, Sistan, and Baluchistan, with a few living in other areas. Not all Shi'i are ethnic Persians, and of the five dominant non-Muslim religious minorities, three—the Baha'i, the Jews, and the Zoroastrians—are Persian speakers. The Armenians and the Assyrians identify their own languages as their mother tongues. With the exception of the Baha'i, who emerged in the mid-nineteenth century, these religions have been practiced in Iran since ancient times. Centuries of persecution and the judicial use of the Islamic codes, which treat non-Muslims as second-class citizens, had reduced their numbers and made them isolated and underdeveloped. The twentieth century was a time of major change. The emergence of a secular, powerful government and a new constitution improved these minorities' material life and legal status, with some reservations. The success of the Islamic Revolution in 1979 had major detrimental effects on their welfare and legal status. Many were compelled to emigrate, and as a result their numbers have been reduced even further. However, they have not given up demanding equal rights. International media and human rights agencies and associated organizations outside Iran are making their cases known globally. This publicity has put pressure on the Iranian government, and it is believed that some reforms will occur, although gradually. Many restrictions have been lifted, and less pressure is imposed on religious minorities. However, under the present legal system they are not equal with Muslims, and despite many efforts, demands, and debates they have not succeeded in the quest for equality.

Should the non-Muslim religious minorities be able to effectively change the legal codes to their benefit, it will be a very significant achievement for the global Muslim community and will help advance women's rights as well. No major Islamic institution or prominent clergy in the Muslim world have effectively demanded any change in the Islamic Shari'a. For a long time secular and human rights activists have demanded equal rights for non-Muslims, among other reforms, but to no avail. Secular governments in Muslim countries have made significant improvements, but the events of the past three decades in a number of countries, including Iran, indicate that the Muslim institutions and clergy do not favor such changes, and many strongly oppose them. Any reform in a theocratic state such as Iran will have a significant impact on Islamic institutions worldwide.

The constitution was amended ten years after its inception and is a significant document. It clearly marks the ideology of the state with respect to notions of citizenship; nationality; religious minorities, including non-Shi'i Muslims; and what it means to be Iranian. It guarantees many rights, all within the boundaries of Islam as stated in Article 4, and therefore institutionalizes the different treatment of non-Muslims in the Islamic codes. Articles 12, 13, and 14 of the constitution deal with Sunni and other religious minorities. Ismaili Muslims who have modernized their institutions are not mentioned in the constitution, and *fugaha* (clergy) are clearly in control.

Article 4

All civil, penal, financial, economic, administrative, cultural, military, political, and other laws and regulations must be based on Islamic criteria. This principle applies absolutely and generally to all articles of the Constitution as well as to all other laws and regulations, and the fuqaha of the Guardian Council are judges in this matter.

Article 12

The official religion of Iran is Islam and the Twelfth Ja'fari school, and this principle will remain eternally immutable. Other Islamic schools, including the Hanafi, Shafi'i, Maliki, Hanbali, and Zaydi, are to be accorded full respect, and their followers are free to act in accordance with their own jurisprudence in performing their religious rites. These schools enjoy official status in matters pertaining to religious education, affairs of personal status (marriage, divorce, inheritance, and wills), and related litigation in courts of law. In regions of the country where Muslims following any one of these schools of fiqh constitute the majority, local regulations, within the bounds of the jurisdiction of local councils, are to be in accordance with the respective school of fiqh, without infringing upon the rights of the followers of other schools.

Article 13

Zoroastrians, Jewish, and Christian Iranians are the only legitimate religious minorities who, within the limits of Islamic laws, are free to perform their religious rites, and to act according to their own canon in personal matters and religious education.

Article 14

In accordance with the sacred verse ("God does not forbid you to deal kindly and justly with those who have not fought against you because of your religion and who have not expelled you from your homes" [60:8]), the government of the Islamic Republic of Iran and all Muslims are obliged to treat non-Muslims in conformity with ethical norms and the principles of Islamic justice and equity, and to respect their human rights. This principle applies to all who refrain from engaging in conspiracy or activity against Islam and the Islamic Republic of Iran.

With the exception of the Baha'i, four representatives from the non-Muslim groups were present while the constitution was being drafted. Of the seventy-three deputies elected to draft a constitution, fifty-five were clergy and over fifty were members of the Islamic Republican Party. After three months of debate a new constitution was drafted and approved. The official religion of the country is Shi'i, major leadership positions are reserved for them, and the clergy are exclusively in charge of the most powerful positions. Obedience to God, Islam, and religious leaders prevails over individual and communal rights. Women and religious minorities, including the Sunni, despite being Muslims, have inferior legal status and are excluded from leadership positions, among other disadvantages. The Baha'i were excluded altogether and remain without any legal standing.

In theory the religious minorities, with the exception of the Sunni Muslims, maintained the rights they had before. There was no major change in their status compared to the previous constitution. Even the exclusion of the Baha'i was consistent with their historical treatment. However, the adoption of the Islamic Shari'a made a significant change with respect to the religious minorities. The secular civil and criminal codes of the past had regarded all citizens as equal. The Islamic codes make sharp distinctions between Muslims and non-Muslims, grant superior legal status to male Muslims, and treat the others as second-class citizens. The Islamic penal code was presented to the parliament in 1981 despite protests from many. It was approved in 1982.

The Bill of Retribution (Qesas) included in the code is very damaging for non-Muslims. The codes treat Muslims and non-Muslims differently, and the laws reiterate this inequality. The codes have been criticized for centuries, and their institutionalization, once again, has become subject of international criticism. The reservation of leadership positions exclusively for Shi'i Iranians has practically barred others from positions of power. Major changes in the educational institutions have resulted in segregation, exclusion, and subordination of religious minorities. The Ministry of Culture and Islamic

Guidance has enforced unprecedented measures with respect to religious minorities' publications, sermons, and public talks, although it is becoming more lenient. Members of minorities can publish religious literature, but all such publications have to be approved by the ministry. The texts for public talks must also be submitted to the ministry beforehand for approval. All literature in non-Persian languages must be translated and submitted for review. Although such practices were and are common with regard to most literature, public talks, and printed press, their use with respect to religious texts for the minorities was new.

Following the revolution, Muslims were barred from attending Christian, Jewish, and Baha'i ceremonies and places of worship, and all non-Muslim communities were required to sign forms acknowledging such restrictions. Only one leader, a bishop and the president of the Council of Protestant Churches in Iran, refused to sign such a document. Although many Iranians were under restrictions with respect to travel in the 1980s and during the war, the restrictions were more severe for the religious minorities, and many were not issued passports.

With the exception of the Baha'i, there was no systematic persecution or destruction of property, but sporadic actions against individuals and communal properties existed, increased, and to some extent continue even now. Family matters, personal disputes, marriage, divorce, and inheritance among members of minority groups are handled internally in the communities under their own codes. But they are subject to supervision and final approval by the state authorities, who can overrule internal decisions. The minorities are encouraged to convert to Islam, and the old inheritance rules have been restored that state if one member of a family converts to Islam, only he or she will inherit all the property. Disputes between non-Muslims and Muslims can be dealt with only in the Islamic courts, which immediately puts non-Muslims at a disadvantage because of the law's different treatment of the two groups.

Educational institutions lost their autonomy, and their principals and staff are chosen by the authorities. The appointment of Muslims, particularly clergy and radical elements, to revise and watch over the schools has created resentment and many problems. Instruction in the minority language instructions has been reduced, and the state authorities directly supervise and interfere in the teachings of religious texts. Due to a shortage of schools, Muslim students have been encouraged to enroll in minority schools. If the schools have been attached to churches, temples, or synagogues, they have been closed or separated from the schools by barricades or walls. The Iranian authorities and institutions have been inconsistent with respect to many of these policies. The result has been a diversity of attitudes, enforcement, and implementation strategies in dealing with the minority issues nationally, provincially, and locally.

In the 1980s high-ranking ayatollahs confirmed that non-Muslims were "impure" *(najess),* and measures were taken and restrictions imposed to deal with purity risks. Such claims are not made publicly anymore, but there is no guarantee that they will not be used again. Job discrimination was rampant in the 1980s and has continued. The religious minorities participated in the war mostly as auxiliaries, such as support and medical staff, and less in combat because of the principle that non-Muslims should not be allowed to kill Muslims. However, accusations have frequently been made that they were deliberately sent to more dangerous zones. The Islamic dress code is imposed on all women, including the religious minorities, and they have been instructed not to consume alcohol or eat pork publicly. Random killings, kidnappings, and interruption and harassment of minority gatherings have continued, although they are becoming less frequent. One major change is with respect to the Sunni population. They have become a minority because leadership positions are reserved for Shi'i. Systematic and institutionalized discrimination against them exists. As of yet, they do not have a mosque in Tehran and have not been able to get a permit to build one.

Christians

In the absence of any reliable statistics with respect to the Baha'i, the Armenians are considered to be the largest non-Muslim religious minority. They are the largest Christian group in Iran, and in the 1980s and early 1990s their numbers were estimated to be around 150,000 to 200,000. Such figures are much higher than the official statistics. The government figures from the 1996 census put the number of all Christians at 78,745, which is lower than the number a decade earlier at 97,557. Such discrepancies are common in Iran. One reason is that people will not mark their true religion on the forms or do not state it at all because of fear of discrimination and persecution. The majority of the Armenians still belong to the Apostolic Church, which has three archdioceses in Tehran, Tabriz, and Isfahan. A few are Catholics and Protestants.

They are free to celebrate their major festivals, and such events are acknowledged by the media and the government. The majority of the Armenians celebrate the new year on December 31 and Christmas on January 6, following the Julian calendar. Catholic Armenians celebrate Christmas on

December 25, and Easter is celebrated by all. There are no restrictions with respect to celebrations, and Christmas trees are sold openly. April 24, a day of remembrance for the genocide of the Armenians in Turkey, is also observed by the community. In 2001 close to 10,000 Armenians were given permission to march in Tehran to commemorate this day. Armenian pilgrims from other countries are able to visit holy places such as the Church of Saint Thaddaeus in Urmiya. The church is believed to have been built in the first century A.D. in the memory of Saint Thaddaeus, one of the twelve disciples. He is believed to have lost his life and became a martyr while spreading the gospel in Iran. The oldest part of the church is from the tenth century; it was extensively rebuilt in the thirteenth and seventeenth centuries.

Armenians currently are mainly urban, with a few villages around major cities such as Tabriz and Isfahan and some near Hamadan and Arak. As the largest Christian community, they have had more conflicts with the authorities since 1979 than others. In 1981 the government banned the teaching of the Armenian language in Armenian schools and insisted that all religious teachings must be in Persian. The Armenians refused and continued to resist; they avoided getting help from the international community so as not to jeopardize their situation in Iran, especially during the war with Iraq. The resistance continued for almost three years, and many Armenian schools were closed in the process. In the end the government directives prevailed, with a few compromises. The Armenian language was not eliminated altogether, but classes in it were reduced to two hours per week, compared to daily classes before. The law was not implemented uniformly, and depending on the sensitivity of the government-appointed principals and officials, some schools managed to have more classes in Armenian. Direct interference in religious teachings in minority schools and standard government-issued religious texts in Persian for these schools has remained a major issue. Such actions are directly against Article 13 of the constitution, which guarantees freedom of religious teachings for the recognized minorities. Education at all levels has remained a major issue for the minorities, and despite many appeals and promises, discrimination still exists. They are not required to take Islamic courses but often are discriminated against if they do not know Islamic principles. This prospect forces them to take the courses. Armenians are leaving the country in large numbers, and it is estimated that close to 100,000 might have left Iran since the Islamic Revolution. Currently Armenians have two representatives in the parliament on behalf of the Armenians of the north and the southern territories. They can serve on most house committees except the Foreign Affairs Committee and those dealing with Islamic legislation, such as the Judicial Committee.

The Assyrians and Chaldeans have had similar problems. Due to their small numbers, they have only one representative in the parliament. Their numbers in the 1990s were estimated to be between 16,000 and 18,000, a sharp decrease from their numbers prior to the revolution, 30,000 to 32,000. The majority of the remaining Assyrians live in Tehran and the Chaldeans in Khuzistan, mainly Ahvaz. Their patriarchal seat is still in Baghdad. They have suffered the same restrictions with respect to language and religious and regular education, but their very small numbers prevent them from taking any action.

Other Christians in Iran are not recognized by the state and have undergone systematic persecution. Their presence in Iran, even before the revolution, was not without reservation. They were always opposed by Muslim groups because of the missionary nature of their churches. Some properties were attacked right after the revolution, and one pastor in Shiraz in the Fars province was murdered. The Islamic Propagation Society, an extremist Muslim group, had been opposing the churches for decades, and it organized attacks against churches, individuals, and communal properties, even Christian hospitals. The Anglican Church of Iran was formally declared dysfunctional in Iran in 1981, and all foreign members were expelled. Protestant churches suffered even more. Attacks on the churches were followed by the kidnapping and murder of two evangelical bishops: the head of the Assemblies of God, part of the evangelical Pentecostal Christian church, and the chairman of the Council of Protestant Ministers of Iran. Several churches were closed in a number of cities, and the situation worsened in the 1990s. Of twelve evangelical churches, only two were open for service by 1996. Most followers of these churches were converts from Islam. Such conversions are regarded as blasphemy, and converts are automatically condemned to death. Their bishops early on refused to cooperate and would not give in to pressure, and despite persecution they have remained persistent. They conduct their services in Armenian and Persian. The numbers of these Christian groups are not known. Some estimates in 1994 put the number of Catholic and Protestants in Iran at around 15,000 including both ethnic Christians and Muslim converts.

Jews

Within one year of the revolution of 1979, the number of Jews in Iran declined drastically from 80,000 to 50,000–60,000. By the mid-1990s their numbers were estimated to be around 35,000. The government's census of

1986 and 1996 recorded their numbers at been 26,354 and 12,737, respectively. However, the actual numbers are normally expected to be higher than those cited in government statistics. Anti-Zionist and anti-Israel ideologists and sentiments are central to the Islamic government in Iran. The close relationship of the prerevolutionary government with Israel proved detrimental to the situation of Iranian Jews after the revolution. Some prominent Jewish businessmen and a few community leaders were executed on the pretense that they had collaborated with the enemies of God: imperialism and Israel. Many Jewish teachers, professors, and government officials were expelled or were forced or voluntarily decided to retire early. A chief rabbi left Iran in 1980 and encouraged other Jews to leave the country. Travel restrictions were harsh for Iranian Jews. Originally they were refused passports and exit visas. Some authorities were careful to distinguish between the Iranian Jews and the Zionists, but nevertheless, charges of treason and conspiracy continued. Such charges are still used occasionally when there is pressure on the Iranian Jews. Their situation has relaxed since the mid-1990s; however, their exodus continues. Their economic position has deteriorated since the revolution, they are cut off from the elite, and it is harder for them to participate in large-scale economic and industrial ventures they once were part of. They are subjected to the same restrictions as other non-Muslims and are represented by one deputy in the parliament. Before the revolution there were about twenty Jewish schools in Iran; some have closed because of a reduction in the Jewish population. Hebrew instruction is allowed, but the authorities discourage the distribution of Hebrew texts, which makes teaching the language a difficult task. Iran's Jewish population is still the largest in the Middle East, with the exception of Israel.

Iranian Jews celebrate all traditional Jewish festivals, and there is little interference in such practices. The Jewish new year (Rosh Hashanah), Purim festival, Passover (Pesach), Day of Atonement (Yom Kippur), and Festival of Lights (Hanukkah) are celebrated, among others. One of their most holy places, the mausoleum of Esther and Mordecai in Hamadan, is open for pilgrimage. They also have a celebration that is more common among the Jewish communities in Iran and Russia; the Festival of Blessing the Trees (Birkhat Ha'ilanot) is celebrated more or less around the same time that the Yalda Festival is celebrated by the Iranians. Both celebrate the end of winter and resemble ancient crop or harvest festivals with many treats, mostly fruits and other produce from the earth. *Yalda* is a Syriac word in origin and means birth. In the pre-Islamic Iran, a festival celebrating the rebirth of the sun on the morning following the longest night of the year was celebrated on the

An Iranian woman jumps over a fire during a traditional ceremony in Tehran, March 15, 2005. Iranians mark the last Tuesday of the Iranian calendar year with traditional fireworks and fire-jumping. The Iranian new year starts on March 21. (Morteza Nikoubazl/Reuters/Corbis)

exact same night under a different name. Jews also celebrate the Iranian New Year (No Ruz), which is a pre-Islamic celebration of the spring equinox.

Zoroastrians

Zoroastrians were mostly concentrated in Tehran by the late 1970s. Some still lived in Yazid and Kirman, and most were urbanized, with a few villages near Yazd. Government censuses show their numbers to have been reduced from 32,589 in 1986 to 27,920 in 1996. Independent estimates vary, and some even report an increase in their numbers from around 35,000 before the revolution to 50,000 (Sanasarian, 2000, p. 50). The increase is unusual. They do not accept converts, but since the revolution they have become very popular; many Iranians, including some Baha'i, declare themselves to be Zoroastrians, and there are some unofficial organizations of these new Zoroastrians with little connection to the old established associations. Their traditional symbols have become very popular among Iranians, especially the youth.

Worldwide their numbers are close to 125,000, concentrated mainly in India, Pakistan, and Iran. They have built new temples in Shiraz, Isfahan, and Ahvaz. Many have moved to Europe and North America, and Zoroastrian temples and associations exist in many major cities on these continents.

The major Zoroastrian festivals celebrated by all Iranians originally faced some opposition by the Islamic authorities. Initially they tried to reduce the length of the No Ruz holidays by half. They were not successful, and the public, particularly youths, continued to celebrate the festival as before. Jumping over the fire was unofficially banned, but people still jump over bonfires after sunset as part of a purification rite. In the process they sing songs, some very ancient in origin, and celebrate the rest of the evening with dance, music, and feasts. Since the election of Khatami and the relaxation of some codes, the festival has become far more pronounced and elaborate, with music and dancing, some publicly by females. Some observers have labeled such practices as open revolt, and the authorities were compelled to acknowledge the issue officially in 2003 in order to impose some control.

There has been a resurgence of interest in Zoroastrianism, both in Iran and among Iranian emigrants outside the country, particularly in North America. The Zoroastrian festivals are celebrated with zest and grandeur by almost all Iranians. Although the celebrations in Iran have evolved into defiance, outside the country they have become instruments for preserving the culture. Iranians both inside and outside Iran have begun observing other occasions that traditionally were exclusive to the Zoroastrians, such as Mihregan, which celebrates the ancient deity Mihr or Mithra, and the Festival of Sadeh ("one hundred"), celebrating the one hundredth day before No Ruz.

Zoroastrians are different from the rest of the religious minorities. They often emphasize the fact that their connection is to the land itself and that they are the true natives of the country. Many Iranians have affinity for them. They are stronger and more unified and have come to represent the other religious minorities in their demands for reform. The resurgence of sympathy for the pre-Islamic Iran has made them more confident. They are subject to all restrictions imposed on non-Muslims but have fared better under the Islamic Republic than other religious minorities.

Baha'i

The Baha'i have historically been the most persecuted religious minority in Iran and remain so up to the present. Their number prior to 1979 was estimated to be 150,000–300,000. They became targets before, during, and after the revolution. The clergy and religious institutions on the whole resented the Baha'i, and historically they are labeled as blasphemers. Such charges in Islam are dealt with severely with harsh punishments, including death. They enjoyed relative peace during the Pahlavi regime, but the prerevolutionary Iranian leaders were not prepared to battle the clergy and give the Baha'i legal status. Once the revolutionary government took over, it did not need to ban them, since they were already illegitimate. They have never been fully accepted by the general public either. Once the persecutions started and until the present day, very few organizations in Iran have defended them or explicitly supported their cause. Most human rights activists in Iran have talked about freedom of religion in general, but none has or can explicitly mention the Baha'i.

During and after the revolution they were attacked, and their properties were ransacked, destroyed, and confiscated. Their communal buildings, including cemeteries, were destroyed. They were dismissed from their workplaces, schools, and universities. By 1981 all nine leaders of the National Spiritual Assembly had vanished and were presumed dead. The new members of the subsequent National Assemblies had the same faith, and many were secretly executed. Travel restrictions were imposed, and the arrested Baha'i were given the choice of converting to Islam; if they refused, as many did, they were executed. An anti-Baha'i group active since the 1950s, called Hojjatieh, carried out or encouraged some of the worst persecutions. One of its members became the minister of education and dismissed all Baha'i from educational institutions. In order to provide education for their children, they set up private educational institutions that were repeatedly raided and destroyed. The Hojjatieh group itself came under attack in the mid-1980s, and its activities stopped. However, the persecution continued well into the late 1990s, when some relief came mainly due to international pressure. They were permitted to bury their dead as Baha'i in some cemeteries, and their children were allowed to attend grade school and high school. They have established an institute of higher education for their youth in a number of houses and offices. The properties were extensively raided in the late 1990s, but since then they have been unofficially permitted to carry on. But no guarantees have been given that they will not be persecuted again.

The government's unofficial policy states that the Baha'i should not be incarcerated without reason but that their progress and development should be stopped inside the country and their cultural roots outside should be confronted and destroyed. Most of their communal properties have never been returned, and almost all of their main holy places have been destroyed and even leveled. Islamic principles state that Islam is the last revealed religion; therefore, no religion after Islam is accepted. As a result the Baha'i are condemned as apostates. Although many have left Iran, many have remained and despite persecution still practice their religion secretly. The postwar Islamic Republic entered a new era with the election of President Khatami. The religious minorities in particular welcomed his election and expected some improvements, and some changes have occurred.

A New Era, 1997–2004

According to the constitution, Iran is headed by a supreme leader who is chosen from among the clergy by the clergymen who form the Assembly of Experts. This leader appoints the head of the judiciary and is the commander in chief of the armed forces. He also appoints six clergymen to the Guardian Council; the other six, mainly lawyers and nonclergy, are chosen by the parliament, renamed the Islamic Consultative Assembly (Majlis). The Guardian Council can veto all bills passed by the parliament and certifies the legitimacy of candidates for the parliament and presidency. The first decade of the Islamic Republic was dominated by individuals fully approved by the supreme leader and the Guardian Council. The election of President Khatami in 1997 was a deviation from this norm. The president is elected by universal suffrage to a four-year term by an absolute majority of votes. Khatami, a well-educated clergyman, rose to popularity in the Ministry of Culture and Islamic Guidance. He eased media censorship, promoted many cultural activities such as concerts and film festivals, and talked about women's rights and the nation of Iran as opposed to the nation of Islam. He developed a reputation as a reformist and defeated the government-sponsored candidates in the presidential election. His victories in the elections in 1997 and 2001 and two successive reformist parliaments created enthusiasm and hope that change for the better was inevitable. Most of his supporters during both of his terms were women and the young. Despite many efforts by his administration, due to many factors, including the limited powers of both the parliament and the president, neither was able to impose fundamental reforms. However, many serious questions were raised and became the subjects of debate that is still going on. Questions related to the compatibility and legitimacy of Islam in a modern world, women's rights, religious minorities, and individual freedoms are still debated. One such major question is nationalism and a new understanding of what constitutes a modern nation.

Kish Island, south of Iran, where Iranians go to relax. Today they enjoy more freedom than in the early days of the Islamic Republic. This young woman puts her chador back on after a horseback ride, July 2003. (Kaveh Kazemi/Corbis)

New Notions of Nationhood

Persians constitute 51 percent of the population in Iran, and the majority is Shi'i. Traditionally they live in central Iran, Fars, Khurasan, the northern territories near the Caspian area, and Tehran and its vicinity, among other places. They are Persian speaking, with close to fifty-two associated dialects. The Persian language is Indo-European in origin, and all major Persian language groups are spoken in Iran. Persians have a strong affinity for their language and identify closely with being Iranian. They supported many of the early Pahlavi reforms, and many oppose the Islamization and Arabization policies of the current government.

The Persian language is playing an increasingly important role in creating national sentiments in the country. The compulsory universal education for all was started by Reza Shah and continued very successfully under his son and the Islamic Republic. The literacy rate for people under the age of twenty-four is very high, close to 87 percent. Well over 60 percent of the population is under nineteen years old, and nearly 94 percent finish grade five.

The standard curriculum is in Persian, and, with the exception of the religious minorities who have limited instruction in other languages, no ethnic languages are taught at schools. The most popular second language in Iran is English, with thousands of private institutions and private tutors. Although major universities teach European languages and there are many English departments, none have Turkish or, until recently, Kurdish departments. Arabic is also taught extensively at the schools and at the university level but has very little use except in Islamic studies.

The very young population of the country and the predominance of Persian as the primary language of instruction have already introduced major changes in the country. The Persianization that started during the Pahlavi era in the early twentieth century is becoming a reality in the realm of modern education. The population migration in massive numbers has significantly altered the population distribution in the country. The urban population of Iran was estimated to be close to 46 percent in 1979; in 2002 it was close to 66 percent. The 1996 census put the population of Tehran at 11.5 million; more current estimates are close to 14 million, although no official statistics have been available since 1996. All major cities have become multiethnic and cosmopolitan, with major sociocultural changes in every aspect of life.

Such major changes have brought people together, and new and stronger notions of nationhood are taking shape, particularly among the younger people. Such notions of nationhood are antireligion, prodemocracy, and emphasize individual liberties and freedoms; they are taking shape because of necessity and the harsh realities of life under the current regime. In the absence of political parties and leaders, they are not influenced either by the state apparatus or by political trends such as communism or socialism, as was the case in the earlier twentieth century in Iran. What shape they will take will very likely determine the future of nationalism in Iran. The government is well aware of the hostility and the problems imposed by such trends among the younger generation. It has taken a few steps to reduce tensions and ease living conditions, but with little success. In their relationship with the different ethnic groups, the authorities have remained consistent in imposing central authority and official policies. They have had less success in dealing with major social changes that are affecting every aspect of life in twenty-first-century Iran.

Kurdistan

The political activities of the Kurds in Kurdistan have been halted for more than a decade. The assassination of Ghassemlou in 1989 and further assas-

Iranian girls take a break from skiing at the top of a hill at Shemshak ski resort, about 35 miles (57 kilometers) from Tehran, 2004. Shemshak and its sister resort, Dizin, are favorite getaways for well-to-do young Tehranis during the winter and spring months. (Damir Sagolj/Corbis)

sinations of other key figures of the KDPI made a significant impact on this organization. However, it has survived, and its publications in Europe continue to support Kurdish autonomy in Iran. It has remained the most organized and articulate opposition group among the Kurdish Iranians. The Kurds voted for the reformist president Khatami, and some measures were taken by his administration to ease relations with Kurds and other minorities. President Khatami's election in 1997 created some enthusiasm, and at one point the number of Kurdish representatives in the parliament increased and a parliamentary faction was formed to deal with Kurdish problems. However, neither the representative nor the government was able to implement any major reform. The armed struggle of the Kurds in Iran has failed, and the remnants of their leadership live as refugees either in Iraqi Kurdistan or Western Europe. The present struggles of the Iranian Kurds are primarily for recognition and cultural rights rather than an independent Kurdistan. As it stands, the emergence of an autonomous Kurdistan in Iraq may give this cultural struggle a boost but will not necessarily transform it into a political or military struggle. The most serious problem facing the government in Kurdistan at the moment is the economic development of the area. The challenges are evident in the patterns of employment and migration. Large numbers are migrating to larger cities outside Kurdistan. It is in the slums of major cities, such as Tehran, that the displaced Kurds, many far better educated than the previous generations of migrant workers, may find new voices or leadership options to lead them to questions of autonomy or ethnic identity.

With religion being at the forefront of all activities, the Shi'i-Sunni division has deepened in Kurdistan. It has resulted in the assassination of some prominent Sunni clergy and violent clashes. The marginal and mystical sects are criticized and are labeled as heretical by both the Shi'i and Sunni clergy. The Sufi orders are still prominent, and centuries-old divisions between the two major orders still persist. The older Qaderi order has been in the area since the twelfth century and is famous for its eccentric practices, such as eating glass, walking over fire, and piercing the body with knives or swords. Such practices are alien to Islam, and government officials have harassed the followers of this order. The other prominent order, the Naqshbandi, originated in central Asia and prefers a more contemplative practice. The order gained massive popular support among the Kurds in Iraq and presently is the most popular among Iranian Kurds. Some of its leaders played a significant part in the development of Kurdish nationalism and have maintained loyalty among their followers.

Other smaller sects, such as Alevid and Ahl-i Haqqi, despite their veneration of Ali, a central character in Iranian Shi'ism, are not received well by the authorities. One exception has been the Ahl-i Haqqi tribes of Guran and Sanjab. One of their prominent shaikhs supported the government; defended the border against Iraq; and gained prestige, a good reputation, and support from the central authorities. Like the previous governments, the Islamic Republic takes advantage of divisions among the Kurds and supports groups that could be useful to it. Some Kurds went back to seminomadic practices and livestock breeding with more ease than before and received support from the government.

The mystical cults and minor religions are more popular in the rural areas of Kurdistan and have many communal affairs and practices. They rely on oral traditions, and supporters follow their leaders religiously and have been persistent in their regional loyalties. This might be one reason that the authorities intend to keep them under control and have been building mosques and other religious institutions in the areas they consider troublesome. They are promoting state-sponsored religious practices and loyalties through such establishments. Yazidi, another minor sect, is believed by most to be heretical, but its very small following in Iran has made it insignificant, even in Kurdistan. The most serious threat to all these minor sects is the socioeconomic change in the region. A high literacy rate among the young, emigration and assimilation into the national culture, military service, new roads, and accessibility to modern media have created divisions inside the sects. Such divisions are increasing and have created more factionalism. The survival of these sects may depend on the ability of the traditional leaders or shaikhs to effectively manage such internal rifts and changes.

Persecutions, wars, the worsening socioeconomic problems, and inability to articulate freely in the Kurdish language have pushed Kurdish cultural expressions to the privacy of family life. It is in the safety of homes and among extended families that the language, religion, dress, music, and a newly emerging Kurdish literature are flourishing. Kurdish music in particular has prospered in Iran, mainly because there are no restrictions on performing ethnic music as long as it does not involve solo female singers. One major change that has helped the survival and continuation of Kurdish culture and literature is the presence of a large number of Kurds in Western countries, particularly in Europe. The beginning of a substantial Kurdish literature and press goes back to Iraq under the British mandate, when minorities such as Kurds were granted limited cultural rights in the 1920s. The Kurds in Russia under the Soviets were also able to publish freely in Kurdish. However, their literature is in Cyrillic script and not accessible to many Kurds.

After the 1991 Kurdish massacres by the Iraqi government, the two groups in Iraq, the KDP and the PUK, managed to control certain areas in northern Iraq. They have promoted Kurdish culture and language in the areas under their control and broadcast Kurdish programs into Iran. Modern Kurdish is written mainly in three scripts: Arabic, Latin, and Cyrillic. The mass emigration of Kurds, particularly from Iraq and Turkey, in the 1990s created a boom in the publication and production of Kurdish press and literature in Western countries. Radio broadcasts; TV programs; and thousands of websites, many in Kurdish, have resulted in an unprecedented flourishing of Kurdish in the Kurmanji language. This literature of exile has made a significant impact on the continuity of Kurdish literature in Iran, Iraq, and Turkey. Kurdish cultural associations in Sweden, France, England, Germany, and many other countries have emerged and contribute greatly to the continuity of Kurdish culture.

The Iranian constitution supports the freedom of publication in minority languages. During the first decade of the Islamic Republic and following the events in Kurdistan and the war with Iraq, many restrictions were imposed on minority-language publications. The situation has improved, and

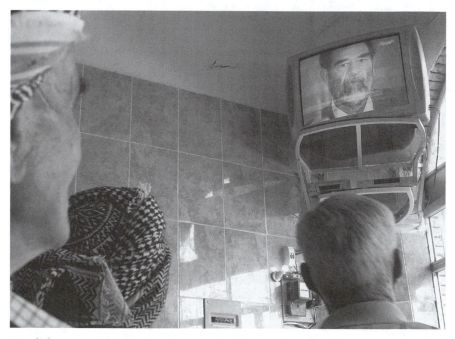

Kurdish men watch television in a tea shop in central Arbil, northern Iraq, July 14, 2004, as they follow Saddam Hussein's trial after the U.S. occupation of Iraq. One of the charges directed against the former Iraqi president was the use of chemical weapons against the Kurdish town of Hlabja, which led to the deaths of thousands of Kurds. (Sasa Kralj/Reuters/Corbis)

since the late 1980s there have been a few publications in Kurdish along with some conferences on Kurdish culture and literature in Iran. At the same time, private and state publishing have increased in Kurdistan. Publishing houses owned by the government have published a number of titles in Kurdish, and the radio and television broadcasting agencies have produced programs in Kurdish. Such literature mainly deals with Kurdish culture, both in Kurmanjii and Surani. However, censorship exists, and there are no daily or weekly papers in Kurdish and no provision for instruction in the Kurdish language in Kurdistan. The universities do not have major courses in Kurdish history, literature, or languages. There have been some changes. The Provincial University of Kurdistan in July 2004 announced the formation of the first Kurdish Language Department in Iran. This is a first for a minority language, and the development is being closely watched by the people from Azerbaijan.

One major change is the existence of thousands of Internet cafes through-out Iran. These cafes have made it possible for all, including the Kurds, to view thousands of Kurdish sites globally, and this access has transformed the traditional ways of communication. This is in sharp contrast to the period from 1900 to 1978, where altogether less than 100 titles were printed in Kurd-ish. Another significant change in Iran is the popularity of satellite TV, ex-tensively used by all Iranians, which provides access to foreign TV channels in a number of languages, including Persian, Arabic, Kurdish, and Turkish. The popularity of cinema in Iran and the existence of an internationally ac-claimed cinema, with some very well-known Kurdish directors concentrat-ing on Kurdish life and issues, have exposed Iranians to the dilemmas of life in Kurdistan. Kurdish issues are openly discussed in the media, and recent translations of Western scholarly works on ethnic problems in Iran will no doubt increase awareness. The Institute of National Studies has published a number of credible and well-researched books on ethnic issues and intends to produce a whole series on ethnic questions in Iran.

The massive attacks of the Iraqi government on the Kurds and the use of chemical weapons against a number of villages in Iraqi Kurdistan in the 1990s made the plight of the Kurds an international issue. They became the subject of intensive research by many Western scholars, journalists, and me-dia personalities who traced Kurdish history and culture through major pub-lications and documentaries. Such information is used and sometimes abused and distorted by the many Kurdish groups outside the Middle East to produce reconstructed histories and mythical ancestries and to promote Kurdish nationalism and identity. The occupation of Iraq and the removal of Saddam Hussein have been welcomed by the Kurds in Iraq. Their success in establishing an autonomous Kurdistan, or at least a prosperous and peaceful Kurdistan, will have major implications for the Kurds in Iran and Turkey. These two countries have started collaborating to curtail Kurdish in-surgencies in the border areas. Militant Kurds from Turkey have been killed or arrested at the border by Iranian forces. At times the Iranian government has provided assistance to the Kurdistan's Workers' Party (PKK) from Turkey in rebellions against the Turkish government. Such policies are contradictory, but they enable the security forces in Iran to have resources in Turkey; they probably use the PKK to create divisions among local Kurdish groups. The Iranian government has been consistently involved with the Iraqi Kurds and has been trying to promote Shi'i Islam among them. With the demise of communism and the collapse of the Soviet Union and its agents in the area, Islam has returned as a significant factor in Kurdish politics. The Islamic gov-ernment has taken many measures to establish its own supporters. It has not been very successful in gaining the support of pious Kurdish Muslims in Iran, but it has had more success in Iraq. During the war, it initially supported the secular Kurdish groups in Iraq to fight the Iraqi government. In the process it sent Shi'i preachers to Iraq. It also supported a prominent Barazani Naqshbandi shaikh to establish an armed force known as Hezbollah al-Kurdi in Iraq. By the mid-1980s, all support for the Iraqi communist and socialist forces had stopped, and they were expelled from territories under the control of the Hezbollah al-Kurdi. The Iranian influence was countered by the Saudis, who established their own Islamic group in Iraqi Kurdistan. In the 1990s another revolutionary Hezbollah group under the leadership of the same Barazani shaikh separated from the original one. The new offshoot was more loyal to Iran than to Saudi Arabia. The Islamic groups backed by Iran are finding more support among the Kurds in Iraq. Their future will depend on U.S. policy in Iraq and how well the new Iraqi government can control such groups.

Azerbaijan

Azerbaijan has remained relatively calm, with the exception of occasional clashes. There were protests and clashes between the supporters of Khatami and those of the government-sponsored presidential candidates in 1997 in Azerbaijan, as in other areas in Iran. But no major disturbances have happened in recent times. The most important active group, the National Liberation Movement of Southern Azerbaijan, has a strong voice; it was restructured in 1999 when a few other groups amalgamated into a united front. The organization is illegal, and the authorities have accused Turkey of supporting it. It is very vocal in its support of minority rights, has accused the central government of trying to Persianize the Turkic minorities, and has organized demonstrations in Tabriz. Because of the availability of Internet cafes, broadcasts from abroad, and satellite television, the central government in Iran has been unable to suppress the flow of information and propaganda through these modern media. The presence of major oil fields in the Caspian area has added to the significance of both Azerbaijans and has complicated matters further. The main oil fields are in Kazakistan and the Republic of Azerbaijan, with limited sources in Turkmenistan. Should a pro-U.S. government appear in Iran, a new pipeline could connect the Caspian oil fields with the Iraqi oil terminals currently under the control of the United States in Iraq. However, at present the U.S. emphasis is on building a pipeline that will connect the Caspian oil fields to Turkey and reduce the monopolizing powers of the Gulf states, Iran, and OPEC in general.

Many of the problems the Azeri face in Iran are shared by all, such as high unemployment, mismanagement of economic and national resources, and lack of basic rights and freedoms. Barring popular candidates from participating in elections or disallowing their credentials after they are elected is common; it happens everywhere and is not unique to the minorities. There are specific ethnic grievances as well, such as the lack of freedom with respect to language use and the appointment of non-Azeri (sometimes hostile to Azeri) officials from Tehran. There is a very large Azeri population in Tehran, and they have a wide range of effective networks and a very strong presence in retail and many other businesses. Compared to other minorities, they have a strong presence in the government as well. The current supreme leader, Ayatollah Khameini, is from Azerbaijan, and there are several Azeri ministers in the government. So far they have not taken sides with the Azeri and have remained loyal to the basic principles of the regime.

The relative freedom of the press in recent years has enabled some to express their wants and needs in local and national newspapers. However, the response from the government has been insignificant. Some problems are due to the inability of the government to run the country effectively, and others are partly due to its centralization and unification policies. The government is fearful of separatist movements and the disintegration of the country. Its central ideology favors a united Muslim state with Shi'i supremacy. It promotes unity, downplays ethnic distinctions, and believes that Islam has the power to unite the nation despite ethnic and religious divisions. So far it has not succeeded in implementing such unity. The Azerbaijanis strive for cultural rights, as do the Kurds.

The prospect of an independent Azerbaijan and separation from Iran does not have popular support. Azeri entrepreneurs have massive business and trade networks in Tehran, which have created a relatively large prosperous Azeri group in the capital. For many, the priority is to send their children to Europe and North America for a better education and life rather than supporting the formation of a new republic. Prosperous Azerbaijanis, like other Iranians, are investing their money and capital in Western countries, which they consider to be safe places. However, regional autonomy and language rights are immensely popular issues among the Azeri in Iran and will have to be dealt with at some point. Recently the government has taken steps to legalize private broadcasting networks such as television stations. Whether ethnic minorities will be able to get licenses to have their own media and use them to promote their own goals remains to be seen. There are regional programs and broadcasts in Azeri, but they are neither enough nor independent of government control. Most other groups and provinces are in more or less the same situation as in the 1980s, with the exception of Baluchistan, due to both the war in Afghanistan and the narcotics business in the area.

Baluchistan

Baluchistan has remained the most backward region in Iran. The government's response to the problems and poverty in the area has been insignificant. Despite some attempts by President Khatami's administration and the creation of a number of agencies and some planning, the situation has barely improved. Shortage of water is a major problem, and a major drought is entering its third year. Many villages and tribal groups are entirely dependent on clean water supplies provided by government agencies. This dependence in turn has increased the government's presence in the area.

The creation of a number of educational institutes in Iranian Baluchistan has led to some improvements, and a new class of educated Baluchis has emerged. They have some connection with opposition groups in Pakistan, but so far no major group has emerged or could emerge due to political restrictions. Most opposition groups from Baluchistan are active only in Pakistan, with little impact in Iran. However, the Baluchi are familiar with the nationalist literature that is evolving in Pakistan. Such literature portrays the Baluchi as a separate group with distinct Baluchi kingdoms and no link to Iranians. They have reconstructed histories and emphasize a distinct origin and language, but these theories are based on little evidence or documentation. The Baluchi language is Iranian in origin and belongs to the northwestern Iranian language groups. The language is divided into two main groups, southern and western Baluchi, and both these and their related dialects are used widely in Iran.

One of the most significant changes in the area following the revolution has been the narcotics and smuggling businesses. These pursuits have emerged as the most profitable economic option for many in the border areas of Iran and the neighboring countries, such as Pakistan and particularly Afghanistan. In 2003 Afghanistan produced around three-quarters of the world's opium. Close to 70 percent of all farming in Afghanistan produces opium. The drug goes through Iran and Pakistan before reaching its main destinations of Europe and North America. Most of it is used to make heroin. The scale of the narcotics business has created very powerful drug lords and criminal networks. None of the three governments in the region is able or willing to combat the problem. The narcotics economy has transformed the traditional power structures in the region, and its impact on the social, political, and economic structures is not yet fully understood or realized.

The smugglers and the drug lords have emerged as the most serious problem in the area. Many members of different tribes are involved in the drug networks, as are some local authorities. Not everyone in the clans or tribes is active in drug trafficking, and some prominent members of chiefly families refuse to get involved, but none oppose the situation either. This lack of opposition is mostly because no one in the area is strong enough to seriously challenge the extensive networks operating in Afghanistan, Pakistan, and Iran. The government troops and agencies, despite massive loss of life in fighting the bandits and smugglers, have had very little overall success. Despite the significance of the narcotics-based economy in the region, the rate of drug addiction is lower among the local population than in other areas such as Kirmanshah. However, this situation could change. Iran has around two million drug addicts, out of a population of nearly seventy million, one of the highest per capita rates in the world.

Clan and tribal ties are used extensively by the smugglers, who are well equipped and heavily armed with modern artillery, travel in large convoys, and use vehicles and animals such as camels for trafficking. Some tribal groups have been in the smuggling business for centuries and have multiple citizenships. Even most of the liberation organizations that favor a united Baluchistan are involved in the narcotics business. Government statistics indicate that on the average Iran loses three people per day fighting the drug trade. There is no international help, and the government's control over the area is very limited. The drug economy is a new phenomenon in the area, and its long-term effects on entire regions or tribal organizations are not yet known. It has consolidated tribal and clan loyalties, but around new criminal elements in these groups rather than the traditionally respected chiefs or khans. In the absence of effective government development plans for the region and owing to discrimination against the Sunni elements, the drug lords might yet prove either the government's worst enemies or its best friends.

Minorities in the Twenty-first Century

President Khatami's administration produced some improvement but no fundamental changes with respect to the legal status of minorities. Among the tribal groups, the chiefly families have become irrelevant and have lost most of their power. In the past the khans had extensive marriage and economic-social ties to the power groups, which saved them at times. The emergence of a new ruling class with no connections to the old aristocracy and bureaucracy, tribal lords, and regular army has disconnected the old ruling groups from their traditional power bases. Different groups have responded differently, and some such as the Shahsevan have benefited from new experimental projects. The boom in nomadic produce during the war has ended, and most groups face competition from major agroindustrial projects and foreign imports. Most pastoral nomads rely on government agencies for pasture allocation, water, and migration planning in order to survive. The Organization of Pastoral Nomadic Affairs has proved relatively effective and has improved management at the local level. A few postgraduate students from the universities have been able to conduct research among the nomads, including the Qashqa'i, and a number of recommendations have been made to improve management and migrations. However, such reforms have been insignificant in the face of major economic and social changes in Iran, and more nomads are settling down.

Religious minorities have seen some improvements as well. In 1999 President Khatami publicly stated that no one in Iran should be discriminated against because of their religion. Subsequently the parliament and, more importantly, the Guardian Council, which has the right to veto the parliament's approved bills, passed the Right of Citizenship bill confirming the social and political rights of all citizens and equality before the law. Following this legislation, the registry offices and public notaries were instructed to register all marriages without the need to state religion on the registry forms. This policy allows the Baha'i to register their marriages and improves the legal status of their children.

However, another bill, approved by the parliament in 2002, to improve the penal code and to eliminate discriminatory sentencing and monetary compensation, or "blood money" payment, between Muslims and non-Muslims was rejected by the Guardian Council. For example, in the current law if a non-Muslim kills a Muslim, he will be executed and his family will have to pay compensation. If a Muslim kills a non-Muslim, he is exempted from the death penalty and pays compensation that is half what a non-Muslim has to pay. Eliminating such discriminatory codes would have been a significant step in Islamic jurisdiction. The bill was rejected on the basis that it directly contradicted the Quran and was non-Islamic. Diversity in the implementation of laws regionally and nationally has allowed some flexibility and at the same time enables the more fanatical elements to act on their own beliefs.

Despite improvements, sporadic arrests and persecutions are still common. In 1999 thirteen Jews in Shiraz were accused of maintaining illegal contact with Israel and conspiracy to form an illegal organization in Iran. They were sentenced to lengthy periods of imprisonment. However, an appeals court overruled the accusation of conspiracy and reduced their sentences. Several have been freed since then, and three were pardoned by the supreme leader. Jewish Iranians are suspected of cooperation with Israel, and the Jewish community is therefore closely watched in Iran. Although Jews are given passports and exit visas, the authorities sometimes make it difficult for all members of the same family to travel together outside the country. Such restrictions may apply to all Iranians, but they are more common for religious minorities. It is also more difficult for Jews to get multiple-exit visas. Despite restrictions and the usual limitations imposed on religious minorities, Jews are not harassed systematically. They are left to themselves as long as they comply with the regulations. Despite the high rate of emigration, some have chosen to stay, and their situation has improved compared to the early days of the revolution.

Sunnis, despite being Muslims, are discriminated against. The policy of appointing Shi'i officials and imams for Friday prayers and as governors, some with no local or ethnic connections, has continued. The official support for Shi'i religious institutions and building of large mosques in Sunni areas with little financial support for Sunni institutions has intensified these divisions.

Evangelical Christians and the Baha'i have suffered more persecutions since the success of the fundamentalists in the July 2004 parliamentary elections. Close to seventy evangelical Christians, including several priests, were arrested by the authorities in a single raid in autumn 2004. This act was followed by destruction of the most important Baha'i site in Iran, the house of Bahaullah in Mazandaran. The destruction was carried out despite major protests by cultural heritage authorities declaring the 150-year-old house to be of national historical importance. The Baha'i' community in North America and Europe responded by placing large ads in prominent newspapers condemning the acts. The authorities have lifted some restrictions on the Baha'i in Iran, including restrictions on travel permits, but future improvements are doubtful.

Women and the Islamic Republic

Iranian women had a major presence during the demonstrations leading to the Islamic Revolution. Millions from all classes participated in every aspect of the movement. Many modern secular individuals adopted the Islamic dress code to indicate their support for the new regime. The Islamic Republic was inaugurated in January 1979, and by March women had been barred from becoming judges. The Family Protection Laws were annulled in April. The marriage age for girls was reduced, and married women were barred from attending regular schools. In summer 1980 a new bill introduced compulsory veiling. Family planning was deemed un-Islamic, and many women were forced or chose to resign from government institutions. Segregation of sexes was implemented in schools, and unsuccessful attempts were made to impose such segregation throughout the society as a whole. Women maintained their electoral rights and can be and were elected to the parliament.

The staff involved in an Iranian children's educational show produced by Mrs. Soheila Ghodsi. Mrs. Ghodsi, a graduate of the San Francisco School of Fine Arts, moved back to Iran with her two American-born children in pursuit of an Islamic lifestyle that she lacked in the United States. She produces English-language programming for Iran's state-run television and radio stations. Her team includes many women working behind and in front of the camera. Unlike other Islamic countries in the region, women in Iran play a major role in all levels of society and the professions. They are still not considered equal to men; however, since reformers took power, many things have changed. This television program targets children born in Europe and the United States, teaching them Farsi through English. (Ramin Talaie/Corbis)

The response to the changes has been varied, but on the whole the set-backs resulted in the formation of a significant and articulate women's movement that continues today. Modern classes have regarded the changes as an outright attack on their rights. However, the segregation of sexes and compulsory veiling has enabled millions of females from the lower classes and the more traditional families to enter schools, employment, and public life and participate more freely than in the past. The adult literacy rate is high, and the gap between males and females is getting smaller. At the primary school level the percentage of males and females attending school in 2002 has been 98 and 96 percent, respectively (according to UNICEF statistics). The literacy rate for adolescents was close to 60 percent in 1976. In the last census in 1996, it was recorded as close to 95 percent. The rise was greater among females; it increased from nearly 48 percent in 1976 to almost 92 percent in 1996. For males the increase was from close to 72 percent to around 98 percent for the same period. The rise in the number of literate females in the rural areas for the same period has been equally impressive (according to UNESCO). Currently more women than men are entering universities. The University of Tehran Center for Women's Studies reported in 2002 that 52.9 percent of students entering the universities were women. The figure is closer to 65 percent for 2004, but it has not yet been substantiated.

Women are in the same position as members of religious minorities. The constitution guarantees their rights and equal treatment, but conformity with the Islamic codes and criteria annuls such equality. The Islamic Shari'a awards superior legal status to males, so discrimination against women is institutionalized in the legal system. The notion of Islamic criteria and the use of Shari'a have come under extensive criticism by many in the country, and the debate still continues. Articles 20 and 21 of the constitution clearly state women's rights.

Article 20
All citizens of the country, both men and women, equally enjoy the protection of the law and enjoy all human, political, economic, social, and cultural rights, in conformity with Islamic criteria.

Article 21
The government must ensure the rights of women in all respects, in conformity with Islamic criteria, and accomplish the following goals: 1. create a favorable environment for the growth of woman's personality and the restoration of her rights, both the material and intellectual; 2. the protection of mothers, particularly during pregnancy and childbearing, and the protection of

children without guardians; 3. establishing competent courts to protect and preserve the family; 4. the provision of special insurance for widows, and aged women and women without support; 5. the awarding of guardianship of children to worthy mothers, in order to protect the interests of the children, in the absence of a legal guardian.

Despite setbacks, the rise in the literacy rate among females and their increasing participation in public life and employment have made significant changes. In over two decades the women's movement in Iran has grown to become one of the most significant women's movements in the world. Women have changed the concept of compulsory veiling by introducing modern styles, color, and fashionable trends in major cities. The marriage age has been increased, and they have gained small but steady progress with respect to family codes. Youth movements have become the most significant opposition to the government, and both groups were instrumental in the elections of the reformist president and the two subsequent reformist parliaments since 1997. Women have a small but consistent presence in leadership positions and the parliament. At the middle and lower levels of management they have a significant presence. Their struggle was acknowledged internationally when an Iranian lawyer activist, Shirin Ebadi, received the Nobel Peace Prize in 2003. It is unlikely that the new parliament will reverse the few gains women have made in Iran, but it is not clear if any more gains can be made with the fundamentalists in control.

Iranians in Exile

The information regarding Iranians in exile is scarce and fragmented. President Khatami in his earlier days in office made a few brief efforts to encourage exiles to return to Iran. Some statistics appeared, and it was casually mentioned by government officials that close to three million Iranians had left since the 1979 revolution. Many have moved to India, Turkey, Japan, the Persian Gulf states, Europe, and North America, among other places. Recently, due to the large number of Iranians in the United States and Canada, Iranian exiles have become the subject of interest and research in both Iran and North America.

One well-documented article, produced for the Iranian government in 2002 by a government agent, Seyed Mehdi Mousavi, sheds some light on the statues of Iranians in the United States. According to the author, the official figures on Iranians in the United States indicate that there were around 6,000 in 1965 and close to 120,000 in 1980. The latter included close to 50,000 students. By 2002 the Iranian authorities' files had 620,000 persons on record, and they estimated that 40 percent of the Iranians in the United States had not registered with the Iranian government agencies. The figures do not include second-generation Iranians who do not have Iranian ID cards and passports. On the whole the estimates are that close to a million live in the United States and around 300,000 in Canada (Mousavi, 2002, p. 5).

The same author mentions that according to statistics offered by the Republicans in the United States (1999), about 84 percent of Iranians speak English and are employed, 46 percent hold B.Sc. and higher degrees, and about 43 percent have top professional and management positions. The average annual income of Iranians is $55,000, and 92 percent have private homes.

The majority of Iranians in the United States live in California, mainly Los Angeles. Many Iranians mockingly refer to this city as *Irangeles* or *Tehrangeles*. Preserving the ancient culture and language has been a major issue, and extensive efforts are made to maintain and preserve the Iranian culture and introduce it to non-Iranians. There are numerous Iranian radio stations, publications, political organizations, scientific and industrial associations, and a few sports institutions in the United States, and the numbers are growing. By the end of 2004, close to thirty networks, some twenty-four hours per day, were broadcast into Iran through satellite TV. Most are broadcast from California and a few from Europe. In response, Iranian authorities have created a major TV network that is broadcast from Iran to Europe and North America. However, despite superior programming, it has not attracted a large number of viewers. In California alone there are close to fifty cultural organizations dealing with every aspect of Iranian culture and art. There are hundreds of concerts, dances, and other artistic endeavors by Iranians every year, and Persian cookbooks are selling by the thousands.

The majority of Iranians in the United States are modern and secular. This might explain why there are only six Iranian Islamic institutes or organizations, which have very little support among Iranians. Most Iranians in the United States emphasize and sympathize with pre-Islamic Persia and have been instrumental in popularizing some of the exclusively Zoroastrian festivals such as Mihregan and Sadeh among mainstream Iranians. All the Iranian festivals are celebrated extensively and elaborately in the United States, while the Muslim festivals are barely mentioned. There are close to 500 Iranian lawyers or legal organizations owned by Iranians in the United States and no doubt political figures with Iranian ancestry will soon emerge, at least in California.

There are many non-Muslim Iranians in the United States as well. Iranian Jews and Zoroastrians have maintained their Iranian identity, whereas Assyrians tend to be assimilated into the culture of the host country. Iranian Jews have sponsored a number of Jewish organizations to trace their history and culture in Iran. They have kept their connection with other Iranians and have remained patriotic with respect to their Iranian past. Their numbers are estimated to be close to 30,000 in California. Unofficial estimates put their numbers in the greater New York City area at around 15,000. They are considered Sephardic Jews (with rituals of Babylonian origin) and are different from Ashkenazi Jews with respect to some rituals and foods during Jewish festivals. There are several Iranian yeshivas (Jewish religious schools) and synagogues in California and New York, and many kosher Persian restaurants.

Many wealthy Jewish Iranians have sponsored major Iranian cultural activities, and like Zoroastrians, they have maintained Persian as their mother language. The Zoroastrians have temples in New York, Chicago, San Francisco, and Los Angeles. Close to 35,000 Iranian Armenians live mainly in California. They emphasize their Armenian heritage and take measures to preserve Armenian identity first. However, they have kept close ties with mainstream Iranians. Close to 6,000 Iranian Baha'i live in California alone. They too have maintained close ties with mainstream Iranians.

International pressure on the government has been positive in some cases. The overwhelmingly fundamentalist parliament elected in February 2004 has been closely watched by minorities and international agencies. It is too early to predict what changes it might introduce. However, the recent destruction of the Baha'i holy sites and the arrests of the evangelical Christians are indications that significant reforms might not happen soon.

Conclusion

Iran is a vast country with many different ethnic groups. Most groups have been in Iran for centuries, and in some cases for thousands of years. The diverse peoples of Iran are separated by language, religion, and way of life. At times their loyalties extend beyond the present borders. Historically such diversity was accepted and lived with most of the time. After the Islamic conquest, non-Muslims were conditionally protected, but over the centuries their situation became worse and their numbers decreased. As of the tenth century, the intrusion and invasion of a number of Turkish and later Mongol and Turkmen groups introduced pastoral nomadism as a major mode of production, modified land use, and significantly changed the ethnic character of the country. Although religious persecution existed, ethnic cleansing or wars were not characteristic of the country. Historically, there were no restrictions with respect to the use of ethnic languages or multiple ways of life. Various groups fought among themselves and against each other for military superiority and material gain. They constantly changed sides, even against closely related tribes and siblings, during power struggles.

The sixteenth and twentieth centuries were significant periods in Iranian history. The Safavids introduced Shi'i Islam as the state religion by using force and in the process lost large territories in the east. They united the country after centuries of fragmentation and more or less fixed borders that closely resemble modern Iran, with some exceptions. The twentieth century was a time of nation building, reforms, consolidation of power, and the emergence of a modern nation-state based on European models. This was achieved by building an infrastructure and a modern army and Persianization of the country at the expense of regional and ethnic diversity. Religious minorities and women gained many rights and after centuries of isolation entered public life freely, with some reservations. For most of the century tribes and nomadism were deemed archaic and a barrier to progress and centralization. Many tactics, including coercion at times, were used to settle the nomadic tribes that constituted a large portion of the population at the beginning of the twentieth century. The legal system based on ancient Islamic codes was modernized up to a point, and religious authorities lost many of their powers. The Pahlavi rulers placed the royalty at the center of the new state ideology and unsuccessfully tried to create a bond between the monarchy and the people.

The Islamic Republic, established in 1979, reversed many of the earlier reforms and aimed at creating an Islamic state with a Shi'i leadership composed of clergy at the heart of the new system. They came into power with a popular vote and soon emerged as a theocratic government bidding for control over every aspect of the private and public lives of the citizens. Neither the Pahlavi regime nor the Islamic Republic managed to come to terms with the various ethnolinguistic groups. Some measures taken were essential in terms of building a modern country, such as disarming the many tribal groups, eliminating chiefly warlords, and increasing security. But others, such as forced settlements, were detrimental to the country as a whole and created resentment and resistance. As a result of such policies, among others, the country remained more or less unstable politically. Unity was achieved by using force and relocation, and often through cooperation of willing segments within the diverse groups. The governments throughout the twentieth century downplayed factors that are distinctive to minority groups. Freedom to use ethnic languages or clothing and nomadic ways of life was restricted and manipulated in the name of preserving unity.

Such policies were further complicated and helped to worsen the situation because of foreign involvement and the sensitive geopolitics of the region as a whole. Separatist movements, mostly with help from foreigners, appeared; although they have been defeated so far, they could still reemerge and threaten the very unity the governments want to preserve. The present government has gone further and frowns upon anything that is distinctive or different from the Shi'i Islamic culture it promotes. The adoption of the Islamic codes has institutionalized discrimination against religious minorities and women. The authorities have been more lenient with nomadic groups but envision ultimately settling them down. They have used force to impose central authority and have not hesitated to brutally crush any opposition, uprising, or demands for autonomy in Kurdistan, Azerbaijan, Baluchistan, and Turkmen Sahra. As the supreme leader of the country, Ayatollah Khamenei, has repeatedly mentioned, "The splendid nation gives preference to unity over factors which might divide it."

The state promotes the idea that there are no ethnic problems in Iran and that all see themselves as Iranians first, in the same way that Pahlavi leaders once announced that there was no tribalism in Iran. Globalization, a large number of organized ethnic groups and political activists in Europe and North America, modern communication systems, reconstruction, and occasionally falsification of origins and histories are making significant changes. Ethnic minorities in Iran are bombarded with literature and images and have become aware of their rights to preserve and practice their cultures freely. The government effectively cannot control them or impose censorship. As it stands, unless the leadership comes to terms with ethnic and religious diversity, its territorial integrity and the very unity that it wants to preserve will remain threatened.

Timeline

1979	The shah and his family were forced into exile on January 16. An interim government headed by Shapour Bakhtiyar was appointed by the shah.
1979	Ayatollah Khomeini returned to Iran on February 1 after almost fifteen years of exile in Iraq and a few months in France. The interim government was dismissed.

1979	The Islamic Republic of Iran was proclaimed on April 1 after a referendum. A Kurdish uprising started in Kurdistan. Azerbaijan opposed the referendum.
1979	Fifty-two Americans were taken hostage inside the U.S. embassy by militant students in Tehran on November 4. The militants demanded the extradition of the shah, who was receiving treatment for cancer in the United States.
1980	The first president of the new republic, Bani-Sadr, was elected in January. The shah died in Egypt in July. Iraq invaded Iran in September. The American hostages were released after 444 days in captivity. Bani-Sadr was impeached by a vote of 177-1 in the parliament.
1981	Bani-Sadr, the first president elect, was dismissed; he later fled to France. A massive bomb attack killed many leaders, including the new president, Rajai. The Mujahedin Khalq group was blamed by the government. Khamenei was elected the third president.
1982	Israel invaded Lebanon. Iran sent Revolutionary Guards to Bekaa Valley in Lebanon.
1983	Kurds were defeated throughout Kurdistan.
1985	Khamenei was reelected president.
1988	Iran accepted a cease-fire agreement with Iraq following negotiations in Geneva under the aegis of the United Nations in July. Iraq massacred thousands of Iraqi Kurds for supporting Iran.
1989	Ayatollah Khomeini issued a religious edict (*fatwa*) ordering Muslims to kill British author Salman Rushdie for his novel *The Satanic Verses,* considered blasphemous. Khomeini died in June, and Khamenei became the supreme leader. Rafsanjani, another cleric, became the president.
1990	Iran and Iraq resumed diplomatic relations in September.
1991	Thousands of Kurds fled to Iran following attacks by Saddam Hussein after the invasion of Kuwait and his defeat.
1995	The United States imposed oil and trade sanctions against Iran for alleged sponsorship of terrorism.

1996	The U.S. Congress imposed more sanctions on Iran and Libya.
1997	The moderate clergyman Mohammad Khatami won the presidential election by a 70 percent landslide. He was reelected in 2001.
1999	In July thousands of prodemocracy students started massive demonstrations against the government. They were brutally oppressed.
2000	In the newly elected parliament, liberals and supporters of Khatami won 170 of the 290 seats. Hard-liners won only 44 seats.
2000	A new press law banned publication of many reformist newspapers. Women were given permission to lead religious congregations of women worshippers.
2002	U.S. president George Bush proclaimed Iraq, Iran, and North Korea to be an "axis of evil."
2003	Thousands attended student-led protests in Tehran against the government. The Nobel Peace Prize was awarded to an Iranian woman, Shirin Ebadi, in October.
2004	Conservatives gained control of the parliament in controversial elections. Kurdistan University announced the formation of the first Kurdish Language Department in Iran.

Significant People, Places, and Events

ASSEMBLY OF EXPERTS: The eighty-six members of the assembly are chosen by public vote for eight years. They are all clergy, and the Guardian Council decides who can run for the elections.

BAKHTIYAR, SHAPUR: The last prime minister appointed by the shah. Bakhtiyar was a member of the National Front, supporting Dr. Musaddiq. He became prime minister on January 3, 1979, and lasted only thirty-seven days. He was assassinated in Paris by agents of the Islamic Republic in 1991.

GUARDIAN COUNCIL: Composed of clergy, the group has the power to veto all legislation passed by the parliament. The council has twelve members, six of whom are appointed by the supreme leader; the rest are elected by the parliament, but they are nominated by the Supreme Judicial Council (clergy).

KURDISTAN DEMOCRATIC PARTY (KDP): The party was founded by Mustafa Barazani in 1946 in Iraq and is dedicated to the creation of an independent Kurdistan.

PATRIOTIC UNION OF KURDISTAN (PUK): The leftist organization was set up by Jalal Talabai, a Kurdish leader, in 1975 in Iraq. With the KDP, it has jointly administered northern Iraqi territories since the Gulf War. It has been opposing Barazani's group for decades.

PESHMERGES ("READY TO DIE"): Kurdish guerrilla fighters who perform suicide attacks. They were very active in Iraq against Saddam Hussein. Currently they are helping U.S. troops in Iraq.

SUPREME SPIRITUAL LEADER: The highest position in the Islamic Republic. The leader has extensive powers and can veto any decisions made by all other government organs in the country. Ayatollahs Khomeini and Khamenei have been the two leaders so far.

Bibliography

Atabaki, Touraj. *Azerbaijan: Ethnicity and the Struggle for Power in Iran.* London and New York: I. B. Tauris, 2000.

Bonnie, Michael E., and Nikki Keddie. *Modern Iran: The Dialectics of Continuity and Change.* Albany, NY: State University of New York Press, 1981.

Chaqueri, Cosroe. *The Armenians of Iran: The Paradoxical Role of a Minority in a Dominant Culture.* Harvard Middle Eastern Monographs, No. 30. Cambridge, MA: Harvard University Press, 1998.

Kamrava, Mehran. *The Political History of Modern Iran: From Tribalism to Theocracy.* Westport, CT: Praeger Publishers, 1992.

Karsh, Efraim. *The Iran-Iraq War, 1980–1988.* Essential Histories, No. 20. London: Osprey Publishing, 2002.

Keddie, Nikki R. *Religion and Politics in Iran: Shi'ism from Quietism to Revolution.* New Haven, CT: Yale University Press, 1983.

Keddie, Nikki R., and Eric Hooglaund. *The Iranian Revolution and the Islamic Republic.* Syracuse, NY: Syracuse University Press, 1986.

Kreyenbroke, Philip G., and Christine Allison. *Kurdish Culture and Identity.* London: Zed Books, Centre for Near and Middle Eastern Studies, School of African and Oriental Studies, London University, 1996.

Kreyenbroke, Philip G., and Stefan Sperl. *The Kurds: A Contemporary Overview.* London and New York: Routledge, 1992.

Mousavi, Seyed Mehdi. "A Glance at the Situation of Iranians in America." *Sedaye Edalat,* No. 149, March 5, 2002, p. 5. http://www.netiran.com/?fn=artd(672).

Sanasarian, Eliz. *Religious Minorities in Iran.* Cambridge: Cambridge University Press, 2000.

UNICEF: "At a glance: Iran (Islamic Republic of)." http://www.unicef.org/infobycountry/iran_statistics.html.

Appendix A:
Chronology and Origin
of the Ruling Groups

Ruling Dynasty	Chronology and ethnic origin of the ruling dynasties
Predynastic period: Many different and mixed groups occupied territories throughout the Iranian plateau. The area was dominated by the Sumerians, Babylonians, and Assyrians at times.	3000–2000 B.C. Hurrians, Kassites, Quti, Lullubi, and Mannians, among others
Elamite period: In modern Khuzistan, the ancient kingdom of Elam with Susa as its capital has been inhabited extensively from 3300 B.C.	2000–700 B.C. Origin unknown
Medes: Ancient Indo-Iranian tribes who became the first Iranian rulers of Mesopotamia and Iran, occupying parts of Azerbaijan, Kirmanshah, and Kurdistan.	728–550 B.C. Iranian
Achaemenids: The first major Iranian dynasty formed by the Persians. At their peak, their empire extended from India to Egypt.	550–330 B.C. Iranian
Alexander and the Seleucids: The Macedonian king defeated the Persians in 330 B.C. Seleucids were Greek rulers of Persia and heirs to Alexander's empire.	305–125 B.C. Greek
Parthians (Arcasids): Belonging to the Parni tribe, these Iranian tribes moved south and created a major empire. They were settled in northwest Iran before expanding.	247 B.C.–A.D. 228 Iranian
Sasanians: They organized a national state competing with Rome. The name of the country, *Iran*, is derived from the Sasanian concept of Eranshahr (empire of the Aryans) in the third century A.D.	A.D. 224–651 Iranian

Arab dynasties: The defeat of the Sasanians resulted in the establishment of the Arab Umayyad and the following Abbasid rulers in Iran.

A.D. 651–945
Arabs

Tahirids: They created an autonomous Iran in the east and played an important role in the dissolution of the political unity of the caliphate in Baghdad.

821–873
Iranian

Saffarids: From Sistan, they were instrumental in the revival and renaissance of the New Persian literature and culture.

867–903
Iranian

Samanids: The first independent Iranian kingdom after the Arab conquest. They revived the Persian language.

873–999
Iranian

Buyids: They occupied Baghdad and promoted Shi'ism and Persian culture.

945–1055
Iranian

Ghaznavids: Originally slaves from central Asia, they replaced the Iranian Samanids. Oghuz Turks arrived in massive numbers during this period.

994–1030
Turkic

Saljuqs: Oghuz Turks, they occupied central and western Iran and expanded from there. Azerbaijan acquired its Turkish character from this period.

1045–1217
Turkic

Mongol/Ilkhanid dynasties: Mongols were pastoral nomadic tribes from north of present-day Mongolia. They were followed by many other Turkish and Turkmen tribes and made a significant impact on the ethnic composition of Iran.

1221–1383
Mongols and Turkicized Mongols

Timurids and Turkmen: Timur's conquest was followed by the arrival of many Turkmen such as the Qra Quyunlu and Aq Quyunlu groups. A significant Turco-Persian culture and literature was developed.

1383–1501
Turkish and Turkmen

Safavids: Of Turkmen and Persian ancestry, they consolidated power against the Ottoman Turks. They made Shi'i the state religion in Iran.

1501–1722
Turkmen/Iranian

Afshars: A Turkic group, they moved to Iran with the Mongols in the thirteenth century from Turkistan and originally settled in Azerbaijan.

1736–1747
Turkish

Zands: A Luri tribe, they established the first Iranian dynasty after centuries of rules by Arab and Turkish groups.

1750–1779
Iranian

Qajars: Turkmen groups from Oghuz ancestry, they became very Persianized by the nineteenth century.

1796–1925
Persianized Turkmen

Pahlavi: The founders of modern Iran, promoted Persianization and created the most powerful centralized government in Iran.

1925–1979
Iranian

The Islamic Republic: Established following the collapse of the Pahlavi rule.

1979–present
Iranian

Appendix B: Ethnic Groups

Ethnic Group	Religion	Population Estimates Late 1990s	Languages	Main Locations
Arabs	Sunni and Shi'i	615,000–2 million	Arabic	Khuzistan, Persian Gulf Coast
Azeri Turks	Shi'i	8.8–10 million	Turkic	West and East Azerbaijan, Tehran
Bakhtiyari Haft Lang Chahar Lang	Shi'i	300,000–1 million	Luri	Central and western Zagros, Khuzistan, Luristan, Isfahan, Chahar Mahal, and Bakhtiyari
Baluchis	Sunni	500,000–1 million	Baluchi	Sistan and Baluchistan
Kurds	Majority Sunni, some Shi'i and Sufi	4–8 million	Kurdish Kurmanji Surani Gurani Zaza	Kurdistan, West Azerbaijan, Kirmanshah
Lurs	Shi'i	300,000–580,000	Luri	Luristan
Persians	Shi'i	41–45 million	Persian	Central provinces, including Fars and Khurasan, Caspian provinces, Tehran

(continues)

Ethnic Group	Religion	Population Estimates Late 1990s	Languages	Main Locations
Shahsevan Ardabili Meshgini	Shi'i	310,000	Turkic	Northwest Iran, East Azerbaijan
Turkmen Yomut Guklan Tekke Salour	Sunni	1.2 million	Turkic	Turkmen Sahra, Gorgan plains

Note: Population estimates after Eliz Sanasarian, *Religious Minorities in Iran,* Cambridge Middle Eastern Studies no. 13 (Los Angeles: University of Southern California Press, 2000).

Appendix C:
Non-Muslim Religious Minorities

Group	Population 1970s	Population Late 1990s	Religion	Location
Armenian	250,000	150,000–200,000	Apostolic Catholics, Protestants	Major cities, including Tehran, Isfahan, and Tabriz
Assyrians and Chaldeans	30,000	16,000–18,000	Nestorian, Chaldean, Roman Catholic	Major cities, including Tehran, Urmiya, and Ahvaz
Baha'is	150,000–300,000	Not available	Baha'i	Major cities, including Tehran
Jews	80,000	20,000–30,000	Judaism	Major cities, including Tehran, Hamadan, and Shiraz
Zoroastrians	30,000–35,000	50,000	Zoroastrianism	Major cities, including Tehran, Yazid, and Kirman

Note: Population estimates after Eliz Sanasarian, *Religious Minorities in Iran,* Cambridge Middle Eastern Studies no. 13 (Los Angeles: University of Southern California Press, 2000).

Index